AF541810

# Performance Management

# Performance Management

**Dr. Parul Agarwal**

RANDOM PUBLICATIONS
NEW DELHI (INDIA)

**Performance Management**

---

ISBN 978-93-5111-450-5


Published in 2014 in India by

**RANDOM PUBLICATIONS**

4376-A/4B, Gali Murari Lal, Ansari Road
New Delhi-110 002
Phone : +91-11-43580356, +91-11-23289044
e-mail: randomexports@gmail.com, sales@randompublications.com,
info@randompublications.com

*Type Setting by* : Keystoneprintads, Delhi-110051
*Digitally Printed at* : Replika Press Pvt. Ltd.

# Preface

Performance management (PM) includes activities which ensure that goals are consistently being met in an effective and efficient manner. Performance management can focus on the performance of an organization, a department, employee, or even the processes to build a product of service, as well as many other areas. PM is also known as a process by which organizations align their resources, systems and employees to strategic objectives and priorities.

This is used most often in the workplace, can apply wherever people interact — schools, churches, community meetings, sports teams, health setting, governmental agencies, social events and even political settings - anywhere in the world people interact with their environments to produce desired effects.

Armstrong and Baron (1998) defined it as a "strategic and integrated approach to increase the effectiveness of companies by improving the performance of the people who work in them and by developing the capabilities of teams and individual contributors." It may be possible to get all employees to reconcile personal goals with organizational goals and increase productivity and profitability of an organization using this process. It can be applied by organizations or a single department or section inside an organization, as well as an individual person.

The performance process is appropriately named the self-propelled performance process (SPPP). Managing employee or system performance and aligning their objectives facilitates the effective delivery of strategic and operational goals. There is a clear and immediate correlation between using performance management programs or software and improved business and organizational results.

For employee performance management, using integrated software, rather than a spreadsheet based recording system, may deliver a significant return on investment through a range of direct and indirect sales benefits, operational efficiency benefits and by unlocking the latent potential in every employees work day.

I thank all members of my team who have helped in the preparation of the book. My special thanks go to "Random Publications" who have published the book.

*– Dr. Parul Agarwal*

# Contents

# 1

# Introduction

Performance management includes activities which ensure that goals are consistently being met in an effective and efficient manner. Performance management can focus on the performance of an organization, a department, employee, or even the processes to build a product of service, as well as many other areas. PM is also known as a process by which organizations align their resources, systems and employees to strategic objectives and priorities. Performance management as referenced on this page in a broad term coined by Dr. Aubrey Daniels in the late 1970s to describe a technology (i.e. science imbedded in applications methods) for managing both behavior and results, two critical elements of what is known as performance.

## APPLICATION

This is used most often in the workplace, can apply wherever people interact — schools, churches, community meetings, sports teams, health setting, governmental agencies,social events and even political settings - anywhere in the world people interact with their environments to produce desired effects. Armstrong and Baron defined it as a "strategic and integrated approach to increase the effectiveness of companies by improving the performance of the people who work in them and by developing the capabilities of teams and individual contributors." It may be possible to get all employees to reconcile personal goals with organizational goals and increase productivity and profitability of an organization using this process. It can be applied by organizations or a single department or section inside an organization, as well as an individual person. The performance process is appropriately named the self-propelled performance process (SPPP). First, a commitment analysis must be done where a job mission statement is drawn up for each job. The job mission statement is a job definition in terms of purpose, customers, product and scope. The aim with this analysis is to determine the continuous key objectives and performance standards for each job position. Following the commitment analysis is the work analysis of a particular job in terms of the reporting structure and job description. If a job description is not available, then a systems analysis can be done to draw up a job description. The aim with this analysis is to determine the continuous critical objectives and performance standards for each job.

## BENEFITS

Managing employee or system performance and aligning their objectives facilitates the effective delivery of strategic and operational goals. There is a clear and immediate correlation between using performance management programs or software and improved business and organizational results.

For employee performance management, using integrated software, rather than a spreadsheet based recording system, may deliver a significant return on investment through a range of direct and indirect sales benefits, operational efficiency benefits and by unlocking the latent potential in every employees work day (i.e. the time they spend not actually doing their job). Benefits may include:

Direct financial gain,

- Grow sales
- Reduce costs in the organization
- Stop project overruns
- Aligns the organization directly behind the CEO's goals
- Decreases the time it takes to create strategic or operational changes by communicating the changes through a new set of goals

Motivated workforce

- Optimizes incentive plans to specific goals for over achievement, not just business as usual
- Improves employee engagement because everyone understands how they are directly contributing to the organizations high level goals
- Create transparency in achievement of goals
- High confidence in bonus payment process
- Professional development programs are better aligned directly to achieving business level goals

Improved management control

- Flexible, responsive to management needs
- Displays data relationships
- Helps audit / comply with legislative requirement
- Simplifies communication of strategic goals scenario planning
- Provides well documented and communicated process documentation

## ORGANIZATIONAL DEVELOPMENT

In organizational development (OD), performance can be thought of as Actual Results vs Desired Results. Any discrepancy, where Actual is less than Desired, could constitute the performance improvement zone. Performance management and improvement can be thought of as a cycle:

1. Performance planning where goals and objectives are established
2. Performance coaching where a manager intervenes to give feedback and adjust performance
3. Performance appraisal where individual performance is formally documented and feedback delivered

A performance problem is any gap between Desired Results and Actual Results. Performance improvement is any effort targeted at closing the gap between Actual Results and Desired Results. Other organizational development definitions are slightly different. The U.S. Office of Personnel Management (OPM) indicates that Performance Management consists of a system or process whereby:

1. Work is planned and expectations are set
2. Performance of work is monitored
3. Staff ability to perform is developed and enhanced
4. Performance is rated or measured and the ratings summarized
5. Top performance is rewarded

## IMPLEMENTATION

Erica Olsen notes that "Many businesses, even those with well-made plans, fail to implement their strategy. Their problem lies in ineffectively managing their employees once their plan is in place. Sure, they've conducted surveys, collected data, gone on management retreats to decide on their organization's direction-- even purchased expensive software to manage their process-- but somewhere their plan fails." Performance management and performance appraisals have a significant overlap. In general, there are three type of performance management: long-cycle, short-cycle, and micro.

### LONG-CYCLE PERFORMANCE MANAGEMENT

Long-cycle Performance Management is usually done on an annual, every 6 months, or quarterly basis. From implementations standpoint, this area is the one that has traditionally received the most attention. This is so for historical reasons, as most performance management techniques/styles predate use of computers.

### SHORT-CYCLE PERFORMANCE MANAGEMENT

Short-cycle Performance Management (which overlaps with principles of [Agile Software Development]) is usually done on a weekly, by-weekly, or monthly basis. From thc implementation standpoint, this sort of management is industry-specific.

### MICRO PERFORMANCE MANAGEMENT

Micro Performance management is generally done on a by-minute/hour/day basis.

# 2

# Performance Appraisal

## DEFINITION

The history of performance appraisal is quite brief. Its roots in the early 20th century can be traced to Taylor's pioneering Time and Motion studies. But this is not very helpful, for the same may be said about almost everything in the field of modern human resources management. As a distinct and formal management procedure used in the evaluation of work performance, appraisal really dates from the time of the Second World War - not more than 60 years ago. Yet in a broader sense, the practice of appraisal is a very ancient art. In the scale of things historical, it might well lay claim to being the world's second oldest profession!

There is, says Dulewicz (1989), "... a basic human tendency to make judgements about those one is working with, as well as about oneself." Appraisal, it seems, is both inevitable and universal. In the absence of a carefully structured system of appraisal, people will tend to judge the work performance of others, including subordinates, naturally, informally and arbitrarily. The human inclination to judge can create serious motivational, ethical and legal problems in the workplace. Without a structured appraisal system, there is little chance of ensuring that the judgements made will be lawful, fair, defensible and accurate. Performance appraisal systems began as simple methods of income justification. That is, appraisal was used to decide whether or not the salary or wage of an individual employee was justified. The process was firmly linked to material outcomes. If an employee's performance was found to be less than ideal, a cut in pay would follow. On the other hand, if their performance was better than the supervisor expected, a pay rise was in order.

Little consideration, if any, was given to the developmental possibilities of appraisal. If was felt that a cut in pay, or a rise, should provide the only required impetus for an employee to either improve or continue to perform well. Sometimes this basic system succeeded in getting the results that were intended; but more often than not, it failed. For example, early motivational researchers were aware that different people with roughly equal work abilities could be paid the same amount of money and yet have quite different levels of motivation and performance. These observations were confirmed in empirical studies. Pay rates were important, yes; but they were not the only element that had an impact on employee performance. It was found that other issues, such as morale and self-esteem, could also have a major influence. As a result, the traditional emphasis on reward outcomes was progressively rejected. In the 1950s in the United States, the potential usefulness of appraisal as tool for motivation and development was gradually recognized. The general model of performance appraisal, as it is known today, began from that time.

## MODERN APPRAISAL

Performance appraisal may be defined as a structured formal interaction between a subordinate and supervisor, that usually takes the form of a periodic interview (annual or semi-annual), in which the work performance of the subordinate is examined and discussed, with a view to identifying weaknesses and strengths as well as opportunities for improvement and skills development. In many organizations - but not all - appraisal results are used, either directly or indirectly, to help determine reward outcomes. That is, the appraisal results are used to identify the better performing employees who should get the majority of available merit pay increases, bonuses, and promotions. By the same token, appraisal results are used to identify the poorer performers who may require some form of counseling, or in extreme cases, demotion, dismissal or decreases in pay. (Organizations need to be aware of laws in their country that might restrict their capacity to dismiss employees or decrease pay). Whether this is an appropriate use of performance appraisal - the assignment and justification of rewards and penalties - is a very uncertain and contentious matter.

## CONTROVERSY

Few issues in management stir up more controversy than performance appraisal. There are many reputable sources - researchers, management commentators, psychometricians - who have expressed doubts about the validity and reliability of the performance appraisal process. Some have even suggested that the process is so inherently flawed that it may be impossible to perfect it. At the other extreme, there are many strong advocates of performance appraisal. Some view it as potentially "... the most crucial aspect of organizational life".

Between these two extremes lie various schools of belief. While all endorse the use of performance appraisal, there are many different opinions on how and when to apply it. There are those, for instance, who believe that performance appraisal has many important employee development uses, but scorn any attempt to link the process to reward outcomes - such as pay rises and promotions. This group believes that the linkage to reward outcomes reduces or eliminates the developmental value of appraisals. Rather than an opportunity for constructive review and encouragement, the reward-linked process is perceived as judgmental, punitive and harrowing.

For example, how many people would gladly admit their work problems if, at the same time, they knew that their next pay rise or a much-wanted promotion was riding on an appraisal result? Very likely, in that situation, many people would deny or downplay their weaknesses. Nor is the desire to distort or deny the truth confined to the person being appraised. Many appraisers feel uncomfortable with the combined role of judge and executioner. Such reluctance is not difficult to understand. Appraisers often know their appraisees well, and are typically in a direct subordinate-supervisor relationship. They work together on a daily basis and may, at times, mix socially. Suggesting that a subordinate needs to brush up on certain work skills is one thing; giving an appraisal result that has the direct effect of negating a promotion is another. The result can be resentment and serious morale damage, leading to workplace disruption, soured relationships and productivity declines.

On the other hand, there is a strong rival argument which claims that performance appraisal must unequivocally be linked to reward outcomes. The advocates of this approach say that organizations must have a process by which rewards - which are not an unlimited resource - may be openly and fairly distributed to those most deserving on the basis of merit, effort and results. There is a critical need for remunerative justice in organizations. Performance appraisal - whatever its practical flaws - is the only process available to help achieve fair, decent and consistent reward outcomes. It has also been claimed that appraisees themselves are inclined to believe that appraisal results should be linked directly to reward outcomes - and are suspicious and disappointed when told this is not the case. Rather than feeling relieved, appraisees may suspect that they are not being told the whole truth, or that the appraisal process is a sham and waste of time.

## PROCESS OF PERFORMANCE APPRAISAL

### ESTABLISHING PERFORMANCE STANDARDS

The first step in the process of performance appraisal is the setting up of the standards which will be used to as the base to compare the actual performance of the employees. This step requires setting the criteria to judge the performance of the employees as successful or unsuccessful and the degrees of their contribution to the organizational goals and objectives. The standards set should be clear, easily understandable and in measurable terms. In case the performance of the employee cannot be measured, great care should be taken to describe the standards.

## COMMUNICATING THE STANDARDS

Once set, it is the responsibility of the management to communicate the standards to all the employees of the organization. The employees should be informed and the standards should be clearly explained to the. This will help them to understand their roles and to know what exactly is expected from them. The standards should also be communicated to the appraisers or the evaluators and if required, the standards can also be modified at this stage itself according to the relevant feedback from the employees or the evaluators.

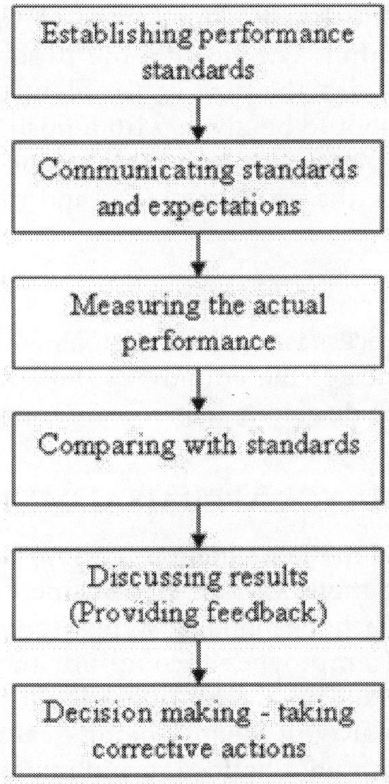


## MEASURING THE ACTUAL PERFORMANCE

The most difficult part of the Performance appraisal process is measuring the actual performance of the employees that is the work done by the employees during the specified period of time. It is a continuous process which involves monitoring the performance throughout the year. This stage requires the careful selection of the appropriate techniques of measurement, taking care that personal bias does not affect the outcome of the process and providing assistance rather than interfering in an employees work.

## COMPARING THE ACTUAL WITH THE DESIRED PERFORMANCE

The actual performance is compared with the desired or the standard performance. The comparison tells the deviations in the performance of the employees from the standards set. The result can show the actual performance being more than the desired performance or, the actual performance being less than the desired performance depicting a negative deviation in the organizational performance. It includes recalling, evaluating and analysis of data related to the employees' performance.

### DISCUSSING RESULTS

The result of the appraisal is communicated and discussed with the employees on one-to-one basis. The focus of this discussion is on communication and listening. The results, the problems and the possible solutions are discussed with the aim of problem solving and reaching consensus. The feedback should be given with a positive attitude as this can have an effect on the employees' future performance. The purpose of the meeting should be to solve the problems faced and motivate the employees to perform better.

### DECISION MAKING

The last step of the process is to take decisions which can be taken either to improve the performance of the employees, take the required corrective actions, or the related HR decisions like rewards, promotions, demotions, transfers etc.

## PERFORMANCE APPRAISAL METHODS

Performance appraisal methods include 11 appraisal methods / types as follows: Critical incident method: The critical incidents for performance appraisal is a method in which the manager writes down positive and negative performance behavior of employees throughout the performance period Weighted checklist method: This method describe a performance appraisal method where rater familiar with the jobs being evaluated prepared a large list of descriptive statements about effective and ineffective behavior on jobs

Paired comparison analysis: Paired comparison analysis is a good way of weighing up the relative importance of options. A range of plausible options is listed. Each option is compared against each of the other options. The results are tallied and the option with the highest score is the preferred option. Graphic rating scales: The Rating Scale is a form on which the manager simply checks off the employee's level of performance. This is the oldest and most widely method used for performance appraisal. Essay Evaluation method: This method asked managers / supervisors to describe strengths and weaknesses of an employee's behavior. Essay evaluation is a non-quantitative technique. This method usually use with the graphic rating scale method.

Behaviorally anchored rating scales: This method used to describe a performance rating that focused on specific behaviors or sets as indicators of effective or ineffective performance. It is a combination of the rating scale and critical incident techniques of employee performance evaluation. Performance ranking method: Ranking is a performance appraisal method that is used to evaluate employee performance from best to worst. Manager will compare an employee to another employee, rather than comparing each one to a standard measurement. Management By Objectives (MBO) method: MBO is a process in which managers / employees set objectives for the employee, periodically evaluate the performance, and reward according to the result. MBO focuses attention on what must be accomplished (goals) rather than how it is to be accomplished (methods) 360 degree performance appraisal: 360 Degree Feedback is a system or process in which employees receive confidential, anonymous feedback from the people who work around them. This post also include information related to appraisal methods such as 720, 540, 180... Forced ranking (forced distribution): Forced ranking is a method of performance appraisal to rank employee but in order of forced distribution. For example, the distribution requested with 10 or 20 percent in the top category, 70 or 80 percent in the middle, and 10 percent in the bottom. Behavioral Observation Scales: Behavioral Observation Scales is frequency rating of critical incidents that worker has performed.

## ABSOLUTE STANDARDS

### CONFIDENTIAL REPORT

It is mostly used in government organizations. It is a descriptive report prepared, generally at the end of every year, by the employee's immediate superior. The report highlights the strengths and weaknesses of the subordinate. The report is not databased. The impressions of the superior about the subordinate are merely recorded there. It does not offer any feedback to the appraisee. The appraisee is not very sure about why his ratings have fallen despite his best efforts, why others are rated high when compared to him, how to rectify his mistakes, if any; on what basis he is going to be evaluated next year, etc. Since the report is generally not made public and hence no feedback is available, the subjective analysis of the superior is likely to be hotly contested. In recent years, due to pressure from courts and trade unions, the details of a negative confidential report are given to the appraisee.

### ESSAY EVALUATION

Under this method, the rater is asked to express the strong as well as weak points of the employee's behavior. This technique is normally used with a combination of the graphic rating scale because the rater can elaborately present the scale by substantiating an explanation for his rating. While preparing the essay on the employee, the rater considers the following factors: (i) Job knowledge and potential of the employee; (ii) Employee's understanding of the company's programmes, policies, objectives, etc.; (iii) The employee's relations with co-workers and superiors; (iv) The employee's general planning, organizing and controlling ability; (v) The attitudes and perceptions of the employee, in general. Essay evaluation is a non-quantitative technique. This method is advantageous in at least one sense, i.e., the essay provides a good deal of information about the employee and also reveals more about the evaluator. The essay evaluation method however, suffers from the following limitations:

- It is highly subjective; the supervisor may write a biased essay. The employees who are sycophants will be evaluated more favorably then other employees.
- Some evaluators may be poor in writing essays on employee performance. Others may be superficial in explanation and use flowery language which may not reflect the actual performance of the employee. It is very difficult to find effective writers nowadays.
- The appraiser is required to find time to prepare the essay. A busy appraiser may write the essay hurriedly without properly assessing the actual performance of the worker. On the other hand, appraiser takes a long time, this becomes uneconomical from the view point of the firm, because the time of the evaluator (supervisor) is costly.

## CRITICAL INCIDENT TECHNIQUE

Under this method, the manager prepares lists of statements of very effective and ineffective behavior of an employee. These critical incidents or events represent the outstanding or poor behavior of employees on the job. The manager maintains logs on each employee, whereby he periodically records critical incidents of the workers behavior. At the end of the rating period, these recorded critical incidents are used in the evaluation of the workers' performance. An example of a good critical incident of a sales assistant is the following:

- The sales clerk patiently attended to the customers complaint. He is polite, prompt, enthusiastic in solving the customers' problem.

On the other hand the bad critical incident may appear as under:

- The sales assistant stayed 45 minutes over on his break during the busiest part of the day. He failed to answer the store manager's call thrice. He is lazy, negligent, stubborn and uninterested in work.

This method provides an objective basis for conducting a thorough discussion of an employee's performance. This method avoids recency bias (most recent incidents get too much emphasis). This method suffers however from the following limitations:

- Negative incidents may be more noticeable than positive incidents.

- The supervisors have a tendency to unload a series of complaints about incidents during an annual performance review session.
- It results in very close supervision which may not be liked by the employee.
- The recording of incidents may be a chore for the manager concerned, who may be too busy or forget to do it.

Most frequently, the critical incidents technique of evaluation is applied to evaluate the performance of superiors rather than of peers of subordinates.

## CHECKLISTS AND WEIGHTED CHECKLISTS

Another simple type of individual evaluation method is the checklist. A checklist represents, in its simplest form, a set of objectives or descriptive statements about the employee and his behavior. If the rater believes strongly that the employee possesses a particular listed trait, he checks the item; otherwise, he leaves the item blank. A more recent variation of the checklist method is the weighted list. Under this, the value of each question may be weighted equally or certain questions may be weighted more heavily than others. The following are some of the sample questions in the checklist.

- Is the employee really interested in the task assigned? Yes/No
- Is he respected by his colleagues (co-workers) Yes/No
- Does he give respect to his superiors? Yes/No
- Does he follow instructions properly? Yes/No
- Does he make mistakes frequently? Yes/No

A rating score from the checklist helps the manager in evaluation of the performance of the employee. The checklist method has a serious limitation. The rater may be biased in distinguishing the positive and negative questions. He may assign biased weights to the questions. Another limitation could be that this method is expensive and time consuming. Finally, it becomes difficult for the manager to assemble, analyze and weigh a number of statements about the employee's characteristics, contributions and behaviors. In spite of these limitations, the checklist method is most frequently used in the employee's performance evaluation.

## GRAPHIC RATING SCALE

Perhaps the most commonly used method of performance evaluation is the graphic rating scale. Of course, it is also one of the oldest methods of evaluation in use. Under this method, a printed form, as shown below, is used to evaluate the performance of an employee. A variety of traits may be used in these types of rating devices, the most common being the quantity and quality of work. The rating scales can also be adapted by including traits that the company considers important for effectiveness on the job. A model of a graphic rating scale is given.

**Table. Typical Graphic Rating Scale**

Employee Name.................. Job title................
Department........................ Rate..............
Data.................................

| Quantity of work: Volume of work under normal working conditions | Unsatisfactory | Fair | Satisfactory | Good | Outstanding |
|---|---|---|---|---|---|
| Quality of work: Neatness, thoroughness and accuracy of work Knowledge of job | | | | | |
| A clear understanding of the factors connected with the job | | | | | |
| Attitude: Exhibits enthusiasm and cooperativeness on the job | | | | | |
| Dependability: Conscientious, thorough, reliable, accurate, with respect to attendance, reliefs, lunch breaks, etc. | | | | | |
| Cooperation: Willingness and ability to work with others to produce desired goals. | | | | | |

From the graphic rating scales, excerpts can be obtained about the performance standards of employees. For instance, if the employee has serious gaps in technical-professional knowledge (knows only rudimentary phases of job); lacks the knowledge to bring about an increase in productivity; is reluctant to make decisions on his own (on even when he makes decisions they are unreliable and substandard); declines to accept responsibility; fails to plan ahead effectively; wastes and misuses resources; etc., then it can safely be inferred that the standards of the performance of the employee are dismal and disappointing.

The rating scale is the most common method of evaluation of an employee's performance today. One positive point in favor of the rating scale is that it is easy to understand, easy to use and permits a statistical tabulation of scores of employees. When ratings are objective in nature they can be effectively used as evaluators. The graphic rating scale may however suffer from a long standing disadvantage, i.e., it may be arbitrary and the rating may be subjective. Another pitfall is that each characteristic is equally important in evaluation of the employee's performance and so on.

## BEHAVIORALLY ANCHORED RATING SCALES

Also known as the behavioral expectations scale, this method represents the latest innovation in performance appraisal. It is a combination of the rating scale and critical incident techniques of employee performance evaluation. The critical incidents serve as anchor statements on a scale and the rating form usually contains six to eight specifically defined performance dimensions. The following chart represents an example of a sales trainee's competence and a behaviorally anchored rating scale.

**Table. An Example of Behaviorally Anchored Rating Scale (BARS)**

| Performance | Points | Behavior |
|---|---|---|
| Extremely good | 7 | Can expect trainee to make valuable suggestions for increased sales and to have positive relationships with customers all over the country. |
| Good | 6 | Can expect to initiate creative ideas for improved sales. |
| Above average | 5 | Can expect to keep in touch with the customers throughout the year. |
| Average | 4 | Can manage, with difficulty, to deliver the goods in time. |
| Below average | 3 | Can expect to unload the trucks when asked by the supervisor. |
| Poor | 2 | Can expect to inform only a part of the customers. |
| Extremely poor | 1 | Can expect to take extended coffee breaks and roam around purposelessly. |

How to construct BARS? Developing a BARS follows a general format which combines techniques employed in the critical incident method and weighted checklist ratings scales. Emphasis is pinpointed on pooling the thinking of people who will use the scales as both evaluators and evaluees.

*Step 1:* Collect critical incidents: People with knowledge of the job to be probed, such as job holders and supervisors, describe specific examples of effective and ineffective behavior related to job performance.

*Step 2:* Identify performance dimensions: The people assigned the task of developing the instrument cluster the incidents into a small set of key performance dimensions. Generally between five and ten dimensions account for most of the performance. Examples of performance dimensions include technical competence, relationships with customers, handling of paper work and meeting day-to-day deadlines. While developing varying levels of performance for each dimension (anchors), specific examples of behavior should be used, which could later be scaled in terms of good, average or below average performance.

*Step 3:* Reclassification of incidents: Another group of participants who are knowledgeable about the job is instructed to retranslate or reclassify the critical incidents generated (in Step II) previously. They are given the definition of job dimension and told to assign each critical incident to the dimension that it best describes. At this stage, incidents for which there is not 75 per cent agreement are discarded as being too subjective.

*Step 4:* Assigning scale values to the incidents: Each incident is then rated on a one-to-seven or one-to-nine scale with respect of how well it represents performance on the appropriate dimension. A rating of one represents ineffective performance; the top scale value indicates very effective performance. The second group of participants usually assigns the scale values. Means and standard deviations are then calculated for the scale values assigned to each incident. Typically incidents that have standard deviations of 1.50 or less (on a 7-point scale) are retained.

*Step 5:* Producing the final instrument: About six or seven incidents for each performance dimension – all having met both the retranslating and standard deviation criteria – will be used as behavioral anchors. The final BARS instrument consists of a series of vertical scales (one for each dimension) anchored (or measured) by the final incidents. Each incident is positioned on the scale according to its mean value.

Because the above process typically requires considerable employee participation, its acceptance by both supervisors and their subordinates may be greater. Proponents of BARS also claim that such a system differentiates among behavior, performance and results and consequently is able to provide a basis for setting developmental goals for the employee. Because it is job-specific and identifies observable and measurable behavior, it is a more reliable and valid method for performance appraisal.

Researchers, after surveying several studies on BARS, concluded that "despite the intuitive appeal of BARS, findings from research have not been encouraging". It has not proved to be superior to other methods in overcoming rater errors or in achieving psychometric soundness. A specific deficiency is that the behaviors used are activity oriented rather than results oriented. This creates a potential problem for supervisors doing the evaluation, who may be forced to deal with employees who are performing the activity but not accomplishing the desired goals. Further, it is time consuming and expensive to create BARS. They also demand several appraisal forms to accommodate different types of jobs in an organization. In a college, lecturers, office clerks, library staff, technical staff and gardening staff all have different jobs; separate BARS forms would need to be developed for each. In view of the lack of compelling evidence demonstrating the superiority of BARS over traditional techniques such as graphic rating scales. Decotis concluded that: "It may be time to quit hedging about the efficacy of behavioral scaling strategies and conclude that this method has no clear-cut advantages over more traditional and easier methods of performance evaluation".

## FORCED CHOICE METHOD

This method was developed to eliminate bias and the preponderance of high ratings that might occur in some organizations. The primary purpose of the forced choice method is to correct the tendency of a rater to give consistently high or low ratings to all the employees. This method makes use of several sets of pair phrases, two of which may be positive and two negative and the rater is asked to indicate which of the four phrases is the most and least descriptive of a particular worker. Actually, the statement items are grounded in such a way that the rater cannot easily judge which statements apply to the most effective employee. The following box is a classic illustration of the forced choice items in organizations.

**Table. Forced Choice Items**

| | | | |
|---|---|---|---|
| 1. | Least | | Most |
| | A | Does not anticipate difficulties | A |
| | B | Grasps explanations easily and quickly | B |
| | C | Does not waste time | C |
| | D | Very easy to talk to | D |
| 2. | Least | | Most |
| | A | Can be a leader | A |
| | B | Wastes time on unproductive things | B |
| | C | At all times, cool and calm | C |
| | D | Smart worker | D |

The favorable qualities earn a plus credit and the unfavorable ones earn the reverse. The worker gets over plus when the positive factors override the negative ones or when one of the negative phrases is checked as being insignificantly rated. They overall objectivity is increased by using this method in evaluation of employee's performance, because the rater does not know how high or low he is evaluating the individual as he has no access to the scoring key. This method, however, has a strong limitation. In the preparation of sets of phrases trained technicians are needed and as such the method becomes very expensive. Further, managers may feel frustrated rating the employees 'in the dark'. Finally, the results of the forced choice method may not be useful for training employees because the rater himself does not know how he is evaluating the worker. In spite of these limitations, the forced choice techniques is quite popular.

## MANAGEMENT BY OBJECTIVES (MBO)

MBO represents a modern method of evaluating the performance of personnel. Thoughtful managers have become increasingly aware that the traditional performance evaluation systems are characterized by somewhat antagonistic judgments on the part of the rater. There is a growing feeling nowadays that it is better to make the superior work with subordinates in fixing goals. This would inevitably enable subordinates to exercise self-control over their performance behaviors. The concept of management by objectives is actually the outcome of the pioneering works of Drucker, McGregor and Odiorne in management science. Management by objectives can be described as "a process whereby the superior and subordinate managers of an organization jointly identify its common goals, define each individuals' major areas of responsibility in terms of results expected of him and use these measures as guides for operating the unit and assessing the contributions of each of its members". MBO thus represents more than an evaluation programme and process. Practicing management scientists and pedagogues view it as a philosophy of managerial practice; it is a method by which managers and subordinates plan, organize, control, communicate and debate.

Features:

- MBO emphasizes participatively set goals that are tangible, verifiable and measurable.
- MBO focuses attention on what must be accomplished (goals) rather than how it is to be accomplished (methods).
- MBO, by concentrating on key result areas translates the abstract philosophy of management into concrete phraseology. The technique can be put to general use (non-specialist technique). Further it is "a dynamic system which seeks to integrate the company's need to clarify and achieve its profit and growth targets with the manager's need to contribute and develop himself".
- MBO is a systematic and rational technique that allows management to attain maximum results from available resources by focusing on achievable goals. It allows the subordinate plenty of room to make creative decisions on his own.

## MANAGEMENT BY OBJECTIVES

The concept of 'Management by Objectives' (MBO) was first given by Peter Drucker in 1954.

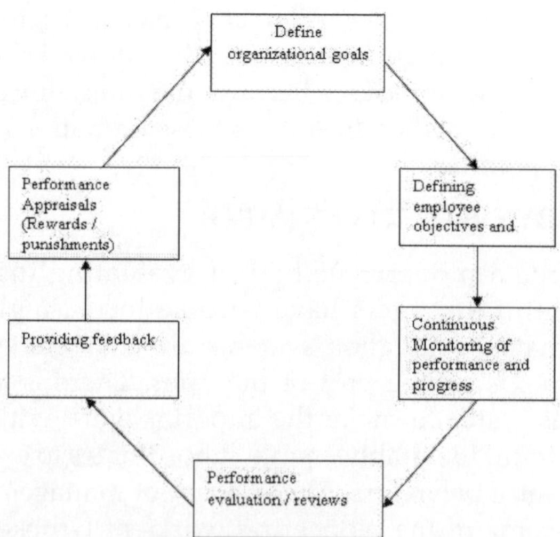


It can be defined as a process whereby the employees and the superiors come together to identify common goals, the employees set their goals to be achieved, the standards to be taken as the criteria for measurement of their performance and contribution and deciding the course of action to be followed. The essence of MBO is participative goal setting, choosing course of actions and decision making. An important part of the MBO is the measurement and the comparison of the employee's actual performance with the standards set. Ideally, when employees themselves have been involved with the goal setting and the choosing the course of action to be followed by them, they are more likely to fulfill their responsibilities.

## THE MBO PROCESS

## UNIQUE FEATURES AND ADVANTAGES OF MBO

The principle behind Management by Objectives (MBO) is to create empowered employees who have clarity of the roles and responsibilities expected from them, understand their objectives to be achieved and thus help in the achievement of organizational as well as personal goals.

Some of the important features and advantages of MBO are:

- Clarity of goals – With MBO, came the concept of SMART goals i.e. goals that are:
  Specific
  Measurable
  Achievable
  Realistic, and
  Time bound.
  The goals thus set are clear, motivating and there is a linkage between organizational goals and performance targets of the employees.
- The focus is on future rather than on past. Goals and standards are set for the performance for the future with periodic reviews and feedback.
- Motivation – Involving employees in the whole process of goal setting and increasing employee empowerment increases employee job satisfaction and commitment.
- Better communication and Coordination – Frequent reviews and interactions between superiors and subordinates helps to maintain harmonious relationships within the enterprise and also solve many problems faced during the period.

# COMMON APPRAISAL ERRORS

## CONTRAST EFFECT

Tendency of a rater to evaluate people in comparison with other individuals rather than against the standards for the job

**FIRST IMPRESSION ERROR**

Tendency of a rater to make an initial positive or negative judgment of an employee and allow that first impression to color or distort later information.

**HALO/HORNS EFFECT**

Inappropriate generalizations from one aspect of an individual's performance to all areas of that person's performance.

**SIMILAR-TO-ME EFFECT**

The tendency of individuals to rate people who resemble themselves more highly than they rate others.

**CENTRAL TENDENCY**

The inclination to rate people in the middle scale even when their performance clearly warrants a substantially higher or lower rating.

**NEGATIVE AND POSITIVE SKEW**

The opposite of central tendency: the rating of all individuals as higher or lower than their performance warrants.

**ATTRIBUTION BIAS**

The tendency to attribute performance failings to factors under the control of the individual and performance successes to external causes.

**RECENCY EFFECT**

The tendency of minor events that have happened recently to have more influence on the rating than major events of many months ago.

**STEREOTYPING**

The tendency to generalize across groups and ignore individual differences.

# 3

# Performance Development and Assessment

## INTRODUCTION

Performance assessment helps organizations to determine how employees can help to achieve the goals of organizations. It has two important activities included in it. First has to do with determining the performance and other with the process of evaluation. In this unit, concept of performance assessment and the processes involved in it have been discussed.

## CONCEPT OF PERFORMANCE ASSESSMENT

### WHAT IS PERFORMANCE?

What does the term performance actually mean? Employees are performing well when they are productive. Productivity implies both concern for effectiveness and efficiency, effectiveness refers to goal accomplishment. However it does not speak of the costs incurred in reaching the goal. That is where efficiency comes in. Efficiency evaluates the ratio of inputs consumed to outputs achieved. The greater the output for a given input, the greater the efficiency. It is not desirable to have objective measures of productivity such as hard data on effectiveness, number of units produced, or percent of crimes solved etc and hard data on efficiency (average cost per unit or ratio of sales volume to number of calls made etc.). In addition to productivity as measured in terms of effectiveness and efficiency, performance also includes personnel data such as measures of accidents, turnover, absences, and tardiness. That is a good employee is one who not only performs well in terms of productivity but also minimizes problems for the organisation by being to work on time, by not missing days, and by minimizing the number of work-related accidents.

### WHAT IS ASSESSMENT

Assessments are judgments of the characteristics, traits and performance of others. On the basis of these judgments we assess the worth or value of others and identify what is good or bad. In industry performance assessment is a systematic evaluation of employees by supervisors. Employees also wish to know their position in the organization. Assessments are essential for making many administrative decisions: selection, training, promotion, transfer, wage and salary administration etc. Besides they aid in personnel research. Performance Assessment thus is a systematic and objective way of judging the relative worth of ability of an employee in performing his task. Performance assessment helps to identify those who are performing their assigned tasks well and those who are not and the reasons for such performance.

## GOALS OF PERFORMANCE ASSESSMENT

Conducting performance assessments on employee's performance should be more than a simple checklist of Do's and Don'ts. Performance evaluation should serve as a vital component, one that is of interest to both the organization and the employee. From the organizational perspective, sound performance assessments can ensure that correct work is being done, work that assists in meeting department goals simply put. Each employee's work should support the activities needed to action his or her supervisor's performance objectives.

This should ultimately continue up the hierarchy, with all efforts supporting corporate strategic goals. From the employee perspective, properly operating performance assessment systems provide a clear communication of work expectations. Knowing what is expected is a first step in helping one to cope better with the stress usually associated with a lack of clear direction. Secondly, properly designed performance assessments should also serve as a means of assisting an employee's personal development. To make effective performance assessments a reality, four criteria need to be present. These are:

- Employees should be actively involved in the evaluation and development process.
- Supervisors need to enter performance assessments with a constructive and helpful attitude.
- Realistic goals must be mutually set.
- Supervisors must be aware, and have knowledge of the employee's job and performance.

## OBJECTIVES OF PERFORMANCE ASSESSMENT

Performance assessment has a number of specific objectives. These are given below:

- To review past performance;
- To assess training needs;
- To help develop individuals;
- To audit the skills within an organizations;

- To set targets for future performance;
- To identify potential for promotion.

Some employees may believe that performance assessment is simply used by the organization to apportion blame and to provide a basis for disciplinary action. They see it as a stick that management has introduced with which to beat people. Under such situations a well thought out performance assessment is doomed to failure. Even if the more positive objectives are built into the system, problems may still arise because they may not all be achievable and they may cause conflict. For Example, an appraise is less likely to be open about any shortcomings in past performance during a process that affects pay or promotion prospects, or which might be perceived as leading to disciplinary action. It is therefore important that performance assessment should have specific objective. Not only should the objectives be clear but also they should form part of the organization's whole strategy. Thus incorporating objectives into the assessment system may highlight areas for improvement, new directions and opportunities.

## THE PERFORMANCE ASSESSMENT PROCESS

Following steps are involved in assessment process:

- The assessment process begins with the establishment of performance standards. These should have evolved out of job analysis and the job description. These performance standards should also be clear and objective enough to be understood and measured. Too often, these standards are articulated in some such phrase as "a full day's work" or "a good job." Vague phrases tell us nothing. The expectations a manager has in term of work performance by the subordinates must be clear enough in their minds so that the managers would be able to at some later date, to communicate these expectations to their subordinates and appraise their performance against these previously established standards.
- Once performance standards are established, it is necessary to communicate these expectations. It should not be part of the employees' job to guess what is expected of them. Unfortunately, too many jobs have vague performance standards. The problem is compounded when these standards are not communicated to the employees. It is important to note that communication is a two-way street. Mere transference of information from the manager to the subordinate regarding expectations is not communication. Communication only takes place when the transference of information has taken place and has been received and understood by subordinate. Therefore feedback is necessary. Hence the information communicated by the manager has been received and understood in the way it was intended.

- The Third step in a assessment process is measurement of performance. To determine what actual performance is, it is necessary to acquire information about it. We should be concerned with how we measure and what we measure. Four common sources of information are frequently used by mangers to measure actual performance: personal observation, statistical reports, oral reports, and written reports. Each has its strengths and weaknesses; however, a combination of them increases both the number of input sources and the probability of receiving reliable information. What we measure is probably more critical to the evaluation process than how we measure. The selection of the wrong criteria can result in serious dysfunctional consequences. What we measure determines, to a great extent, what people in a organization will attempt to excel at. The criteria we choose to measure must represent performance as stated in the first two steps of the assessment process.
- The fourth step in the assessment process is the comparison of actual performance with standards. The attempt in this step is to note deviations between standard performance and actual performance. One of the most challenging tasks facing managers is to present an accurate assessment to the subordinate and then have the subordinate accept the assessment in a constructive manner. The impression that subordinates receive about their assessment has a strong impact on their selfesteem and, very important, on their subsequent performance. Of course, conveying good news is considerably less difficult than conveying the bad news that performance has been below expectations. Thus, the discussion of the assessment can have negative as well as positive motivational consequences.

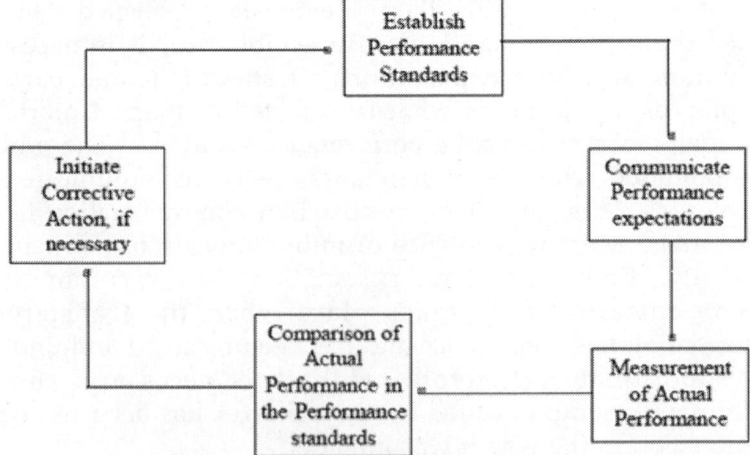

- The final step in the assessment is the initiation of corrective action when necessary. Corrective action can be of two types; one is immediate and deals predominantly with symptoms. The other is basic and delves into causes. Immediate corrective action is often described as "putting out fires", where as basic corrective action gets to the source of deviation and seeks to adjust the differences permanently. Immediate action corrects something right now and gets things back on track. Basic action asks how and why performance deviated. In some instances, managers may rationalize that they do not have the time to take basic corrective action and therefore must be content to "perpetually put out fires." Figure shows the performance process in summary.

## BENEFITS OF PERFORMANCE ASSESSMENT

The benefits of an effective assessment scheme can be summed up under three categories. These are for the organization, for appraiser and for appraisee.

- For the Organizations: Following benefits would accrue to the organization. a) Improved performance throughout the organization due to more effective communication of the organization's objectives and values, increased sense of cohesiveness and loyalty and improved relationships between managers and staff.
  - Improvement in the tasks performed by each member of the staff.
  - Identification of ideas for improvement.
  - Expectations and long-term plans can be developed.
  - Training and development needs can be identified more clearly.
  - A culture of continuous improvement and success can be created and maintained.
  - People with potential can be identified and career development plans can be formulated for future staff requirements.
- For the appraiser: The following benefits would accrue to the appraiser:
  - The opportunity to develop an overview of individual jobs and departments.
  - Identification of ideas for improvements.
  - The opportunity to link team and individual objectives and targets with departmental and organizational objectives.
  - The opportunity to clarify expectations of the contribution the manager expects from teams and individuals.
  - The opportunity to re-prioritize targets.
  - A means of forming a more productive relationship with staff based on mutual trust and understanding.

- For the appraisee: For the appraisee the following benefits would accrue:
  - Increased motivation.
  - Increased job satisfaction.
  - Increased sense of personal value.

## PERFORMANCE ASSESSMENT METHODS

This section looks at how management can actually establish performance standards and devise instruments that can be used to measure and appraise an employee's performance. A number of methods are now available to assess the performance of the employees.

### CRITICAL INCIDENT METHOD

Critical incident assessment focuses the rater's attention on those critical or key behaviors that make the difference between doing a job effectively and doing it ineffectively. What the appraiser does is write down little anecdotes that describe what the employee did that was especially effective or ineffective. In this approach to assessment, specific behaviors are cited, not vaguely defined personality traits. A behaviorally based assessment such as this should be more valid than trait-based assessments because it is clearly more job related. It is one thing to say that an employee is "aggressive" or "imaginative or "relaxed," but that does not tell anything about how well the job is being done. Critical incidents, with their focus on behaviors, judge performance rather than personalities. Additionally, a list of critical incidents on a given employees provides a rich set of examples from which the employee can be shown which of his or her behaviors are desirable and which ones call for improvement. This method suffers from following two drawbacks:

- Supervisors are reluctant to write these reports on a daily or even weekly basis for all of their subordinates as it is time consuming and burdensome for them
- Critical incidents do not lend themselves to quantification. Therefore the comparison and ranking of subordinates is difficult.

### CHECKLIST

In the checklist, the evaluator uses a bit of behavioral descriptions and checks of those behaviors that apply to the employee. The evaluator merely goes down the list and gives "yes" or "no" responses. Once the checklist is complete, it is usually evaluated by the staff of personnel department, not the rater himself. Therefore the rater does not actually evaluate the employee's performance; he/she merely records it. An analyst in the personnel department then scores the checklist, often weighting the factors in relationship to their importance. The final evaluation can then be returned to the rating manager for discussion with the subordinate, or someone from the personnel department can provide the feedback to the subordinate.

## GRAPHIC RATING SCALE

One of the oldest and most popular methods of assessment is the graphic rating scale. They are used to assess factors such as quantity and quality of work, job knowledge, cooperation, loyalty, dependability, attendance, honesty, integrity, attitudes, and initiative etc. However, this method is most valid when abstract traits like loyalty or integrity are avoided unless they can be defined in more specific behavioral terms. The assessor goes down the list of factors and notes that point along the scale or continuum that list of factors and notes that point along the scale or continuum that best describes the employee. There are typically five to ten points on the continuum. In the design of the graphic scale, the challenge is to ensure that both the factors evaluated and the scale pints are clearly understood and unambiguous to the rater. Should ambiguity occur, bias is introduced. Following are some of the advantages of this method:

- They are less time-consuming to develop and administer.
- They permit quantitative analysis.
- There is greater standardization of items so comparability with other individuals in diverse job categories is possible.

## FORCED CHOICE METHOD

The forced choice assessment is a special type of checklist, but the rater has to choose between two or more statements, all of which may be favorable or unfavorable. The appraiser's job is to identify which statement is most (or in some cases least) descriptive of the individual being evaluated. To reduce bias, the right answers are not known to the rater. Someone in the personnel department scores the answers based on the key. This key should be validated so management is in a position to say that individuals with higher scores are better-performing employees.

The major advantages of the forced choice method are:

- Since the appraiser does not know the "right" answers, it reduces bias.
- It looks at over all performance.
- It is based on the behavior of the employees.

## BEHAVIOURALLY ANCHORED RATING SCALES

These scales combine major elements from the critical incident and graphic rating scale approaches. The appraiser rates the employees based on items along continuum, but the points are examples of actual behavior on the given job rather than general descriptions or traits. Behaviorally anchored rating scales specify definite, observable, and measurable job behavior.

Examples of job-related behavior and performance dimensions are generated by asking participants to give specific illustrations on effective and ineffective behavior regarding each performance dimension. These behavioral examples are then retranslated into appropriate performance dimensions. Those that are sorted into the dimension for which they were generated are retained. The final group of behavior incidents are then numerically scaled to a level of performance that each is perceived to represent. The incidents that are retranslated and have high rater agreement on performance effectiveness are retained for use as anchors on the performance dimension. The results of the above processes are behavioral descriptions, such as anticipates, plans, executes, solves immediate problems, carries out orders, and handles emergency situations. This method has following advantages:

- It does tend to reduce rating errors.
- It assesses behavior over traits.
- It clarifies to both the employee and rater which behaviors connote good performance and which connote bad.

## GROUP ORDER RANKING

The group order ranking requires the evaluator to place employees into a particular classification, such as "top one-fifth" or "second one-fifth." Evaluators are asked to rank the employees in the top 5 per cent, the next 5 per cent, the next 15 per cent. So if a rater has twenty subordinates, only four can be in the top fifth and, of course, four must also be relegated to the bottom fifth. The advantage of this method is that it prevent raters from inflating their evaluations so everyone looks good or from homogenizing the evaluations for everyone is rated near the average outcome that are usual with the graphic rating scale. It has following disadvantages:

- It is not good if the number of employee being compared is small. At the extreme, if the evaluator is looking at only four employees, it is very possible that they may all be excellent, yet the evaluator may be forced to rank them into top quarter, second quarter, third quarter, and low quarter!
- Another disadvantage, which plagues all relative measures, is the "zero-sum game": consideration. This means, any change must add up to zero. For example, if there are twelve employees in a department performing at different levels of effectiveness, by definition, three are in the top quarter, three in the second quarter, and so forth. The sixth-best employee, for instance, would be in the second quartile. Ironically, if two of the workers in the third or fourth quartiles leave the department and are not replaced, then our sixth best employee now fit into the third quarter.
- Because comparison are relative, an employee who is mediocre may score high only because he or she is the "best of the worst" Similarly,

an excellent performer who is matched against "stiff" competition may be evaluated poorly, when in absolute terms his or her performance is outstanding.

## INDIVIDUAL RANKING

The individual ranking method requires the evaluator merely to list all the employees in an order from highest to lowest. Only one can be the "best." If the evaluator is required to appraise thirty individuals ranking method carries the same pluses and minuses as group order ranking.

## PAIRED COMPARISON

The paired comparison method is calculated by taking the total of [n (n-1)]/2 comparisons. A score is obtained for each employee by simply counting the number of pairs in which the individual is the preferred member. It ranks each individual in relationship to all others on a one-on-one basis. If ten people are being evaluated, the first person is compared, with each of the other nine, and the number of items this person is preferred in any of the nine pairs is tabulated. Each of the remaining nine persons, in turn, is compared in the same way, and a ranking is evolved by the greatest number of preferred "victories". This method ensures that each employee is compared against every other, but the method can become unwieldy when large numbers of employees are being compared.

## MANAGEMENT BY OBJECTIVES

Management by objectives (MBO) is a process that converts organizational objectives into individual objectives. It can be thought of as consisting of four steps: goal setting, action planning, self-control, and periodic reviews:-

- In goal setting, the organization's overall objectives are used as guidelines from which departmental and individual objectives are set. At the individual level, the manager and subordinate jointly identify those goals that are critical for the subordinate to achieve in order to fulfill the requirements of the job as determined in job analysis. These goals are agreed upon and then become the standards by which the employee's results will be evaluated.
- In action planning, the means are determined for achieving the ends established in goals setting. That is, realistic plans are developed to attain the objectives. This step includes identifying the activities necessary to accomplish the objective, establishing the critical relationships between these activities, estimating the time requirement for each activity, and determining the resources required to complete each activity.
- Self-control refers to the systematic monitoring and measuring of performance. Ideally, by having the individual review his or her

own performance. The MBO philosophy is built on the assumptions that individuals can be responsible, can exercise self-direction, and do not require external controls and threats of punishment.

- Finally, with periodic progress reviews, corrective action is initiated when behavior deviates from the standards established in the goal-setting phase. Again, consistent with MBO philosophy, these manager-subordinate reviews are conducted in a constructive rather than punitive manner. Reviews are not meant to degrade the individual but to aid in future performance. These reviews should take place at least two or three times a year.

Following are the advantages of MBO:

- It is result –oriented. It assists the planning and control functions and provides motivation.
- Employees know exactly what is expected of them and how they will be evaluated.
- Employees have a greater commitment to objectives that they have participated in developing than to those unilaterally set by their bosses.

## 360 DEGREE ASSESSMENT

The 360 degree feedback process involves collecting perceptions about a person's behaviour and the impact of that behaviour from the person's boss or bosses, direct reports, colleagues, fellow members of project teams, internal ad external customers, and suppliers. Other names for 360 degree feedback are multi-rater feedback, multisource feedback, full-circle assessment, and group performance review. 360 degree feedback is a method and a tool that provides each employee the opportunity to receive performance feedback from his or her supervisor and four to eight peers, subordinates and customers. 360 degree feedback allows each individual to understand how his effectiveness as an employee, co-worker, or staff member is viewed by others. The most effective processes provide feedback that is based on behaviours that other employees can see. The feedback provides insight about the skills and behaviours desired in the organization to accomplish the mission, vision, goals and values. The feedback is firmly planted in behaviours needed to exceed customer expectations. People whoe are chosen as raters are usually those that interact routinely with the person receiving feedback. The purpose of the feedback is to:

- Assist each individual to understand his or her strengths and weaknesses.
- Contribute insights into aspects of his or her work needing professional development.

Following are some of the major considerations in using 360 degree feedback. These are basically concerned with how to:

- Select the feedback tool and process;
- Select the raters;
- Use the feedback
- Review the feedback; and
- Manage and integrate the process into a larger performance management system.

**Features of 360 degree assessment**

Organizations that are using with the 360 degree component of their performance management systems identify following positive features of the process. These features will manifest themselves in well-managed, well-integrated 360 degree processes.

- Improved Feedback from more sources: Provides well-rounded feedback from peers, reporting staff, co-workers, and supervisors. This can be a definite improvement over feedback from a single individual. 360 feedback can also save managers' time in that they can spend less energy providing feedback as more people participate in the process. Co-worker perception is important and the process helps people understand how other employees view their work.
- Team Development: Helps team members learn to work more effectively together. Team members know more about how other members are performing than their supervisor. Multirater feedback makes team members more accountable to each other as they share the knowledge that they will provide input on each member's performance. A well-planned process can improve communication and team development.
- Personal and Organizational Performance Development: 360 degree feedback is one of the best methods for understanding personal and organizational developmental needs.
- Responsibility for Career Development: For many reasons, organizations per se are no longer responsible for developing the careers of thei employees. Multirater feedback can provide excellent information to individuals about what they need to do to enhance their career. Additionally, many employees feel 360 degree feedback is more accurate, more reflective of their performance, and more validating than feedback from the supervisor along. This makes the information more useful for both career and personal development.
- Reduced Discrimination Risk: When feedback comes from a number of individuals in various job functions, biases because of varying reasons are reduced. The judgemental errors of the supervisors are eliminated as the feedback comes from various sources.
- Improved Customer Services: Feedback process involves the internal or external customer. Each person receives valuable feedback about the quality of his product or services. This feedback should enable

the individual to improve the quality, reliability, promptness, and comprehesiveness of these products and services to his/her customers.

- Training Needs Assessment: Multirater feedback provides comprehensive information about organization training needs and thus helps in mounting relevant training programmes. Such programmes add value to the contribution made by the individual employee.

**Benefits of 360 degree Assessment**

Following benefits of 360 degree Assessment accrue to the individual, team and organization:

To the individual:

- This process helps individuals to understand how others perceive them
- It uncovers blind spots
- It provides feedback that is essential for learning
- Individuals can better manage their own performance and careers
- Quantifiable data on soft skills is made available.

To the team:

- It increases communication between team members
- It generates higher levels of trust ad better communication as individuals identify the causes of breakdowns
- It creates better team environment as people discover how to treat others and how they want to be treated
- It supports teamwork by involving team members in the development process
- It increased team effectiveness.

To the Organization:

- It reinforces corporate culture and openness and trust
- It provides better opportunities for career development for employees
- Employees get growth and promotional opportunities
- It improves customer service by having customers contribute to evaluation
- It facilitates the conduct of relevant training programmes.

## PERFORMANCE COUNSELLING

The main objective of performance counselling is to help the employee to overcome his weaknesses and to reinforce his strengths. In this sense it is a developmental process where the supervisor and the subordinate discuss the past performance with a view to help the subordinate to improve and become more effective in future. Assessment reports serve as spring board for discussion. One of the fallout effects of this dyadic interaction is the identification of training needs. Counselling provides an opportunity to the supervisor to give feedback to the subordinate on the performance and performance related behavior. Feedback can be an effective tool provided:

- Both negative and positive feedbacks are communicated.
- It is not just an opinion but is backed by data. In other words it should be descriptive and not evaluative.
- It focuses on behavior rather than on the individual.
- It is timely. Delayed feedback is neither helpful nor effective. On the other hand, it might be seen as criticism which may further deteriorate the relationship. As time passes, details are forgotten and recall may be jeopardized by distortions.

Several conditions for effective counseling are identified. The Following are some of the important ones:

- A climate of openness and trust is necessary. When people are tense and hostile, attempts should be made to counsel and help rather than be critical.
- The counselor should be tactful and helpful rather than critical and fault finding.
- The subordinate should feel comfortable to participate without any hesitation or inhibition.
- The focus should be on the work-related problems and difficulties rather than personality or individuals likes, dislikes or idiosyncrasies.
- It should be devoid of all discussions on salary, reward and punishment. Any discussion on compensation changes the focus from performance improvement to the relationship between performance and reward.

Since counselling is a difficult activity, the supervisor should be specially trained in social competence to handle these aspects of his job. The skill required to do well in these situations is often referred to as the use of non-directive technique. It is a methodology of generating information and using this information to help employees. A sample of non-directive technique could be to start the interview by asking "tell me how you think you are doing". This provides an environment for the subordinate to talk about his part of the story first. The essential feature is to provide an employee an opportunity to talk and share his experience which the supervisor should be able to listen and then process and provide feedback to him. Many supervisors are hesitant to initiate performance counseling sessions because the subordinates may raise uneasy questions for which they may not have answers. Or they may question their judgments and decisions which may lead to argument, debate and misunderstanding. That is why there is a need to train supervisors in the techniques of counseling sessions. One major outcome of performance counseling is identification of the potential of the employee's skills and abilities not known and utilized by the organization. Potential assessment is different from performance assessment as the latter limits evaluation to what the subordinate has done on the job (or his performance) whereas the former on the other hand, seeks to examine what the subordinate can do?. The distinct advantage of a thoroughly carried out potential assessment are given below:

- The organizations are able to identify individuals who can take higher responsibilities.
- It also conveys the message that people are not working in dead-end jobs in the organization.

## PROBLEMS IN PERFORMANCE ASSESSMENT

While it is assumed that performance assessment process and techniques present an objective system it would be naïve to assume, however, that all practicing managers impartially interpret and standardize the criteria upon which their subordinates will be appraised. In spite of our recognition that a completely error-free performance assessment can only be idealized a number of errors that significantly impede objective evaluation. Some of these errors are discussed below:

### LENIENCY ERROR

Every evaluator has his/her own value system that acts as a standard against which assessments are made. Relative to the true or actual performance an individual exhibits, some evaluators mark high and others low. The former is referred to as positive leniency error, and the latter as negative leniency error. When evaluators are positively lenient in their assessment, an individual's performance becomes overstated; that is rated higher than it actually should. Similarly, a negative leniency error understates performance, giving the individuals as lower assessment.

### HALO EFFECT

The halo effect or error is a tendency to rate high or low on all factors due to the impression of a high or low rating on some specific factor. For example, if an employee tends to be conscientious and dependable, the supervisor might become biased toward that individual to the extent that he will rate him/her high on many desirable attributes.

### SIMILARITY ERROR

When evaluators rate other people in the same ways that the evaluators perceive themselves they are making a similarity error. Based on the perception that evaluators have of themselves, they project those perceptions onto others. For example, the evaluator who perceives him self or herself as aggressive may evaluate others by looking for aggressiveness. Those who demonstrate this characteristic tend to benefit, while others are penalized.

## LOW APPRAISER MOTIVATION

What are the consequences of the assessment? If the evaluator knows that a poor assessment could significantly hurt the employee's future particularly opportunities for promotion or a salary increase the evaluator may be reluctant to give a realistic assessment. There is evidence that it is more difficult to obtain accurate assessments when important rewards depend on the results.

## CENTRAL TENDENCY

It is possible that regardless of whom the appraiser evaluates and what traits are used, the pattern of evaluation remains the same. It is also possible that the evaluator's ability to appraise objectively and accurately has been impeded by a failure to use the extremes of the scale, that is, central tendency. Central tendency is the reluctance to make extreme ratings (in either directions); the inability to distinguish between and among ratees; a form of range restriction.

## RECENCY VS. PRIMACY EFFECT

Recency refers to the proximity or closeness to assessment period. Generally an employee takes it easy for the whole year and does little to get the punishment. However, comes assessment time, he becomes very active. Suddenly there is an aura of efficiency, files move faster, tasks are taken seriously and the bosses are constantly appraised of the progress and problems. All this creates an illusion of high efficiency and plays a significant role in the assessment decisions. The supervisor gets railroaded into believing that the employee is alert and hence, rates him high. In reality though it refers only to his two to three month's performance. The opposite of recency is primacy effect. Here the initial impression influences the decision on year end assessment irrespective of whether the employee has been able to keep up the initial impression or not. First impression is the last impression is perhaps the most befitting description of this error.

# EFFECTIVE PERFORMANCE ASSESSMENT

The issues raised above essentially focus on the problems of reliability and validity of performance assessment. In other words, how do we know whether what is appraised is what was supposed to be appraised. As long as assessment format and procedure continues to involve subjective judgment, this question cannot be fully answered and perhaps, will not be answered completely because no matter how objective a system is designed it will continue to be subjective. Perhaps, the following steps can help improve the system.

- The supervisors should be told that performance assessment is an integral part of their job duties and that they themselves would be evaluated on how seriously they have taken this exercise.
- To help them do this task well, they should be provided systematic training on writing performance reports and handling performance interviews.
- Conduct job evaluation studies and prepare job descriptions/roles and develop separate forms for various positions in the organization.
- Design the system as simple as possible so that it is neither difficult to understand nor impossible to practice
- Generally after the assessment interview the employee is left alone to improve his performance on the dimensions. The supervisor should monitor now and then whether the improvement in performance in the areas found weak is taking place or not and, if not, help the employee to achieve the required improvement.
- Finally, reviewing, the assessment systems every now and then help updating it, and making suitable evolutionary changes in it. This is the most important factor in making performance assessment effective. As time passes changes in technology and work environment necessitate changes in tasks, abilities and skills to perform these tasks. If changes in the format are not incorporated the reports may not generate the kind of date needed to satisfy assessment objectives.

## BEHAVIORALLY BASED MEASURES

The evidence strongly favors behaviorally based measures over those developed around traits. Many traits often considered to be related to good performance may, in fact have little or no performance relationship. Traits like loyalty, initiative, courage, reliability, and self-expression are intuitively appealing as desirable characteristics in employees. But the relevant question is, Are individuals who are evaluated as high on those traits higher performers than those who rate low? Traits like loyalty and initiative may be prized by managers, but there is no evidence to support that certain traits will be adequate synonyms for performance in large cross-section of jobs. Behaviorally derived measures can deal with this objection. Because they deal with specific examples of performance-both good and bad, they avoid the problem of using inappropriate substitutes.

## ONGOING FEEDBACK

Employees like to know how they are doing. The annual review, where the manager shares the subordinates evaluations with them, can become a problem. In some cases, it is a problem merely because managers put off such reviews. This is particularly likely if the assessment is negative. The solution lies in having the manager share with the subordinate both expectations and disappointments on a day-today basis. By providing the employee with frequent opportunities to discuss performance before any reward or punishment consequences occur, there will be no surprises at the time of the annual formal review. In fact, where ongoing feedback has been provided, the formal sitting down step should not be particularly traumatic for either party.

## MULTIPLE RATERS

As the number of raters increase, the probability of attaining more accurate information increases. If rater error tends to follow a normal curve, an increase in the number of raters will tend to find the majority congregating about the middle. If a person has had ten supervisors, nine having rated him or her excellent and one poor, we can discount the value of the one poor evaluation.

## PEER EVALUATIONS

Periodically managers find it difficult to evaluate their subordinates' performance because they are not working with them every day. Unfortunately, unless they have this information, they may not be making an accurate assessment. One of the easiest means is through peer evaluations. Peer evaluations are conducted by employees' coworkers, people explicitly familiar with the jobs involved mainly because they too are doing the same thing, they are the ones most aware of co-workers' day to-day work behavior and should be given the opportunity to provide the management with some feedback. The main advantages to peer evaluation are that (a) there is tendency for co-workers to offer more constructive insight to each other so that, as a unit, each will improve; and (b) their recommendations tend to be more specific regarding job behaviors-unless specificity exists, constructive measures are hard to gain.

# 4

# Project Performance Measurement

## METRICS AND MEASUREMENT

Most of us have heard some version of the standard performance measurement cliches: "what gets measured gets done, if you don't measure results, you can't tell success from failure and thus you can't claim or reward success or avoid unintentionally rewarding failure, if you can't recognize success, you can't learn from it; if you can't recognize failure, you can't correct it," "if you can't measure it, you can neither manage it nor improve it, but what eludes many of us is the easy path to identifying truly strategic measurements without falling back on things that are easier to measure such as input, project or operational process measurements.

Performance Measurement is addressed in detail in Step Five of the Nine Steps to Success TM methodology. In this step, Performance Measures are developed for each of the Strategic Objectives. Leading and lagging measures are identified, expected targets and thresholds are established, and baseline and benchmarking data is developed. The focus on Strategic Objectives, which should articulate exactly what the organization is trying to accomplish, is the key to identifying truly strategic measurements. Strategic performance measures monitor the implementation and effectiveness of an organization's strategies, determine the gap between actual and targeted performance and determine organization effectiveness and operational efficiency.

- Good Performance Measures:
- Provide a way to see if our strategy is working
- Focus employees' attention on what matters most to success
- Allow measurement of accomplishments, not just of the work that is performed
- Provide a common language for communication
- Are explicitly defined in terms of owner, unit of measure, collection frequency, data quality, expected value(targets), and thresholds
- Are valid, to ensure measurement of the right things
- Are verifiable, to ensure data collection accuracy

- If you would like to learn more about how the Balanced Scorecard Institute can help your organization develop strategic performance measures, call (919) 460-8180 or contact us electronically.

**ROLE**

The role of the PMO has become more critical than ever in supporting strategic business priorities. As PMOs become more successful, they also need to be more accountable and prove their value. In this blog post we outline our top 10 metrics to track PMO performance. Although a PMO may not be able to track all these metrics immediately, as a PMO grows and matures, it should be able to track the majority of these metrics on a quarterly performance scorecard.

We've organized the ten metrics to map to four business drivers of a PMO:

- Strategic Alignment,
- Operational Efficiency,
- Execution
- Business Value Delivered.

**STRATEGIC ALIGNMENT**

- % of Projects Aligned with Strategic Objectives. The number of projects, or weighted cost of projects, that are aligned with at least one strategic objective over the total of projects.
- Investment Class Targets ($). Set investment targets for Run, Grow, and Transform type of projects and analyze spend variance against these. A simpler alternative is to report the percent of effort/cost going toward 'Keeping the Lights On' (KLO) activities for IT.
- Business Unit Investment Targets ($). Set investment targets for cost and effort devoted to each business unit and analyze spend variance against these.

**OPERATIONAL EFFICIENCY**

- % Resource Utilization. The percentage of time spent on productive activities such as project work, ticket resolution, etc.
- % Project Effort. For IT PMOs, the percentage of time spent working on projects, as opposed to maintenance, enhancements and tickets. This should be measured against a target to show delivery of new business/technology investments.
- % Project Churn. The number of projects put on hold or cancelled over the total number of projects in a given period.

**EXECUTION**

- % Increase in Project Success Rate (or % Decrease in Failure Rate). This assumes success is defined not just by time and budget, but by delivering the business requirements (based on satisfaction surveys of the business stakeholders post-delivery).

- Variance to Budget ($). Cost savings measured by positive variances to budget. This assumes project costs are accurately estimated during planning. Earned Value can also be used for this, for instance looking at the % of projects with a Cost Performance Index (CPI) over 1. CPI = Budgeted Cost of Work Performed (BCWP)/Actual Cost of Work Performed (ACWP). BCWP is Earned Value (this is the PMI definition). PMO will need to monitor CPI on a per project basis.

## BUSINESS VALUE DELIVERED

- Customer Satisfaction (%). A measure of stakeholder/customer satisfaction of business value delivered based on surveys post-delivery.
- Business Value Realized. Business value is realized when the right projects are selected and executed at the right time. Selecting the right projects involves estimating Economic Value Add from a project. This is best if based on actual benefits measurements post-project, but in reality the estimated benefits are simpler to calculate tied back to the project delivery date. This can be measured in cost savings, additional revenue, increased customer satisfaction etc. A standard scoring model can be used to normalize across different benefits, and business value points used to demonstrate value delivered.

# PERFORMANCE MEASUREMENT PROCESS

## INTRODUCTION

Performance measures are recognized as an important element of all Total Quality Management programs. Managers and supervisors directing the efforts of an organization or a group have a responsibility to know how, when, and where to institute a wide range of changes. These changes cannot be sensibly implemented without knowledge of the appropriate information upon which they are based. In addition, among many organizations within the Department of Energy (DOE) complex, there is currently no standardized approach to developing and implementing performance measurement systems. As a result, performance measures have not been fully adopted to gauge the success of the various quality management programs practiced by members of the Department of Energy Nevada Operations Office Family Quality Forum.

To address these issues, the steering committee members commissioned a work group to study the development, implementation, and operation of performance measurement systems. This guidance document, the product of the work group, provides a comprehensive, step-by-step explanation of how to develop performance measurements at any level within an organization and how to evaluate their effectiveness.

The implementation of performance measurements for a specific process should involve as many cognizant employees as possible to stimulate ideas and reinforce the notion that this is a team effort requiring buy-in from all involved in order to succeed. Substantial benefits are realized by organizations implementing performance measurement programs. These benefits are realized almost immediately through an improved understanding of processes by all employees. Furthermore, individuals get an opportunity to receive a broadened perspective of the organization's functions, rather than the more limited perspective of their own immediate span of control. As a process, performance measurement is not simply concerned with collecting data associated with a predefined performance goal or standard. Performance measurement is better thought of as an overall management system involving prevention and detection aimed at achieving conformance of the work product or service to your customer's requirements.

Additionally, it is concerned with process optimization through increased efficiency and effectiveness of the process or product. These actions occur in a continuous cycle, allowing options for expansion and improvement of the work process or product as better techniques are discovered and implemented.

Performance measurement is primarily managing outcome, and one of its main purposes is to reduce or eliminate overall variation in the work product or process. The goal is to arrive at sound decisions about actions affecting the product or process and its output.

## PERFORMANCE MEASURES

Performance measures quantitatively tell us something important about our products, services, and the processes that produce them. They are a tool to help us understand, manage, and improve what our organizations do. Performance measures let us know:

- How well we are doing
- If we are meeting our goals
- If our customers are satisfied
- If our processes are in statistical control
- If and where improvements are necessary.

They provide us with the information necessary to make intelligent decisions about what we do. A performance measure is composed of a number and a unit of measure. The number gives us a magnitude (how much) and the unit gives the number a meaning (what). Performance measures are always tied to a goal or an objective (the target). Performance measures can be represented by single dimensional units like hours, meters, nanoseconds, dollars, number of reports, number of errors, number of CPR-certified employees, length of time to design hardware, etc. They can show the variation in a process or deviation from design specifications.

Single-dimensional units of measure usually represent very basic and fundamental measures of some process or product. More often, multidimensional units of measure are used. These are performance measures expressed as ratios of two or more fundamental units. These may be units like miles per gallon, number of accidents per million hours worked (a performance measure of the companies safety program), or number of on-time vendor deliveries per total number of vendor deliveries. Performance measures expressed this way almost always convey more information than the single-dimensional or single-unit performance measures. Ideally, performance measures should be expressed in units of measure that are the most meaningful to those who must use or make decisions based on those measures.

Most performance measures can be grouped into one of the following six general categories. However, certain organizations may develop their own categories as appropriate depending on the organization's mission:

1. Effectiveness: A process characteristic indicating the degree to which the process output (work product) conforms to requirements.(Are we doing the right things?)
2. Efficiency: A process characteristic indicating the degree to which the process produces the required output at minimum resource cost. (Are we doing things right?)
3. Quality: The degree to which a product or service meets customer requirements and expectations.
4. Timeliness: Measures whether a unit of work was done correctly and on time. Criteria must be established to define what constitutes timeliness for a given unit of work. The criterion is usually based on customer requirements.
5. Productivity: The value added by the process divided by the value of the labor and capital consumed.
6. Safety: Measures the overall health of the organization and the working environment of its employees.

The following reflect the attributes of an ideal unit of measure:

- Reflects the customer's needs as well as our own
- Provides an agreed upon basis for decision making
- Is understandable
- Applies broadly
- May be interpreted uniformly
- Is compatible with existing sensors (a way to measure it exists)
- Is precise in interpreting the results
- Is economical to apply

Performance data must support the mission assignment(s) from the highest organizational level downward to the performance level. Therefore, the measurements that are used must reflect the assigned work at that level. Within a system, units of measure should interconnect to form a pyramid. Technological units start at the base. These are measures of individual units of products and of individual elements of service. The next level of units serves to summarize the basic data (e.g., percent defective for specific processes, documents, product components, service cycles, and persons.) Next are units of measure that serve to express quality for entire departments, product lines, and classes of service. In large organizations, there may be multiple layers of this category. At the top are the financial and upper management units (measures, indexes, ratios, etc.), which serve the needs of the highest levels in the organization: corporate, divisional, and functional.

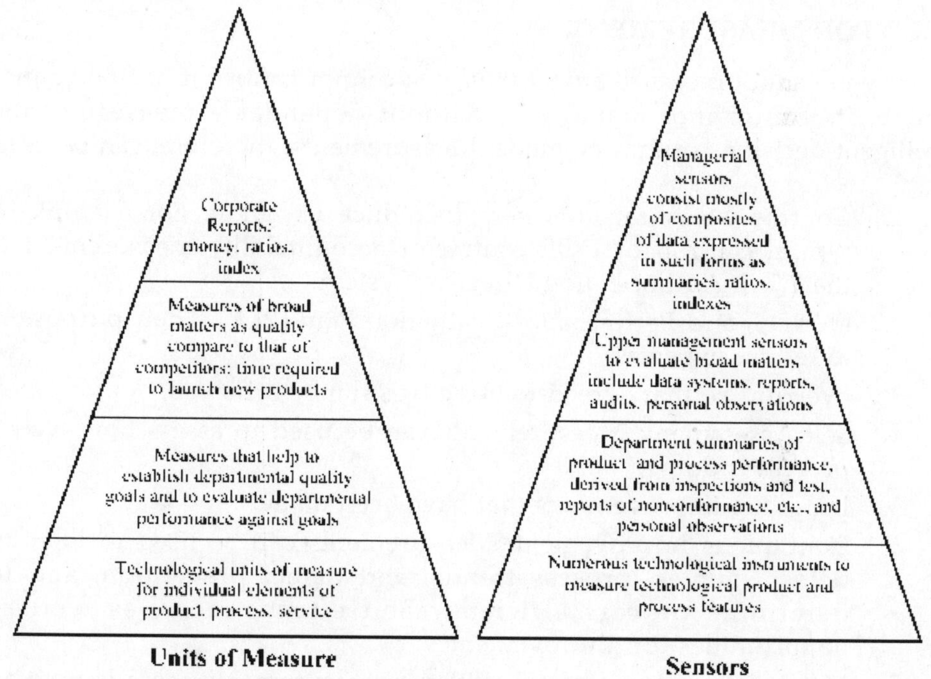


## BENEFITS OF MEASUREMENTS

Listed below are seven important benefits of measurements:

1. To identify whether we are meeting customer requirements. How do we know that we are providing the services/products that our customers require?
2. To help us understand our processes. To confirm what we know or reveal what we don't know. Do we know where the problems are?

3. To ensure decisions are based on fact, not on emotion. Are our decisions based upon well documented facts and figures or on intuition and gut feelings?
4. To show where improvements need to be made. Where can we do better? How can we improve?
5. To show if improvements actually happened. Do we have a clear picture?
6. To reveal problems that bias, emotion, and longevity cover up. If we have been doing our job for a long time without measurements, we might assume incorrectly that things are going well. (They may or may not be, but without measurements there is no way to tell.)
7. To identify whether suppliers are meeting our requirements. Do our suppliers know if our requirements are being met?

## NEED FOR MEASUREMENT

If you cannot measure an activity, you cannot control it. If you cannot control it, you cannot manage it. Without dependable measurements, intelligent decisions cannot be made. Measurements, therefore, can be used for:

1. Control: Measurements help to reduce variation. For example, a typical control for DOE contractor accountability measurement is the Work Authorization Directive System
2. (WADS) and Performance Evaluation Plan (PEP). Their purpose is to reduce expense
3. overruns so that agreed-to objectives can be achieved.
4. Self-Assessment: Measurements can be used to assess how well a process is doing,
5. including improvements that have been made.
6. Continuous Improvement: Measurements can be used to identify defect sources, process trends, and defect prevention, and to determine process efficiency and effectiveness, as well as opportunities for improvement.
7. Management Assessment: Without measurements there is no way to be certain we are
8. meeting value-added objectives or that we are being effective and efficient. The basic
9. concept of performance measurement involves
   - planning and meeting established operating goals/standards;
   - detecting deviations from planned levels of performance;
   - restoring performance to the planned levels or achieving new levels of performance.

## FOUNDATION FOR A PERFORMANCE MEASUREMENT SYSTEM

Successful performance measurement systems adhere to the following principles:

1. Measure only what is important. Do not measure too much; measure things that impact customer satisfaction.
2. Focus on customer needs. Ask our customers if they think this is what we should measure.
3. Involve employees (workers) in the design and implementation of the measurement system.

Give them a sense of ownership, which leads to improvements in the quality of the measurement system. The basic feedback loop shown in Figure presents a systematic series of steps for maintaining conformance to goals/ standards by communicating performance data back to the responsible worker and/or decision maker to take appropriate action(s).

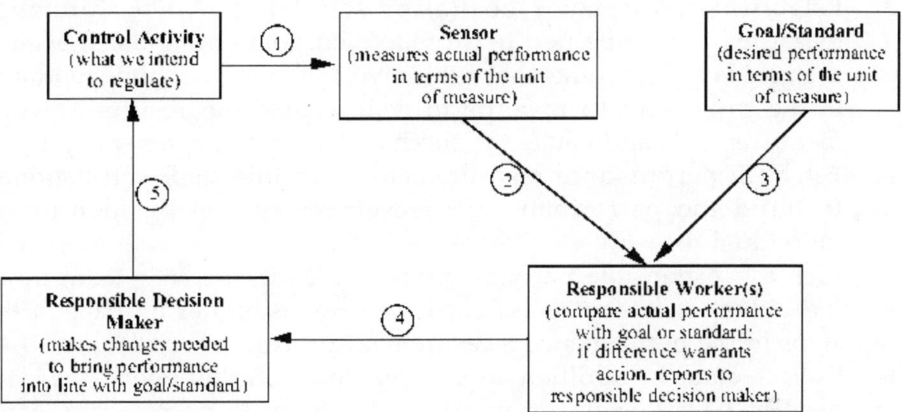


**Fig.** shows a high level block diagram of the performance measurement process

Without the basic feedback loop, no performance measurement system will ever ensure an effective and efficient operation, and, as a result, conformance to customers' requirements. The message of the feedback loop is that to achieve the goal or standard, those responsible for managing the critical activities must always be in a position to know

- What is to be done;
- What is being done;
- When to take corrective action;
- When to change the goal or standard.

The basic elements of the feedback loop and their interrelations are:

- The Sensor evaluates actual performance.
- The Sensor reports this performance to a Responsible Worker.
- The Responsible Worker also receives information on what the goal or standard is.

- The Responsible Worker compares actual performance to the goal. If the difference warrants action, the worker reports to a Responsible Decision Maker.
- The Responsible Decision Maker verifies variance, determines if corrective action is necessary, and, if so, makes the changes needed to bring performance back in line with the goals.

A brief description of each of the process shown in fig follows:

1. Identify the process flow. This is the first and perhaps most important step. If your employees cannot agree on their processes, how can they effectively measure them or utilize the output of what they have measured?
2. Identify the critical activity to be measured. The critical activity is that culminating activity where it makes the most sense to locate a sensor and define an individual performance measure within a process.
3. Establish performance goal(s) or standards. All performance measures should be tied to a predefined goal or standard, even if the goal is at first somewhat subjective. Having goals and standards is the only way to meaningfully interpret the results of your measurements and gauge the success of your management systems.
4. Establish performance measurement(s). In this step, you continue to build the performance measurement system by identifying individual measures.
5. Identify responsible party(s). A specific entity (as in a team or an individual) needs to be assigned the responsibilities for each of the steps in the performance measurement process.
6. Collect data. In addition to writing down the numbers, the data need to be pre-analyzed in a timely fashion to observe any early trends and confirm the adequacy of your data collection system.
7. Analyze/report actual performance. In this step, the raw data are formally converted into performance measures, displayed in an understandable form, and disseminated in the form of a report.
8. Compare actual performance to goal(s). In this step, compare performance, as presented in the report, to predetermined goals or standards and determine the variation (if any).
9. Are corrective actions necessary? Depending on the magnitude of the variation between measurements and goals, some form of corrective action may be required.
10. Make changes to bring back in line with goal. This step only occurs if corrective action is expected to be necessary. The actual determination of the corrective action is part of the quality improvement process, not the performance measurement process. This step is primarily concerned with improvement of your management system.

11. Are new goals needed? Even in successful systems, changes may need to be revised in order to establish ones that challenge an organization's resources, but do not overtax them. Goals and standards need periodic evaluation to keep up with the latest organizational processes.

## HIGH LEVEL BLOCK DIAGRAM

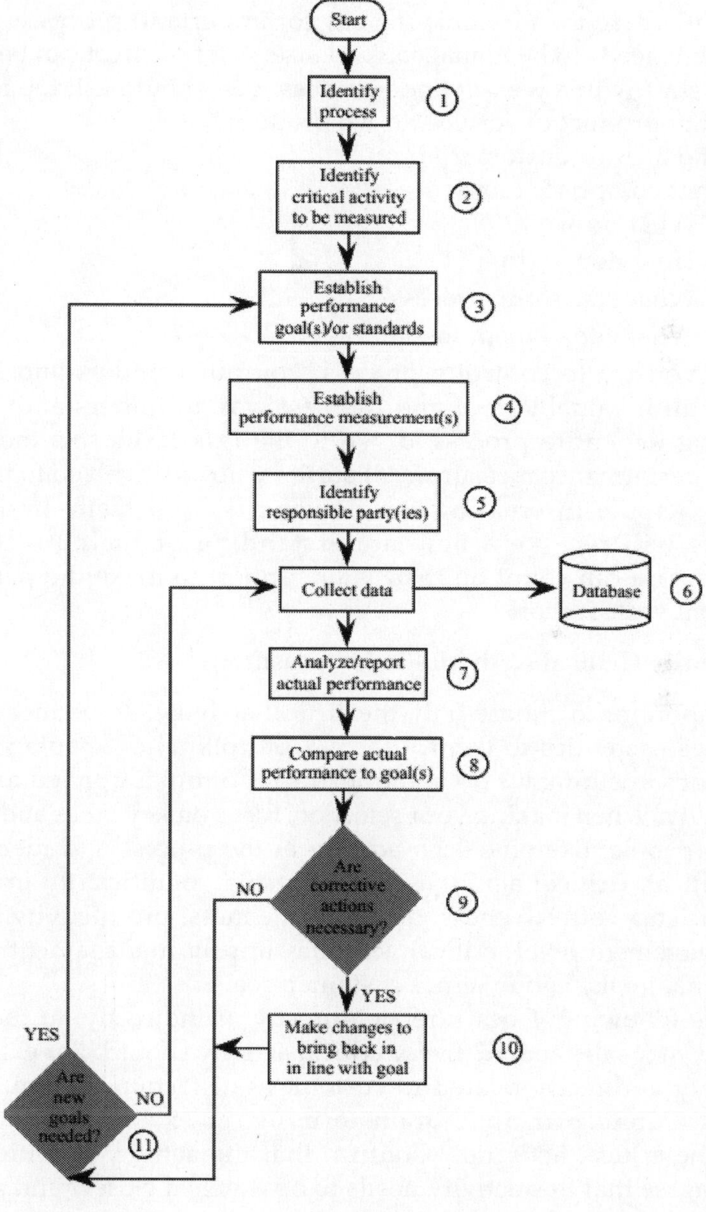

**Step 1: Identify Process**

In identifying the process, an understanding of what you want to measure is of critical importance. Usually there are many processes and functions, each potentially needing performance measures. If there are multiple processes, consider the business impacts, and select those processes that are most important to the customer (both internal and external) to satisfy their requirements and/or those processes with problem areas identified by management. These then become the key (or important) processes.

A process needs to be manageable in size. A lot of effort can be wasted if you do not start with a well-defined process. You should ask the following:

- What product or service do we produce?
- Who are our customer(s)?
- What comprises our process?
  - What do we do?
  - How do we do it?
  - What starts our process?
  - What ends our process?

Before you try to control a process, you must understand it. A flow diagram is an invaluable tool and the best way to understand a process. Flowcharting the entire process, down to the task level, sets the stage for developing performance measures. All parties who are involved in the process should participate in creating the flowcharts. In a team environment, individuals will receive a new understanding of their processes. As participants, you can count on their later support to make the performance measurement system work.

**Step 2: Identify Critical Activities to be measured**

It is important to choose only the critical activities to be measured. We measure these activities to control them. Controlling, or keeping things on course, is not something we do in the abstract. Control is applied to a specific critical activity. When making your selection, focus on key areas and processes rather than people. Examine each activity in the process and identify those that are critical. Critical activities are those that significantly impact total process efficiency, effectiveness, quality, timeliness, productivity, or safety. At the management level, critical activities impact management priorities, organizational goals, and external customer goals.

Ask the following: Does it relate, directly or indirectly, to the ultimate goal of customer satisfaction? Every critical activity should. For example, on-time delivery is directly related to customer satisfaction. Use quality tools such as the Pareto principle, brainstorming, or examining data to help prioritize the critical activities. Confirm that the activity is critical. Do all concerned agree that this activity needs to be watched closely and acted on if its performance is less than desirable? Is it something that should be continuously improved? Does the benefit exceed the cost of taking the measurement? If the answer is "no" to any of these questions, you should reevaluate why you consider it critical.

Each critical activity becomes the hub around which a feedback loop is constructed. It is at this step you begin to think about what you want to know or understand about the critical activity and/or process. Perhaps the most fundamental step in establishing any measurement system is answering the question, "What do I want to know." The key issue then becomes, "How do we generate useful information?" Learning to ask the right questions is a key skill in effective data collection. Accurate, precise data collected through an elaborately designed statistical sampling plan is useless if it does not clearly address a question that someone cares about. It is crucial to be able to state precisely what it is you want to know about the activity you are going to measure.

Without this knowledge, there is no basis for making measurements. To generate useful information, planning for good data collection proceeds along the following lines:

- What question do we need to answer?
- How will we recognize and communicate the answers to the question?
- What data-analysis tools (Pareto diagram, histogram, bar graph, control charts, etc.) do we envision using? How will we communicate the results?
- What type of data do the data analysis tools require?

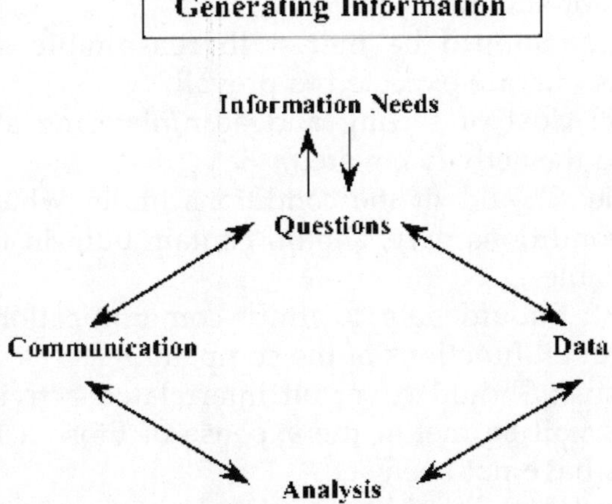


Notice how this planning process essentially works backward through the model for generating useful information. We start by defining the question. Then, rather than diving into the details of data collection, we consider how we might communicate the answer to the question and what types of analysis we will need to perform. This helps us define our data needs and clarifies what characteristics are most important in the data. With this understanding as a foundation, we can deal more coherently with the where, who, how, and what else issue of data collection.

**Step 3: Establish Performance Goals or Standards**

Goals and standards are necessary; otherwise there is no logical basis for choosing what to measure, what decisions to make, or what action to take. Goals can be a management directive or can be set in response to customer needs or complaints. Know your customers and their expectations. For each critical activity selected for measurement, it is necessary to establish a performance goal or standard. This is an "aimed-at" target, an achievement toward which effort is expended. Standards often are mandated by external sources (e.g., Occupational Safety and Health Administration, government regulations, etc.). Knowledge of performance is not enough; you must have a basis for comparison before you can decide or act. The concept of establishing performance goals/standards is not limited to numbered quantities, i.e., budget, deliveries. Neither is it limited to "things." The concept of standards extends to business practices, routines, methods, and procedures as well.

Performance goals can be established for:

- The overall process output,
- The critical activities that produce the output.

In any case, if this is the first set of goals or standards to be established, and no basis for setting goals or standards exists, a baseline period of observation is appropriate prior to establishing the goal or standard. Good performance goals or standards are:

- Attainable: Should be met with reasonable effort under the conditions that are expected to prevail.
- Economic: Cost of setting and administering should be low in relation to the activity covered.
- Applicable: Should fit the conditions under which they are to be used. If conditions vary, should contain built-in flexibility to meet these variables.
- Consistent: Should help to unify communication and operations throughout all functions of the company.
- All-inclusive: Should cover all interrelated activities. Failing this, standards will be met at the expense of those activities for which standards have not been set.
- Understandable: Should be expressed in simple, clear terms, so as to avoid misinterpretation or vagueness. Instructions for use should be specific and complete.
- Measurable: Should be able to communicate with precision.

- Stable: Should have a long enough life to provide predictability and to amortize the effort of preparing them.
- Adaptable: Should be designed so that elements can be added, changed, and brought up to date without redoing the entire structure.
- Legitimate: Should be officially approved.
- Equitable: Should be accepted as a fair basis for comparison by the people who have the job of meeting the goal or standard.
- Customer Focus: Should address areas important to the customer (internal/external) such as cycle time, quality, cost schedule performance, and customer satisfaction.

**Step 4: Establish Performance Measurement(s)**

This step involves performing several activities that will continue to build the performance measurement system. Each performance measurement consists of a defined unit of measure, a sensor to measure or record the raw data, and a frequency with which the measurements are made. To develop a measure, the team performs the following activities:

- Translates "what do I want to know" into a performance measure
- Identifies the raw data that will generate the performance measure
- determines where to locate the raw data
- identifies the sensor or measurement instrument that will collect the data for the performance measures
- determines how often to make the measurements

At this point, your team has agreed upon which process to measure (Step 1), identified the critical activities of your process with emphasis on those that impact quality, efficiency, timeliness, customer satisfaction, etc. (Step 2), looked at goals for these activities, products, and services (where they exist), and has quantified these goals where possible (Step 3). Your team should use the knowledge gained from these previous steps to help state precisely what you want to know about the critical activities or the process as a whole. Think of this step as one that will allow you to generate useful information rather than just generating data. The purpose of this information is to provide everyone involved with an agreed-upon basis for making sensible decisions about your processes, products, and services. Don't move on until the team agrees on what information you are trying to extract from the measurements.

***Translate into Performance Measures***

Having identified precisely what you want to know or understand about your process, you must now assemble this knowledge into a performance measure. Performance measures, and the data necessary to generate them, should be chosen to answer the questions you have just posed above. At this point, your team must decide how you will "say it in numbers." Performance measures are generally easiest to determine for activities or processes that have established and quantified goals. In such cases, the performance measures are usually stated in the same units as or similar units to the goals.

**Step 5: Identify Responsible Parties**

Steps 1 through 4 are primarily team activities. To continue the performance measurement process, the responsible worker(s) and the responsible decision maker must be defined. (In some instances, one person may be responsible for the entire system.) It is now appropriate to determine who should:

- Collect the data
- Analyze/report actual performance
- Compare actual performance to goal/standard
- Determine if corrective action is necessary
- Make changes

Ideally, responsibility should be assigned to individuals commensurate with authority. This means that each responsible party should:

- Know what the goals are
- now what the actual performance is
- ave the authority to implement changes if performance does not conform to goals and standards

To hold someone responsible in the absence of authority prevents them from performing their job and creates the risk of unwarranted blame.

**Step 6: Collect Data**

The determination of conformance depends on meaningful and valid data. Before you start out to collect a lot of new data, it is always wise to look at the data you already have to make certain you have extracted all the information you can from it. In addition, you may wish to refer back to Step 2 and review planning for good data collection. Information, as a term, comprises the answers to your questions. Data are a set of facts presented in quantitative or descriptive form. Obviously, data must be specific enough to provide you with relevant information. There are two basic kinds of data:

***Measured or variables data***

Data that may take on any value within some range. This type of data provides a more detailed history of your business process. This involves collecting numeric values that quantify a measurement and therefore require small samples. If the data set is potentially large, consider recording a representative sample for this type of data.

Examples:

- Cost of overnight mail
- Dollar value of stock

- Number of days it takes to solve a problem
- Diameter of a shaft

***Counted or attribute data***

Data that may take on only discrete values. Attribute data need not be numeric. These kinds of data are counted, not measured, and generally require large sample sizes to be useful. Counting methods include defective/non defective; yes/no; accept/reject.

Examples

- Was the letter typed with no errors?
- Did the meeting start on time?
- Was the phone answered by the second ring?
- Was the report turned in on schedule?

***Data Collection Forms***

There are two types of forms commonly used to aid in data collection. Often combinations of these are used:

- Checksheet: A form specially designed so that the results can be readily interpreted from the form itself. This form of data collection is ideal for capturing special (worker controlled) cause of process variation since the worker can interpret the results and take corrective actions immediately.
- Data Sheet: A form designed to collect data in a simple tabular or column format (often related to time-dependent data). Specific bits of data–numbers, words, or marks–are entered in spaces on the sheet. As a result, additional processing is typically required after the data are collected in order to construct the tool needed for analysis. This form of data collection is usually used for capturing common (manager controlled) causes of process variations.

# 5

# Planning Tools and Performance Measures for Projects and Divisions

## CAPITAL BUDGETING

Capital budgeting (or investment appraisal) is the planning process used to determine whether a firm's long term investments such as new machinery, replacement machinery, new plants, new products, and research development projects are worth pursuing. It is budget for major capital, or investment, expenditures.

Many formal methods are used in capital budgeting, including the techniques such as

- Accounting rate of return
- Net present value
- Profitability index
- Internal rate of return
- Modified internal rate of return
- Equivalent annuity

These methods use the incremental cash flows from each potential investment, or project Techniques based on accounting earnings and accounting rules are sometimes used - though economists consider this to be improper - such as the accounting rate of return, and "return on investme

### NET PRESENT VALUE

In finance, the net present value (NPV) or net present worth (NPW) of a time series of cash flows, both incoming and outgoing, is defined as the sum of the present values (PVs) of the individual cash flows. In the case when all future cash flows are incoming (such as coupons and principal of a bond) and the only outflow of cash is the purchase price, the NPV is simply the PV of future cash flows minus the purchase price (which is its own PV). NPV is a central tool in discounted cash flow (DCF) analysis, and is a standard method for using the time value of money to appraise long-term projects. Used for capital budgeting, and widely throughout economics, finance, and accounting, it measures the excess or shortfall of cash flows, in present value terms, once financing charges are met.

The NPV of a sequence of cash flows takes as input the cash flows and a discount rate or discount curve and outputting a price; the converse process in DCF analysis, taking as input a sequence of cash flows and a price and inferring as output a discount rate (the discount rate which would yield the given price as NPV) is called the yield, and is more widely used in bond trading.

**Formula**

Each cash inflow/outflow is discounted back to its present value (PV). Then they are summed. Therefore NPV is the sum of all terms,

$$\frac{R_t}{(1+i)^t}$$

where

t - the time of the cash flow

i - the discount rate (the rate of return that could be earned on an investment in the financial markets with similar risk.)

Rt - the net cash flow (the amount of cash, inflow minus outflow) at time t. For educational purposes, R0 is commonly placed to the left of the sum to emphasize its role as (minus) the investment. The result of this formula if multiplied with the Annual Net cash in-flows and reduced by Initial Cash outlay will be the present value but in case where the cash flows are not equal in amount then the previous formula will be used to determine the present value of each cash flow separately. Any cash flow within 12 months will not be discounted for NPV purpose.

**The discount rate**

The rate used to discount future cash flows to their present values is a key variable of this process. A firm's weighted average cost of capital (after tax) is often used, but many people believe that it is appropriate to use higher discount rates to adjust for risk or other factors. A variable discount rate with higher rates applied to cash flows occurring further along the time span might be used to reflect the yield curve premium for long-term debt.

Another approach to choosing the discount rate factor is to decide the rate which the capital needed for the project could return if invested in an alternative venture. If, for example, the capital required for Project A can earn five percent elsewhere, use this discount rate in the NPV calculation to allow a direct comparison to be made between Project A and the alternative. Related to this concept is to use the firm's Reinvestment Rate. Reinvestment rate can be defined as the rate of return for the firm's investments on average. When analyzing projects in a capital constrained environment, it may be appropriate to use the reinvestment rate rather than the firm's weighted average cost of capital as the discount factor. It reflects opportunity cost of investment, rather than the possibly lower cost of capital.

An NPV calculated using variable discount rates (if they are known for the duration of the investment) better reflects the real situation than one calculated from a constant discount rate for the entire investment duration. Refer to the tutorial article written by Samuel Baker for more detailed relationship between the NPV value and the discount rate. For some professional investors, their investment funds are committed to target a specified rate of return. In such cases, that rate of return should be selected as the discount rate for the NPV calculation. In this way, a direct comparison can be made between the profitability of the project and the desired rate of return.

To some extent, the selection of the discount rate is dependent on the use to which it will be put. If the intent is simply to determine whether a project will add value to the company, using the firm's weighted average cost of capital may be appropriate. If trying to decide between alternative investments in order to maximize the value of the firm, the corporate reinvestment rate would probably be a better choice. Using variable rates over time, or discounting "guaranteed" cash flows differently from "at risk" cash flows may be a superior methodology, but is seldom used in practice. Using the discount rate to adjust for risk is often difficult to do in practice (especially internationally), and is difficult to do well. An alternative to using discount factor to adjust for risk is to explicitly correct the cash flows for the risk elements using rNPV or a similar method, then discount at the firm's rate.

**What NPV Means**

NPV is an indicator of how much value an investment or project adds to the firm. With a particular project, if Rt is a positive value, the project is in the status of discounted cash inflow in the time of t. If Rt is a negative value, the project is in the status of discounted cash outflow in the time of t. Appropriately risked projects with a positive NPV could be accepted. This does not necessarily mean that they should be undertaken since NPV at the cost of capital may not account for opportunity cost, i.e. comparison with other available investments. In financial theory, if there is a choice between two mutually exclusive alternatives, the one yielding the higher no-no should be selected.

| If... | It means... | Then... |
|---|---|---|
| NPV > 0 | the investment would add value to the firm | the project may be accepted |
| NPV < 0 | the investment would subtract value from the firm | the project should be rejected |

| | | |
|---|---|---|
| NPV = 0 | the investment would neither gain nor lose value for the firm | We should be indifferent in the decision whether to accept or reject the project. This project adds no monetary value. Decision should be based on other criteria, e.g. strategic positioning or other factors not explicitly included in the calculation. |

**Example**

A corporation must decide whether to introduce a new product line. The new product will have startup costs, operational costs, and incoming cash flows over six years. This project will have an immediate (t=0) cash outflow of $100,000 (which might include machinery, and employee training costs). Other cash outflows for years 1–6 are expected to be $5,000 per year. Cash inflows are expected to be $30,000 each for years 1–6. All cash flows are after-tax, and there are no cash flows expected after year 6. The required rate of return is 10%. The present value (PV) can be calculated for each year:

| Year | Cash flow | Present value |
|---|---|---|
| T=0 | $\frac{-100,000}{(1+0.10)^0}$ | -$100,000 |
| T=1 | $\frac{30,000-5,000}{(1+0.10)^1}$ | $22,727 |
| T=2 | $\frac{30,000-5,000}{(1+0.10)^2}$ | $20,661 |
| T=3 | $\frac{30,000-5,000}{(1+0.10)^3}$ | $18,783 |
| T=4 | $\frac{30,000-5,000}{(1+0.10)^4}$ | $17,075 |
| T=5 | $\frac{30,000-5,000}{(1+0.10)^5}$ | $15,523 |
| T=6 | $\frac{30,000-5,000}{(1+0.10)^6}$ | $14,112 |

The sum of all these present values is the net present value, which equals $8,881.52. Since the NPV is greater than zero, it would be better to invest in the project than to do nothing, and the corporation should invest in this project if there is no mutually exclusive alternative with a higher NPV.

The same example in Excel formulae:

- NPV(rate,net_inflow)+initial_investment
- PV(rate,year_number,yearly_net_inflow)

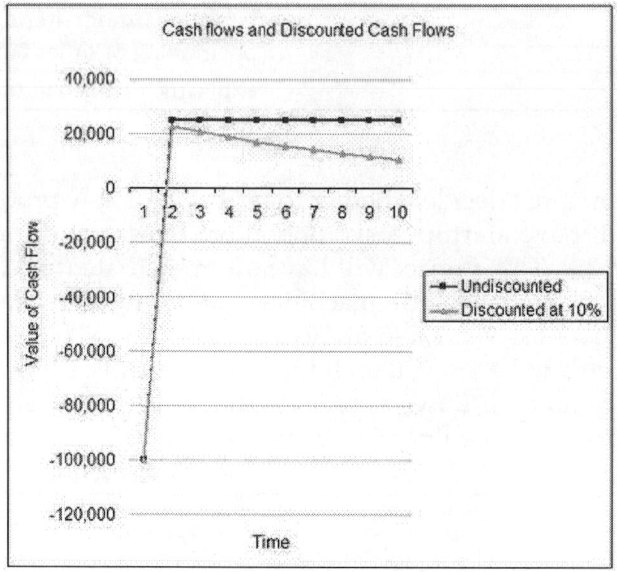


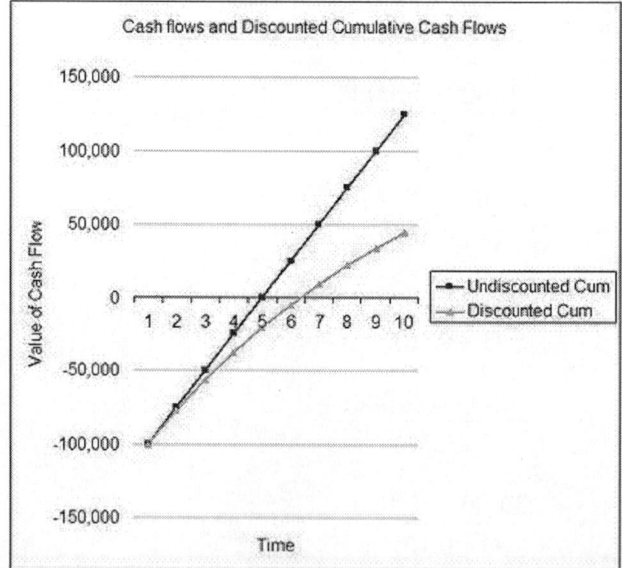


More realistic problems would need to consider other factors, generally including the calculation of taxes, uneven cash flows, and salvage values as well as the availability of alternate investment opportunities.

**Common pitfalls**

- If, for example, the Rt are generally negative late in the project (e.g., an industrial or mining project might have clean-up and restoration costs), then at that stage the company owes money, so a high discount rate is not cautious but too optimistic. Some people see this as a problem with NPV. A way to avoid this problem is to include explicit provision for financing any losses after the initial investment, that is, explicitly calculate the cost of financing such losses.
- Another common pitfall is to adjust for risk by adding a premium to the discount rate. Whilst a bank might charge a higher rate of interest for a risky project, that does not mean that this is a valid approach to adjusting a net present value for risk, although it can be a reasonable approximation in some specific cases. One reason such an approach may not work well can be seen from the following: if some risk is incurred resulting in some losses, then a discount rate in the NPV will reduce the impact of such losses below their true financial cost. A rigorous approach to risk requires identifying and valuing risks explicitly, e.g. by actuarial or Monte Carlo techniques, and explicitly calculating the cost of financing any losses incurred.
- Yet another issue can result from the compounding of the risk premium. R is a composite of the risk free rate and the risk premium. As a result, future cash flows are discounted by both the risk-free rate as well as the risk premium and this effect is compounded by each subsequent cash flow. This compounding results in a much lower NPV than might be otherwise calculated. The certainty equivalent model can be used to account for the risk premium without compounding its effect on present value.
- If NPV is negative the project should not be immediately rejected. Sometimes companies have to execute an NPV-negative project if not executing it creates even more value destruction.
- Another issue with relying on NPV is that it does not provide an overall picture of the gain or loss of executing a certain project. To see a percentage gain relative to the investments for the project, usually, Internal rate of return or other efficiency measures are used as a complement to NPV.

**Alternative capital budgeting methods**

- Adjusted present value (APV): adjusted present value, is the net present value of a project if financed solely by ownership equity plus the present value of all the benefits of financing.
- Payback period: which measures the time required for the cash inflows to equal the original outlay. It measures risk, not return.

- Cost-benefit analysis: which includes issues other than cash, such as time savings.
- Real option method: which attempts to value managerial flexibility that is assumed away in NPV.
- Internal rate of return: which calculates the rate of return of a project while disregarding the absolute amount of money to be gained.
- Modified internal rate of return (MIRR): similar to IRR, but it makes explicit assumptions about the reinvestment of the cash flows. Sometimes it is called Growth Rate of Return.
- Accounting rate of return (ARR): a ratio similar to IRR and MIRR

## INTERNAL RATE OF RETURN

The internal rate of return (IRR) is a rate of return used in capital budgeting to measure and compare the profitability of investments. It is also called the discounted cash flow rate of return (DCFROR) or simply the rate of return (ROR). In the context of savings and loans the IRR is also called the effective interest rate. The term internal refers to the fact that its calculation does not incorporate environmental factors (e.g., the interest rate or inflation).

The internal rate of return on an investment or project is the annualized effective compounded return rate or discount rate that makes the net present value of all cash flows (both positive and negative) from a particular investment equal to zero. In more specific terms, the IRR of an investment is the interest rate at which the net present value of costs (negative cash flows) of the investment equal the net present value of the benefits (positive cash flows) of the investment. Internal rates of return are commonly used to evaluate the desirability of investments or projects. The higher a project's internal rate of return, the more desirable it is to undertake the project. Assuming all other factors are equal among the various projects, the project with the highest IRR would probably be considered the best and undertaken first.

A firm (or individual) should, in theory, undertake all projects or investments available with positive IRRs. Investment may be limited by availability of funds to the firm and/or by the firms capacity or ability to manage numerous projects.

### Uses

Because the internal rate of return is a rate quantity, it is an indicator of the efficiency, quality, or yield of an investment. This is in contrast with the net present value, which is an indicator of the value or magnitude of an investment. An investment is considered acceptable if its internal rate of return is greater than an established minimum acceptable rate of return or cost of capital. In a scenario where an investment is considered by a firm that has equity holders, this minimum rate is the cost of capital of the investment (which may be determined by the risk-adjusted cost of capital of alternative investments). This ensures that the investment is supported by equity holders since, in general, an investment whose IRR exceeds its cost of capital adds value for the company (i.e., it is economically profitable).

**Calculation**

Given a collection of pairs (time, cash flow) involved in a project, the internal rate of return follows from the net present value as a function of the rate of return. A rate of return for which this function is zero is an internal rate of return. Given the (period, cash flow) pairs (n, Cn) where n is a positive integer, the total number of periods N, and the net present value NPV, the internal rate of return is given by r in:

$$NPV = \sum_{n=0}^{N} \frac{C_n}{(1+r)^n} = 0$$

Note that the period is usually given in years, but the calculation may be made simpler if r is calculated using the period in which the majority of the problem is defined (e.g., using months if most of the cash flows occur at monthly intervals) and converted to a yearly period thereafter. Note that any fixed time can be used in place of the present (e.g., the end of one interval of an annuity); the value obtained is zero if and only if the NPV is zero. In the case that the cash flows are random variables, such as in the case of a life annuity, the expected values are put into the above formula.

Often, the value of r cannot be found analytically. In this case, numerical methods or graphical methods must be used.

***Example***

If an investment may be given by the sequence of cash flows

| Year (n) | Cash Flow (Cn) |
|---|---|
| 0 | -4000 |
| 1 | 1200 |
| 2 | 1410 |
| 3 | 1875 |
| 4 | 1050 |

then the IRR r is given by

$$NPV = -4000 + \frac{1200}{(1+r)^1} + \frac{1410}{(1+r)^2} + \frac{1875}{(1+r)^3} + \frac{1050}{(1+r)^4} = 0.$$

In this case, the answer is 14.3%.

***Numerical solution***

Since the above is a manifestation of the general problem of finding the roots of the equation NPV(r), there are many numerical methods that can be used to estimate r. For example, using the secant method, r is given by

$$r_{n+1} = r_n - NPV_n\left(\frac{(r_n - r_{n-1})}{NPV_n - NPV_{n-1}}\right)$$

where $r_n$ is considered the nth approximation of the IRR.

This formula initially requires two unique pairs of estimations of the IRR and NPV (r0,NPV0) and (r1,NPV1), and produces a sequence of $(r_0, NPV_0), (r_1, NPV_1), \ldots, (r_{n-1}, NPV_{n-1}), (r_n, NPV_n), (r_{n+1}, NPV_{n+1})$ that may converge to $(r, 0)$ as $n \to \infty$. If the sequence converges, then iterations of the formula can continue indefinitely so that r can be found to an arbitrary degree of accuracy.

The convergence behaviour of the sequence is governed by the following:

- If the function NPV(i) has a single real root r, then the sequence will converge reproducibly towards r.
- If the function NPV(i) has n real roots f**, then the sequence will converge to one of the roots and changing the values of the initial pairs may change the root to which it converges.
- If function NPV(i) has no real roots, then the sequence will tend towards +8.

Having $r_1 > r_0$ when NPV or $r_1 < r_0$ when NPV0 < 0 may speed up convergence of $r_n$ to r.

***Calculation of IRR with the help of Trial and error method***

IRR can also be calculated by Trial and error method if the data satisfy the following conditions

- Outflow take place one time
- Inflows are constant as per interval and amount
- Time period involve is significant so that the other methods become complicated for example in a case there is a project with initial investment of $100 (year 0) and annual cash inflows of $20 at the end of each year till 10th year now here one want to calculate the IRR. IRR is the rate with which if all the cash inflows are discounted then the resultant figure will be equal to initial investment so here we use Trial and error method in this method one formula for aggression is used That is as below

$$\text{IRR} = \text{Lower rate} + \frac{\text{NPV at lower rate}}{\text{NPV at lower rate} - \text{NPV at higher rate}}$$

$$*(\text{Higher rate} - \text{Lower rate})$$

Here as we will calculate IRR at lower rate that will be in positive and NPV at Higher rate will negative and as we will put this value in NPV at lower rate - NPV at Higher rate the Minus sign will become positive as NPV at Higher rate also contain negative sign with it so the 2nd important thing is to guess higher rate and lower rate like in the case given above suppose 10% as lower rate and 20% as higher rate NPV@10% will be 22.89 and NPV@20% will be -16.15 and at last if we apply the formula above we will get 15% that is IRR of the project Now if all the inflows are discounted @15% the resultant figure will be 100 as the Present value factor @15% for 10years is 5.0 and 20*5 = $100.

This method is also called Hit and Trial Method.

**Problems with using internal rate of return**

As an investment decision tool, the calculated IRR should not be used to rate mutually exclusive projects, but only to decide whether a single project is worth investing in. In cases where one project has a higher initial investment than a second mutually exclusive project, the first project may have a lower IRR (expected return), but a higher NPV (increase in shareholders' wealth) and should thus be accepted over the second project (assuming no capital constraints).

IRR assumes reinvestment of interim cash flows in projects with equal rates of return (the reinvestment can be the same project or a different project). Therefore, IRR overstates the annual equivalent rate of return for a project whose interim cash flows are reinvested at a rate lower than the calculated IRR. This presents a problem, especially for high IRR projects, since there is frequently not another project available in the interim that can earn the same rate of return as the first project. When the calculated IRR is higher than the true reinvestment rate for interim cash flows, the measure will overestimate — sometimes very significantly — the annual equivalent return from the project. The formula assumes that the company has additional projects, with equally attractive prospects, in which to invest the interim cash flows.

This makes IRR a suitable (and popular) choice for analyzing venture capital and other private equity investments, as these strategies usually require several cash investments throughout the project, but only see one cash outflow at the end of the project (e.g., via IPO or M&A).

Since IRR does not consider cost of capital, it should not be used to compare projects of different duration. Modified Internal Rate of Return (MIRR) does consider cost of capital and provides a better indication of a project's efficiency in contributing to the firm's discounted cash flow.

In the case of positive cash flows followed by negative ones (+ + - - -) the IRR may have multiple values. In this case a discount rate may be used for the borrowing cash flow and the IRR calculated for the investment cash flow. This applies for example when a customer makes a deposit before a specific machine is built. In a series of cash flows like (-10, 21, -11), one initially invests money, so a high rate of return is best, but then receives more than one possesses, so then one owes money, so now a low rate of return is best. In this case it is not even clear whether a high or a low IRR is better. There may even be multiple IRRs for a single project, like in the example 0% as well as 10%. Examples of this type of project are strip mines and nuclear power plants, where there is usually a large cash outflow at the end of the project.

In general, the IRR can be calculated by solving a polynomial equation. Sturm's theorem can be used to determine if that equation has a unique real solution. In general the IRR equation cannot be solved analytically but only iteratively. When a project has multiple IRRs it may be more convenient to compute the IRR of the project with the benefits reinvestmented. Accordingly, MIRR is used, which has an assumed reinvestment rate, usually equal to the project's cost of capital.

Despite a strong academic preference for NPV, surveys indicate that executives prefer IRR over NPV. Apparently, managers find it easier to compare investments of different sizes in terms of percentage rates of return than by dollars of NPV. However, NPV remains the "more accurate" reflection of value to the business. IRR, as a measure of investment efficiency may give better insights in capital constrained situations. However, when comparing mutually exclusive projects, NPV is the appropriate measure.

**Mathematics**

Mathematically the value of the investment is assumed to undergo exponential growth or decay according to some rate of return (any value greater than -100%), with discontinuities for cash flows, and the IRR of a series of cash flows is defined as any rate of return that results in a net present value of zero (or equivalently, a rate of return that results in the correct value of zero after the last cash flow). Thus internal rate(s) of return follow from the net present value as a function of the rate of return. This function is continuous. Towards a rate of return of -100% the net present value approaches infinity with the sign of the last cash flow, and towards a rate of return of positive infinity the net present value approaches the first cash flow (the one at the present). Therefore, if the first and last cash flow have a different sign there exists an internal rate of return. Examples of time series without an IRR:

- Only negative cash flows - the NPV is negative for every rate of return.
- (-1, 1, -1), rather small positive cash flow between two negative cash flows; the NPV is a quadratic function of 1/(1+r), where r is the rate of return, or put differently, a quadratic function of the discount rate r/(1+r); the highest NPV is -0.75, for r = 100%.

In the case of a series of exclusively negative cash flows followed by a series of exclusively positive ones, consider the total value of the cash flows converted to a time between the negative and the positive ones. The resulting function of the rate of return is continuous and monotonically decreasing from positive infinity to negative infinity, so there is a unique rate of return for which it is zero. Hence the IRR is also unique (and equal). Although the NPV-function itself is not necessarily monotonically decreasing on its whole domain, it is at the IRR.

Similarly, in the case of a series of exclusively positive cash flows followed by a series of exclusively negative ones the IRR is also unique.

- Extended Internal Rate of Return: The Internal rate of return calculates the rate at which the investment made will generate cash flows. This method is convenient if the project has a short duration, but for projects which has an outlay of many years this method is not practical as IRR ignores the Time Value of Money. To take into consideration the Time Value of Money Extended Internal Rate of Return was introduced where all the future cash flows are first discounted at a discount rate and then the IRR is calculated. This method of calculation of IRR is called Extended Internal Rate of Return or XIRR.

## EQUIVALENT ANNUITY METHOD

The equivalent annuity method expresses the NPV as an annualized cash flow by dividing it by the present value of the annuity factor. It is often used when assessing only the costs of specific projects that have the same cash inflows. In this form it is known as the equivalent annual cost (EAC) method and is the cost per year of owning and operating an asset over its entire lifespan. It is often used when comparing investment projects of unequal lifespans. For example if project A has an expected lifetime of 7 years, and project B has an expected lifetime of 11 years it would be improper to simply compare the net present values (NPVs) of the two projects, unless the projects could not be repeated.

The use of the EAC method implies that the project will be replaced by an identical project. Alternatively the chain method can be used with the NPV method under the assumption that the projects will be replaced with the same cash flows each time. To compare projects of unequal length, say 3 years and 4 years, the projects are chained together, i.e. four repetitions of the 3 year project are compare to three repetitions of the 4 year project. The chain method and the EAC method give mathematically equivalent answers.

The assumption of the same cash flows for each link in the chain is essentially an assumption of zero inflation, so a real interest rate rather than a nominal interest rate is commonly used in the calculations.

## REAL OPTIONS

In finance, real options analysis or ROA (not to be confused with return on assets) applies put option and call option valuation techniques to capital budgeting decisions. A real option itself, is the right — but not the obligation — to undertake some business decision; typically the option to make, abandon, expand, or shrink a capital investment. For example, the opportunity to invest in the expansion of a firm's factory, or alternatively to sell the factory, is a real option. ROA, as a discipline, extends from its application in Corporate Finance, to decision making under uncertainty in general, adapting the mathematical techniques developed for financial options to "real-life" decisions. For example, R&D managers can use Real Options Analysis to help them determine where to best invest their money in research; a non business example might be the decision to join the work force, or rather, to forgo several years of income and to attend graduate school. Thus, in that it forces decision makers to be explicit about the assumptions underlying their projections, ROA is increasingly employed as a tool in business strategy formulation.

**Comparison with standard techniques**

ROA is often contrasted with more standard techniques of capital budgeting, such as net present value (NPV), where only the most likely or representative outcomes are modelled, and the "flexibility" available to management is thus "ignored"; see Valuing flexibility under Corporate finance. The NPV framework therefore (implicitly) assumes that management will be "passive" as regards their Capital Investment once committed, whereas ROA assumes that they will be "active" and may / can modify the project as necessary. The real options value of a project is thus always higher than the NPV - the difference is most marked in projects with major uncertainty (as for financial options higher volatility of the underlying leads to higher value).

More formally, the treatment of uncertainty inherent in investment projects differs as follows. Under ROA, uncertainty inherent is usually accounted for by risk-adjusting probabilities (a technique known as the equivalent martingale approach). Cash flows can then be discounted at the risk-free rate. Under DCF analysis, on the other hand, this uncertainty is accounted for by adjusting the discount rate, (using e.g. the cost of capital) or the cash flows (using certainty equivalents, or applying "haircuts" to the forecast numbers). These methods normally do not properly account for changes in risk over a project's lifecycle and fail to appropriately adapt the risk adjustment.

In general, since ROA attempts to predict the future, the quality of the output will only ever be as good as the quality of the inputs, which by their nature are sketchy. This comment also applies to net present value analysis, although NPV does not require volatility information. Opinion is thus divided as to whether Real Options Analysis provides genuinely useful information to real-world practitioners. ROA is therefore increasingly used as a discussion framework, as opposed to as a valuation or modelling technique.

**Valuation**

As above, ROA is distinguished from other approaches in that it takes into account uncertainty about the future evolution of the parameters that determine the value of the project, and management's ability to respond to the evolution of these parameters. It is the combined effect of these, that makes ROA technically more difficult than its alternatives.

***Valuation inputs***

Generically, the inputs required for modelling the real option correspond to those required for a financial option valuation.

- The option's underlying is the project in question - it is modelled in terms of:
  - Spot price: the starting or current value of the project is required: this is usually based on management's best guess as to NPV; some analysts use a listed security as a proxy;
  - Volatility: uncertainty as to the change in value over time is required: when the underlying project is used, the volatility of project NPV is used (sometimes the volatility of the first period's cash flows are preferred); when a proxy is used, this is either the volatility of the price of the security (historical volatility), or, if options exist on this security, their implied volatility.
- Option characteristics:
  - Strike price: this usually corresponds to sunk costs. In general, management would proceed (i.e. the option would be in the money) given that the present value of expected cash flows exceeds this amount;
  - Option term: the time during which management may decide to act, or not act, corresponds to the life of the option. Examples include the time to expiry of a patent, or of the mineral rights for a new mine.
- Option style. Management's ability to respond to changes in value is modeled at each decision point as a series of options:
  - The option to contract the project (an American styled put option);
  - The option to abandon the project (also an American put);
  - The option to expand or extend the project (both American styled call options);
  - Switching options, composite options or rainbow options which may also apply to the project.

***Valuation methods***

The valuation methods employed are generally adapted from techniques developed for valuing financial options. The most commonly employed are Closed form solutions - often modifications to Black Scholes - and binomial lattices; the latter are probably more widely used due to their flexibility.

Specialised Monte Carlo Methods have also been developed and are increasingly applied particularly to high dimensional problems. When the Real Option can be modelled using a partial differential equation, then Finite difference methods for option pricing are sometimes applied. Although many of the early ROA articles discussed this method, its use is relatively uncommon today - particularly amongst practitioners - due to the required mathematical sophistication.

In general, these methods are limited either as regards dimensionality, or as regards early exercise, or both; in selecting a model, analysts must usually trade off between these considerations. Additionally, sometimes, the stochastic nature of such projections can make analysis using the Monte Carlo method infeasible, necessitating other investigatory methods, such as Robinson differentials. Other new methods have recently been introduced to simplify the calculation of the real option value and thus make the numerical use of the methods easier for practitioners.

### *Technical considerations*

Limitations as to the use of these models arise due to the contrast between Real Options and financial options, for which these were originally developed. The main difference is that the underlying is often not tradeable - e.g. the factory owner cannot easily sell the factory upon which he has the option. As above, this results in difficulties as to estimating the value (i.e. spot price) and volatility of the underlying which are key valuation inputs - this is further complicated by uncertainty as to management's actions in the future. Further, and relatedly, difficulties arise in applying the rational pricing assumptions which underpin these option models: often the "replicating portfolio approach", as opposed to Risk neutral valuation, must be applied.

Additional difficulties include the fact that the real option itself is also not tradeable — e.g. the factory owner cannot sell the right to extend his factory to another party, only he can make this decision; however, some real options can be sold, e.g., ownership of a vacant lot of land is a real option to develop that land in the future. Some real options are proprietary (owned or exercisable by a single individual or a company); others are shared (can be exercised by many parties). Therefore, a project may have a portfolio of embedded real options; some of them can be mutually exclusive.

### History

Whereas business operators have been making capital investment decisions for centuries, the term "real option" is relatively new, and was coined by Professor Stewart Myers at the MIT Sloan School of Management in 1977. It is interesting to note though, that in 1930, Irving Fisher wrote explicitly of the "options" available to a business owner. The description of such opportunities as "real options", however, followed on the development of analytical techniques for financial options, such as Black–Scholes in 1973. As such, the term "real option" itself is closely tied to these new methods.

Real options are today an active field of academic research. Professor Eduardo Schwartz (UCLA) was a pioneering academic in the field. Professor Lenos Trigeorgis (University of Cyprus) has been a leading name for many years, publishing several influential books and academic articles. An academic conference on real options is organized yearly. Amongst others, the concept was "popularized" by Michael J. Mauboussin, the chief U.S. investment strategist for Credit Suisse First Boston and an adjunct professor of finance at the Columbia Business School. Mauboussin uses real options in part to explain the gap between how the stock market prices some businesses and the "intrinsic value" for those businesses as calculated by traditional financial analysis, specifically using discounted cash flows. Trigeorgis also has broadened exposure to real options through layman articles in publications such as The Wall Street Journal. This popularization is such that ROA is now a standard offering in postgraduate finance degrees, and often, even in MBA curricula at many Business Schools.

Recently, real options have been employed in business strategy, both for numerical-valuation purposes and as a conceptual framework. The idea of treating strategic investments as options was conceived by Timothy Luehrman in two HBR articles: "In financial terms, a business strategy is much more like a series of options, than a series of static cash flows". Using Luehrman's framework, investment opportunities are plotted in an "option space" with dimensións "volatility" & value-to-cost ("NPVq"). The higher either of these, the greater the option value inherent in the investment.

## RANKED PROJECTS

The real value of capital budgeting is to rank projects. Most organizations have many projects that could potentially be financially rewarding. Once it has been determined that a particular project has exceeded its hurdle, then it should be ranked against peer projects (e.g. - highest Profitability index to lowest Profitability index). The highest ranking projects should be implemented until the budgeted capital has been expended.

## FUNDING SOURCES

When a corporation determines its capital budget, it must acquire said funds. Three methods are generally available to publicly traded corporations: corporate bonds, preferred stock, and common stock. The ideal mix of those funding sources is determined by the financial managers of the firm and is related to the amount of financial risk that corporation is willing to undertake. Corporate bonds entail the highest financial risk and therefore generally have the lowest interest rate. Preferred stock have no financial risk but dividends, including all in arrears, must be paid to the preferred stockholders before any cash disbursements can be made to common stockholders; they generally have interest rates higher than those of corporate bonds. Finally, common stocks entail no financial risk but are the most expensive way to finance capital projects.

## OPERATING BUDGET

A budget is a quantitative plan for the future that assists the organization in coordinating activities. All large organizations budget. Many organizations prepare detailed budgets that look one year ahead, and budgets that look further into the future that contain relatively less detail and more general strategic direction.

The budget assists in the following activities:

- Planning. A budget helps identify the resources that are needed, and when they will be needed.
- Control. A budget helps control costs by setting spending guidelines.
- Motivating Employees. A budget can motivate employees and managers. Budgets are more effective motivational tools if employees and managers "buy into" the budget, which is more likely to occur if they participate in the preparation of the budget in a meaningful way.
- Communication. A budget can provide either one-way (top-down) or two-way communication within the organization.

A company's overall budget, which is sometimes called a master budget, consists of many supporting budgets. These supporting budgets include:

- Sales budget
- Pro forma income statement
- The production budget and supporting schedules
- Budgets for capital assets and for financing activities
- Budgets for individual balance sheet accounts and departmental expenses
- Cash budget, including cash disbursements and cash receipts budgets
- Pro forma balance sheet

There is a logical sequence for the preparation of these budgets. The first step in a corporate setting is almost always to forecast sales and to assemble a sales budget.

### THE SALES BUDGET

The individuals who are best able to forecast sales are usually the sales force and product managers. Their ability to accurately forecast sales depends on the nature of the industry and on characteristics of the product. Demand is seasonal for many products, in which case each month's forecast usually incorporates information about sales for the same month last year. Accurately forecasting sales of new products and fashion products can be difficult. Demand for some products is sensitive to macroeconomic forces such as interest rates and foreign exchange rates. On the other hand, given the seemingly arbitrary way in which most of us decide where to each lunch, restaurants can usually predict each day's lunch revenue with astounding accuracy. Most companies face a downward-sloping demand curve for their products, which implies that forecasting sales revenue requires predicting sales volume at the planned sales price.

## PRO FORMA INCOME STATEMENT

With planned sales prices, forecasted sales volumes, and an understanding of the cost structure of the business, the company can assemble a pro forma income statement (an anticipated income statement for the upcoming period). This process is illustrated below, in a simple one-product setting, for the Guess Who Jeans Company. The planned sales price is $40 per unit. Assume that the sales manager's best guess of sales volume at this price is 20,000 units for October. Then anticipated revenue for October is $800,000. The company's cost structure is characterized by $30 of variable manufacturing costs per unit, and $150,000 in fixed manufacturing and S.G.&A. (selling, general and administrative) costs. This information is sufficient to complete the pro forma income statement that is shown below.

Guess Who Jeans
Pro Forma Contribution Margin
Income Statement for October

| Income Statement Account | Budgeted amount Per unit | Sale of 20,000 ur |
|---|---|---|
| Revenue | $40 | $800,000 |
| Variable manufacturing costs: | | |
| Materials | 15 | 300,000 |
| Labor | 10 | 200,000 |
| Overhead | 5 | 100,000 |
| Total | 30 | 600,000 |
| Contribution margin | $10 | 200,000 |
| Fixed costs: | | |
| Manufacturing overhead | | 100,000 |
| Selling, general & admin. | | 50,000 |
| Total fixed costs | | 150,000 |
| Operating income | | $50,000 |

## THE PRODUCTION BUDGET

The next step in the budgeting process is more complicated for manufacturing firms than for merchandising firms, because manufacturing companies have three types of inventory accounts: raw materials, work-in-process and finished goods. However, regardless of the number of asset accounts involved, the goal is to determine the required additions to each account (purchases or transfers-in from an upstream account). The calculation to determine required additions is derived by expanding the Sources = Uses equality as follows:

⇒ Beginning balance + additions = transfers out + ending balance

This calculation sometimes uses physical quantities, and sometimes uses dollar values, depending on which makes the most sense under the circumstances.

The beginning balance equals the ending balance for the prior period, which is available either from actual results (the ending balance sheet), or from another budget if the start of the period being budgeted is in the future. The ending balance is a target established by the company, and is usually based on anticipated activity for the following period (that is, the period following the one for which the current budget is being prepared). Transfers-out equals the demand for the asset derived from a previous step in the budgeting process:

- If the asset account is finished goods inventory, the demand is based on cost of goods sold, as derived from the pro forma income statement.
- If the asset account is work-in-process inventory, the demand is based on the additions to the finished goods account, as calculated by applying the sources = uses equation shown above to the finished goods account.
- If the asset account is raw materials inventory, the demand is based on the additions to the work-in-process account for materials, as calculated by applying the sources = uses equation shown above to the work-in-process account.

The unknown in the sources = uses equation is additions, which can be solved for, thus completing the production budget. The following table provides balance sheet information for Guess Who Jeans for September 30, which is the period just ended. (This is also the beginning balance for October 1, the period for which the budget is being prepared, because balance sheet amounts at the end of the day on September 30 are the same as the opening balances on the morning of October 1). We will use the information in this table to budget for October's production. Because Guess Who Jeans makes only one product, it is more convenient to use physical quantities in the sources = uses equations than dollars. We assume that the budget for October is being prepared on October 1st.

## GUESS WHO JEANS BALANCE SHEET SEPTEMBER 30 (THE MONTH JUST ENDED)

| Assets | Amount | Liabilities | Amount |
|---|---|---|---|
| Cash | $ 67,000 | Accounts Payable | $ 295,000 |
| Accounts Receivable | 676,000 | Line of Credit | 345,000 |
| Inventory: | | Stockholders' Equity: | |
| Raw Materials (1,800 yards) | 13,500 | Common stock | 100,000 |
| Work in Process (1,500 units) | 35,000 | Additional paid-in capital | 72,500 |
| Finished Goods (5,000 units) | 150,000 | Retained earnings | 1,009,000 |
| Total inventory | 198,500 | Total | 1,181,500 |
| Property, Plant & Equipment, net of accumulated depreciation | 880,000 | | |
| Total | $1,821,500 | Total | $1,821,500 |

## REQUIRED ADDITIONS TO FINISHED GOODS INVENTORY

Guess Who Jeans expects to sell 20,000 units each month for the next two months (October and November). The company would like to have on hand, at the beginning of each month, 20% of next month's sales. The company did not achieve this operational goal for October, because 5,000 units are on hand on October 1, and expected sales are 20,000 units, but the company came close to its goal (25% versus 20%). At the end of October, the company would like to have 4,000 units on hand (20% of 20,000 units expected to be sold in November).

Beginning balance + additions = transfers out + ending balance 5,000 units + additions = 20,000 units in expected sales + 4,000 units for desired ending inventory ⇒ additions = 19,000. Hence, Guess Who Jeans should plan to transfer out 19,000 units from work-in-process to finished goods inventory during the month of October.

## REQUIRED ADDITIONS TO WORK-IN-PROCESS

Guess Who Jeans would like to have on hand, at any point in time, 1,200 units in work-in-process. The company has determined that this level of work-in-process provides optimal efficiency on the production line.

Beginning balance + additions = transfers out + ending balance 1,500 units + additions = 19,000 units transferred to finished goods + 1,200 units for desired ending WIP ⇒ additions = 18,700. Hence, Guess Who Jeans should plan to start production of 18,700 units during the upcoming month of October.

## REQUIRED ADDITIONS TO RAW MATERIALS

On average, 2 yards of fabric are required for each unit of product. Guess Who Jeans would like to maintain 2,000 yards of fabric on hand at any point in time. (The company had less fabric on hand than desired at the end of September.)

Beginning balance + additions = transfers out + ending inventory

⇒ 1,800 yards + additions = (2 yards per unit x 18,700 units) + 2,000 yards desired in ending inventory on October 31

⇒ 1,800 yards + additions = 37,400 yards + 2,000 yards

⇒ Additions = 37,600 yards of fabric

Hence, Guess Who Jeans should plan to purchase 37,600 yards of fabric during the month of October. Using the budgeted cost of $7.50 per yard, the expected expenditure for these fabric purchases is $282,000.

## ACCOUNTS RECEIVABLE AND ACCOUNTS PAYABLE BUDGETS

### Accounts Receivable

To budget for the ending balance of accounts receivable, the company incorporates information about the rate at which receivables are collected. Guess Who Jeans makes all sales on credit, and past experience indicates that the following collection schedule can be anticipated:

50% of sales are collected in the month of sale

30% of sales are collected in the month following the sale

20% of sales are collected two months following the sale

This collection schedule implies that on October 31, accounts receivable will consist of:

50% of October sales

20% of September sales

Nothing from sales that occurred prior to September

(E.g., August sales would be collected in August, September, and October)

Actual sales for September were 25,000 units.

Anticipated sales for October are 20,000 units.

Therefore, the budget for accounts receivable at the end of October can be calculated as follows:

| | |
|---|---|
| 50% of October sales | 20,000 units x $40 per unit x 50% = $400,00 |
| 20% of September sales | 25,000 units x $40 per unit x 20% = 200,000 |
| | $600,000 |

However, this calculation does not incorporate information available about September collections of September sales and September collections of prior month sales. Possibly, September collections of September sales differed from the 50% that is budgeted, or perhaps not all of August's sales were collected by the end of September. This additional information would normally be used to refine the budget of Accounts Receivable at the end of October.

### Accounts payable

To budget for the ending balance of accounts payable, the company incorporates information about the extent to which the company makes purchases on credit. Guess Who Jeans pays cash for all types of purchases except for fabric purchases. The company pays for fabric 30 days after the fabric is purchased, on average. This payment policy implies that at the end of October, accounts payable will consist of all October purchases of fabric, and nothing else. In the raw materials budget, we determined that $282,000 would be incurred for fabric purchases in October. Hence, this amount is the anticipated the balance in Accounts Payable on October 31.

## THE CASH BUDGET

One of the most important components of the budgeting process for most organizations is the cash budget. The cash budget indicates how much cash the company will have on hand at the end of each period, and also indicates when the company will need to borrow funds to cover temporary cash shortfalls, and when the company will have excess funds to invest in short-term financial instruments. Cash flow is so important that in some organizations, cash balances are projected for the end of each week, or even on a daily basis.

Often, the cash budget is assembled from supporting schedules. These schedules show, for the period being budgeted, anticipated cash disbursements and cash receipts that arise from (1) operating activities, (2) additions and disposals of fixed assets, and (3) financing activities.

Cash receipts: the company anticipates that the only cash receipts that will occur in October will come from collections of receivables. Cash receipts in October are based on anticipated collections of sales that were made in August and September, and anticipated sales for October, and are projected as follows:

Sales made in the month of    Sales volume during    Unit sales p
percentage collected d Collections

| | month | | October | October |
|---|---|---|---|---|
| August | 22,000 | $40 | 20% | $176,000 |
| September | 25,000 | $40 | 30% | 300,000 |
| October | 20,000 | $40 | 50% | 400,000 |
| | | | | $876,000 |

Cash disbursements are anticipated as follows:

| | |
|---|---|
| Fabric purchases (for fabric acquired in September) | 189,000 |
| Manufacturing labor | 189,000 |
| Manufacturing variable overhead | 94,500 |
| Fixed manufacturing overhead (excluding non-cash items) | 50,000 |
| Fixed selling, general and admin. (excluding non-cash items) | 35,000 |
| Cash payments for capital acquisitions (from the capital budget) | 110,000 |
| Payments of short-term borrowings | 60,000 |
| Total disbursements for October | $833,500 |

This information about receipts and disbursements is used to project the ending cash balance for the month, as follows:

- Beginning balance + cash receipts ? cash disbursements = ending balance
- $67,000 + $876,000 ? $833,500 = $109,500

## PRO FORMA BALANCE SHEET

The foregoing analysis can be used to assemble a pro forma balance sheet, projecting the balance sheet at the end of the October. The amounts in the pro forma balance sheet are derived as follows:

Cash: from the cash budget, shown above.

Accounts receivable: from the accounts receivable budget, shown above.

Raw materials inventory: from the projected ending inventory of 2,000 yards multiplied by the budgeted price of $7.50 per yard.

Work-in-process inventory:

| | |
|---|---|
| Beginning balance | |
| + Fabric additions (37,400 yards x $7.50 per yard) | $ 35,000 |
| + Manufacturing labor (from the cash disbursements budget) | 280,500 |
| + Manufacturing variable overhead (from the cash disbursements budget) | 189,000 |
| – Transfers out to finished goods inventory (19,000 units x | 94,500 |
| $30 per unit) | 570,000 |
| Ending balance | $ 29,000 |

Finished goods inventory: from the projected ending inventory of 4,000 units, multiplied by the budgeted cost of $30 per unit. (Note: the company uses Variable Costing for internal reporting.)

Property, plant & equipment, net of accumulated depreciation:

| | |
|---|---|
| Beginning balance | $880,000 |
| + Capital acquisitions (from the cash disbursements budget) | 110,000 |
| – Depreciation expense | 65,000 |
| Ending balance | $925,000 |

The $65,000 in depreciation expense reconciles to the non-cash portion of the $150,000 in fixed manufacturing and selling, general and administrative costs shown on the pro forma income statement. The difference of $85,000 (i.e., the cash portion of these fixed costs) is shown on the cash disbursements budget as $50,000 for fixed manufacturing overhead and $35,000 for fixed selling, general and admin. overhead.

Accounts payable: from the accounts payable budget, shown above.

Short-term borrowings: beginning balance of $345,000 less the anticipated payment of $60,000 as per the cash disbursements budget.

Common stock and Additional paid-in capital: no change.

Retained earnings: beginning balance of $1,009,000 + October income of $50,000, as per the pro forma income statement.

**Guess who Jeans Pro-forma Baance Sheet October 31**

| Assets | Amount | | Liabilities | Amount |
|---|---|---|---|---|
| Cash | $109,500 | | Accounts Payable | $282,000 |
| Accounts Receivable | 600,000 | | Line of Credit | 285,000 |
| Inventory: | | | | |
| Raw Materials (2,000 yards) | 15,000 | | Stockholders' Equity: | |
| Work in Process (1,200 units) | 29,000 | | Common stock | 100,000 |
| Finished Goods (4,000 units) | 120,000 | | Additional paid-in capital | 72,500 |
| Total inventory | 164,000 | | Retained earnings | 1,059,000 |
| Property, Plant & Equipment, | | | Total | 1,231,500 |
| net of accumulated depreciation | 925,000 | | | |
| Total | $1,798,500 | | Total | $1,798,500 |

It is interesting to note that whereas the pro forma income statement can be prepared early in the budgeting process (at least for the results of operating activities), the pro forma balance sheet is one of the last schedules to be prepared, because it depends on information obtained from numerous supporting budgets and schedules.

## BUDGETARY INCENTIVE SCHEMES

Most budgets are built on sales forecasts, and hence, budgets are only as accurate as those forecasts. The sales force has the most accurate and complete information about future sales prospects. Therefore, sales personnel are the best source for the sales forecast, and one would expect the budgeting process to begin with input from the sales force.

Furthermore, the success of most companies depends in large part on the ability of the sales force to generate sales. In order to motivate sales personnel to work hard, many companies include sales commissions as an important component of sales personnel compensation packages: the more they sell, the more they earn.

For many companies, and in many industries, a straight commission is not viewed as equitable. Some sales representatives have "easier" sales territories or product lines. A fixed percentage commission applied to all members of the sales force seems unfair to sales representatives who are assigned more difficult product lines or territories. Many companies solve this problem by paying sales representatives a bonus based on actual sales relative to budgeted sales. The budget can be tailored for each sales representative, so that the difficulty of meeting and exceeding budget is comparable for all sales personnel. Such a bonus scheme rewards sales representatives for incremental effort and sales volume, relative to some baseline.

Taken together, the preceding three paragraphs create an obvious dilemma. The company relies on the sales force to accurately forecast sales for budgeting purposes, yet sales representatives, when asked for their forecasts, will budget conservatively. In so doing, they give themselves easy targets that help ensure that they will maximize their bonuses.

One possible solution to this dilemma is to not pay bonuses based on actual performance relative to budget. An alternative solution is to not ask the sales representatives for their forecasts, but simply to assign targeted sales goals. Neither solution is optimal, because the first solution limits the company's ability to motivate the sales force using a bonus scheme that is generally perceived as effective and fair, and the second solution ignores information that would materially assist in the budgeting process.

One might wonder whether a better solution is possible. In fact, budgetary incentive schemes that simultaneously address these two apparently conflicting objectives have been used for at least 25 years. The example described in the rest of this chapter is adapted from a bonus scheme that was used by IBM in Brazil, as described in an article by Joshua Gonek that appeared in the Harvard Business Review in the 1970s. However, the following example is set in the context of students in an accounting class, not sales representatives working for a company.

## EXAMPLE OF A BUDGETARY INCENTIVE SCHEME

Instructors want students to work hard and to study diligently for exams. If an instructor also wants students to predict their performance on an upcoming exam, then the instructor faces the same dilemma as described above: how does one encourage students to provide accurate forecasts of future performance, and also provide incentives for students to exert maximum effort after the forecasts have been delivered. (In the absence of an incentive mechanism to encourage accurate forecasts, students are notoriously optimistic.)

Consider an exam with ten multiple choice questions, where credit on each question is "all or nothing" (no partial credit). Each question is worth five points, for a total of fifty points. Now consider the following extra credit opportunity related to that exam. One week before the exam, students are asked to forecast how many of the ten questions they will answer correctly. After the exam, they receive extra credit based on the number of points indicated in the box at the intersection of their forecast and their actual score. For example, if a student forecasts that she will answer six questions correctly, and actually answers seven questions correctly, she receives 13 extra credit points (the intersection of row 7 and column 6) in addition to her score of 35 (7 questions x 5 points per question), for a total of 48 points.

This scheme encourages students to forecast accurately, and once the students have made their forecasts, to study hard for the exam. When the student makes her forecast, she is choosing the column that will be used to determine her extra credit. Therefore, once the forecast has been delivered, students want to score as high as possible to maximize both the extra credit score and the total exam score.

Extra Credit Grid for Exam

| | Forecast Exam Score | | | | | | | | | | | |
|---|---|---|---|---|---|---|---|---|---|---|---|---|
| Actual Exam Score | | 0 | 1 | 2 | 3 | 4 | 5 | 6 | 7 | 8 | 9 | 10 |
| | 0 | -- | -- | -- | -- | -- | -- | -- | -- | -- | -- | -- |
| | 1 | 1 | 2 | 1 | -- | -- | -- | -- | -- | -- | -- | -- |
| | 2 | 2 | 3 | 4 | 3 | 2 | 1 | -- | -- | -- | -- | -- |
| | 3 | 3 | 4 | 5 | 6 | 5 | 4 | 3 | 2 | 1 | -- | -- |
| | 4 | 4 | 5 | 6 | 7 | 8 | 7 | 6 | 5 | 4 | 3 | 2 |
| | 5 | 5 | 6 | 7 | 8 | 9 | 10 | 9 | 8 | 7 | 6 | 5 |
| | 6 | 6 | 7 | 8 | 9 | 10 | 11 | 12 | 11 | 10 | 9 | 8 |
| | 7 | 7 | 8 | 9 | 10 | 11 | 12 | 13 | 14 | 13 | 12 | 11 |
| | 8 | 8 | 9 | 10 | 11 | 12 | 13 | 14 | 15 | 16 | 15 | 14 |
| | 9 | 9 | 10 | 11 | 12 | 13 | 14 | 15 | 16 | 17 | 18 | 17 |
| | 10 | 10 | 11 | 12 | 13 | 14 | 15 | 16 | 17 | 18 | 19 | 20 |

Now consider the question of whether students have incentives to forecast accurately. At the time that the student makes her forecast, she has an idea of what her actual score will be. Hence, she has a best-guess of the row that will be used to determine her extra credit. In any given row, the maximum bonus occurs in the column for which the row heading equals the column heading. For example, if the student thinks she will answer five questions correctly, then her maximum extra credit from row "5" is ten, which occurs in the column labeled "5." Therefore, if she thinks she will score five, she cannot expect to do better than to forecast five, the same as her expected performance. If she intentionally forecasts low (choosing a column to the left of column 5) or forecasts high (choosing a column to the right of column 5), she can anticipate earning less than ten extra credit points if she actually answers five questions correctly, as she predicts.

This extra credit scheme is an example of a budgetary incentive scheme that encourages individuals to both forecast accurately, and to exert maximum effort after the forecast has been delivered. Implicit in this scheme, and all such schemes, is a "baseline" performance level. For example, in the extra credit scheme, if the instructor anticipates that the median on the exam will be six, then it is important that students have approximately the same expectation. If the exam turns out to be more difficult or easier than anticipated, then students' forecasts will be "high" or "low" on average, and the amount of extra credit earned will be less than otherwise would have been the case. The extra credit scheme would still encourage accurate forecasts and maximum effort, but it probably would not be perceived as "fair" after the scores are in. Hence, this specific scheme and all such schemes rely on some level of accuracy in management's (or the instructor's) information, but then uses that information to obtain still more accurate information from the individuals who are best informed (sales representatives or students, as the case may be).

## DIVISIONAL PERFORMANCE MEASURES

### DIVISIONAL INCOME

Divisional income is a measure of divisional performance that is analogous to corporate net income for evaluating overall company performance. Similar to related-party transactions in the context of financial accounting, the calculation of divisional income must consider transactions that occur between divisions, and between the division and corporate headquarters. One type of intra-company transaction is the transfer of goods between divisions. These transfers, which represent revenue to the selling division and a cost of inventory to the buying division, are discussed in Chapter 23. Another type of transaction is the receipt of services from corporate headquarters or from other responsibility centers within the company. Examples of such services are human resources, legal, risk management, and computer support. In many companies, these services are "charged out" to the divisions that utilize them. These service department cost allocations were discussed in Chapter 12.

Because divisional income fails to account for the size of the division, it is ill-suited for comparing performance across divisions of different sizes. Divisional income is most meaningful as a performance measure when compared to the same division in prior periods, or to budgeted income for the division.

### RETURN ON INVESTMENT

Return on investment (ROI) is calculated as:

$$\text{Return on Investment} \; \frac{\text{Divisional Income}}{\text{Divisional Investment}}$$

The same issues arise in determining the numerator in ROI as arise in the previous subsection with respect to deriving divisional income. As regards the denominator, senior management must decide whether and how to allocate shared assets among divisions, such as service departments at the corporate level, or shared manufacturing facilities. Also, management must decide how to value the capital assets that comprise the division's investment. These assets can be valued at their gross book value (the acquisition cost), their net book value (usually the acquisition cost minus depreciation expense), or less often, some other valuation technique such as replacement cost, net realizable value or fair market value. The calculation of the numerator should be consistent with the choice of valuation technique in the denominator. For example, if divisional investment is calculated using gross book value, then divisional income in the numerator should not be reduced by depreciation expense.

One advantage of using gross book value instead of net book value in the ROI calculation is that net book value can discourage divisional managers from replacing old equipment, even if new equipment would be more efficient and would increase the economic profits of the division. This dysfunctional managerial incentive occurs because if the existing equipment is fully depreciated, but is still functional, its replacement can reduce the division's ROI by lowering the numerator (due to increased depreciation expense) and increasing the denominator (because fully depreciated assets have a net book value of zero).

ROI can be broken down into the following two components:

$$\text{ROI} = \frac{\text{Divisional Income}}{\text{Divisional Investment}} = \frac{\text{Divisional Income}}{\text{Divisional Revenue}} = \frac{\text{Divisional Revenue}}{\text{Divisional Investment}}$$

The first term on the right-hand side is called the return on sales (ROS). It is also called the operating profit percentage. This ratio measures the amount of each dollar of revenue that "makes its way" to the bottom line. ROS is often an important measure of the efficiency of the division, and the divisional manager's ability to contain operating expenses.

The second term on the right-hand side is called the asset turnover ratio or the investment turnover ratio. This ratio measures how effectively management uses the division's assets to generate revenues. Interestingly, this ratio seems to hover around one for many companies in a wide range of industries, particularly in the manufacturing sector of the economy. Breaking ROI into these two components often provides more useful information than looking at ROI alone, and it is an example of the type of financial ratio analysis that stock analysts conduct in evaluating company-wide performance. In this context, two common specifications for the denominator in the ROI calculation are assets and equity. The resulting ratios are called return on assets (ROA) and return on equity (ROE).

At the divisional level, ROI controls for the size of the division, and hence, it is well-suited for comparing divisions of different sizes. On the other hand, similar to the Internal Rate of Return for evaluating capital projects, ROI can discourage managers from making some investments that shareholders would favor. For example, if a divisional manager is evaluated on ROI, and if the division is currently earning an ROI in excess of the company's cost of capital, then the manager would prefer to reject an additional investment opportunity that would earn a return above the cost of capital but below the division's current ROI. The new investment opportunity would lower the division's ROI, which is not in the manager's best interests. However, because the investment opportunity provides a return above the cost of capital, shareholders would favor it.

## RESIDUAL INCOME

One way in which financial accounting practice fails to follow corporate finance theory is that the cost of debt is treated as an expense in arriving at net income, but the cost of equity is not. Specifically, interest expense appears as a deduction to income on the income statement, but dividends are shown on the statement of changes in shareholders' equity. Hence, net income is affected by the company's financing strategy as well as by its operating profitability, which can obscure the economic performance of the firm.

A simple solution to this problem is to add back interest expense (net of the tax effect) to net income, to arrive at operating income after taxes. The performance measure called residual income makes this adjustment, and then goes one step further, by deducting a charge for capital based on the organization's total asset base:

Residual Income = Operating Income ? (Investment Base x Required Rate of Return) The company's cost of capital is often appropriate for the required rate of return. Residual income is probably the closest proxy that accounting provides for the concept of economic profits; hence, residual income probably comes close to measuring what shareholders really care about (to the extent that shareholders only care about maximizing wealth). Residual income can be calculated both at the corporate level and at the divisional level. Many companies that use residual income at the divisional level do so because management believes that residual income aligns incentives of divisional managers with incentives of senior management and shareholders.

One type of residual income calculation is called Economic Value Added. EVA was developed by the consulting firm of Stern Stewart & Co., and is a registered trademark of that firm. The calculation of EVA includes a deduction for the cost of capital, and also adjusts accounting income to more accurately reflect the economic effect of transactions and the economic value of assets and liabilities. In general, these adjustments move the income calculation further from the reliability-end of the relevance-versus-reliability continuum, and closer to the relevance-end of that continuum. Since the 1990s, EVA has helped revive the popularity of residual income. However, it should be emphasized that although Stern Stewart has obtained trademark protection on the term "EVA," the concept of residual income precedes EVA by almost half a century, and it is in the public domain. Anyone can use residual income for any purpose whatsoever without violating trademark, copyright or patent law, and this includes making obvious adjustments to net income to more accurately reflect the underlying economic reality of the firm.

## TRANSFER PRICING

### DEFINITION AND OVERVIEW

A transfer price is what one part of a company charges another part of the same company for goods or services. In the excerpt from Casablanca, Rick apparently loaned Ferrari 100 cartons of cigarettes for which he was never repaid. Now that Ferrari owns both the Blue Parrot and Rick's Café, he jokes about the fact that what was previously a debt that he owed to Rick, is now a "debt" from one nightclub that he owns to another nightclub that he owns. If Ferrari continues to transfer cartons of cigarettes between the two clubs, he might wish to establish a "transfer price" for cigarettes, but knowing Ferrari, he won't bother.

We will restrict attention to transfers that involve a tangible product, and we will refer to the two corporate entities engaged in the transfer as divisions. Hence, the transfer price is the price that the "selling" division charges the "buying" division for the product. Because objects that float usually flow downstream, the selling division is called the upstream division and the buying division is called the downstream division.

Transferred product can be classified along two criteria. The first criterion is whether there is a readily-available external market price for the product. The second criterion is whether the downstream division will sell the product "as is," or whether the transferred product becomes an input in the downstream division's own production process. When the transferred product becomes an input in the downstream division's production process, it is referred to as an intermediate product.

Transfer pricing serves the following purposes.

1. When product is transferred between profit centers or investment centers within a decentralized firm, transfer prices are necessary to calculate divisional profits, which then affect divisional performance evaluation.
2. When divisional managers have the authority to decide whether to buy or sell internally or on the external market, the transfer price can determine whether managers' incentives align with the incentives of the overall company and its owners. The objective is to achieve goal congruence, in which divisional managers will want to transfer product when doing so maximizes consolidated corporate

profits, and at least one manager will refuse the transfer when transferring product is not the profit-maximizing strategy for the company.

3. When multinational firms transfer product across international borders, transfer prices are relevant in the calculation of income taxes, and are sometimes relevant in connection with other international trade and regulatory issues.

The transfer generates journal entries on the books of both divisions, but usually no money changes hands. The transfer price becomes an expense for the downstream division and revenue for the upstream division. Following is a representative example of journal entries to record the transfer of product:

Upstream Division:

1. Intercompany Accounts Receivable $9,000
   Revenue from Intercompany Sale $9,000
2. Cost of Goods Sold – Intercompany Sales $8,000
   Finished Goods Inventory $8,000

(To record the transfer of 500 cases of Clear Mountain Spring Water, at $18 per case, to the Florida marketing division, and to remove the 500 cases from finished goods inventory at the production cost of $16 per case.)

Downstream Division:

1. Finished Goods Inventory $9,000
   Intercompany Accounts Payable $9,000

(To record the receipt of 500 cases of Clear Mountain Spring Water, at $18 per case, from the bottling division in Nebraska)

## TRANSFER PRICING OPTIONS

There are three general methods for establishing transfer prices.

- Market-based transfer price: In the presence of competitive and stable external markets for the transferred product, many firms use the external market price as the transfer price.
- Cost-based transfer price: The transfer price is based on the production cost of the upstream division. A cost-based transfer price requires that the following criteria be specified:
  - Actual cost or budgeted (standard) cost.
  - Full cost or variable cost.
  - The amount of markup, if any, to allow the upstream division to earn a profit on the transferred product.
- Negotiated transfer price: Senior management does not specify the transfer price. Rather, divisional managers negotiate a mutually-agreeable price.

Each of these three transfer pricing methods has advantages and disadvantages.

## MARKET-BASED TRANSFER PRICES

Microeconomic theory shows that when divisional managers strive to maximize divisional profits, a market-based transfer price aligns their incentives with owners' incentives of maximizing overall corporate profits. The transfer will occur when it is in the best interests of shareholders, and the transfer will be refused by at least one divisional manager when shareholders would prefer for the transfer not to occur. The upstream division is generally indifferent between receiving the market price from an external customer and receiving the same price from an internal customer. Consequently, the determining factor is whether the downstream division is willing to pay the market price. If the downstream division is willing to do so, the implication is that the downstream division can generate incremental profits for the company by purchasing the product from the upstream division and either reselling it or using the product in its own production process. On the other hand, if the downstream division is unwilling to pay the market price, the implication is that corporate profits are maximized when the upstream division sells the product on the external market, even if this leaves the downstream division idle. Sometimes, there are cost savings on internal transfers compared with external sales. These savings might arise, for example, because the upstream division can avoid a customer credit check and collection efforts, and the downstream division might avoid inspection procedures in the receiving department. Market-based transfer pricing continues to align managerial incentives with corporate goals, even in the presence of these cost savings, if appropriate adjustments are made to the transfer price (i.e., the market-based transfer price should be reduced by these cost savings).

However, many intermediate products do not have readily-available market prices. A disadvantage of a market-based transfer price is that the prices for some commodities can fluctuate widely and quickly. Companies sometimes attempt to protect divisional managers from these large unpredictable price changes.

## COST-BASED TRANSFER PRICES

Cost-based transfer prices can also align managerial incentives with corporate goals, if various factors are properly considered, including the outside market opportunities for both divisions, and possible capacity constraints of the upstream division.

First consider the case in which the upstream division sells the intermediate product to external customers as well as to the downstream division. In this situation, capacity constraints are crucial. If the upstream division has excess capacity, a cost-based transfer price using the variable cost of production will align incentives, because the upstream division is indifferent about the transfer, and the downstream division will fully incorporate the company's incremental cost of making the intermediate product in its production and marketing decisions. However, senior management might want to allow the upstream division to mark up the transfer price a little above variable cost, to provide that division positive incentives to engage in the transfer.

If the upstream division has a capacity constraint, transfers to the downstream division displace external sales. In this case, in order to align incentives, the opportunity cost of these lost sales must be passed on to the downstream division, which is accomplished by setting the transfer price equal to the upstream division's external market sales price.

Next consider the case in which there is no external market for the upstream division. If the upstream division is to be treated as a profit center, it must be allowed the opportunity to recover its full cost of production plus a reasonable profit. If the downstream division is charged the full cost of production, incentives are aligned because the downstream division will refuse the transfer under only two circumstances:

- First, if the downstream division can source the intermediate product for a lower cost elsewhere;
- Second, if the downstream division cannot generate a reasonable profit on the sale of the final product when it pays the upstream division's full cost of production for the intermediate product.

If the downstream division can source the intermediate product for a lower cost elsewhere, to the extent the upstream division's full cost of production reflects its future long-run average cost, the company should consider eliminating the upstream division. If the downstream division cannot generate a reasonable profit on the sale of the final product when it pays the upstream division's full cost of production for the intermediate product, the optimal corporate decision might be to close the upstream division and stop production and sale of the final product. However, if either the upstream division or the downstream division manufactures and markets multiple products, the analysis becomes more complex. Also, if the downstream division can source the intermediate product from an external supplier for a price greater than the upstream division's full cost, but less than full cost plus a reasonable profit margin for the upstream division, suboptimal decisions could result.

## NEGOTIATED TRANSFER PRICES

Negotiated transfer pricing has the advantage of emulating a free market in which divisional managers buy and sell from each other in a manner that simulates arm's-length transactions. However, there is no reason to assume that the outcome of these transfer price negotiations will serve the best interests of the company or shareholders. The transfer price could depend on which divisional manager is the better poker player, rather than whether the transfer results in profit-maximizing production and sourcing decisions. Also, if divisional managers fail to reach an agreement on price, even though the transfer is in the best interests of the company, senior management might decide to impose a transfer price. However, senior management's imposition of a transfer price defeats the motivation for using a negotiated transfer price in the first place.

## SURVEY OF PRACTICE

Roger Tang (Management Accounting, February 1992) reports 1990 survey data on transfer pricing practices obtained from approximately 150 industrial companies in the Fortune 500. Most of these companies operate foreign subsidiaries and also use transfer pricing for domestic interdivisional transfers. For domestic transfers, approximately 46% of these companies use cost-based transfer pricing, 37% use market-based transfer pricing, and 17% use negotiated transfer pricing. For international transfers, approximately 46% use market-based transfer pricing, 41% use cost-based transfer pricing, and 13% use negotiated transfer pricing. Hence, market-based transfer pricing is more common for international transfers than for domestic transfers. Also, comparison to an earlier survey indicates that market-based transfer pricing is slightly more common in 1990 than it was in 1977.

Tang also finds that among companies that use cost-based transfer pricing for domestic and/or international transfers, approximately 90% use some measure of full cost, and only about 5% or 10% use some measure of variable cost.

## EXTERNAL REPORTING

For external reporting under Generally Accepted Accounting Principles, no matter what transfer price is used for calculating divisional profits, the effect should be reversed and intercompany profits eliminated when the financial results of the divisions are consolidated. Obviously, intercompany transfers are not arm's-length transactions, and a company cannot generate profits or increase the reported cost of its inventory by transferring product from one division to another.

## DUAL TRANSFER PRICING

Under a dual transfer pricing scheme, the selling price received by the upstream division differs from the purchase price paid by the downstream division. Usually, the motivation for using dual transfer pricing is to allow the selling price to exceed the purchase price, resulting in a corporate-level subsidy that encourages the divisions to participate in the transfer. Although dual transfer pricing is rare in practice, a thorough understanding of dual transfer pricing illustrates some of the key bookkeeping and financial reporting implications of all transfer pricing schemes.

In the following example, the Clear Mountain Spring Water Company changes from a negotiated transfer price of $18 per case to a dual transfer price in which the upstream division receives the local market price of $19 per case, and the downstream division pays $17 per case.

Upstream Division:

1. Intercompany Receivable/Payable $9,500
   Revenue from Intercompany Sale $9,500
2. Cost of Goods Sold – Intercompany Sales $8,000
   Finished Goods Inventory $8,000

(To record the transfer of 500 cases of Clear Mountain Spring Water, at $19 per case, to the Florida marketing division, and to remove the 500 cases from finished goods inventory at the production cost of $16 per case.)

Downstream Division:

1. Finished Goods Inventory $8,500
   Intercompany Receivable/Payable $8,500

(To record the receipt of 500 cases of Clear Mountain Spring Water at $17 per case, from the bottling division in Nebraska)

Corporate Headquarters:

1. Interco. Receivable/Payable – Florida $8,500
   Corporate Subsidy for Dual Transfer Price $1,000
   Interco. Receivable/Payable – Nebraska $9,500

(To record the transfer of 500 cases of Clear Mountain Spring Water from Nebraska to Florida, at a dual transfer price of $19/$17 per case.)

Corporate Subsidy for Dual Transfer Price is an expense account at the corporate level. This account and the revenue account that records the intercompany sale affect the calculation of divisional profits for internal reporting and performance evaluation, but these accounts—as well as the intercompany receivable/payable accounts—are eliminated upon consolidation for external financial reporting. To the extent that the Florida Division has ending inventory, the cost of that inventory for external financial reporting will be the company's cost of production of $16 per case. In other words, the transfer price has no effect on the cost of finished goods inventory.

## TRANSFER PRICING AND MULTINATIONAL INCOME TAXES

When divisions transfer product across tax jurisdictions, transfer prices play a role in the calculation of the company's income tax liability. In this situation, the company's transfer pricing policy can become a tax planning tool. The United States has agreements with most other nations that determine how multinational companies are taxed. These agreements, called bilateral tax treaties, establish rules for apportioning multinational corporate income among the nations in which the companies conduct business. These rules attempt to tax all multinational corporate income once and only once (excluding the double-taxation that occurs at the Federal and state levels). In other words, the tax treaties attempt to avoid the double-taxation that would occur if two nations taxed the same income. Since transfer prices represent revenue to the upstream division and an expense to the downstream division, the transfer price affects the calculation of divisional profits that represent taxable income in the nations where the divisions are based.

For example, if a U.S.-based pharmaceutical company manufactures a drug in a factory that it operates in Ireland and transfers the drug to the U.S. for sale, a high transfer price increases divisional income to the Irish division of the company, and hence, increases the company's tax liability in Ireland. At the same time, the high transfer price increases the cost of product to the U.S. marketing division, lowers U.S. income, and lowers U.S. taxes. The company's incentives with regard to the transfer price depend on whether the marginal tax rate is higher in the U.S. or in Ireland. If the marginal tax rate is higher in the U.S., the company prefers a high transfer price, whereas if the marginal tax rate is higher in Ireland, the company prefers a low transfer price. The situation reverses if the drug is manufactured in the U.S. and sold in Ireland. The general rule is that the company wants to shift income from the high tax jurisdiction to the low tax jurisdiction. There are limits to the extent to which companies can shift income in this manner. When a market price is available for the goods transferred, the taxing authorities will usually impose the market-based transfer price. When a market-based transfer price is not feasible, U.S. tax law specifies detailed and complicated rules that limit the extent to which companies can shift income out of the United States.

## OTHER REGULATORY ISSUES

Transfer pricing sometimes becomes relevant in the context of other regulatory issues, including international trade disputes. For example, when tariffs are based on the value of goods imported, the transfer price of goods shipped from a manufacturing division in one country to a marketing division in another country can form the basis for the tariff. As another example, in order to increase investment in their economies, developing nations sometimes restrict the extent to which multinational companies can repatriate profits. However, when product is transferred from manufacturing divisions located elsewhere into the developing nation for sale, the local marketing division can export funds to "pay" for the merchandise received. As a final example, when nations accuse foreign companies of "dumping" product onto their markets, transfer pricing is often involved. Dumping refers to selling product below cost, and it generally violates international trade laws. Foreign companies frequently transfer product from manufacturing divisions in their home countries to marketing affiliates elsewhere, so that the determination of whether the company has dumped product depends on comparing the transfer price charged to the marketing affiliate with the upstream division's cost of production.

# 6

# Mentoring and Performance Coaching

## CONDITIONS FOR EMPLOYEE DEVELOPMENT

For helping an employee to grow and develop in any Organisation, it is necessary to understand the conditions associated with development. The following are some such conditions.

### THE INDIVIDUAL SHOULD BE INTERESTED IN DEVELOPING HIMSELF

Development cannot take place if the person himself is not interested in it. The first condition for Human Resources Development is to ensure the interest of the individual in developing himself. Quite often, higher level officers in the organisations write off some of their employees as not growing or not willing to grow. Such perceptions only show bias. No individual wants to stagnate. Only others, because of their expectations and their limited perspectives, brand people as stagnating. This may be because of the difference between the observer's interest in the employee's development in one direction, being different from the employee's own desire to learn something else. It is useful to know in which areas the employee is interested in developing. Through such an understanding and mutual discussion, it may be possible to create interest in individuals for new areas of development that are congruent with organisational goals and plans.

### THE INDIVIDUAL SHOULD KNOW THE AREAS OF HIS POTENTIAL DEVELOPMENT

Although the recent researches in behaviour suggest that individuals can learn any skills, there is also ample evidence to show that some individuals can grow faster on some dimensions that on others. These are called aptitudes. While in the developed countries there are enough opportunities for an individual to know about his potential through psychological tests, school coaching services, family guidance services, etc., we do not have such services easily available in India. An individual himself may discover, quite often too late, that he is good at certain things and he is not as good at certain other things. A person's insight into his strengths and weaknesses may depend on his introspective capability and the opportunities he gets to test himself. In organisations where fresh graduates are exposed to a variety of jobs through job rotation procedures, the young men get opportunities to test themselves and their aptitudes in relation to various functions. In organisations which do not have such a job rotation policy at the early stages of employee's career, the chances of round pegs being put in square holes increase. While every individual should attempt to discover his own potential, the organisation also has an obligation to create conditions for such a discovery.

### THE INDIVIDUAL SHOULD MAKE A CLEAR CHOICE ABOUT THE DIRECTION IN WHICH HE WOULD LIKE TO GROW AND DEVELOP

Besides discovering his aptitude, the individual should be in a position to make a clear choice about his career. He might discover that he has more than one strength. A combination of his strengths may indicate that he is good at a number of things. Some careers may be more paying than others. Sometimes the individual may have the strengths required for a particular career, which according to him is rewarding only in a limited way. In such a case, he should be able to take the risk and create opportunities for himself to develop strengths required for new careers. Through a good career planning and training system, the organisation should attempt to help him to develop himself. The organisation should also help in setting such career goals realistically.

### HE SHOULD BE ABLE TO IDENTIFY OPPORTUNITIES FOR DEVELOPMENT WITHIN AND OUTSIDE THE ORGANIZATION

Identification of potential, strengths, weaknesses, etc., may have a demoralising effect on the employees if no system exists for developing or overcoming them. Opportunities for the development of individual employees within and outside the organisation should be created.

### HE SHOULD IDENTIFY MECHANISMS OF USING THESE OPPORTUNITIES AND GET THE SUPPORT HE NEEDS FROM HIS SUPERIORS AND THE ORGANIZATION

While the organisation should plan for the growth of the employees according to their career plan, it is unrealistic to expect it to support the career goal of each individual employee. However, it should help the individual to understand the limitations and work out alternative strategies.

### HE SHOULD MAKE EFFORTS TO DEVELOP

Mere interest in development does not serve any purpose if the individual is not prepared to invest himself and his energies in his development. Such an investment would depend upon how much he is prepared to act. Development can take place only through concentrated efforts to acquire knowledge and the ability to experiment with that knowledge. High-activity level and risk-taking orientation 'accelerate learning.

## HE SHOULD TAKE OUTSIDE HELP TO PERIODICALLY REVIEW HIS PROGRESS

Persons cannot develop in isolation. Most of the development at higher levels is facilitated through human interaction. A person should have either a reference group or a few selected helpers in the environment for periodical reviews. The reference group or selected helpers act as mirrors so that the individual can continuously look at himself in the direction in which he is growing.

## A POSITIVE EMOTIONAL AND PROFESSIONAL CLIMATE SHOULD BE CREATED IN THE WORK PLACE FOR THE EMPLOYEE TO PROGRESS AND REVIEW HIMSELF

The responsibility for creating such a climate lies at every level with higher level officers and the top management of the organisation. Such a climate facilitates free expression of feelings, emotions, free exchange of views, opinions and, at the same time fostering of mutual trust. The identification of potential and development of the employee is a joint responsibility of the employee himself and the organisation. While the latter should provide opportunities for the individual to grow, the former should get interested in identifying opportunities, strengths and weaknesses, set himself realistic career goals, and continuously review his growth. The individual has the responsibility to make use of such opportunities and act with drive and determination. One of the most effective instruments in the hands of an employee for development is performance review. Performance review can be done at several stages. While it is the responsibility of the supervisors to guide and counsel their employees in relation to their past, present and future, a formal system of performance review can be employed by organisations. Performance review can be done both for the individual and the group.

## THE OBJECTIVES OF PERFORMANCE COACHING

Coaching aims at developing employees in an organization, by the following.

1. Helping them to realise their potential as managers.
2. Helping them to understand themselves – their strengths and weaknesses
3. Providing them opportunity to acquire more insight into their behaviour and analyse the dynamics of such behaviour.
4. Helping them to have a better understanding of the environment.

5. Increasing their personal and interpersonal effectiveness by giving them feedback about their behaviour and assisting them in analysing their inter-personal competence.
6. Encouraging them to set goals for further improvement.
7. Encouraging them to generate alternatives for dealing with various problems.
8. Providing them empathic atmosphere for sharing and discussing tensions, conflicts, concerns and problems.
9. Helping them to develop various action plans for further improvement.
10. Helping them to review in a non-threatening way their progress in achieving various objectives.
11. Strengthening the dyadic relationship between the employee and his boss.

## INDIVIDUAL-LEVEL REVIEW

The purpose of performance review is to help the employee grow and develop. Others can help him as quite often he may not be aware of his own strengths, just as he may be blind to his weaknesses. Those who continuously interact with the person can act as mirrors. However, such a feedback should be specific and purposeful. It serves three main purposes:

1. General improvement of the person,
2. Improvement of his performance in specific tasks, and
3. Identification and development of his potential for higher level responsibilities.

### General Improvement

Feedback for the general improvement of an employee is a continuous process. It occurs either inside or outside the organisation through colleagues, friends, subordinates, family members, etc. Within the organisation, people who work closely can be instrumental in helping the employee continuously assess the impact he is making on people and the environment. Such an assessment would help him to understand his own characteristics and develop as a mature person. No formal system can help in such a continuous interpersonal feedback. However, it can be facilitated through an open climate, a climate of psychological security, and positive attitudes towards one another in the organisation.

### Improved Performance

While the senior officer help their subordinates to perform gains. Usually, managers guide their subordinates more in relation to specific, immediate task-related problems rather than on other aspects of behaviour. For example, whenever a subordinate faces a problem, his officer may give a solution for that particular problem. Merely providing the solution to a problem does not amount to giving feedback. This will not necessarily help the employee to develop the ability to solve future problems by himself This ability to solve problems by himself can be developed through continuous education. The formal appraisal system is another mechanism of giving feedback discussion. In such a formal system, the tasks are set much in advance. The qualities on which the individual is going to be rated are also identified in advance. At the end of a specified period of time, both the individual and his senior officer sit together for performance review. Feedback is a critical factor in such a review. In the performance review, the individual points out his own accomplishments in relation to the objectives decided upon. He may also identify the factors that have helped him in achieving whatever he could achieve, and the factors that prevented him from doing better. The individual may also highlight the qualities he has shown in that particular period. After he presents his own assessment, his senior officer tries to help him analyse his own performance in greater depth. He might add a number of other factors which have helped him to achieve whatever he has achieved, and a number of other factors that prevented him from doing better. The senior officer may also focus on the strengths and weaknesses of the appraises. He might also point out the consistencies or inconsistencies of behaviour he observed in the employee. Both the manager and his employee jointly identify the developmental needs and ways of meeting the needs.

**Potential Development of the Employee**

Employees develop their potential if they are aware of the opportunities in the organisation and also of the mechanisms for developing this potential. Some organisations use mechanisms to appraise the potential of an employee. Usually, data are collected about all the employees whose potential is being assessed. It may be useful to give feedback to the employee on such data. Feedback on potential assessment would help the employee to understand his strengths and weaknesses, and help him to modify his career plans accordingly. If the employee has no opportunity to explore the feedback further, it is likely to demoralise him. Since emotions are involved here, it should be handled delicately. Such review should better be done either by one whom the employee trusts, or by an outside expert who has used objective measures of assessing the potential, or by a group of people from the top management who have a broader perspective and who can coach the employee. The officers one or two levels above the employee can give such feedback, either formally or informally, after a system of potential appraisal has been introduced in the organisation. In such a review with the employee, they would have with them the employee's ratings and other data on his potential. The following points may be kept in mind in the potential appraisal review of the employees.

- The employee should be given the source of feedback;
- The employee should be told the limits of the feedback;
- The employee should be helped to view alternative career opportunities;
- Before giving such feedback, it should be ensured that the employee believes that there are opportunities to develop his potential and that human behaviour is dynamic and changeable; and
- While giving the feedback, the relationship of the employee with others who work with him should also be kept in mind.

### FEEDBACK TO GROUPS OR TEAMS

Feedback needs to be given to a group of people who constitute a small unit or a department within a large organisation. It may help the group to grow and develop as such. Feedback to groups is generally useful in terms of the process mechanisms operating in the group, like decision-making styles, collaborative orientation of the group with other groups, delegation, supervisory styles, morale, etc Feedbacks can be given either by the organisational leader or through an external agent using the research and surveys. Mechanisms of giving group feedback using survey research are described in the section on research and organisation development.

## CONDITIONS FOR EFFECTIVE COACHING

Coaching is a means and not an end in itself. Development does not occur just because there is coaching. Coaching could be an effective instrument in helping people integrate with their organisations and have a sense of involvement and satisfaction. The following conditions are necessary for coaching to be effective:

### GENERAL CLIMATE OF OPENNESS AND MUTUALITY

If the organisation or department in which the employee is working is full of tension, and people do not trust each other, coaching cannot be effective. A climate of minimum trust and openness is essential for effective coaching.

### GENERAL HELPFUL AND EMPATHIC ATTITUDE OF MANAGEMENT

Coaching involves effective helping, which is not possible unless the coach has a general helping attitude and has empathy for the counselled.

### UNINHIBITED PARTICIPATION BY THE SUBORDINATES IN THE REVIEW PROCESS

Unless the subordinates in a department or organisation feel free enough to participate without inhibition in the process of review and feedback, coaching cannot be effective. Coaching is not a one-way process of communicating to the employee what he should or should not do. It is a process of developing a dialogue which eventually contributes to a better understanding on the part of the counsellee.

## DIALOGIC RELATIONSHIP IN GOAL SETTING AND PERFORMANCE REVIEW

Performance coaching focuses on the counsellee's achievement of the performance goals set in consultation with his manager. Joint participation by the employee and his reporting officer is necessary both in goal-setting and performance review. Without such collaborative effort, coaching cannot achieve its purpose.

## FOCUS ON WORK-ORIENTED BEHAVIOUR

The main purpose of performance coaching is to help the employee to improve his performance. Coaching can be effective if the focus is kept on the work-related goals rather than on diffusing attention into various other areas. While doing so, discussion may involve other related and personal issues, but these are used to refocus on improvement on organisation roles rather than on personal or general personality problems.

## FOCUS ON WORK-RELATED PROBLEMS AND DIFFICULTIES

Performance coaching is not only related to the achievement of goals, but also to the contextual problems in achieving or not achieving the goals. Analysis of performance therefore becomes the basis of coaching.

## AVOIDANCE OF DISCUSSION OF SALARY AND OTHER REWARDS

Performance coaching may not serve its purpose if it includes discussion about salary raise, rewards, etc. The main purpose of performance coaching is to use performance appraisal in planning and improvement of the employee, rather than in understanding the relationship between performance and rewards like salary, etc. Bringing such discussion in the performance coaching may vitiate the main purpose of coaching.

# THE PROCESS OF COACHING

Coaching is given by one who is senior to the person, receiving the help—in competence, knowledge, psychological expertise, or in the hierarchical position in an organisation. There are three main processes involved in coaching—communication, influencing and helping. The coach essentially communicates with the employee. Communication involves receiving messages, giving messages, and giving feedback. The person who provides coaching does all the three things. Coaching also involves influencing the counsellee in several ways. The manager cannot deny the fact that he is influencing his employee in such a way that the latter is able to move in some direction. However, this influence is of a special that is, enabling the other person to exercise more autonomy, providing positive reinforcement so that desirable behaviour is further strengthened, and creating conditions in which the person is able to learn from the behaviour of the coach through the process of identification. The third element in the process, i.e., helping, also functions in a similar way. It involves three different elements. Firstly, helping behaviour is based on the concern and empathy the coach has for his counselee. Secondly, it is also based on the mutuality of relationship; the counselee responds as much to the coach's needs as the latter does to the former's. Finally, helping primarily involves identification of developmental needs of the counselee so that he may be able to develop and increase his effectiveness. This dynamic process of coaching is shown.

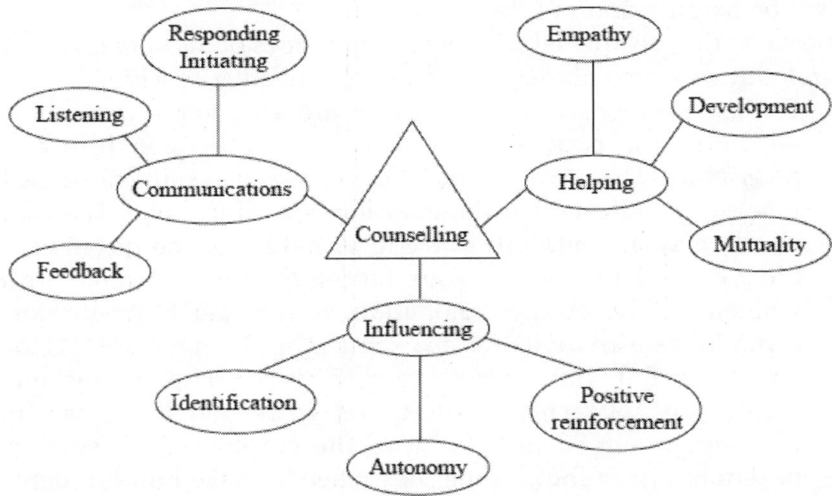


The Process of Coaching

## COMMUNICATION

Interpersonal communication is the basis of performance review in which both the employee and his reporting officer are involved. Such a conversation in performance review should be congenial, which may help the employee to be in a receptive mood. It is important to keep in mind that communication is greatly influenced by how problems and issues are perceived by the two persons involved in the conversation. It may get distorted if people are not empathic to each other and do not try to understand each others' point of view. Non-verbal communication is as important as verbal communication. People speak much more through their gestures and postures than through words. The tone and manner of speaking is also important. There are three main elements in communication. Listening: Listening is the first effective step in communication. Listening involves paying attention to the various messages being sent by the other person. The obvious message is the ideas being communicated. But there may be hidden feelings and concerns which the other person may not be able to put clearly in words. Listening to feelings and concerns is very important for effective coaching. This involves skills which can be practised. Some exercises can be used to improve listening of such hidden messages.

Asking Questions and Responding: Questions can facilitate or hinder the process of communication. They can serve several purposes: they can help in getting more information, establishing mutuality, clarifying matters, stimulating thinking. Questions play a very important role in coaching. Some questions can shut off the employee, or make him dependent on the coach, while some others can build the autonomy of the employee. Obviously, the latter will be helpful, and not the former.

Questions that do not Help: The following types of questions are not only unhelpful, but they also hinder the process of effective coaching:

- Critical questions: Questions which are used to criticise, reprimand or doubt the counsellee, create a gap between him and the counsellor. The way the question is asked (skeptical or sarcastic tone) may indicate that the question is a critical one. The choice of words may also indicate the critical nature of the question. "Why did you fail to achieve your targets?" communicates criticism, whereas "Why could you not attain your targets?" would normally communicate an invitation to examine hindering factors. "How did you again fall short of your target?" is a reprimanding question. "How can you achieve this target since you failed last time?" indicates doubt in the ability of the employee. All such critical questions either shut off the counsellee or make him diffident.
- Testing questions: Questions that are asked to find out whether a person is right or wrong, or how much he knows, are evaluating or testing questions. Such questions may tend to put the other person on the defensive. In a testing question, the person asking the question takes a superior attitude, while the other person is put in a kind of witness box. Such questions may also take the form of a crossexamination. A reporting officer who proposes to find out why his employee was not able to meet his target can easily slip into a cross-examination, testing or evaluating posture. Again, the tone of the interviewer may determine whether the question is a testing question. Such questions are sometimes similar to critical questions.
- Resenting questions: A person may ask questions to indicate his resentment of the behaviour of the other person. When an employee in a coaching situation asks: "How should I attain a higher target?", it may indicate his resentment depending on the tone in which such a question is asked.

- Leading questions: Quite often unknowingly, the questions asked indicate what kind of answers are wanted and such answers are actually received. Such a question may be asked after making a statement. For example, a reporting officer may say to his employee: "You could not attain the target because maintenance department did not cooperate. Is that true?", or it may be put in the question form: "Were you not able to attain the target because the maintenance department did not cooperate?" Both are leading questions. A leading question almost seduces the other person to go along the line of thinking of the one who asks the question. This tends to stop further exploration and is not helpful

Questions that are Helpful: The following types of questions may be of help in developing a more healthy relationship and in increasing the effectiveness of the other person.

- Trusting questions: Questions which are asked to that the questioner is seeking help or suggestions may indicate the trust he has in the other person. The question "How do you think I can deal with the problem I am facing?" is seeking help from the other person. Such questions may be asked both by the employee and the supervisor.
- Clarifying questions: Questions may be asked to collect information, more facts and figures. Such questions are very helpful. If a coach asks his employee several questions to help him to get more information about various aspects, the employee, in turn, would provide him with relevant information to understand his problems. After listening to a person for some time, the coach may paraphrase the counsellee's statement (also called mirroring), and then he may ask a question to confirm whether his understanding is correct. For example, the question, "Are you worried about your lack of knowledge of the new system?" is a clarifying question. A clarifying question helps the manager and the employee to remain at the same level throughout the conversation.
- Empathic questions: Questions about the feelings of a person, his concern, his problem, not so much for finding solutions as to indicate and express concern, may be classified as empathic questions. When a manager asks an employee: "How is your son feeling now?", he is not merely seeking information, but in fact indicating his personal concern about the health of the employee's son and thereby expressing empathy with the employee. Such questions help to generate more trust, and the necessary rapport with the employee. Empathic questions create a climate of mutual trust and human understanding.
- Open questions: The most useful questions are those which stimulate reflection and thinking in the employee. "Why do you

think we have not achieved the targets this year while the other company has?" is an open question inviting the other person to explore the various possible dimensions, and to share them with the person who is asking such a question. Open questions encourage creativity, and a tendency to explore several directions which might have been neglected so far. Such questions are very useful.

- Responding to questions: Coaches sometimes use certain responses, some of which are useful and some dysfunctional. Some coaches may be using certain types of responses more often than others. It is necessary to be aware of this. Responses that alienate the employee, criticise him or order him, are more likely to be dysfunctional. Empathic, supportive, and exploring responses are more functional. Various verbal behaviours in a coaching situation that characterise these responses are shown in Exhibit 1.

**Exhibit : Coach Responses**

| Unhelpful | Effective and helpful |
|---|---|
| Alienating | Empathic |
| Continuous stress on conformity | Leveling |
| Not encouraging creative acts | Rapport building |
| Passive listening | Identifying feelings |
| Lack of verbal response | Supportive |
| Critical | Recognising |
| Criticising | Communicating availability |
| Pointing inconsistencies | Committing support |
| Repeated mention of weaknesses | Trusting |
| Belittling | Exploring Questions |
| Reprimanding | Questions |
| Directive | Reflecting |
| Prescribing | Sharing |
| Ordering | Probing |
| Threatening | Closing |
| Giving no options | Summarising |
| Pointing out only one aceptable way | Concluding |
| Quoting rules and regulations | Contracting for follow up and help |

## Feedback

Feedback will be effective if the person giving feedback (coach) makes sure that it is:

1. Descriptive and not evaluative;
2. Focused on the behaviour of the person and not on the person himself;
3. Data-based and specific and not impressionistic;
4. Reinforces positive new behaviour;
5. Suggestive and not prescriptive;
6. Continuous;
7. Mostly personal, giving data from one's own experience;
8. Need-based and solicited;
9. Intended to help;
10. Focused on modifiable behaviour;
11. Satisfying the needs of both (giver and receiver of feedback)
12. Checked and verified;
13. Well timed; and
14. Contributes to mutuality and building up of relationship.

From the point of view of the one who receives the feedback, it is necessary that the reaction to feedback is more in terms of exploring ways of improving behaviour rather than of defensive behaviour. The following defensive behaviour might not help in using feedback properly; the behaviour which are opposite of these may be helpful.

1. Denying feedback as opposed to owning up responsibility for behaviour.
2. Rationalisation (explaining away feedback by giving reasons) as opposed to self-analysis to find why such behaviour was shown.
3. Projection (contributing negative feelings to the other persons) as opposed to empathy (trying to understand the point of view of the other persons).
4. Displacement (expressing negative feelings to one who may not fight back) as opposed to exploration (taking help of the other person in knowing more about the feedback given).
5. Quick acceptance without exploration as opposed to collecting more information and data to understand the behaviour.
6. Aggression towards the person giving feedback as opposed to seeking his help in understanding the feedback.
7. Humour and wit as opposed to concern for improvement.
8. Counterdependence (rejecting the authority) as opposed to listening carefully to the person giving feedback.
9. Cynicism (generally strong skepticism that things cannot improve) as opposed to a positive, critical attitude to accept some feedback and to question some other.
10. Generalisation (explaining things in a general way) as opposed to experimenting.

## INFLUENCING

Influencing would mean making an impact on the person in relationship. Such impact need not necessarily be of a restrictive type. Influencing in coaching would involve the following three aspects:

- Increasing Autonomy of the Person Usually, influencing is understood only in the sense of restricting the autonomy of the person and directing him into channels which are predetermined by the person exerting influence. Positive influencing is the opposite of this; the autonomy of the other person is increased, and he has larger scope of making his own choice. Even this is influencing, but of a different kind. Flanders makes a distinction between the two modes of influence, viz., the direct mode of influence (which restricts the freedom of the other person), and the indirect mode of influence (which increases the freedom of the other person). Flanders has developed some categories to indicate the two modes. He classifies criticism and punishment in the first category, and encouraging a person in the second category of influence. The reason is obvious. When a person is criticised or punished, some actions for which he is criticised or punished are inhibited and the person avoids doing those in future. This restricts his freedom. On the other hand, if a person is praised or recognised, he feels encouraged to take more initiative in exploring new directions. This results in an increase in the field of his autonomy. In coaching, much more use is made of the indirect mode of influence, by recognising and expressing feelings, acknowledging and praising good ideas given by the counsellee, and raising questions which promote thinking and exploration.
- Positive Reinforcement: It has been established by Skinner that change in behaviour cannot be brought about in human beings through punishment or negative reinforcement, but only through positive reinforcement. Influencing would involve providing encouragement and reinforcing success so that the person takes more initiative and is able to experiment with new ideas. Change cannot take place without experiment and risk taking. And these are encouraged through positive reinforcement.
- Identification: One major influence which helps an employee to develop is the opportunity for him to identify himself with individuals having more experience, skill and influence. This is the first stage in the development of psycho-social maturity, or power motivation. This legitimate need should be fulfilled. Levinson states several barriers which may come in the way of such a legitimate process of identification: lack of time, intolerance for mistakes, complete rejection of dependency needs, repression of rivalry, and

unexamined relationship. Levinson suggests that, to help the development of the process of identification it is necessary that the manager also examines his own process, and needs of interacting with the subordinates.

## HELPING

Coaching is essentially helping. Helping involves several processes but the following three are mainly important.

- Concern and Empathy: Without the manager's concern for his employee, effective helping cannot be provided in a coaching session. Such concern is shown when the coach is able to feel for his subordinate and is able to empathise with him. This would be reflected in the kinds of questions asked and the tone in which the conversation takes place. Managers may constantly ask themselves how much concern and genuine empathy they have for the employees they are coaching. Without such genuine concern, coaching may only degenerate into a ritual and cannot achieve its goals.
- Mutuality of Relationship: Coaching should not be regarded as merely giving help. It is also receiving help on various aspects. Unless such a relationship is established— i.e., both persons involved in the relationship feeling free to ask for and provide help to each other—coaching cannot be effective. Mutuality is based on trust and the genuine perception that each person has enough to contribute. Although the coach is in a superior position, he continues to learn and to receive help from the counsellee.
- dentifying Developmental Needs: The main purpose of performance coaching is to identify the development needs of the employee which can be met through various ways. It is necessary that coaching results in clear and systematic identification of such needs and in subsequent plans as to how these needs will be fulfilled. Sperry and Hess (1974) have advocated the use of contact coaching, which they defined as " the process by which the manager aids the employee in effective problemsolving, and develop using the techniques or keying, responding and guiding." Contact coaching is based on a transactional analysis approach and makes use of several skills already discussed. Keying refers to reading people. The supervisor uses an appropriate frame of reference to perceive what the employee means by his verbal and non-verbal responses. Responding concerns what the supervisor communicates back to the employee. What is learnt from keying is replayed in a manner which adds to, on subtracts from, the interchanges with the meaning the employee communicates.

Guiding is the techniques the supervisor uses to motivate or help the employee to change his behaviour. The supervisor as motivator can increase the employee's drive and direct it so that he accomplishes his objectives better. Morrisey (1972) has suggested a few other techniques, such as a you-we technique, second-hand compliment, advice-request and summary. In the you-we technique, one uses you to compliment and we to criticise ("you are doing a great job, we have a problem"). The second-hand compliment is communicating to the subordinate a compliment for him received from a third party. The advice-request is asking the employee for suggestions and advice. Summarising at the end helps in clarifying the decisions taken and fixing the responsibilities and integrating the whole discussions.

Values in the Helping Process: The central issue in a helping process relates to the values of the helper. The helping behaviour and strategies flow out of the basic stand he takes in relation to the client. The helper should ask himself/herself what values he/ she holds, and with what consequences. Okun (1976) has suggested that the following set of images of people is essential for an effective helping process:

1. People are responsible, and capable of making their own choices and decisions.
2. People are controlled to a certain extent by their environment, but they are able to direct their lives more than they realise. They always have choices and freedom, along with responsibility, even if they have restricted options due to environmental variables or inherent biological or personality predispositions.
3. Behaviours are purposive and goal-directed. People are continuously striving towards meeting their own needs, ranging from basic physiological needs to abstract self-actualisation ones (fulfilling physiological, psychological and aesthetic needs).
4. People want to feel good about themselves and continuously need positive confirmation of their own self-worth from significant persons. They want to feel and behave congruently, to reduce dissonance between internal and external realities.
5. People are capable of learning new behaviours and unlearning existing ones and they are subject to environmental and internal consequences of their behaviours, which in turn, serve as reinforcements. They strive for reinforcements that are meaningful and congruent with their personal values and belief systems.
6. People's personal problems may arise from unfinished business (unresolved conflicts) stemming from the past (concerning events and relationships) and, although some exploration of causation may be beneficial in some cases, most problems can be worked through by focusing on the here and now, on what choices the person has now. Problems are also caused by incongruence between internal

(how you see things inside) and external (how you see things outside) perceptions in the present.

7. Many problems experienced by people today are societal or systemic rather than personal or interpersonal. People are capable of learning to effect choices and changes within the system as well as from without.

## PHASES OF PERFORMANCE COACHING

Coaching is helping the employee to grow and develop in the organisation. Every manager is coaching his employee, knowingly or unknowingly, in his day-to-day work-life. An effective manager coach is one who helps his employees to become more aware of their strengths and weaknesses and helps them to improve further on the strong points and overcome weaknesses. By the process of mutuality and support, he helps the employee to develop, by providing the proper emotional climate. Mutuality involves working together with the employee and developing future plans of action for the employee's growth and contribution to the organisation. Support involves acceptance of the employee as a total person, with his strengths and weaknesses, and encouraging him with warmth. Coaching requires certain interpersonal skills which can be acquired easily if a manager is genuinely interested in developing his subordinates. Coaching skills are important for a manager, particularly at the time of performance review.

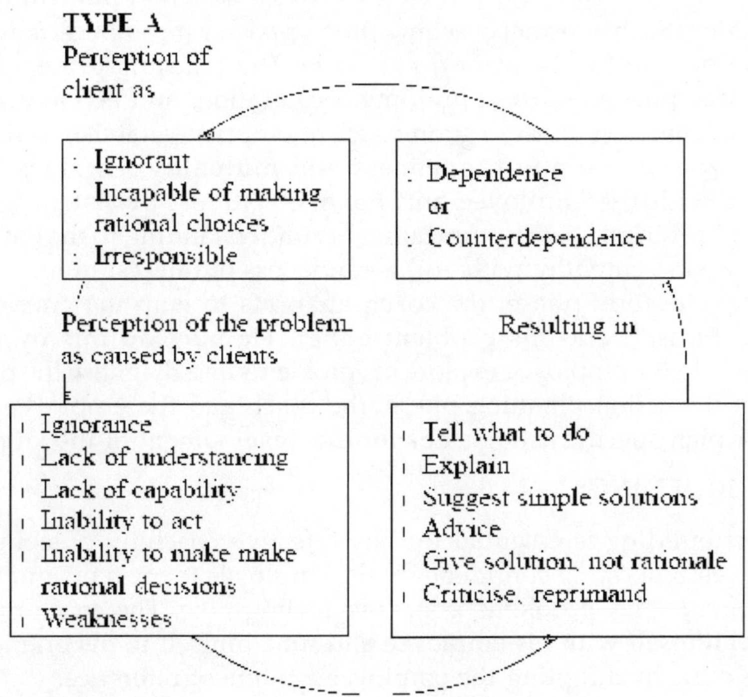

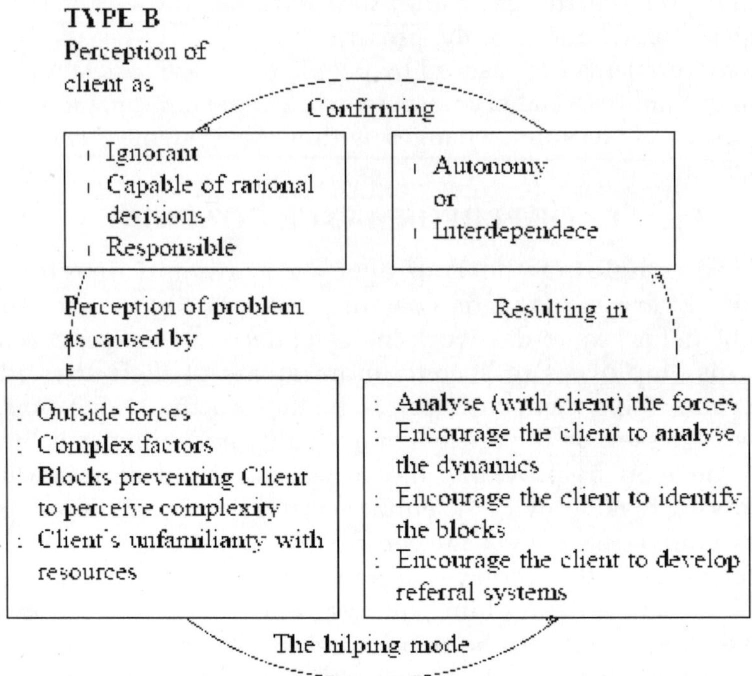


Good managers, whenever the necessity arises, coach their employees in their jobs. Annual performance reviews provide formal opportunities for formal coaching. Such a formal coaching process passes through certain stages, which are important for the managers to note. The coaching process has the following three phases: rapport building, exploration, and action planning. In the rapport-building phase, a good coach attempts to establish a climate of acceptance, warmth, support, openness and mutuality. He does this by empathising with the employee and his orientations, by listening to his problems and feelings, by communicating his understanding to the employee, and by expressing empathy with and genuineness of interest in him.

In the exploration phase, the coach attempts to help the employee to understand himself and his problem better. He may do this by raising questions to help the employee explore his problems and diagnose the problem properly. In the action planning phase, the coach and the employee jointly work out or plan specific action steps for the development of the latter.

## RAPPORT BUILDING

Rapport building is essential for any effective coaching outcome. This phase involves generating confidence in the employee to open up and frankly share his perceptions, problems, concerns, feelings, etc. The coach-manager should level himself with his employee and tune himself to his orientations. This can be done by adopting the employee's frame of reference.

**Attending**

The opening phase of coaching is very important in rapport building. General opening rituals may communicate messages of attending to the employee and give importance to the coaching transaction. Inviting rituals like offering the chair, closing the door to indicate privacy, asking the secretary not to disturb or not to connect telephonic calls during the conversation, may indicate that the coach is attending to the employee. However, all such rituals should come out of the genuine concern for and full attention to the employee during the coaching session.

**Listening**

It has already been discussed that listening is important for effective coaching. As already stated it is important to listen to what the employee says, as well as to his feelings and concerns. Physical posture (e.g., leaning forward) and keeping eye contact with the employee are indicators of listening.

**Acceptance**

Establishing a climate of acceptance is a necessary part of establishing rapport. The employee must feel that he is wanted and that his coach is interested in understanding him as a person rather than as a role or a position in an organisation. The coach communicates this to the employee by listening to all the problems of the employee and communicating back to the employee that he is listening. The coach can communicate back to the employee by paraphrasing or mirroring or reflecting what the employee says. For example, when an employee says, "I am really mad. I have tried to do my best in the past year. I have worked twice as hard as anyone else in the office. But I never get promotion," he is expressing his anger. The coach may reflect back and say, "You feel that your superiors have not shown proper recognition for your hard work." Such a reflection or mirroring would help the employee feel that he is being understood and that his coach is interested in him. This builds a climate of acceptance and facilitates the process.

**Exploration**

Besides accepting the employee, listening to him, and establishing a climate of openness, the coach should attempt to understand as well as help the employee understand his own situation, strengths, weaknesses, problems and needs. Nobody would like to be directly told his weaknesses. Coaching skill lies in making the employee discover his own weaknesses, and identify his problem. At the most, the coach may use open and exploring questions. Exploring helps an employee to search various dimensions of the problems, or discover unidentified problems and bring to the surface unnoticed issues. Exploring can be done by using questions and suggesting to the employee to talk more on a problem he mentions. As already discussed, a variety of questions may be used.

**Problem Identification**

After general exploring, questions may be asked to help the employee focus on the problem. It is necessary for the coach to use questions, both to generate information on some concerns and problems and to narrow down focus to identify a more probable problem. For example, if an employee feels that his problem is that others do not cooperate with him, the coach may ask questions to narrow down the problem to the employee's relationship with a few colleagues, and then questions may be asked to help the employee see what he does that prevents possible cooperation. Eventually, the problem may turn out as to how the employee may deal with competitive relationship, and yet collaborate. Identification of a problem is the necessary step in planning for improvement.

**Diagnosis**

Diagnosis of the problem is the next step in exploration. Explorations should lead to the diagnosis. Without diagnosis there is little scope for solving any problem. Open questions like "Why do you think people are put off when you talk with them?", "Can you recall occasions when you got full cooperation?", "What do you attribute it to?", "What personal limitations mainly bother you?" may help the employee more towards a better diagnosis. The main attempt should be to generate several alternative causes of a problem.

**Action Planning**

Managers are expected to guide their employees and contribute to their development. Coaching interviews should end with specific plans of action for the development of the employee. Identifying a training need, job rotation, sponsoring for further training, increased responsibility, role clarity, etc., are some of the likely outcomes in such action plans. Three sub-phases can be identified in action planning.

**Searching**

The main contribution of the coach to action planning is the help he provides to the employee in thinking of alternative ways of dealing with a problem. In addition to encouraging the employee in brain-storming such alternatives, the coach at a later stage can also add to this list of alternatives for further exploration. This should, however, be done only after some time. The employee should primarily take the responsibility of generating alternatives.

**Decision Making**

After the alternatives have been generated, the coach may help the employee assess the advantages and disadvantages of each alternative, raise questions on the feasibility of the various alternatives, and help finalise a plan to be implemented. This may, however, be regarded as a contingency plan, to be altered in the light of further experience.

**SUPPORTING**

The final and, crucial stage of coaching is to communicate support and plan for such support in implementing the agreed action plan. Psychological contract of providing help should emerge after considerable exploration and discussion. Support and help should facilitate in further increasing the autonomy of the employee, and not his dependence on the coach. A system for monitoring and follow up of the action plan may be prepared. This closes the coaching interaction.

## MAKING COACHING EFFECTIVE

In performance coaching formally organised by the organisation, the employee may not ask for coaching but his superior may organise coaching interviews as an organisational requirement. On such occasions, the employee may be forced into a coaching situation. If coaching is given without having been sought, it is likely to be of limited value. It may prove frustrating both to the coach and to the employee. In such situations, the coach would do well by forgetting about performance coaching and talk to the employee about his lack of interest in growth. The employee is likely to open up if the coach establishes an open climate. If the employee has serious emotional block in dealing with his superior, there is no use organising a coaching interview. They need a problem-solving session before that. Hence, before coaching, it must be ensured that the employee is willing to learn from this interview. Some employees are so loyal and some superiors so protective, that there is a danger of employees becoming totally dependent on the coach. The coach should check from time to time through reflection, if he is making the employee too dependent on him. The coach must allow the employee to make his own decisions and perhaps help him in making decisions, but must not take decisions for him.

The employee must understand the purpose of coaching. If he does not understand, or has wrong expectations, he may not receive whatever is said to him in the proper perspective. If it is felt that he has some misunderstandings, it is better to use the first session to clarify them and then schedule another session. Arguments should be minimised. One argument is sufficient to make both parties defensive. The coach should accept everything the employees says and try to build on it. Acceptance is the best way of bringing about self-realisation in the person. Good coaching sessions fail to produce effective results due to lack of follow up. Follow ups through informal exchanges go a long way in communicating interest in the employee. Otherwise, he may feel that the coaching is only artificial and may lose interest in it eventually.

## THE PROCESS OF MENTORING

The word "mentor" comes from the Greek epic story about Odysseus who wandered the world seeking adventure and—you could say—personal development. Before going on his ten-year voyage (none of this weekend workshop stuff for Odysseus!), he left his son Telemachus in the care of an older and trusted friend whose name was Mentor. In Odysseus' absence, Mentor not only helped the boy become a competent young man but also saved his life. This relationship, and the name of the older man who assisted the younger man in developing himself, became a model for what is now known as mentoring.

Mentoring is the process where a person (the mentor) provides support, training, and guidance to a less experienced, usually younger person (the mentee, mentoree, or protege). Some benefits of mentoring are that it enhances productivity and teamwork, it encourages continued learning, it improves the self-esteem of the protege, and it improves the chances of success in the protege's endeavours. Levinson et al. (1978) have contributed the most to the understanding of the mentoring process. Levinson's concept of a mentor includes being a teacher, sponsor, counsellor, developer of skills and intellect, host, guide, exemplar, and most importantly supporter and facilitator in the realization of the vision the young person has about the kind of life he wants as an adult. Mentoring integrates characteristics of the parent-child relationship and peer support without being either. According to Levinson not having a mentor in formative years of a young person could be a great handicap to one's psychological and career development. Although young person during their professional journey, unknowingly research and discover appropriate mentors, organisations are increasingly paying attention to this phenomenon.

Generally, more promising young managers are given mentoring experience. A young manager assigned to a mentor, who is senior in position and age sometimes several levels senior to the protege; not necessarily from the protege's department. Mentors are selected on the basis of their interest, availability, and "mentoring competence" (image of competence, empathy, and ability to provide emotional support). One mentor may have not more than five protege. Tata Iron successfully used this arrangement. There are two main phases in mentoring process: dependence and inter-dependence, although counter-dependence may in some cases be an intermediary phase between the two. During dependence phase admiration for the mentor is followed by identification with him, followed by approval (getting guidance and checking alternative action ideas). The inter-dependence phase is characterised by trust-building and mutuality when the mentor and the protege may begin to collaborate and provide emotional support to each other, If the mentor is experienced as overwhelming and overpowering, counter-dependence may develop before inter-dependence. The protege may reject the mentor and may develop his own independence. Search of one's own identity may later lead to appreciation of the mentor's role and relationship, leading to inter-dependence. Several well-known persons in the west having famous mentors passed through the counter-dependence phase, and some could not make much progress to inter-dependence.

Mentoring process is quite similar to the counselling process. The dynamics of the phases discussed with counselling are also applicable to mentoring. The ultimate goal of both counselling and mentoring is to help an employee attain psychological maturity and effectiveness.

# 7

# Team Goals and Performance Management

## GROUP DYNAMICS AND TEAMS

### THEORIES OF GROUP FORMATION

#### Group Formation

Well functioning groups do not just form out of the blue. It takes time for a group to develop to a point where it can be effective and where all members feel connected to it. Bruce Tuckman has identified four stages that characterize the development of groups. Understanding these stages can help determine what is happening with a group and how to manage what is occurring. These four group development stages are known as forming, storming, norming, and performing as described below and the skills needed to successfully guide a group through these stages are described by clicking here.

#### *Forming*

This is the initial stage when the group comes together and members begin to develop their relationship with one another and learn what is expected of them. This is the stage when team building begins and trust starts to develop. Group members will start establishing limits on acceptable behavior through experimentation. Other members' reactions will determine if a behavior will be repeated. This is also the time when the tasks of the group and the members will be decided.

#### *Storming*

During this stage of group development, interpersonal conflicts arise and differences of opinion about the group and its goals will surface. If the group is unable to clearly state its purposes and goals or if it cannot agree on shared goals, the group may collapse at this point. It is important to work through the conflict at this time and to establish clear goals. It is necessary for there to be discussion so everyone feels heard and can come to an agreement on the direction the group is to move in.

### *Norming*

Once the group resolves its conflicts, it can now establish patterns of how to get its work done. Expectations of one another are clearly articulated and accepted by members of the group. Formal and informal procedures are established in delegating tasks, responding to questions, and in the process by which the group functions. Members of the group come to understand how the group as a whole operates.

### *Performing*

During this final stage of development, issues related to roles, expectations, and norms are no longer of major importance. The group is now focused on its task, working intentionally and effectively to accomplish its goals. The group will find that it can celebrate its accomplishments and that members will be learning new skills and sharing roles. After a group enters the performing stage, it is unrealistic to expect it to remain there permanently. When new members join or some people leave, there will be a new process of forming, storming, and norming engaged as everyone learns about one another. External events may lead to conflicts within the group. To remain healthy, groups will go through all of these processes in a continuous loop.

When conflict arises in a group, do not try to silence the conflict or to run from it. Let the conflict come out into the open so people can discuss it. If the conflict is kept under the surface, members will not be able to build trusting relationships and this could harm the group's effectiveness. If handled properly, the group will come out of the conflict with a stronger sense of cohesiveness then before.

## SKILLS TO MANAGE GROUP DEVELOPMENT

You may know the name of the different stages of development but there are different skills and techniques needed to guide a group through the stages. Here are some suggestions.

### Forming

Be inclusive and empowering. Make sure that everyone connected to the group is involved. Seek out diverse members and talents and model inclusive leadership. Identify common purposes and targets of change. Create an environment that fosters trust and builds commitment to the group.

### Storming

Be ethical and open to other people's ideas. Allow differences of opinion to be discussed. Handle conflict directly and civilly. Keep everyone focused on the purpose of the group and the topic of conflict. Avoid personal attacks. Examine biases that may be blocking progress or preventing another member to be treated fairly.

**Norming**

Be fair with processes. New members should feel welcomed, informed, and involved. Continue to clarify expectations of individuals and of the group. Engage in collaboration and teamwork.

**Performing**

Celebrate accomplishments and find renewal in relationships. Encourage and empower members to learn new skills and to share roles that keep things fresh and exciting. Revisit purpose and rebuild commitment.

## TYPES OF GROUPS

The most common way of distinguishing between groups is to categorizing the groups into formal or informal groups. Formal groups are deliberately created by the organization in order to help the organizational members achieve some of the important the organizational goals. The informal groups, in contrast, develop rather spontaneously among an organization's members without any direction from the organizational authorities.

There are various types of formal groups that are found in an organization. These are:

- Command group which is determined by the organizational chart depicting the approved formal connections between individuals in an organization. Examples of command group are Director and the faculty members in a business school, school principal and teachers, production manager and supervisors, etc.
- Task groups, comprising some individuals with special interest or expertise, are created by the organizational authorities to work together in order to complete a specific task. Task groups are often not restricted to the organizational hierarchy and can be cross functional in nature. Examples of task group might be people working on a particular project.
- Standing committee is a permanent committee in an organization to deal with some specific types of problems that may arise more or less on a regular basis. Examples of standing committees include the standing committee in a university to discuss various academic and administrative issues.
- Task force / ad hoc committee, in contrast, is a temporary committee formed by organizational members from across various functional areas for a special purpose. Meetings can also come under this category.

- Various types of informal groups are:
- Interest groups are formed when a group of employees band together to seek some common objectives, like protesting some organizational policy or joining the union to achieve a higher amount of bonus.
- Friendship groups develop among the organizational members when they share some common interest like participating in some sports activities or staging the office drama, etc.
- Reference groups are the groups, with which individuals identify and compare themselves. These could be within the organization when a middle level executive compares himself with the higher level executive and longs for the perks and benefits enjoyed by the latter. The reference group might exist outside the organization as well when an individual compares himself with his batch mates working in other organizations or an ideal group of people he likes to become.

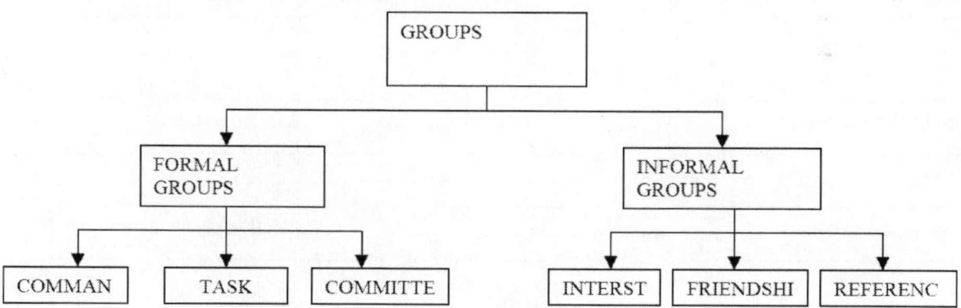


**Types of Groups**

## INDIVIDUAL'S PERFORMANCE IN GROUPS

Groups are formed with individuals, but the output of the groups is not just the sum-total of individual's contribution towards the group. The term group synergy refers to the fact the action of two or more group members result in an effect that is different from the individual summation of their contributions. This occurs because of the social facilitation effect which refers to the tendency for performance of an individual group member to improve in response to the presence of other members. However, the group performance is not always guaranteed to improve as often group members are found to exert less individual effort. This is known as social loafing when members are found to enjoy a 'free ride' which tends to increase with group's size.

## GROUPS AND TEAMS

Do you still remember the excitement during the last world cup and the way the Indian team performed? No matter what they could finally achieve or not, we all used to comment on spirit of the Indian team. A team can be defined as a special type of group whose members have complementary skills and are committed to a common purpose or set of goals for which they hold themselves mutually accountable. In the recent times, a lot of emphasis is being given on developing teams. The importance of teams has long been appreciated in the world of sports, and now it is being used increasingly in the realm of business and industry as well. Though there are similarities between groups and teams and these two terms are often used interchangeably, there are in fact a few striking differences between the two. The following table will help to summarize this.

**Table Groups and Teams**

**Work Groups** **Work Teams**

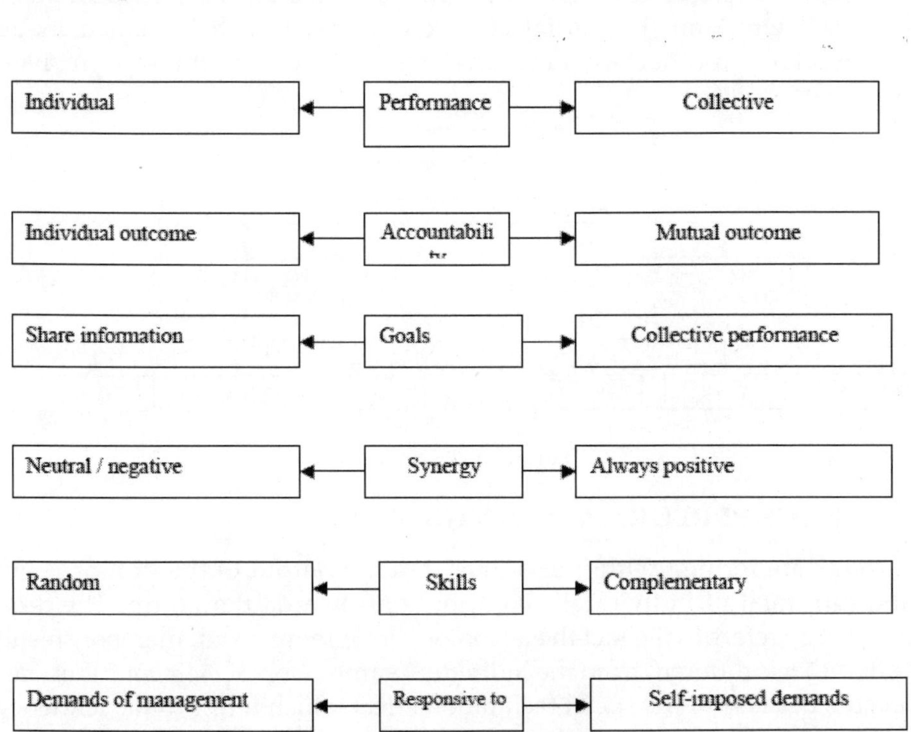


## FORMAL AND INFORMAL ORGANIZATION

### Formal organization

Formal organization is a fixed set of rules of intra-organization procedures and structures. As such, it is usually set out in writing, with a language of rules that ostensibly leave little discretion for interpretation. In some societies and in some organization, such rules may be strictly followed; in others, they may be little more than an empty formalism.

- To facilitate the accomplishment of the goals of the organization: In a formal organization the work is delegated to each individual of the organization. He/She works towards the attainment of definite goals, which are in compliance with the goals of the organization.
- To facilitate the co-ordination of various activities: The authority, responsibility and accountability of individuals in the organization is very well defined. Hence, facilitating the co-ordination of various activities of the organisation very effectively.
- To aid the establishment of logical authority relationship: The responsibilities of the individuals in the organisation are well defined. They have a definite place in the organisation due to a well defined hierarchical structure which is inherent in any formal organisation.
- Permit the application of the concept of specialization and division of Labour, division of work amongst individuals according to their capabilities helps in greater specializations and division of work.
- Create more group cohesiveness

***Characteristics of a formal organization***

- Well defined rules and regulation
- Arbitrary structure
- Determined objectives and policies
- Status symbol
- Limitation on the activities of the individual
- Strict observance of the principle of co-ordination
- Messages are communicated through scalar chain

***Distinction from informal organization***

Formal rules are often adapted to subjective interests — social structures within an enterprise and the personal goals, desires, sympathies and behaviors of the individual workers — so that the practical everyday life of an organization becomes informal. Practical experience shows no organization is ever completely rule-bound: instead, all real organizations represent some mix of formal and informal. Consequently, when attempting to legislate for an organization and to create a formal structure, it is necessary to recognize informal organization in order to create workable structures. However, informal organization can fail, or, if already set in order, can work against mismanagement.

Formal organizations are typically understood to be systems of coordinated and controlled activities that arise when work is embedded in complex networks of technical relations and boundary-spanning exchanges. But in modern societies, formal organizational structures arise in highly institutional contexts. Organizations are driven to incorporate the practices and procedures defined by prevailing rationalized concepts of organizational work and institutionalized in society. Organizations that do so increase their legitimacy and their survival prospects, independent of the immediate efficacy of the acquired practices and procedures. There can develop a tension between on the one hand, the institutionalized products, services, techniques, policies, and programs that function as myths and efficiency criteria on the other hand. To maintain ceremonial conformity, organizations that reflect institutional rules tend to buffer their formal structures from the uncertainties of the technical activities by developing a loose coupling between their formal structures and actual work activities.

***The Hawthorne Experiments***

The deviation from rulemaking on a higher level was documented for the first time in the Hawthorne studies and called informal organization. At first this discovery was ignored and dismissed as the product of avoidable errors, until it finally had to be recognized that these unwritten laws of work of everyday life often had more influence on the fate of the enterprise than those conceived on organizational charts of the executive level. Numerous empirical studies in sociological organization research followed, ever more clearly proving this, particularly during the Human Relations Movement. It is important to analyze informal structures within an enterprise to make use of positive innovations, but also to be able to do away with bad habits that have developed over time.

***Reasons for informal organization***

There are many different reasons for informal organization:

- Informal standards: personal goals and interests of workers differ from official organizational goals.
- Informal communication: changes of communication routes within an enterprise due to personal relations between coworkers.
- Informal group: certain groups of coworkers have the same interests, or the same origin.
- Informal leaders: due to charisma and general popularity, certain members of the organization win more influence than originally intended.
- Different interests and preferences of coworkers.
- Different status of coworkers.
- Difficult work requirements.
- Unpleasant conditions of work.

Managerial organization theory often still regards informal organization as rather disturbing, but sometimes helpful. In the opinion of systems theory and cybernetics, however, formal organization fades into the background and only serves, if necessary, to supplement or to correct. Changes in structure always redevelop because of the conduct and differences among coworkers, and the ability of self-organization is recognized as a natural characteristic of a social system.

**Informal organization**

The informal organization is the interlocking social structure that governs how people work together in practice. It is the aggregate of behaviors, interactions, norms, personal and professional connections through which work gets done and relationships are built among people who share a common organizational affiliation or cluster of affiliations. It consists of a dynamic set of personal relationships, social networks, communities of common interest, and emotional sources of motivation. The informal organization evolves organically and spontaneously in response to changes in the work environment, the flux of people through its porous boundaries, and the complex social dynamics of its members.

Tended effectively, the informal organization complements the more explicit structures, plans, and processes of the formal organization: it can accelerate and enhance responses to unanticipated events, foster innovation, enable people to solve problems that require collaboration across boundaries, and create footpaths showing where the formal organization may someday need to pave a way.

***The informal organization and the formal organization***

The nature of the informal organization becomes more distinct when its key characteristics are juxtaposed with those of the formal organization.

Key characteristics of the informal organization:

- Evolving constantly
- Grass roots
- Dynamic and responsive
- Excellent at motivation
- Requires insider knowledge to be seen
- Treats people as individuals
- Flat and fluid
- Cohered by trust and reciprocity
- Difficult to pin down
- Essential for situations that change quickly or are not yet fully understood

Key characteristics of the formal organization:

- Enduring, unless deliberately altered
- Top-down
- Missionary
- Static
- Excellent at alignment

- Plain to see
- Equates "person" with "role"
- Hierarchical
- Bound together by codified rules and order
- Easily understood and explained
- Critical for dealing with situations that are known and consistent

Historically, some have regarded the informal organization as the byproduct of insufficient formal organization—arguing, for example, that "it can hardly be questioned that the ideal situation in the business organization would be one where no informal organization existed." However, the contemporary approach—one suggested as early as 1925 by Mary Parker Follett, the pioneer of community centers and author of influential works on management philosophy—is to integrate the informal organization and the formal organization, recognizing the strengths and limitations of each. Integration, as Follett defined it, means breaking down apparent sources of conflict into their basic elements and then building new solutions that neither allow domination nor require compromise. In other words, integrating the informal organization with the formal organization replaces competition with coherence.

At a societal level, the importance of the relationship between formal and informal structures can be seen in the relationship between civil society and state authority. The power of integrating the formal organization and the informal organization can also be seen in many successful businesses.

### *Functions of informal organizations*

Keith Davis suggests that informal groups serve at least four major functions within the formal organizational structure.

#### *Perpetuate the cultural and social values*

They perpetuate the cultural and social values that the group holds dear. Certain values are usually already held in common among informal group members. Day-to-day interaction reinforces these values that perpetuate a particular lifestyle and preserve group unity and integrity. For example, a college management class of 50 students may contain several informal groups that constitute the informal organization within the formal structure of the class. These groups may develop out of fraternity or sorority relationships, dorm residency, project work teams, or seating arrangements. Dress codes, hairstyles, and political party involvement are reinforced among the group members.

#### *Provide social status and satisfaction*

They provide social status and satisfaction that may not be obtained from the formal organization. In a large organization, a worker may feel like an anonymous number rather than a unique individual. Members of informal groups, however, share jokes and gripes, eat together, play and work together, and are friends-which contributes to personal esteem, satisfaction, and a feeling of worth.

*Promote communication among members*

The informal group develops a communication channel or system to keep its members informed about what management actions will affect them in various ways. Many astute managers use the grape- vine to "informally" convey certain information about company actions and rumors.

*Provide social control*

They provide social control by influencing and regulating behavior inside and outside the group. Internal control persuades members of the group to conform to its lifestyle. For example, if a student starts to wear a coat and tie to class, informal group members may razz and convince the student that such attire is not acceptable and therefore to return to sandals, jeans, and T-shirts. External control is directed to such groups as management, union leadership, and other informal groups.

***Disadvantages of informal groups***

Informal organizations also possess the following potential disadvantages and problems that require astute and careful management attention.

*Resistance to change.*

Perpetuation of values and lifestyle causes informal groups to become overly protective of their "culture" and therefore resist change. For example, if restriction of output was the norm in an autocratic management group, it must continue to be so, even though management changes have brought about a more participative administration.

*Role conflict*

The quest for informal group satisfaction may lead members away from formal organizational objectives. What is good for and desired by informal group members is not always good for the organization. Doubling the number of coffee breaks and the length of the lunch period may be desirable for group members but costly and unprofitable for the firm. Employees' desire to fulfill the requirements and services of both the informal group and management results in role conflict. Role conflict can be reduced by carefully attempting to integrate interests, goals, methods, and evaluation systems of both the informal and formal organizations, resulting in greater productivity and satisfaction on everyone's behalf.

*Rumor*

The grapevine dispenses truth and rumor with equal vengeance. Ill-informed employees communicate unverified and untrue information that can create a devastating effect on employees. This can undermine morale, establish bad attitudes, and often result in deviant or, even violent behavior. For example, a student who flunks an exam can start a rumor that a professor is making sexually harassing advances toward one of the students in class. This can create all sorts of ill feelings toward the professor and even result in vengeful acts like "egging" the residence or knocking over the mail box.

*Conformity*

Social control promotes and encourages conformity among informal group members, thereby making them reluctant to act too aggressively or perform at too high a level. This can harm the formal organization by stifling initiative, creativity, and diversity of performance. In some British factories, if a group member gets "out of line", tools may be hidden, air may be let out of tires, and other group members may refuse to talk to the deviant for days or weeks. Obviously, these types of actions can force a good worker to leave the organization.

***Benefits of the informal organization***

Although informal organizations create unique challenges and potential problems for management, they also provide a number of benefits for the formal organization.

*Blend with formal system*

Formal plans. policies, procedures, and standards cannot solve every problem in a dynamic organization; therefore, informal systems must blend with formal ones to get work done. As early as 1951, Robert Dubin recognized that "informal relations in the organization serve to preserve the organization from the self-destruction that would result from literal obedience to the formal policies, rules, regulations, and procedures." No college or university could function merely by everyone following the "letter of the law" with respect to written policies and procedures. Faculty, staff, and student informal groups must cooperate in fulfilling the spirit of the law" to effectuate an organized, sensibly run enterprise.

*Lighten management workload*

Managers are less inclined to check up on workers when they know the informal organization is cooperating with them. This encourages delegation, decentralization, and greater worker support of the manager, which suggests a probable improvement in performance and overall productivity. When a professor perceives that students are conscientiously working on their term papers and group projects, there are likely to be fewer "pap tests" or impromptu progress reports. This eases the professors load and that of the students and promotes a better relation- ship between both parties.

*Fill gaps in management abilities*

For instance, if a manager is weak in financial planning and analysis, a subordinate may informally assist in preparing reports through either suggestions or direct involvement. ' Act as a safety valve. Employees experience frustration, tension, and emotional problems with management and other employees. The informal group provides a means for relieving these emotional and psychological pressures by allowing a person to discuss them among friends openly and candidly. In faculty lounge conversations, frustrations with the dean, department head, or students are "blown off" among empathetic colleagues.

*Encourage improved management practice*

Perhaps a subtle benefit of informal groups is that they encourage managers to prepare, plan, organize, and control in a more professional fashion. Managers who comprehend the power of the informal organization recognize that it is a "check and balance" on their use of authority. Changes and projects are introduced with more careful thought and consideration, knowing that the informal organization can easily kill a poorly planned project.

*Understanding and Dealing with the Environmental Crisis*

The The IRG Solution - hierarchical incompetence and how to overcome it1984, argued, that Central media and government type hierarchical organizations. could not adequately understand the environmental crisis we were manufacturing, or how to initiate adequate solutions. It argued that what was required, was the widespread introduction of informal networks or Information Routing Groups which were essentially a description of social networking services prior to the internet.

***Business Approaches***

1. Rapid growth. Starbucks, which grew from 100 employees to over 100,000 in just over a decade, provides structures to support improvisation. In a July 1998 Fast Company article on rapid growth, Starbucks chairman Howard Schultz said, "You can't grow if you're driven only by process, or only by the creative spirit. You've got to achieve a fragile balance between the two sides of the corporate brain."
2. Learning organization. Following a four-year study of the Toyota Production System, Steven J. Spear and H. Kent Bowen concluded

in Harvard Business Review that the legendary flexibility of Toyota's operations is due to the way the scientific method is ingrained in its workers – not through formal training or manuals but through unwritten principles that govern how workers work, interact, construct, and learn.

3. Idea generation. Texas Instruments credits its "Lunatic Fringe"—"an informal and amorphous group of TI engineers," according to Fortune Magazine—for its recent successes. "There's this continuum between total chaos and total order," Gene Frantz, the hub of this informal network, explained to Fortune. "About 95% of the people in TI are total order, and I thank God for them every day, because they create the products that allow me to spend money. I'm down here in total chaos, that total chaos of innovation. As a company we recognize the difference between those two and encourage both to occur."

## A NEW MODEL OF TEAMS

Traditional models of group process tend to treat groups as closed systems that shape individual attitudes and decisions. In other words the emphasis is on the interactions among group members. The research lens sits on the group boundary and points inward, focusing on internal behaviors such as cohesiveness, trust, or member roles. However, since organizational groups have high external demands, it is important to extend the theoretical lens from the team boundary outward.

From an external perspective, the focus shifts to a group in its environment. Here the group is seen as part of an interconnected web of individuals, groups, and departments that depend on one another to get particular organization tasks done. This external perspective raises a whole new set of issues and research questions that complement those raised in traditional models. Added to the question, "How does the group satisfy member needs?" is the question "How does the group meet organizational needs?" Not only do we ask, "How does the team organize itself so that members can work together?" but also "How does the team organize itself so that it can work with other parts of the organization?" Finally, in addition to wanting to understand group dynamics, we want to understand the interaction between teams and their environment. The external perspective does not solely emphasize team initiatives or environmental influence; it also looks at the interplay between team and environment. Environments can clearly constrain action, but teams can mold their environments, too.

Part of the motivation behind this expanded perspective is to understand better how groups actually behave in real organizations rather than in training sessions or laboratories, where most research on the traditional model is tested and where context is sharply attenuated. Early research that takes this external focus indicates that external initiatives, rather than internal dynamics are a better predictor of team performance for real groups operating in organizational settings. Unfortunately, the external perspective remains relatively unexplored. Although many research questions exist, this study addresses three questions, applying them to five consulting teams within one organization. The questions are: What strategies, if any, did these teams use to meet environmental demands? What impact did these external strategies have on internal processes and team performance? What role did their environment play in team context interaction?

## METHODS

### Teams and Organization

This study examines five teams within a government agency. The agency provides educational consulting services to school districts within a state. The teams were created during a reorganization of the agency designed to improve coordination across divisions, provide more uniform service across geographic areas, and improve the reputation of the agency in the field. To accomplish these goals, consultants--a reading specialist, for example--would report to both a functional boss and a regional team leader. Regional teams were composed of six to ten consultants. Most of the consultants, who came from a variety of units, knew each other by sight but had never worked together. The teams were to act as generalists, diagnosing and serving the needs of their regions and improving interunit coordination. Thus, team members might go into a school district and interview teachers about their curriculum needs and then utilize agency resources to design a new course to meet those needs.

From a research point of view, these regional teams were exemplars of an increasingly popular form of group: they had a general task, the autonomy to complete that task as they liked, part-time members, and external demands. Because the teams were new, they had to define a role and learn to relate to existing parts of the organization. Members had to work interdependently to produce a service of importance to the organization. The teams had formal leadership and welldefined boundaries. Upper levels of management evaluated the teams, which served the needs of an external client. Hence, the field was open for teams to define both internal and external behavior. This chapter traces the mechanisms teams used to manage those tasks.

## TEAM STRATEGIES

### Informing

One striking difference among team leaders' strategies was their view of when and how to interact with their regions. The informing team leader had a primary goal of creating an enthusiastic team with open communication among members and clear group goals. Initially, the level of outside contact was to be low; only "somewhere along the line" did he anticipate a lot of interaction with the field. Even when this leader discussed learning about his team's districts, he spoke of "sharing our experiences"--the data team members already had--and the need to "sift through...information," or to reference data that were written and stored, rather than newly collected. Furthermore, judgments about what was important in the field were to be made by the group "deciding if it is important or not" and only later communicated to the districts. In short, this team would inform outsiders when it decided what its approach would be. Indeed,.this team did have the lowest number of visits to the school districts, and it did concentrate on internal team building. Unfortunately, the team experienced a high level of internal conflict and never got around to communicating a coherent approach to its clients. Instead, the team got mired in controversy both within its borders and with top management. Members began to seek direction from top management and became angry when it was not forthcoming.

**Parading**

The strategy of parading adds the need for visibility in the field to the emphasis on internal team building. Like the informing team, these teams wanted to create a "smooth operating group" and to map the environment or "figure out what the region looks like" by using data team members already had. In contrast to the informing team, however, these teams planned a higher level of interaction with people in the field. One team leader said she would "try and visit all the superintendents, and visit all the schools...find out about their unique styles...take a different member of the team out each time." She continued, "I want to circulate, to be familiar, to go to superintendents' meetings and be introduced to improve my reputation." Thus, the goal of work in the field was obtaining visibility, a goal that differentiated the parading from the informing strategy. The parading teams did follow their initially stated strategy, with some minor variations. They had much higher levels of interaction with the environment than the informing team, but each was responsive to only one part of the environment. One team had minimal contact with its region and relied on member knowledge to plan interventions, but maintained high levels of visibility within the organization. Another team was very visible in the field but was isolated from top management. Both teams had relatively smooth relations among team members.

**Probing**

The probing strategy called for high levels of two-way communication with the external environment intended to broaden the perspective of team members, to diagnose the region's needs, to obtain feedback on team ideas, and to "sell" the services of the team to the "customer." In contrast to the other teams, these teams saw external activity as the team's first and primary goal. In addition, their leaders did not believe that the team had all the data needed to put together a plan. Team members might have information about the districts, but it was considered limited because it came from "one point of view," meaning from a specialist rather than a generalist, regional consultant. One team leader planned a very interactive approach with the environment, consisting of hearing the needs of the region, then testing whether the team's plans met those needs.

Another probing team leader planned to talk to different people in the regions, asking, "Are things different now? Are things better? Are you being serviced better over the total educational picture?" He wanted to discover the needs of the region and "develop strategies to meet those needs." To obtain a broader perspective, he wanted people to work outside their existing area of expertise: "If a consultant is in special education, I'm going to have him investigate the science labs." Team leaders who planned to follow a probing strategy did so both within the organization and within the regions. They did not use existing member knowledge alone to map their external environment; members were encouraged to take on new perspectives and bring in new data. These teams had the highest level of external contact, were aggressive not only in testing potential interventions but also in actually implementing new programs, and convinced people in both the field and top management that they were doing a good job. In other words, members of these teams promoted the accomplishments of the teams throughout the organization and the regions. However, these teams suffered somewhat in the short term. Several months after the reorganization, team members reported that internal communications were a problem; members were missing meetings and often felt confused about what other members were doing and about the goals of the team. Gradually these teams improved. Initially, however, the teams were not cohesive and were held together through directive leadership. For example, one team leader's style was described like this: "He gets requests from the field or generates ideas and asks a particular individual to do a piece of the work."

## TEAM-CONTEXT INTERACTION

Thus far I have described a group as a free actor following a strategy toward the external environment. In reality, this picture is much too simple. An environment reacts to a team, and then both team and context influence each other. Just as a team develops patterns of interaction between members and the group itself, so too does it develop a pattern of interaction with the environment. In this organization, we saw three patterns of team-environment interaction. These patterns were setting limits on team activity, choosing best practices, and spreading performance news.

**Setting Limits**

When the new organization structure was put in place, there was some uncertainty as to how much autonomy the teams would have. Team members knew in general that they had to diagnose the needs of the region and meet those needs, and they were told that they had autonomy to do so, but since this task was new to the organization many questions were left unanswered. Could teams do anything they wanted to do? How much coordination had to take place among teams? How would this be accomplished? How often did teams have to "check in" with top management? For top management, issues existed as well. While providing autonomy sounded like the right thing to do, when teams started to take off in new directions, old patterns of wanting control reasserted themselves. As teams and context negotiated the limits of autonomy, emotions ran high and many teams expended energy fighting power battles rather than working on the task at hand.

Several situations exemplify the struggle over autonomy. When the teams were first formed and the leaders chosen, but before teams had officially met, one team leader scheduled informal meetings of the leaders so that they could act as a sounding board for one another. When the vice commissioner found out these meetings were taking place without him, he forbade them. The head of human resources reported that the team leaders, particularly the leader who had started the meetings, were all very angry about this occurrence.

In the ensuing months, the teams began to generate plans for serving their regions. The commissioner decided he did not want teams doing different things, so he told the leaders to plan a unified approach. When a few weeks went by and he saw no results, he told the teams to create regional profiles and to develop a workshop that would communicate "promising practices" observed in particular schools to the rest of the region. The commissioner expressed frustration with the lack of visible team activity and explained that he wanted something done to justify the reorganization. One team resisted this interference, tried to fight the direction, and got caught up in a power struggle. Other teams tried to shape management directives, while still others became dependent and wanted to be told exactly what to do.

What this situation makes clear is that the balance of autonomy and control evolved over time and was more of an issue for some teams than for others. As teams began to act, top management realized that it wanted to maintain some control, so it set limits and provided direction. Yet both teams and management seemed ambivalent about control. Teams both resisted it and asked for it, while management preached the advantages of autonomy even as it set limits on power and action.

This process of defining autonomy parallels what goes on inside the group. As Schein illustrates, during a team's early formation process, members define what their role within the group will be, what the balance between individual and team goals will be, and how much they will succumb to the will of others. This process is necessary if teams are to progress, yet it may stall work in early stages. As one takes an external perspective, it becomes evident that similar issues between the team and its environment must be resolved.

**Choosing Best Practices**

As teams begin work on a new task, both the precise task and how performance will be measured are often unclear. Yet teams begin to act; by watching their actions, top management comes to a clearer idea of what it wants the teams to do. In order to communicate that notion, management holds up particular practices as models of good team behavior. Thus, an environment influences a team by setting limits on activity and by picking particular teams as models defining task and performance. A team can influence its environment by promoting its activities as the ones that should shape the definition of task and performance. Teams are not equally skilled in this influence process.

For example, four months after the teams were formed, an official team leader meeting was held at which leaders reported on their activities. One leader reported on problems within the team, including poor attendance at meetings and internal conflict, while another reported on the creation of a communication network, whereby one team member was assigned to each district. Obviously, the latter became the team most often used as the exemplar of effective interventions with the clients. The promotion of team accomplishments occurred not only in formal team meetings, but also one-on-one, as the team leader and members met with the commissioner and vice commissioner.

On the one hand, this communication of best practices allowed the organization to gain from the trial-and-error learning each team experienced. When one team found an innovative solution to a problem, it was diffused to other teams. On the other hand, choosing best practices led to labeling, and teams having difficulty were punished for communicating bad news.

**Labeling**

The external environment plays yet another role: it becomes an echo chamber. Early on, not much concrete information was available, so the tearms were not labeled. Yet after the formal review described above, information about team performance and top management preferences were channeled to the rest of the organization and amplified. The team that reported trouble reported it to the other team leaders and top management, but soon the whole organization knew. This team was surely in trouble then, because it developed a reputation as a problem team. On the positive side, the team that set up a communication network was praised and the news reinforced a positive image, making it easier for this team to continue on the right track. Thus, the first time there was comparative, evaluative information--even though it was based on limited data- -it became big news.

Since many environments change whispers into roars, teams must manage the information and images they broadcast. These images appear to become permanent even though they may be biased and premature. Here, the initial reputations were intact a year later despite efforts to change them, and indeed new data were interpreted to support the images; for example, superintendent ratings, which differed from top management ratings, were discounted. In short, early evaluations became self-fulfilling prophecies.

## PREDICTING PERFORMANCE

Perhaps the most intriguing research finding is that the way in which a team interacts with its environment seems to be a better predictor of team performance than is the way that team members interact with one another. If I had predicted performance using the traditional internal model, the informing and parading teams would have been prime candidates for top ratings. Their leaders planned to be participative and to engage members in debate and decision making. They considered goal clarity and member satisfaction as important. Yet, the informing team failed, and although the parading teams rated their satisfaction as high early in the observation period, they became only mediocre performers. It was the probing teams who became the highest performers. Thus, the study's key proposition is this: for the new kinds of teams being created in today's organizations probing activities will lead to the highest performance ratings. These teams face new, unstructured tasks and a set of external constituencies that allocate tasks, have their own set of demands, and evaluate performance. Probing teams understand outsiders' demands and initiate field interventions. They do not presume to understand their constituents, but rather venture out to revise assumptions in light of a new charter. Those who probe promote their team and its activities to customers and to those who judge performance.

Those teams that probe for new ideas and reactions to possible interventions do pay a price, however. The cost of probing in this study was low cohesion and satisfaction in the short run. High levels of interaction with outsiders take up a lot of time and bring divergent views into a group, which can lead to conflict and inhibit team building. Groups with an external emphasis run the risk of becoming "underbounded" —having external knowledge but not enough cohesion to motivate members to pull different perspectives together. Group members in this study also expressed a lot of early confusion about team goals. Team leaders partially overcame this problem through directive leadership. Despite these problems externally oriented teams in this study did better than the informing team. That team did have to contend with a negative reputation and poor facilitator skills in addition to isolation, but it is possible that no leader can help a group that is isolated from those upon whom it depends. One of the greatest levers team success may be choosing the right approach to the environment from the start.

## LEARNING TO USE THE EXTERNAL PERSPECTIVE

The findings from this and other studies suggest that teams in today's organizations must learn to use this new external model. Doing so involves using a new way of thinking about group process, team building, and the role of the environment in understanding group behavior. Perhaps with these changes in the way we think about and manage teams, actual team performance can begin to catch up with promises made in the popular press.

### Rethinking Group Process

This study suggests that teams with high external demands will be better performers to the extent that they follow a probing strategy. In order to carry out such a strategy, team members need an expanded view of their activities, they need to have the skills and training to carry them out, and team composition has to reflect the importance of these activities.

If you ask a set of team members and leaders to describe a high-performing team, they will usually recite the traditional group process variables, e.g., trust, commitment, allocation of work according to skill level, open communication, and clear goals and priorities. Yet to carry out a probing strategy a whole new set of activities is needed. Included would be testing ideas in the field, promoting the team to top management and to the client, and updating the team model of the environment as new information is collected. While some team leaders and members intuitively carry out such activities, to many others the internal model dominates. Unless this external perspective is grasped by those managing teams, it will be hard to get any changes in activity. Understanding alone, however, is not enough. Often team members lack the necessary skills. Members' job skills often do not include negotiation skills, and the ability to probe for client needs. Thus, training in these areas is necessary. If training is not possible, then teams need access to resources. For example, if one person in an organization was particularly good at probing activities, this person could be shared by several teams until such skills became more distributed.

Often management selects team members, and this selection may well be made on technical grounds rather than on the basis of group process skills. Management needs to understand that the best set of consultants may be doomed to failure if their product is not accepted by the organization and client. Thus, team composition needs to encompass the skills necessary for meeting external demands.

**Team Building**

Traditional team building often emphasizes the need to let team members work through issues of power and affiliation and to develop clear goals and priorities. This study suggest that team members also need time to work through issues of power and affiliation with the environment, that goals and priorities cannot be established until external demands are understood, and that team building may involve more than just the team. Just as it is difficult for team members to concentrate on the task at hand when they have questions about who is in charge and how to combine individual and group goals, so too do difficulties arise as the team works through these issues with different parts of the environment. As top management and team leaders negotiate limits to autonomy, task work will suffer. Team members and management need to understand that this is a normal part of the development process. Recognition that this is taking place may help people to understand the conflict and discomfort that accompanies the process.

The team must be careful not to set goals and priorities prematurely. Obviously, goals based on old information may not reflect the current environment. Thus, rather than have team members start by brainstorming for possible approaches to their stated task, team leaders might better start with external activities: having each member interview five clients about their current needs, for example, or having everyone ask a senior manager for perceptions of team goals and how to achieve them. Then, the team can brainstorm using this new information. This plan may leave the team dissatisfied, since it expands the time with no clear agenda. Team leaders can acknowledge the discomfort with this unusual start, but explain that gathering external information is the agenda at the beginning. As team members interview outsiders and test ideas, internal processes seem to become smoother. Cohesiveness often follows successful interventions in the field rather than the other way around. And by this time, the team has built more than just a team. It has built up a temporary system of contacts, supporters, sources of feedback, and information nodes that can be used throughout its life cycle. So team building needs to be seen in this broader sense: building a web of outside connections that helps the group to accomplish its task.

**The Role of the Environment**

Thus far my language has implied that the responsibility for team performance is on the team. Yet this study clearer outlines the direct role that the environment plays in team development and success. Since top management is a key part of the environment, it should be aware of its ambivalence about autonomy, the potential damaging effect of labeling, and the danger of rewarding those who promote their teams. In this study, top management was ambivalent about autonomy. While teams were told they could serve their regions in any way they chose, when they actually started to act their actions were sometimes curbed, and directives from the top followed. This double message led to power struggles and resentment. These struggles might have been less difficult if top management had realized its own impact. The commissioner might not have promised so much z :tonomy in the first place, or he might have explained why the teams' different directions made him so uncomfortable, or he might have tried to work with the teams to set goals and priorities. The problem, is that management often has great difficulty giving up control.

When management labels teams early in their life cycle, those labels become difficult to shed. While labeling helps some teams it is quite damaging to others. Management might want to curb this labeling process to lower the risk of shutting some teams down at an early stage. Teams that have initial problems and are open about them may never get a chance to make a useful contribution, while other teams that get a fast start may be rewarded, only to lose momentum later on.

The labeling process can be related to teams' self-promotion. That was not a problem is this study since teams did seem to make significant interventions in the field. However, there is the possibility that management will reward the teams that have the best internal marketing skills and not the ones doing the best work. In fact, one of the parading team leaders complained that she had done a good job but that she had not "played politics," so her team's contribution was not noticed. The key issue here is that a probing strategy involves promoting the team's achievements, as well as testing ideas, approaching the task with a new mindset, and trying out solutions. Management needs to ascertain that the promotional activities are backed up by substance. The external perspective offers lessons for teams and management alike. It directs attention to the ways teams approach their environment, to team-environment dynamics, and to improving team performance. This perspective can help organizations to garner the benefits and avoid the pitfalls of the new teams within their borders.

## TAKING YOUR TEAM TO MARKET

### GOING TO MARKET: LEADERSHIP AND RESPONSIBILITY

In the last business downturn, to cut costs, companies focused on doing more with less. This challenged sales managers to reduce personnel and increase the productivity of those who remained. In the latest business upturn, many businesses refocused from cost cutting to growth. This challenged sales managers to increase headcount and goose everyone's productivity to pay for growth. In the next business downturn... well, you can spot the pattern here. Business cycles do repeat, and each time they do, sales managers are challenged to adapt their organizations without delay. It is a critical point often missed, however, that while the major ups and downs may look similar, the required sales management skills are in constant evolution. In Death of a Salesman, Willy Loman laments the good old days of dull competition, account control, and customer loyalty. He tells his sales manager about his idol, who could blow into towns in thirty-one states, check into a nice hotel, put on green velvet slippers, and take orders over the phone. Willy believes selling is now dead. "In those days... Howard... there was respect, and comradeship, and gratitude in it. Today it's all cut and dried, and there's no chance for bringing friendship to bear—or personality." The Internet and information-age technology add their own flavors to the constantly changing environmental mix in which companies operate. Companies can wither or shine under the 24/7 spotlights of the information age; the lights shine as brightly on the losers as on the winners. The pressure to win is relentless, and so is the demand for growth. Last month's financial darling may be this month's goat. CEOs and boards who cannot achieve their results honestly take ethical shortcuts and even risk prison to sustain the appearance that they are winners. Behind the real winners, it is the 363,000 men and women in professional sales management, often unsung heroes, who deliver the all-important results that make the boss look good.

**"The Ultimately Accountable Job... "**

In a September 2006 Harvard Business Review special sales double issue, sales guru Jerry Colletti described sales leadership as "The Ultimately Accountable Job...." Schering-Plough CEO Fred Hassan observed what sales managers have always known—namely that no company's strategy can succeed without control of its top line. In corporate America, it seems as if sales is taking over the playing field as engineering recedes. Hence, sales is where the big money is today with more than half of sales managers earning six-figure incomes. Sales managers are the top earners of all corporate managers below CEO. And why not? Sales managers routinely have responsibility for teams producing tens of millions of dollars from single accounts. Today's stakes are higher and the challenges more sophisticated than ever. In all of this, the most successful sales managers will see ripe opportunities for personal, career, and earnings growth.

**It Takes a Leader—and Sometimes a Lucky Break**

Despite all their emergent visibility and responsibility, CSOs do not have the direct power or resources to assure the results demanded of them. To succeed in a world defined by the decisions of others, they must be masterful leaders, influencers, marketers, financiers, salesmen, and recipients of a few lucky breaks! Sometimes they look for their breaks outside the rules. The Gallup organization found that more than a third of sales managers knew that their reps lied to make a sale. These managers contributed to consumers' perceptions of sales as at the bottom of consumer honesty and ethical standards.

**Realities**

CSOs must produce their results within the macro economic, political, technological, regulatory, and competitive environment set by others—nationally and globally. At the company level, CSOs operate under conditions set by their superiors and peers—who often make decisions with barely a glance at their effect on sales. Take a well-meaning CFO who argues for a cap on individual sales earnings so that finance can budget sales commissions more predictably. He may not understand that he is also killing sales incentive. In another example, Verizon's sales agency program had an unusual feature for more than a decade: When agent companies exceeded compensation budgets, Verizon told its agents they would not be paid and advised them to stop selling! Often, the CSO has no say in sales decisions. After all, sales neither chooses the products it sells, nor funds its compensation plan, nor controls competition. It does not schedule manufacturing, manage operations, or dispatch service personnel. Sales neither quality checks production nor designs the capacity of plants. It neither determines the company's financial structure nor establishes its purchasing efficiency. At lower levels within the organization, sales personnel are often in political conflict with others outside of sales. Motives are secondguessed, and envy is common due to the apparent freedom sales people enjoy—let alone their nice sales trips. All this has the effect of diluting a company's integration behind the sales program. And then, there are the customers. It is not easy to attend their mercurial demands and maintain their (supposed) loyalty while also selling them products and services at a good profit. Even in this age of expensive CRM systems, just 20% of customers are happy with the sales coverage assigned to their accounts. All of these constraints occur in every sales environment, and they are not necessarily problems. They come with the job—and they are surely surmountable.

**Going to Market**

The chief sales executive takes the company to market. Eight primary go-to-market elements influence the CSO's world and the world of his or her people. Internal decisions determine four elements. These decisions are changeable, sometimes relatively quickly:

- The sales force
- The sales environment
- Sales controls and policies
- Sales alliances

The other four elements are external decisions driven by

- The product/market match
- Competition

- Customers
- The market

***Understanding the Terrain***

Success in going to market results from the sales manager's ability to understand the interplay of these eight elements and to maintain a harmony within them adequate to achieve assigned objectives. With misalignment of even one element, a sales program can fail. To emphasize this, I call these potentially catastrophic yet avoidable problems Hindenburg Omens. Finding and defusing them is your first order of business when you take command. Hence, each of the next eight chapters examines a single go-tomarket element so that you can evaluate its adequacy or inadequacy (a Hindenburg Omen) for the success of your program. This is particularly important at the beginning of a new job or promotion into sales management. This follows advice of the famous military strategist Sun Tzu, who wrote in The Art of War 2,400 years ago, "As a leader there are few things more important than understanding your terrain." A commander "ignorant of the conditions of mountains, forests, dangerous defiles, swamps and marshes... cannot conduct the march of an army." To help evaluate factors of your terrain, you will find insights from experienced managers, interesting examples to illustrate key points, and fascinating research you can apply practically. You will learn to spot problems quickly, and if you find an Omen, there are solutions and ideas to help you prioritize and manage it.

***The Hindenburg***

Longer than three Boeing 747s, the 804-foot Hindenburg Zeppelin was the largest manmade airship ever to fly. It was the Titanic of the sky, designed and built with confidence that it was an engineering pinnacle. It was, however, like the Titanic of the sea, spectacularly ill fated. The Hindenburg was a luxury, hydrogen-filled airship that crossed the Atlantic seventeen times, logging 190,000 miles carrying thousands of passengers in luxury. The airship's designers were so confident in their craft that they positioned a smoking room aboard just below 7 million cubic feet of highly flammable hydrogen. On May 6, 1937, at 9:15 PM, the Hindenburg began mooring at New Jersey's Lakehurst Naval Air Station. Suddenly, hundreds of people on the ground saw a flash near the airship's tail. In less than one minute, the Hindenburg fell to the ground destroyed by fire.

***Sales Omens***

The Hindenburg saga has parallels and lessons for sales leaders. For example, past success is no guarantee of the future. Even after seventeen smooth flights across the Atlantic, calamities can occur. To those who examine with the benefit of hindsight, the tragedy will always seem to have been predictable. There may have been a tripwire awaiting some unfortunate person or event to trigger it. Perhaps the problem was in plain sight and deemed trivial, but grew imperceptibly until, like an avalanche, it crashed down. Whatever the cause, there is always a requirement to fix the blame on those whom it is claimed ought to have foreseen the tragedy. In sales, you are the one who ought to have foreseen unpleasant surprises. This is why you must flag Hindenburg Omens before they trigger and derail your program. For instance, a high attrition rate of good performers eventually leads to failure over time. In hindsight, this is obvious. However, because the trend occurs over time, it may go unrecognized until it is well established.

***Constant Vigilance***

Past success may cause managers to become overconfident and dull their awareness of environmental shifts. Becoming less aware of change, they develop blind spots and assure themselves that the good, old ways still hold. For them, this is the beginning of the end. With change itself occurring at an exponential rate, nothing remains static very long. Former Intel Chairman Andy Grove recognized how this tendency grows from success. To guard against it, Dr. Grove put it succinctly, "only the paranoid survive." Professor Mad Eye Moody in the Harry Potter series adds a corollary that survival is the result of "constant vigilance"! These admonitions are good advice for everyone's sake particularly when taking command as a company's new CSO. One of your critical responsibilities is vigilance to find and fix Hindenburg Omens.

***Do It Now***

Finally, there is a lesson to apply from watching high-profile CEOs take command of troubled companies. The most astute CEOs do all they can to open a clean page in the corporate history book when they first take command. They announce downsizing decisions; sell underperforming assets; make personnel changes; make financial write offs, and even restate prior years' results. They deliver the bad news early and as a package. Savvy new CEOs use their honeymoon period to get all they can behind them, knowing there will never be a more opportune time. The first Ford Motor CEO from outside the family, Alan Mulally, is a textbook example. Mulally joined Ford in September 2006. The following month he announced a quarterly loss of $5.8 billion, and he said the loss for the fourth quarter would be even larger. He reserved $9.5 to $10.5 billion for restructuring costs, warned of negative cash flow for the next several years, and suggested the sale of Aston Martin, Jaguar, and Land Rover. He said in an early interview, "I came in with my eyes wide open. What's good is we are dealing with the reality now." Likewise, the lesson for new sales managers is to draw a firm line separating themselves from the misadventures of their predecessors. As Mulally did, build in reality rather than overcommit. As you examine each of these major components of the go-tomarket process, determine if you find yourself with an element of your program that is "adequate" or "inadequate" to attain your objectives. This is a simple way to prioritize your work. Since any "inadequate" rating stands in the path of reaching your objectives, these are your priorities. "Adequate" means that the element is OK for now. Explore each area and all its related processes and procedures carefully, so you can thoroughly understand what is required to correct or work around it. To do this, you will find helpful ideas in each chapter. The table is a triage tool. Its purpose is to quickly sort critical items and identify potential points of failure. When you spot an inadequate element, you must drill down to all of its component parts.

**Table Triage Table: Rating Eight Go-to-Market Elements**

| Element | Adequate | Inadequate/Hindenburg Omen |
|---|---|---|
| 1. Sales Force | | |
| 2. Sales Environment | | |
| 3. Sales Policies | | |
| 4. Channels | | |
| 5. Product/Market Match | | |
| 6. Competition | | |
| 7. Customers | | |
| 8. Market | | |

This requires thorough preparation, digging through details, and understanding the situation so well that you become an expert on the issue. Your next step is to educate the CEO about the strengths and weaknesses of the company's go-to-market plan. You are going on record to gain consensus and help, if you need it.

### *Prepare Thoroughly for CEO Presentation*

Sales executives are not famous for mastering the kind of detail that their colleagues in marketing use to nail their points, according to several CEOs we interviewed. Rather, CEOs know sales managers as likely to present anecdotal evidence supported by relatively little research. This puts them in the position of having their case easily challenged. By thorough preparation that anticipates questions and challenges, you will make your point and demonstrate that you are no average sales executive. There are two main objectives in this preparation. The first is to verify that a problem actually exists and affects your ability to achieve the company's sales objectives. It puts you on record early and provides the greatest possible time to address the inadequate element and turn the sales plan around. Your second objective is to rally commitment and support to align others in the company behind the essential changes required.

### *Your Leadership in Action*

I believe the best way to present your assessment of the company's go-to-market strategy is to use a few simple visuals and tell a story around them. It visually depicts the key chapters of your story. Use it to show how parts interact to achieve or hinder sales results. It allows you to walk a CEO, board, or your peers through the goto- market terrain describing what you found. As you move from element to element discussing how everything interacts to create a positive or negative influence, take the opportunity to explain what you have already done or plan to do to make changes or build on the strong capabilities that are already in place.

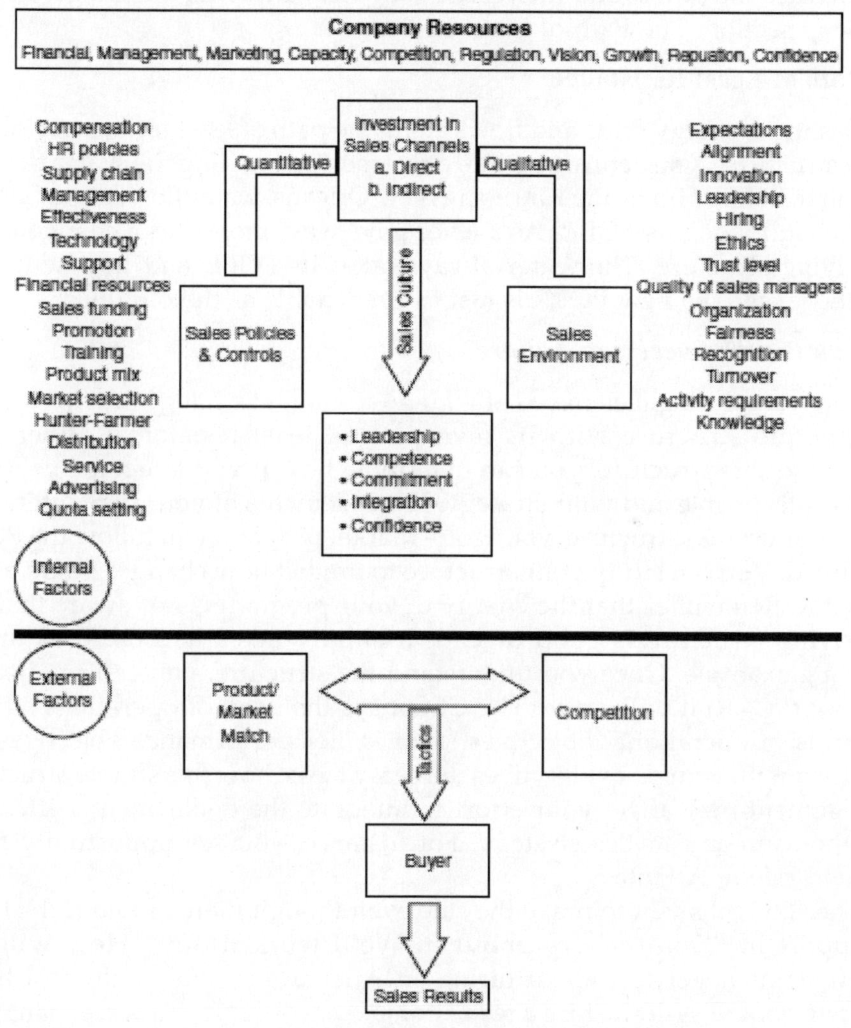


Forces responsible for Sales Result

Upon completion of your session, you have developed a common awareness of the challenges and opportunities you see, described the changes you think are essential, heard suggestions from others, put yourself on record for requesting help where needed, and acquainted everyone with a comprehensive program that won't leave them guessing what sales is doing to achieve its objectives. Keep your presentation handy for review and update. Let it serve as a reminder of:

- What you found,
- What you have accomplished, and
- What others acknowledged, promised, and delivered.

Increase the power and interest of your story by using the imagery of the following section: The Path of Least Resistance.

**The Path of Least Resistance**

In nature, energy finds and flows along the path of least resistance (POLR) in any structure. A structure acts like a riverbed channeling the water flowing through it. Before Hurricane Katrina in New Orleans, water flowed predictably into the Gulf along its POLR. As a levee gave way, there was a change in the underlying structure. The water always takes its POLR and now will flow over the levee. The new POLR is just as predictable as the old one.

***You Can Predict Success or Failure***

Likewise, the eight elements of your go-to-market strategy interact to form your unique structure with its own path of least resistance. When you understand this structure, you can determine how it will affect the behavior of your salespeople and your strategy. If the elements of your plan interact to create your desired structure, your goto- market program will follow the POLR as planned. You can study your structure to predict how changes might affect the POLR. Remember that the energy of your program is not aware that the underlying structure is good or bad. It simply takes its POLR, as in the following example. Once you understand the structure, you can predict the behavior (POLR) it will cause. The CEO pays the head of operations strictly on results of operational objectives. That is, her performance objectives are unaligned with your sales objectives. It is easy to see how this simple structural misalignment may affect your effort to integrate the department's attention with the company's sales strategy. For instance, you see opportunity for a high-end sale in Atlanta.

The CEO tells you to make the sale even though there are no techs there to support it. "Don't worry about it. We'll work it out." How will the operations manager feel about hiring an Atlanta tech that could cost her a quarterly bonus? Will she hire a tech after just one sale? If you were managing operations, when would you hire a tech? People take their path of least resistance. In this actual case, operations decided to fly in a tech until business built enough to hire one locally. Unfortunately, that was not good enough for the customer, who travels his own path of least resistance, fearing that the proposed arrangement would be inadequate for his company. Successful sales managers understand conflicts such as this. They understand how an underlying structure channels the behavior of anyone within it. In fact, they can predict it. When they need to change behavior, they do not tell people to buck up and try harder. They know they must change the underlying structure. Only that will change the POLR. To do this they look for the best leverage points. In this case, if operations had a compensation plan supportive of an expansion strategy to achieve sales growth, we would have seen better alignment of objectives (change in the underlying structure) and thus different behavior (a new path of least resistance). With all this background information in mind, let us move through the eight elements of going to market, beginning with the sales force.

## THE SALES FORCE

Most companies find the cost of going to market is their secondlargest expense—just behind COGS, the cost of goods sold. Depending on the mix of goods and services, companies may spend up to 40% of revenue marketing their products. As CSO, you are a steward of this investment. In your role, just a few strategic decisions will add to or subtract from the company's return on its investment. One of your first decisions is whether the current sales force is adequate or inadequate for its mission. Do you or don't you have the right people? According to Caliper, an organization specializing in recruitment and selection, 80% of salespeople are in the wrong jobs. After a study of 78,000 sales representatives, Caliper concluded that 55% should not be in sales at all, and that 25% were in the wrong kind of sales. If Caliper's findings describe your salespeople, you have a Hindenburg Omen on your hands. You have also discovered an area where your leadership as an agent of change will make you a valuable corporate asset.

### How to Assess Your New Team

How do you determine if your reps and staff are a match for the mission you are leading? You need clarity on two things. The first is your company's objectives, which flow from its mission. The company's mission might be: "To make money for the Hunter family and to cure cancer." More specific objectives flow from that: "Achieve $5 billion in sales this year." Second, you must create a sales strategy to achieve the objective(s). You can only begin your sales force assessment with these ends in mind. For example, to achieve $5 billion in sales, you decide upon a fundamental change in field tactics. Your new strategy requires a solution selling approach to corporate-level (C-level) executives. In the past, the sales force called primarily at the department level using product-oriented tactics. It was effective, but meeting your new assigned objectives requires high growth in existing accounts. The sales force must expand its skills to include effectiveness at the corporate level. Now, assessing your sales force becomes more straightforward. Do they have the polish and technical expertise to be credible at the C-level? Have they demonstrated it before?

***Collecting Data***

Examine the results of existing sales teams and individuals sales reps.

- Socialize your sales vision with colleagues in other departments, and gather their feedback.
- Talk to some of your customers.
- Review team performance with your sales managers, meet one-on-one with top-performing sales reps.
- Review performance reports on sales and team activity.

At the earliest possible time, begin making field calls with your salespeople. There is no better way to make a confident assessment of your terrain than by experiencing it yourself. Do not accept someone else's assessment, because his or her evaluation criteria may be different from yours. Riding in a car with sales reps always provides deep insights available no other way. After a few days in the field, you will appreciate the sales culture, marketplace, customers, and competition more insightfully than any other way. Then, with the confidence of your own observations, you can make faster, more sound decisions. Remember that you are taking a small sample of the whole organization as you make your calls.

Do not take everything you hear or see as a universal truth. Be aware of what I call "the rep who" influence. Psychologists tell us that we have easy recall of, say, "the rep who" you rode with last week who claimed that the company's tech support was lousy. You must keep an open mind later when the issue of tech support arises, remembering that each of us has a different perspective on the truth. We see through the eyes of one in our personal context. Try to simply flag issues for further investigation rather than assuming you have special insight from that single exposure. Your early need is to see the big context and make decisions about how the structure you inherit facilitates or inhibits the behavior it does. That said, making sales calls can unearth solutions to great mysteries and provide valuable insights. I debriefed a new CEO who had returned from a week's worth of sales calls. Primarily, he had called on large accounts and top executives within those accounts. He learned that while the company believed it had a major account program, all it really had was a product sales program. Most of the executives he called upon had no idea of the diversity of his company's products and the potential benefits available by more integrated partnering. This insight led him to develop, despite protests from his VP of sales, a separate major account group under different management.

***Do It Now***

Many months will pass before the benefits materialize from major sales organization changes. Because of this ramp-up time, a new CSO must determine early if she will make major changes in her channels. This is essential because she also must set expectations early. In clear terms and wary of overconfidence, the CSO must inform her CEO how much time will be required to ramp to achieve expected results from the change. She must also warn the CEO of estimated productivity declines in the interim. Then she must get a firm commitment of support. If you don't get buy-in, at least you have put yourself on record assessing the inadequacy of the current sales team to achieve objectives. In denying your request, the CEO also goes on record with you. What happens next? You begin to limp along with a sales force that you have identified as inadequate to do the job. A smart CEO will be open to reconsider your earlier assessment as it now comes to pass. Inaction will not solve the problem. Loyalty to one's staff is important; however, loyalty can hurt people who are asked to perform tasks incompatible with their attitudes and skills. You cannot send ducks to eagle school. A former VP for an international communications firm shared her experience: "The market need these days is for consultative selling. We could have great product-oriented salespeople, but they just wouldn't have the horsepower to do the job required today." Her experience was that 80% of the existing sales force failed to adapt to consultative selling. "There is no time to waste these days. My advice is to make cuts and changes all at once. Loyalty to you isn't worth much if you don't make your numbers." If you don't, it will be your neck on the block.

***"You Got to Know the Territory!"***

Another sales VP advises new CSOs not to stop with changes to the sales channels. "Also assess political alliances of your staff and field managers." In addition to fourteen years as a sales leader, he has a black belt in karate and is a student of Sun Tzu's The Art of War. "I wish I had taken Sun Tzu's advice myself when I became a sales VP—'know your terrain.' " Sun Tzu says that any commander "ignorant of the conditions of mountains, forests, dangerous defiles, swamps and marshes... cannot conduct the march of an army." "Only after you understand your terrain can you develop an effective strategy." In other words, you must adapt your tactics to the reality of the environment as you find it. To illustrate, he discussed several managers in technical and administrative positions whom he inherited and knew to have political loyalty to others.

***Spies***

"They were essentially spies." By the time he learned that several of these holdovers were actively undermining him, it was too late to move them out of his organization. To his chagrin, he discovered that his boss clandestinely maintained an open door to them. "I should have gotten rid of them immediately and put in people loyal to me. I was reluctant to do that because of their political connections. Now I realize there would have been some of initial discomfort, but it would have been well worth it. In the end, they killed me." With your own loyalists, you can move earlier and more decisively. Most sales executives believe the optimum strategy is to make your personnel changes quickly.

Stringing them out will kill morale and cause your best people to look for companies where shoes are not always dropping. I know this from personal experience. I was a sales executive brought in to AT&T to help its sales force succeed in a deregulated environment. In this environment, AT&T announced that 40,000 employees would be separated from the company. You can well imagine the internal environment after this announcement. The downsizing occurred over several years. During that time, morale was low and stayed there. Instead of a focus on market success, the employee focus turned to and remained on personal survival. I observed a sales organization with a short-term, personally pragmatic outlook. Because the downsizing occurred in stops and starts, predictability vanished. Throughout its 100-year history, perhaps more than anything else, predictability of the company's systems, markets, and policies drove the loyalty and commitment of its employees. Thereafter, virtually nothing became predictable, and the culture collapsed. Who could have predicted that the most recognized company in all the world be sucked into decades of decline, finally culminating in the sale of the company?

### *Assessing the Future*

No one would have predicted the demise of AT&T. Because of the market's unflinching confidence in AT&T, it was able to borrow more money than any corporation in the United States and at favorable rates. Did all of its brilliant employees suddenly become inept? No, they simply became victims of a market environment, which changed because of technology, regulation, and competition. Just because prediction is so difficult does not mean that we should not try. By careful observation, many things are highly predictable. Again, the best time to make your prediction is before accepting the job. There are some good ways to do this:

- Through your networking contacts.
- By interviewing customers.
- Through your interviews with the CEO, peers, and if possible, sales managers.
- By reviewing results.
- By assessing the level of supervision and control in place in the sales organization.

Some CEOs have little feel for the sales department. It is best to know this now to understand whether you will be a good match for each other. With good information and good questions, you should be able to assess your CEO's sales temperature. What is the CEO's policy about compensation? Is he willing to let salespeople and sales managers make big incomes? Where you identify a highly cost-conscious CEO, you can bet that the sales organization will tend to be undersized. If you determine the need for additional salespeople, would you have his support? As a sales professional, you know that more salespeople make more sales than fewer salespeople. Experience also says that in growing a sales force, it may be better to bring on new reps all at once rather than over time. Most CEOs are unfamiliar with the concept of carryover. Depending on the sales cycle and nature of the business, up to 40% of next year's business can be directly attributed to selling that began this year. This is the concept of carryover. There is a reason that many CEOs and CFOs do not understand this principle: It is due to the optical illusion that whenever there is a major sales organization downsizing or management change, sales results may appear unaffected—in the short term. Those who do not understand sales do not understand that the continuing sales are the result of work begun months in the past. Fewer reps do not produce as much as more reps. Unfortunately, this myth becomes the problem of the new CSO who inherits a pipeline with insufficient carryover to buoy future results.

### *Contracting the Selling Activities*

One major decision awaiting CSOs is a review of existing partner relationships, or whether some (additional) segment of the sales program ought to be effectively outsourced to indirect channels. These independent companies perform the selling function primarily by extending your company's reach into segments familiar to them and not you. This subject is a book in itself and beyond the scope of this book, which focuses on the direct sales force. Many management parallels do apply, however. Additionally, there are decisions to be made about the wisdom of deploying other selling technologies such as inside sales and the Internet, to reach additional markets cost effectively. In the next section you'll find a powerful tool to weigh the question of whether to add more personnel to your sales force.

## Sales Channel Sizing and Company Profitability

### *Cost Containment*

Companies are always at work on lowering their cost of goods sold to gain competitive advantage through price reductions or to fatten margins. As you read earlier, sales-related expenses are usually the second largest cost item. In a downturn, some companies also focus on reducing sales expenses and/or improving sales productivity. There is a variety of ways they do this. Some companies reduce direct and channel costs by a percentage ("15% across the board cut"); some reduce costs through straight funding cuts ("take $2.5 million from the budget"); still others contain costs through controls such as mandating a target ratio of revenue to sales expense ("sales will be 15% of revenue"). However, the three approaches above are financial strategies, not necessarily good sales strategies. Even in difficult times, if the company is in a growth market, none of these strategies may recognize the opportunity to maximize profits.

***Productivity Improvements***

Productivity improvement is always in season. Some firms channel expense by purchasing automation software to improve sales productivity. If CRM (customer relationship management) delivers a 10% improvement in sales productivity, there are second-level choices. Is this an opportunity to grow sales without adding headcount? Or is this an opportunity to reduce sales headcount by 10%? In a growth market, the appropriate choice may be to reinvest into sales force growth in order to grow revenue and profits.

**Table Current Situation**

| Results | Rationale |
|---|---|
| $100,000,000 total sales for last year | 77 reps = $1,300,000 average sales per rep |
| Revenue = 3.7 times the breakeven sales cost per rep | $245,000 loaded cost per rep at 70% GM (gross margin) = $350,000 sales required to breakeven |
| The ratio of the cost of the sales force to sales is 19% | $18,865,000 sales force cost/ $100,000,000 sales = 18.9% |

***Invest in Sales or Reduce Costs?***

It also demonstrates for the factors given that containing sales costs in a growth market will not maximize profits. Sales investment helps maximize profits.

*Status Quo*

The company makes no changes: The directive to sales is: Maintain 19% sales expense to revenue with no additional sales hires.

*Investment for Profit Improvement*

In this next example, the directive to sales is: Increase the sales force by eight reps for greater reach and coverage.

**Table Improving Profits**

| Results | Rationale |
|---|---|
| $5,200,000 in incremental sales | $650,000 sales per rep times 8 new reps. (50% of annual quota due to ramp up, etc.). |
| 1.86 times the breakeven sales | $350,000 breakeven sales per rep cost per person with $650,000 average sales |
| $1,690,000 incremental sales cost | 8 reps at $245,000 loaded cost each |
| $3,640,000 incremental gross margin | 70% of total incremental sales of $5,200,000 |
| $1,950,000 added to company bottom line profit total loaded | Incremental profit from subtracting cost from total gross margin |
| Revenue to sales cost ratio is 20% | $20,825,000 sales force cost / 105,200,000 total revenue = 19.8 % |

### *Consider Carryover*

A CFO or CEO could argue that many companies appear to have cut their direct and indirect channel costs with relatively little effect on the current year's production. This can sound like a compelling argument. It is a good argument only in the short term. In the longer term, the company handicaps itself by ignoring sales carryover and market growth. Recall that sales carryover recognizes that sales made today are the culmination of sales groundwork done in the past, months or even years earlier. It follows that a drop in sales effort today will not show up until months later, perhaps even the next year. Depending on the industry and length of a sales cycle, up to 40% of next year's sales result from the previous year's activity. This phenomenon makes carryover an important planning consideration. Furthermore, if you are blessed with a growth market, the company loses the advantage it may have gained by securing a larger share. The foregone growth and profits cannot contribute to the company's financial health and competitive position. Now, you must take all the information you have gathered and weigh it against the task ahead of you. The sales force is either adequate or inadequate to meet the assigned objectives. If the sales force is adequate, it passes the minimum threshold required. Therefore, it will not be an initial priority for you. Of course, everything can be improved, but that is not your task right now. You are looking for Hindenburg Omens. A rating of inadequate signifies a Hindenburg Omen.

## In Pursuit of Rewards: Chocolate, Sex, and Money

Freud saw our minds in constant battle between the forces of rationality (superego) and the forces of "I want it now" (id). When rationality prevails, we are said to display emotional intelligence. We are able to delay gratification.

Of course, this is an important power to have, or at the least, to have others perceive that you have it. We are all familiar with those animal experiments where the lab animals drop from exhaustion after nonstop pushing of control bars to release pleasurable substances. Today an MRI enables us to watch ourselves manage our temptations in living color. Researchers observe that we are often on the edge of performing in irrational ways as the power of our own id skirmishes with rationality. When emotional intelligence loses, according to Freud, pursuit of rewards can inspire our own worst behavior. Like it or not, we are still evolution in process with many of our animal-brain proclivities in good working order. Freud's observation, confirmed in color by MRI, explains some of the unusual things we see in sales management. Now we know why people act the way they do. Here is a simple example.

### *Chocolate and Sex*

What do attractive people, sex, and chocolate have in common with money? They all activate the same region of our brain that lights up an MRI when a person ingests morphine or cocaine. Just as they react to sex and drugs, your sales reps can become chemically buzzed up pursuing money or receiving it. "Whether it's reacting to a sexual conquest, a risky business deal, or an addictive drug, the brain often distinguishes clearly between the thrill of the hunt and the pleasure of the feast." For many sales people the chase is reward enough. Sometimes pursuit pushes the rep into risky, unethical, or uncollegial behavior.

### *Non-Money Rewards*

Sales reps do not do what they are not paid to do. Fortunately, researchers Hans Breiter and Daniel Kahneman have demonstrated the power of psychic rewards are a currency, too. Their experiments demonstrated that even salespeople derive pleasure from the hunt whether the payoff is self-esteem, money, or both. A sales success provides a major high from victory, recognition, and being on top. I saw this principle in action the time my top sales rep won our biggest order ever. In a spectacle right out of The Music Man, he marched into our building escorted by a high school marching band. He was smiling and nodding to onlookers like Professor Harold Hill leading 76 trombones!

### *After the Thrill of the Chase*

Of course, the commotion flags when the chase ends. Sometimes, too little interest remains in implementation. This behavior is reminiscent of a classic sales bait and switch joke: During the sales process, the salesperson lavishes golf, exquisite dining, and the promise of perpetual sunshine under blue skies upon the prospect. The rep creates an indelible image of the pleasures and benefits that lie ahead, if only the prospect will sign the contract. He signs and soon discovers that all of this was an illusion. When the customer asks what happened to all the ruffles and flourishes before the sale, the sales rep responds, "yesterday you were a prospect, but today you're just a customer."

***Astute Observation***

One sales team used this proverbial insight to turn several apparent losses into victories. They encountered a talented competitor named Mike who beat them regularly. They studied him and looked for a weakness, which they found. Mike did not require a signed contract to experience the thrill of victory. All he required was to be told that he was the winning vendor. After that, he appeared to down-shift his activity, even to take a vacation. The result: Weeks passed before Mike negotiated a signed contract. We realized that this lag time made him vulnerable to stealing his deal. There is always some degree of buyer's remorse with a major decision. Add to this a time lag and the potential for unpleasant surprises lurking in an unsigned contract, and you can see the reason for our hope of turning around an occasional loss. Perhaps this example is so unusual that you may never apply it. Perhaps the better lesson is this: We need to take every advantage, even small ones, to win. In baseball, the batting champion ekes out every hit he can, because winning the title or a deal may depend upon it. Viewed in a different context, if you were Mike's manager, you would provide him a valuable coaching service by studying why it takes him so long to reel in his dinner.

***Ethics in Question***

In our research interviews with their non-sales colleagues, we heard allegations that "sales will do anything to get the sale." This is another of those "your greatest strength can be your greatest weakness" paradoxes. Sales should do (almost) anything to get a sale that is moral, legal, and ethical. Losing a sale by doing anything less is apostasy! Not just corporate colleagues question sales' ethics. A Gallup poll of consumers found that of all the business occupations, selling and advertising were ranked at the bottom in terms of honesty and ethical standards. Sales ethics are not a black-and-white thing. Salespeople are expected to be enthusiastic about their products. However, when does enthusiasm spill over into puffery, white lies, or untruths? Sales management must communicate answers, lest they risk their company's future. For Met Life and Putnam, questions about sales ethics have prompted internal reorganizations.

For Prudential, an ethical charge cost it over $425 million because its sales force oversold clients. Ethical problems at Arthur Anderson, WorldCom, and Enron caused prosecution and bankruptcy. Obviously, ethical problems are not limited to unreliable firms. The issue is not going away. I say this because ethics have a large situational component. What is unspeakable in one situation can be excusable in another. Is it ever moral to murder your own baby? U.S.

News & World Report raised this question in an article on moral issues. Many psychologists believe we have several powerful moral precepts that are hard-wired within us through evolution. It is an emotionally settled issue at first pass that we would never murder our own child. Not so fast, claim a team of Princeton researchers who underscore the role situational elements play in accepting or overriding our initial gut reaction. Princeton's Joshua Greene proposes that "a moral judgment is ultimately a balance of several different considerations—the initial, primal reaction; empathy; cultural or religious norms; and individual reasoning. Sometimes these will all be in line and make the decision an easy one, but often they will conflict."

The team ran a study posing the following situation: "Enemy soldiers have taken over your village and will kill any civilians they find. You are hiding in the cellar of a house with a group of townspeople, and you hear the soldiers enter the house. Your baby starts to cry, and the only way to quiet him is to hold your hand over his mouth and, eventually, smother him. But if the baby keeps crying, the soldiers will discover your group and kill everyone, the baby included. What should you do?" In this situation about half the subjects said they would murder their own child. Researchers observed the decision process via MRI and saw the collision of emotion with cognition and conflict control. Situational pressures will increase on our sales forces as they face more capable global competition and smarter, more demanding prospects. The future of the direct sales job is more uncertain than ever. Reps worry about outsourcing, downsizing, sharing territory with indirect channels, mergers, acquisitions, reduced budgets, and higher quotas. The most successful sales managers will anticipate these ethical challenges and address them with their teams.

They will make their standards clear and define the penalty for unethical behavior. Careers, reputations, and the viability of our companies are at stake. Keep in mind that personal standards of conduct are usually higher than business standards. Employees often perceive that business behavior at lower standards levels is acceptable. USA Today, referencing an article by Susan Powell Mantel, found this perception goes across department lines. They reported that nearly half of all workers admitted in a survey that they had committed "unethical or illegal acts." It is not just the brains of salespeople that slosh around with potent doses of reward-seeking chemicals. Money and other situational variables seduce corporate workers and create skullduggery in every department.

**SALES ENVIRONMENT**

Of all these go-to-market elements, the one over which the CSO has most influence is the field sales environment. The culture of a field sales office is the living laboratory demonstrating the level of confidence the sales team has in itself and its company. Sales leadership plays the key role in establishing the department's competence, commitment, and credibility with other functional areas. If the sales team maintains a winning trajectory through its results, the CSO is halfway home. The balance of his effort and that of his managers will be built upon foundational practices that support winning in the long run. Leadership must demonstrate competent decisions in the areas of training, coaching, hiring skill, representing the department's interests to other departments and to senior management, assuring adequate compensation, field support, and ability to maintain a confident sales culture.

**Type 1 or Type 2 Situations**

A new CSO seeking to turn the tide on an unsatisfactory sales performance should answer two questions about the sales culture before setting her strategy. Is the negative sales spiral because of:

- Incompetent leadership within the sales department (internal); or
- Perception of incompetent sales leadership, often the result of poor companywide integration of the sales effort stemming from a company's poor self-confidence, senior management ignorance, or CEO incompetence (external)?

Ostensibly, the company hires a new CSO because the last one didn't work out. This is an incomplete answer, however. The full answer completes the sentence "... didn't work out because... (usually reasons 1 or 2)." It is important to determine which so that you can address the actual underlying problem. The perception of sales by others is a good clue about the extent of sales integration into the actions of other departments. When interviewing for a new position, if you hear someone say: "This is an operations-driven company," you can hypothesize a great deal more. "Operations-driven" is a common code phrase for an organization with silos, local power bases, and a CEO who has not well integrated his resources behind the marketing effort.

The implication is that you will be at a disadvantage to a competitor whose organization believes that everyone's role is to win customers and keep them close. In one company, I heard the pricing executive describe the sales managers this way: "They all lie." His boss, the CFO, told me, "I asked them what price he (sic) needed, gave it to them, and then he lost the deal. These guys are incompetent." In a company with such commonplace disregard for sales, you can bet that the CEO is part of the problem, too. At this company, the CEO had not aligned the objectives and compensation of operations, finance, and sales. Managers were paid for accomplishing their parochial tasks without a single objective— even total revenue—in common with sales. Further, at the CEO's staff meetings the group sport was pummeling the Sales VP for his missed forecasts. That the CEO allowed this to occur sent a clear signal to everyone reflecting his confidence in the sales executive.

### *Monkey-in-the-Middle*

This senior team sport reminded me of a game my children play called Monkey-in-the-Middle. There are few rules because the game is obvious to everyone. "It" is the Monkey in the Middle and play is easy. Players circle around the monkey and toss a ball back and forth keeping it away from the Monkey-in-the-Middle. In the business world, sales is often the Monkey-in-the-Middle. Like the kids' game, this monkey-in-the-middle is isolated while all the others circle around in the camaraderie of a management team consisting of everyone but sales. The game is an apt analogy, particularly in seeking the answers above. In fact, as this book demonstrates, when sales revenue is down, sales is often not the cause. Nevertheless, sales is always the easy target to be perceived as the monkey-in-the-middle. The successful CSO finds the truth and collaborates with other senior executives to solve the company's problems. In short, he must know the truth and tell the truth.

### *Ineffective Outside Intervention*

I coached a CSO who was behind in his numbers, but whose biggest job was managing his CEO. His CEO spent more time looking over his shoulder managing sales than in focusing on the survival strategy of the firm. That made it clear to the sales force who really ran the sales force. It also demoralized them. Salespeople are very observant and understand quickly what's going on.

They intensely dislike interference from anyone outside of sales. So, they were not at all happy when the CEO devised a new contest and had it delivered through their VP. This CEO observed that if the sales force closed just 15% more proposals, sales would meets its numbers. Therefore, ask the sales force to raise its proposal win rate to 30%. That may have been a simple observation for the corner office to make, but achieving the result was a different story. As if by magic, proposal win rates grew to the magic number. Unfortunately, the company did not get a step closer to its targets. How can this be? Salespeople simply delayed reporting losses while continuing to report wins. The term malicious compliance was created for the situation like this. The implication is you do precisely what you have been asked to do but absolutely nothing more. To justify a slowdown in loss reporting, sales decided that loss decisions ought not to be made hastily. After all, who knows when a situation could change and provide the opportunity to win? This is a common sales force ploy when it is required to fulfill tasks it does not perceive in its best interest. Malicious compliance is also a term that means you get what you ask for—and no more.

The problem in this company was not bad people or even bad sales leadership. The issue was loss of confidence throughout the company, a path of least resistance created from years of revenue decline. Skilled corporate observer Rosabeth Moss Kanter describes the effects within companies that lose their confidence after repeated attempts to reverse losses: "When losing makes people feel out of control, and when they give in to the temptations associated with defending against feeling powerless, the seeds of systemic pathologies are sown.... Everyone expects the worst of everyone else— and then acts to make those expectations come true. Self-confidence, confidence in one another, and confidence in the system disappear." An intuitive sales leader sees how a company's loss of confidence hurts the sales effort. Kanter says powerlessness to turn a company around produces actions that are taken to preserve control and power. Of course, their actions actually lessen it. Departmental silos and adversarial tactics at this firm sprang from powerlessness, and department managers attempted to protect management domains. They focused on activities and results where they had relatively more control. They lost confidence in larger efforts to save the company. They did what Kanter predicted they would do. Reinforcement came from the CEO who rewarded achievement for departmental metrics, not for critically needed sales revenue. The path of least resistance was clear. Given then a firm with managers rewarded for their defensive results, why would any of them take risks to help sales? In fact, it was in their own perceived best interest not to help sales. Thus, lacking companywide integration, sales performance suffered, morale declined further, and departmental efforts become even more parochial. It was a terrific time and place to play Monkey-in-the-Middle. Certainly, this toxic environment was a classic Hindenburg Omen for the new CSO and all his people. Here again we see the power of context, of circumstances. At one time, most of those managers were star performers on winning teams. Now, constraints of their current environment drive their behavior within it. Hence, the turnaround solution for this company with a sales culture of losing is almost certainly not to fire the CSO. Successful CSOs carefully assess new opportunities to learn why a predecessor "didn't work out." They determine a company's sales culture before accepting a new job. They check out the CEO's relationship with sales as well as the extent of the firm's integration behind the sales effort.

### *Monitoring and Supervision*

Where would you look for clues about the competence of the previous sales management régime? People are rightly sensitive about how management trusts them and respects their competence. A good proxy for this sentiment is often found by learning how management monitors and supervises sales. Do measurement and control systems focus on managing behaviors, or do they focus more on managing results? Is the answer appropriate for the company's goto- market strategy? As a guideline, a sales organization that requires little monitoring and supervision probably understands and executes activities required to achieve results assigned to it.

This company focuses on results. What if you discover the opposite? For instance, if the focus is on behaviors and the level of supervision required is high, this may indicate a low level of skills and commitment in the sales organization. Then again, it may be perfectly appropriate for the mission. One of our telemarketing groups had a metric of "25 before nine." The goal was 25 dials before 9 AM in order to get the group limbered up for its morning meeting. Again, context is everything. An inappropriate match of behavior management to the sales task can indicate low trust in sales and even lower self-confidence of management. Many of us have suffered under such régimes, and if we did, we may have suffered silently or headed for the exit. Whatever we did, we learned an important lesson about management. Attempts to control or measure a salesperson's every move are folly. Where can you sniff out clues about such practices?

Highly talented sales reps chafe under such treatment, and this should be reflected in the company's sales high turnover metrics. You know well that nothing is black or white. High turnover could also stem from a new compensation program. Information gives you the ability to raise important questions to ask during your discussions with the CEO. Good questions will also help you better discern the understanding and commitment of your new CEO toward the sales program you will be managing. Even in a winning sales environment, things go wrong. Sometimes the explanation is chance or some random cause. You could lose days of production because of a freak snowstorm. At other times, the cause of a problem is simple human error. Over the past decade, researchers have explained that some human error and misjudgment is quite predictable. By understanding how circumstances such as uncertainty influence judgment, we can train our people to be conscious of them. At the very least, our own familiarity with sources of influence will make us wiser, more anticipative managers.

## SALES CONTROL AND POLICIES

### Sales Controls

Controls are the company's method of directing and measuring sales activity across the entire organization. Typical sales controls include quota assignments, compensation, expense budgets, activity or funnel reporting, gift policy, rules, forecasting, travel and entertainment reporting and policies, car policy, territory, account selection, and training programs. Sales controls also include derivative metrics such as call activity, close ratio, turnover, and quota performance. Without controls and policies, sales managers would spend unproductive time making individual decisions that are easily codified by controls and policies. Without controls, chaos would reign. Unfortunately, controls that are unenlightened, inconsistent, or misdirected can also lead to chaos. In the following case, observe how a well-intended compensation plan change boomeranged into a disaster.

***Second-Level Consequences***

Sales reps are extraordinarily aware when it comes to their compensation plans. They do what they are paid to do, and little more. Even when an unpaid activity is of high value to the company, sales reps are reluctant helpers. If you want to drive behavior, write the appropriate carrot into their compensation plan. That sounds easy enough. Unfortunately, it is not. Managers often fail to think through the consequences of new decisions. Nobel Prize winner Tversky terms this "nonconsequentialist reasoning." He concludes that we tend to follow a path of least resistance. It's more work to look ahead, and easier to look back. Yet, as the next illustration demonstrates, the most successful sales managers should always push themselves to consider the second-level consequences of their decisions. My assignment was to coach a new CSO whose sales steadily trended down. I noted that the company's standard contract had a provision for one-, two-, or three-year agreements just by checking a box. According to the marketing staff, almost all the contracts were for one year. Further, marketing believed that the disinterest in longerterm contracts portended a swift decline in the company's offering. This view clashed with other research that showed the company's offering as fairly priced and well supported. I discovered a wellintended compensation plan change that explained everything.

The CEO had made a comp plan change that moved a commission from one product to another. The CEO eliminated compensation on the second and third year's sales. He moved the commission funds to emphasize a new product important for the company's future. He intended that sales would not lose commissions. They would just be shifted in order to change behavior. He knew that new products sell faster when they have extra incentive, i.e., he was looking back to his experience. He had not looked forward to the impact on the current product. In his view, the sales effort was already well rewarded for the first year of a new service contract. All that was required to extend the sale to two or three years was a check mark in a box on the contract. In his view, no more effort was required for a multiyear contract, so why pay for it. Almost immediately, the company had a sharp drop in multiyear service contracts. The sales force regarded the compensation change negatively. It considered these commissions as taken away rather than simply shifted. The CEO had a logically defensible position, and so did the sales force. They felt it was unfair to strip a commission because someone believed the sale was too easy. After all, just getting the contract signed in the first place required lot of effort. Furthermore, they reasoned that the company would receive revenue for years two and three of a contract without any compensation expense. Difficulty of the sale notwithstanding, the revenue dollars were still the same. They felt the company was unfairly receiving a benefit they provided and taking away one that they deserved. Multiyear sales at the same commission as single-year sales would have helped the company. Now there was no incentive to sign them—even if the sale were relatively easier. Actually, the reverse was true. There was now an incentive NOT to get two- and three-year contracts. Reps realized they would get a full commission when they resold the service next year. There were even more unintended consequences. As multiyear sales of contracts continued to drop, more accounts were lost to competitors. The CEO's change and sales' response put their customers into a mode of constant shopping for renewal options. To put it differently, saving a few bucks on commissions cost the company hundreds of thousands of dollars in lost accounts to competitors. Of course, there was another unintended consequence. Instead of stimulating sales of the new product, the reps sold less of it. This was due to the power of the path of least resistance. It is easier to resell an old customer than create a new one. Predictably, when renewal time came, the rep would invest his time to re-sign his existing account for another year.

To summarize, the company added fewer new accounts and never received the expected push for the new product line. When the CEO realized the full implication of what he had done, he restored full commission for each additional year of service signed at the time of the contract. Again, context turns out to be everything. The minute the structure was changed, the path of least resistance changed also. The sales force exhibited predictable behavior. Moral: Think beyond the first-stage implication of every change. Even seemingly small changes can have significant, unintended consequences on revenue, morale, and market share. There are many factors that make a sales culture successful or not. These include training, MBOs, territory sizes, ability to meet targets, and others already mentioned. The compensation plan is the most important of them all. Sales does what it is paid to do. Many CEOs are unfamiliar with how sales compensation works. As in the example above, the CEO may think it is obvious that a sales rep would rationally do what is best for the company. However, as the case illustrates, do not count on it.

### The "Art" of Forecasting

Books have been written on the science of forecasting, but anyone in the real world of sales knows that forecasting is no science at all. Rather, it's more like an art—subjective and inexact. Why then do monthly floggings continue until forecasting improves? Let's start at the top.

#### *CEOs Live by Numbers*

Achieving metrics drives CEO earnings. So, they think in metrics and talk of metrics. They got to where they are because they made their numbers. Remember that more of today's CEOs come from engineering than any other discipline. By experience, they believe numbers can describe nearly everything, that numbers can characterize all activity and make it binary. Any number—such as a sales forecast— is either hit or missed. A contract is signed or it isn't. However, selling and forecasting sales are not simple binary operations. What makes sales different from other corporate functions?

***Apples and Oranges***

When a CEO was, say, VP of Operations, he could accurately forecast many metrics. He had personal control over many of them and, therefore, the power to control a measure of forecasting precision. By not filling a personnel position, for example, expenses would decrease predictably. As VP of Finance, he could be an expert cash manager by not paying or prepaying bills. In these examples, actions are causal of results. With causal control over operations, the VPs demonstrated the "science" of accurate forecasting. So, your boss and colleagues wonder: Why can't sales managers demonstrate this science?

***Shades of Gray***

To be a science, a body of knowledge must demonstrate facts or truths. However, facts and truths are difficult to come by in sales. Most situations are shades of gray. The same "facts" may produce different outcomes. For instance, the CFO yields to sales' request for a price cut and wants to know, "What price do you need to win the deal?" In this case, the discount wins the sale. Another manager gets the same discount only to lose his sale. A sales manager understands immediately why this happens, while many CFOs shake their heads in bewilderment. In truth, the CFO is unaware of how much he doesn't know about sales. Unfortunately, this doesn't restrain him from misperceiving the competence of the sales department. Sales knows of the many nonprice variables that enter into a sale. Variables vary often unpredictably. A sudden spending may delay a certain sale. This is why sales forecasts are not governed by consistently repeatable principles and therefore not a science. Sales forecasts are really an art, more the result of intuition, clairvoyance, and probability. Some 350 years ago, the French mathematician Pascal explained this difference in his famous Pensées. There are, he said, differences between scientific and intuitive matters. Scientific matters are those in which reasonable men would come to the same conclusion by applying the facts. There are 90° in a right triangle; therefore, anyone can spot the error of a claim that there are 89°. This is science because the nature of the matter is perfectly definite once you collect the relevant information.

***The Realm of Probability***

Whether a sale will close is not a perfectly definite idea. In a pending sale, the amount of information that exists to describe the situation is nearly infinite. Which information is relevant? Are there unknown factors that will be more relevant? A sale cannot be described with the precision of a right triangle. It can only be described as a probability.

### *Sales Forecasting Is Intuitive*

Describing a pending sale is more akin to describing other indefinite terms such as "love"! With similar difficulty to providing the definition of "love," the closing date of a sale leaves plenty of room for variation from thoughtful observers. Pascal would call these situations matters of intuition or "finesse." In these matters, as opposed to scientific ones, there is sometimes such a large body of information to be digested that the task becomes increasingly complex because of variables that cannot be assigned values and solved like an equation. How do we even know that we have collected all or at least enough information upon which to base a decision? In other words, how can we know what we don't know?

### *Sales Representatives Have Unequal Skills*

There is a further complication in forecasting accurately. In interpreting the set of facts in a sales situation, not every sales representative has the same experience and discernment to draw the same conclusions. Thus, even with all the facts, there is wide variation due to interpretation. Even experts can disagree on the consequences of the same set of facts. Of course, it depends upon your definition of "all"!

### *Who Is Really in Charge of the Sale?*

Unlike the examples in finance and operations above where an executive had control over variables, sales may influence, but not control the ultimate variable. In sales it is the customer who holds the power to determine when a sale will close, not the salesperson. Therefore, while the sales force pushes for decisions in a timely manner, complex internal customer relationships, shifting politics, competitive wildcards, last-minute demands, and more may conspire against the most eloquent urgings of the sales representative upon his prospect. In a company with large volumes of sales orders, the law of large numbers smooths out the good guesses and the bad. It is a scientific law that the more numbers calculated, the closer the result approaches its true value. The forecasting process is most nervewracking where your desired company results are skewed by a relatively few substantial sales. Every sale becomes high profile because even a single customer delay can destroy your sales forecast.

### *Probability: The Forecast Is Wrong*

The consensus among sales executives I asked is that in a given month, only one in four deals—25%—forecast by the sales force will actually close. That is why most executives filter the field forecast through their first-line managers, or apply their own experience factor, or divide by ??before they send the forecast to the CEO. While you may be in the statistical ballpark for the total monthly number, unfortunately, for any particular deal that the boss asks about, the odds are still against you. There are just too many variables for a sales rep to forecast with dead-on accuracy in a single account. Let us look at the permutations involved in predicting that a particular deal will close this month.

| Three Forecasting Variables | | | |
|---|---|---|---|
| 1. The rep has all information required for an informed forecast.* | 2. The rep interprets the information and forecasts correctly based upon it.* | 3. The customer acts as the rep predicts.* | The Statistical Probability of Forecasting Correctly |
| Combinations of the Variables* | | | |
| Yes | Yes | Yes | 100% |
| Yes | Yes | No | 12.5% |
| Yes | No | No | 12.5% |
| Yes | No | Yes | 12.5% |
| No | No | No | 12.5% |
| No | No | Yes | 12.5% |
| No | Yes | Yes | 12.5% |
| No | Yes | No | 12.5% |

*There are eight ($2^3$) possible combinations. Assume 50% probability for each variable, e.g., the rep may or may not have all the required information for an informed forecast; the rep may have the information, but misinterpret it, etc.

The rep can be right that the deal will close or right that it will not close. If this happened often enough, there would be no need for this chapter on forecasting! However, if her intuition is off, she can be wrong about a deal closing or wrong that a deal that she thought would not close will close. The wildcard is always the customer, who can still sign or not sign regardless of whether the rep read the situation correctly. Pascal was right. Some matters are easily determined to be right or wrong, yes or no. Sales forecasting is not one of them!

### *Nevertheless, Forecasting Is Essential*

The difficulty of forecasting not withstanding, how do you satisfy your CEO and colleagues who require one? As we noted, the difficulty and importance vary by your individual context. Here are some ideas from successful managers in a variety of environments.

- Educate your CEO and colleagues about the specific difficulties that present themselves. With thought you can make a factual case describing the particular factors for your environment. Explain how the set of variables involved adds difficulty to the sales forecasting equation.
- Some CSOs sit down with their most vocal or critical colleagues to negotiate a truce from public criticism. They explain the issues described above. Then they lay out alternatives to address the particular criticisms. For example, would the colleague prefer quarterly forecasts? Then listen and negotiate an agreement that works for both of you.
- Developing agreement like this can have the effect of turning an enemy into an ally. Particularly if the criticism of your forecasting has become public, such as in staff meetings, you can lower the heat by announcing the new approach agreed upon.
- With large account responsibility, quarterly or semi-annual forecasting can even out extreme monthly vicissitudes.
- A successful international manager advises having enough flexibility in your pipeline to add in or take out pending sales in order to smooth out a forecast if a large pending sale suddenly goes awry.
- Be realistic. Don't apply more time or resources for the forecasting task beyond the point of diminishing returns. Instead, devote executive resources to actual customer sales and retention.
- Have a Top Ten list of sales to be personally involved in. You will always know what's really happening in the key accounts.
- One Sales Vice President, now a CEO, maintains a practice he found effective on his way to the top. In addition to his longer term participation in his Top Ten accounts, he watched his "Hot Five." These were the top five hottest situations with short-term decision horizons. This personal account team level involvement helped him forecast accurately.
- Study carefully your sales trends to generate a statistically likely forecast, or...
- Develop a list of objective criteria that any potential sale must satisfy before it can be forecast. For example, an account may not be forecast until your contract been approved by the customer's legal department. This is a highly effective method to improve forecasts. It adds objectivity and can help you hammer out agreements with critical colleagues.
- Understand the quality of your product/market match. No one is better situated than you to use market and competitive trends to keep your company viable. This means spotting opportunities for innovation and creative business relationships.

- Become well educated on your competition. Find out why they win and lose sales. Influence your customers and internal colleagues with valuable intelligence. Tell your colleagues what you see as longer-term trends.
- Finally, stay in constant contact with your top customers. Create close relationships you can use to influence other sales, or to save you when your business with their company is in jeopardy. The degree to which you are intimately knowledgeable of your customer's business and their customers' needs is the measure of the value you bring as a collaborative partner.

**Thin-Slicing, a Productivity Tool**

In his best-selling book on human cognition, Blink, author Malcolm Gladwell introduces readers to a phrase from the world of psychology: "the power of thin-slicing." In the book, Gladwell offers many fascinating examples of people making sense of situations based on the thinnest slice of experience—overhearing as little as one or two seconds of a conversation, for example. Cook County Hospital (CCH) is a wonderful example of identifying just the right amount of information by thin-slicing. At CCH, the approach saved lives and resources. Just ahead, you will see how sales managers can use this same technique to win more bids and save resources. In financial crisis, CCH sought to cut costs for its ER's most costly service—diagnosing heart attacks. A heart attack is not an easy thing to diagnose, and no one wants to send a victim home who is actually experiencing one. Therefore, in exercising due care, ER doctors routinely ordered many tests that in retrospect were unnecessary—and expensive. CCH had no standard best practice to diagnose an actual heart attack in progress. There were as many ways to diagnose heart attacks as there were physicians. The administration believed that it could reduce costs and deliver good care if it could identify the best indicators of a probable heart attack and have every physician use them. The question was, "How much information was enough?" They implemented the findings of a study demonstrating that just four relatively easily determined pieces of information, such as blood pressure, would suffice. CCH had its staff implement the practice. The first step was a successful trial. Then CCH implemented its four-step algorithm as standard practice. Thin-slicing has obvious applications for sales management to identify better prospects particularly from among RFPs.

***Thin-Slicing RFPs***

In many companies, each rep applies his own criteria to select an unsolicited RFP on which he wishes to bid. Choices are subjective and there is no agreement about even what constitutes an "unsolicited" RFP, let alone a good one. Where CCH relied upon each physician's own opinion, the default position in sales often is reliance upon the quality of the rep's own judgment. This practice can lead to the waste of resources, especially since many companies have predetermined their choice of vendor. Our study showed that in more than half of RFP requests, they are shopping you for a comparison price against their preferred vendor. Sometimes, the rep can be drawn to bid on marginal opportunities because he has nothing better to work on. He may even bid an opportunity merely to fulfill an activity requirement or just to look busy. Thin-slicing is an effective way to incorporate the best learning of others to the benefit of all. It helps reps at all experience levels select the best opportunities for investment of the company's resources into winning deals.

### *Creating Your Thin-Slicing Tool for RFPs*

Thin-slicing is not complicated. First, develop a checklist of criteria that appear to have worked in the past to identify the best opportunities. "In retrospect, what did we know or wish we had known to determine if the opportunity were real?" Make a list of all the insights you collect from your analysis and advice of your most successful producers. Then combine and narrow your list to the few best insights. Rate all RFP requests on whether they meet or do not meet your predetermined criteria. In order to receive resources to work on a project not meeting criteria, a sales manager's override is required. Then track the results of your system adjusting it when you learn something new. The steps below break out the process in more detail.

#### *Step 1: Hard Evidence*

Gather some hard evidence and include the opinions of your best performers about characteristics of good RFP opportunities. Your list of favorable factors may include:

- The size of the deal: It is in our sweet spot.
- We can influence proposal development: We have a pre-existing relationship with this prospect.
- This is a leading-edge account: It is a strategic opportunity. This is an attractive account with enormous growth potential.
- We have a competitive advantage: Our offer is superior to the competition, or their current supplier has failed them or is unable to meet their expectations.
- We have a fair chance to win: There is a level playing field. We have access to the key players. The decision maker is personally involved. They are "switchable" from our competitor.
- The purchase is budgeted: This is not just a fishing expedition.
- We are positioned with the decision maker: We have a position of influence, not simply acquaintance.

- We helped write the RFP, the new VP selected us at his former company. We have a good solution. Our product is a great match for this opportunity.
- They want to grow: We add real value to their offer.

*Step 2: Group and Combine*

Now group, combine, and quantify your list. Identify the few pieces of hard evidence that allow you in retrospect to pick what you now know were the best opportunities. These become your thin-slicing criteria going forward. Dig down to collect hard evidence: Did we have a pre-existing relationship? Was it important? What really is a relationship? Were we certain the project was budgeted? Did we have access to decision makers? Did it matter? Did we later find that someone had an inside edge? How could we have known that earlier? How many of our bids were "no decision"? Were we being shopped, euphemistically, the "designated loser"? You will begin to see some patterns. Perhaps having a pre-existing relationship jumped out as predictor. On the laundry list above, there are several items suggesting the importance of a prior relationship. Perhaps you find that you won almost no deals without it. Thus, meeting this criterion then becomes a "must" for bidding on an opportunity. Use "must" criteria sparingly because there are times when you ought to take strategic risks even with low odds of success. Your future success comes from developing new relationships with growing firms who are worth competing for. The trick is to carefully select these situations.

*Step 3: Weighting*

Next, weight your indicators relative to each other. The most important indicator will have a relative weight of three and the least important indicator a relative weight of one. Now, clarify what an indicator means by creating a satisfaction scale to explain it. Leave as little room for interpretation as possible. To rate this indicator for an unsolicited RFP from an account where your team is not positioned, the rep would circle zero. The overall Satisfaction Points awarded to this particular indicator is calculated in this example as "0." If you have four key indicators and their total relative importance weighting is, say, 10 (3, 2, 3, 2), and each indicator has a potential 10 attractiveness points, a perfect opportunity would receive a score of 100. Since few opportunities will be perfect 100s, what is the minimum score for an acceptable opportunity?

*Step 4: Test*

Create several phantom opportunities to test your thin-slicing algorithm. Rate them to develop a feel for how many points an opportunity should score to be worthy of resources for a bid. Take your phantom candidate through each indicator and determine the minimum acceptable rating for each. Add the minimum acceptable scores and that number becomes your threshold score. Anything below the threshold should not be bid or require an override by a sales manager. Keep records and adjust the algorithm as you learn more. Keep in mind that you're not after perfection, just a guide that gives everyone standards, access to the organization's best thinking, and allocates resources wisely.

**How a Super Salesman Avoided Common Decision Traps**

Our sales managers' conference invited the country's leading salesperson to tell us the reasons for his success. Bobby F. talked of the importance of planning and time management, but the part that was most profound was his discussion about prospecting. He explained that his sales manager always provided him with the first refusal on any leads that came in. That was out of respect for his success rate and the need to help him avoid any activity that would be a time waster. When a lead interested him, he met personally with the prospect to qualify him. Bobby had worked out what he called his track. The track was simply an explanation of how the two would agree to proceed toward determining if Bobby's product was a match for the customer's need. If the customer did not meet the criteria Bobby had established, or if he could not agree to cooperate in moving along the track that he thought he had established, then the lead would be turned back in to his sales manager, who would pass it on to another sales rep in the office.

***The Lead Didn't Qualify***

Now here is the key part of the story. The new salesperson receiving the lead would approach him and say,

- "Bobby, I just got this
- lead on one of your prospects. What can you tell me about him?"
- "I will tell you that he did not qualify."
- "But, Bobby, everybody knows how hard you qualify these people.
- Please tell me what you know about him."
- "Again, I'll tell you that he did not qualify."

The difference between his success and the lack of success for others boiled down to whether a prospect qualified for his time and effort. After all, he said all he had to give was his time, and it made no sense to waste it upon a poor prospect. The question arises, then, Why would another rep choose to pursue a prospect that the top salesperson in the country perceived as not qualifying? To answer this critical question we can look to work by Daniel Kahneman as mentioned by and Shoemaker, Russo, and others. It appears that about six common decision traps might entice the less experienced sales rep to take on this unqualified account. The endowment theory observes that we tend to value something in our own possession more highly than another possession of the same value in the hands of another. I saw this demonstrated in a sales management class at Columbia University. The instructor gave mugs and T-shirts of equivalent monetary value to sales managers in the class. They were told that both items were equivalent in value; T-shirts were equivalent to the mugs. The question was asked how many were willing to trade even for a gift in possession of another manager. The answer was very few people. The reason was that once each had possession of his or her own gift, psychologically it assumed greater value than the gift of another. The rookie salesman in our example felt a similar ownership of the lead given him by the sales manager. He owned it, and therefore it must have more value than Bobby perceived to have. In fact, the lead would usually turn out to have a negative value because of the time and effort wasted confirming Bobby's evaluation. Bobby carefully avoided the psychological principle of sunk cost. He invested in the time to prepare for the customer call and to make the call itself without being reluctant to fold his hand and toss the lead back to the sales manager. Kahnemann tells us that most of us are reluctant to admit our losses—in this case the time invested in qualifying the account. Typically, we somehow feel that any cost invested into the customer is a reasonable basis to continue the given the investment that we have already made. The less experienced sales rep was often unable to avoid the status quo effect. This decision trap encourages us psychologically to stay the course of a prior decision, even when an impartial observer could judge that the initial decision was in error. If the sales rep who decided to pursue the unqualified lead simply stopped to think about simple probability, he would have also returned to lead to the sales manager. This is a common error we make in tending to overvalue low-probability situations. Perhaps this is a function of perceiving that the lead from management may be of some value (the endowment effect); however, a salesperson playing the odds would note that an account Bobby considered unqualified would be a low-probability account. By pursuing it, he was overvaluing a low-probability situation. There is also the regret fallacy, which means that we will not gain some potential good result if we never follow a situation through to its denouement. It's common with many of us who hear all the "if only" stories about colossal gains foregone by fearing to make the attempt. Finally, Bobby's story of prospecting shows an additional talent he has that is lacking in his less experienced peers. That talent is mental simulation. It is affiliated with intuition and allows Bobby to quickly think through the steps ahead in the potential prospect relationship to identify high-probability disconnects in the future given the feedback he received from the prospect on his initial call.

## PRODUCT/MARKET MATCH

Marketing guru Ted Levitt once described the difference between marketing and sales by saying that it is sales' responsibility to get the customer to buy what the company has to sell. Today a successful sales organization defines its role well beyond this limiting description. In industrial sales today, the smarter sales organization is the one who has a better sense of integrating sales with marketing. Customers are dealing with fewer suppliers, and businesses are adapting their company's products and services more carefully around their customers. If they can provide ideas and assistance that will help their customers become more successful, their customers will reward them.

**Role of Sales**

One sales leader we interviewed talked of the importance of a sales–marketing relationship. His team has responsibility approaching hundreds of millions of dollars in a single account and believes integrating marketing into the selling process is one of his keys to success. Some future-thinking students of organizational structure see sales as assuming more and more of the marketing role. It only makes sense in making every effort to win large sales and lock in customers by delivering value the customer can see. For many customers, the salesperson can add such value by incorporating marketing solutions that he or she virtually becomes the company, the brand in customers' eyes. This increasing role of the salesperson in delivering value is consistent with the need today to customize solutions such as to accommodate so-called markets of one. This said, salespeople are not magicians. If a company does not have products that are a genuine match for customer-motivated needs, they cannot succeed.

This goes to the point of the matter where earlier we noted that a particular sales group was criticized by a CFO. He said that if only salespeople would make more calls, they would make their commitment. Obviously, this is a remark made from ignorance. A good salesman can indeed lock out competition and thereby generate revenue for some period in the decline of his or her company's products. But even the best sales organization will fail without good products. I believe that products are the most important key to the success of any sales organization. Even with a mediocre sales organization, a company with good products can prosper. Of course, the ideal is to have great products and great distribution to become unstoppable. Therefore, sales is at the mercy of product marketing. In many companies, there is no bridging of sales and product marketing. This is a major stake for both organizations. Repeatedly, we were told of the extraordinary loss in many organizations because sales does not provide feedback for what it sees in the marketplace. Product marketing tends to rely on data and focus groups to provide sales of products to sell. It only makes sense that each should become part of the others planning process. Why doesn't this happen? One marketing executive told us that sales simply did not listen to marketing. He felt it was as if sales said,

- "just give us the product and go away. We'll figure out how to sell it."

In organizations where this mutual disrespect exists, a company could have a nation of sales reps trying to figure out for themselves which segments and target markets are best for their products. You will see this clearly in the following example. In this case, the entrepreneur has a great product, but has it targeted to the wrong market.

## COMPETITION

### Learning from the Fosbury Flop

We are familiar with famous names like Digital Equipment, Howard Johnson, General Motors, and others that lost their edge or became obsolete by failing to react to competitive activity. Competitors bring change, and change can be lethal to our companies. Yet, Peter Drucker observes that competition is one of the things we know least about. Historically, business in any industry might be described as punctuated equilibrium. Things go along steady state for a while, then there is a disruptive technology that portends big trouble for those not on the "S" curve of change early enough. Competition is one of those areas driving Ray Kurzweil's observation that change is changing at an exponential rate. The Internet has democratized information today. Nearly anyone can find infor- mation about any subject online. To prove the point, the U.S. government inadvertently posted captured Iraqi plans for an atom bomb on the net, available to any surfer until they were suddenly removed.

#### *Invisible Competitors*

A former professor at Harvard observed that there is always some new kid in his dorm room practicing to be the fastest gun in the west. We know that is the story of how Michael Dell began to take over an industry as an undergraduate. With information available and competitors often invisible, the business world is less predictable. Indeed, can we even define what constitutes an industry— even when we are in it? In all of this, there are some predictable patterns in how a disruptive competitive technology emerges, gains a foothold, and eventually displaces the old technology. I will use an Olympic athletic event to show how this happens. The high jump became an Olympic event in the late 1800s, about the same time Bell invented the telephone. Since then the high jump evolved through several cycles of change in which competitors developed new technology to challenge the old ways and then obsolete them. The first Olympic high jumpers employed a technique called the scissors. They ran to the bar and leaped, putting one leg forward over the bar, then the other. The scissors became the technique (technology) used by everyone for decades until the Western Roll became popular in the 1930s. To execute the Western Roll, jumpers threw their bodies into a roll parallel to the bar. When the roll emerged as a new jumping technology, the best jumpers were still scissors jumpers, and they pooh-poohed the roll. Others saw potential in the roll and worked diligently to learn it. Scissors jumpers redoubled their effort, but improvement was slow. The roll technique had more upside potential, and in time achieved heights no scissors jumper could match. Years later, the Straddle jump gained popularity. The Straddle jumper leapt over the bar with his chest down, pulling his stomach over the bar. The Straddle appeared to provide incremental improve- ment for those who invested in learning it. Others decided to stay with the Western Roll after observing that the competitive advantage of the Straddle was unclear. There was simply not enough evidence to give up the old way. Western Rollers were convinced that their new technique would supplant the old. Just as before, those who held to the old technology reached the limit of their technology and became obsolete. The Straddle demonstrated continuous improvement and reached heights impossible for rollers to achieve. In the 1960s a new technique again displaced the old. It was a strange, eponymic technique dubbed the Fosbury Flop. An unknown kid named Dick Fosbury emerged from his proverbial dorm room in the Pacific Northwest with a new jumping technology to challenge the jumping world. Fosbury struggled learning the Straddle technique. One day he decided to run at the bar, jump and twist his body to go over the bar backwards with his chest facing up. He sort of flopped over the bar. You can guess what the Straddlers and jumping fans did when they first saw the Fosbury Flop. They howled at his inelegant and improbable technique. Of course, we know how the story ends. Fosbury won the gold medal in the Olympic high jump in Mexico in 1968. Today everybody flops.

***Lessons***

There are some interesting lessons here for sales forces as well as companies. First, competitive change appears only incremental when first introduced. Additionally, the competition may appear far less sophisticated than the existing competitive services. "Incremental" and "less sophisticated" are probably valid descriptions of early competitive changes. The serious mistake to beware is underestimating the future of a disruptive change. A disruptive change is a punctuation point in the competitive equilibrium where new technology changes the market direction. The early telephone and subsequent growth of AT&T parallel the cycles of entry and decay we discussed in Olympic competition. Technology makes a modest entry, gains acceptance by enthusiastic outsiders who see potential, then morphs and develops in unexpected ways, dethroning the old guard as it does. Competitors who observe the unsophisticated state of a new market introduction often believe that by working harder at their own technique or technology, they can overcome the challenge. Ignoring promising competition by digging your own heels in to make incremental improvements in your own technology can be a fatal mistakes. Training yourself to be a close observer of change is one way to keep your career in shape. One easy way to do this is called horizon scanning. All that's required is:

- Selecting a topic(s) to focus on.
- Setting up a file folder and/or a computer file for each topic.
- Searching for and clipping new information at least monthly, or clipping whenever you happen across information serendipitously.

Try these free/inexpensive tools help:

- EverNote, a note organizer and clipper (evernote.com), is a nifty way to clip, store, organize, and recall your information.
- Yahoo permits you to store key search words for your topics.
- StumbleUpon.com will surprise you with unknown, helpful websites on your topic.
- And, of course, there's Google and a raft of add-ins for search specialties.

This is the same approach many futurists use to keep their eye on ideas and trends just over the horizon. It's a tool that will enhance your own career as you develop a reputation for identifying "predictable surprises" early enough for your company to act on the intelligence. Finally, scanning the horizon is a smart way to maintain a personal focus upon changing markets and technology that will structure your future. Alternatively, you can await the future passively. In sales management, passivity is almost never a good strategy.

**THE CUSTOMER**

Customers have changed. After all, they face the same challenges we all do: squeezed margins, increased competition, and everything else related to faster changing change. They are more heterogeneous than ever, and the trend is ever more so toward "markets of one." Relationships still matter, but in a different way. Rather than Willie Loman's "personal" relationships being paramount, it's "business" relationships that take precedence today. There are still differences from one continent to another. U.S. sales executives told us that there is much more emphasis on proving the financial return of any investment. In Europe the trend in buying decisions is headed toward more objectivity and less customer loyalty. Nevertheless, a good relationship still trumps incremental improvements in products or ROIs. It takes more than a slight competitive edge for a company to abandon a good vendor relationship. In an example of the decline of vendor loyalty in the United States, some companies use technology to help them better ration- alize their supply chains. We talked to salespeople at SAS Institute who told us that customers buy their software to consolidate supply chains. One client found over 5,000 vendors providing products and services to its locations throughout North America. Using software, the client can combine same vendor purchases to gain discounts and other advantages with the seller. For instance, a mega-buyer can demand that a supplier develop new marketing programs every thirty days to keep its products fresh—and moving. In industrial sales, power still flows to the buyer. A sales VP at a major international technology firm described the downstream effect at his company of customers consolidating their supply lines. "There are fewer customers, but bigger customers," he said. "Sometimes this means windfall revenue when a client takes money from a smaller supplier and applies it to products and services of a preferred vendor. "However, this is a two-edged sword, for with the additional revenue comes additional responsibility."

## THE MARKET

In time, every product reaches the end of its life cycle and no longer maintains its product/market match. Sales is usually the first to discover this and bring back the bad news from the marketplace. Changes like this do not happen overnight, but build like avalanches from changes in competition, regulation, the economy or customer needs.

### Sales Is Only the Messenger

The sales department cannot change markets. It must take markets as it finds them, succeeding by adapting its tactics to the environment. If a company's product and tactics happen to be an effective match for the market, times will be good. You have probably witnessed success in some markets where a company had a good product but a marginal sales organization and still succeeded. Timing and random chance can turn average people into stars. The reverse is also true. Competent managers fail because of bad luck or being at the wrong company at the wrong time. There is also the explanation offered that success breeds failure. That is because we are unable to see changes that are incompatible with our past success patterns. A remarkable example of this occurred with the Digital Equipment Corporation (DEC). DEC's mini computers enjoyed phenomenal growth in the beginning in the 1960s and peaking in 1990. Its PDP and VAX computers opened computing to millions of companies that were too small for IBM's mainframes. DEC competed on overall cost and technology. Its sales force enjoyed a powerful product/market match so good that DEC paid its salespeople flat salaries.

Then PC technology changed the market. DEC's proprietary software and commitment to a proprietary Alpha chip skewed its product/market match. It had fine products, but its market declined. By the time this was clear, DEC missed the PC market altogether. Regrettably, its CEO said he could not foresee the need people could have for PCs in their homes and offices. However competent DEC's sales force, it had no power to change the market's direction. The sales force was just the canary in the mine reporting a Hindenburg Omen back to the CEO who would not see it.

DEC's old headquarters is just a few miles from me. Ken Olson, DEC's founder and longtime CEO, began the company's rise from a modest corner office on the ground floor of an old Civil War blanket mill directly on the main street. Olson remained there even when his original team of 117 people in 1957 grew to more than 120,000 in 1990. This humility and accessibility contributed to the unusual engineering culture. DEC was one of the early companies where employees could dress casually every day. People loved to work for him. When things began to change, I imagine there were some bonecrunching discussions in that office on Main Street. Perhaps DEC's VP of Sales was instructed, "You sales guys committed to the number. Make more calls and get more into the funnel." Would more pressure on the sales force have helped? What if they added commissions to the compensation plan? Is there anything DEC might have done to convince millions of businesses that PCs were a passing fad? A CSO can alter the field's tactics only for a brief time and only so far to forestall the inevitable product/market dissolution. DEC's failure was not unique. Markets have shifted for thousands of years. When bad news comes as a surprise and when there are no new products and services ready for a counterassault, no one wants to hear that the company's market is in decline.

Denial is the common reaction when sales delivers this message. It is unpleasant news for any CEO. Several CEOs told us why they do not trust sales to make market assessments. In the first place, sales is not an impartial observer. If sales claims the market is declining, these CEOs suspect the observation to be a self-serving excuse to back away from a revenue commitment. CEOs also say sales tends to use anecdotal evidence rather than well-researched business cases to present its claim. Third, the sales department does not coordinate its resources to present a unified position. Sales tends to complain one person at a time. CEOs hear concerns in dribs and drabs at the water cooler, in field visits, or in meetings. Often sales misses the big picture entirely because it does not present a well-researched, quantified case. The CEO may ask a rep why sales are down and get an opinion that sales would improve if only this attribute or that attribute were added to the product. Hint to CEOs: When reps talk about adding attributes, the product may be too long in the tooth to save. CEOs want a comprehensive business case and alternatives for something as serious as a market change. They prefer the hard research that the marketing department provides them. Of course, marketing's information may not be any more accurate than sales' anecdotes. However, perception is important. CEOs like numbers, and value is in the eye of the beholder. In the next example of a market change, senior management provided the field organization with the power of inquisition, torture, and even death to achieve revenue results.

# MOTIVATING THE TEAM

## INTRODUCTION

How you communicate with and support the sales team will affect the general working atmosphere and the desire to perform. We will now look at how you can further encourage a positive working environment to motivate the team. We will focus on how you can influence commitment and affect performance by:

- Understanding the needs and personalities of each individual
- Recognizing the factors that they respond to most positively
- Improving the tone of your communication
- Introducing different ways of rewarding progress and achievement.

While financial rewards play a key part in raising sales performance, we will look at how these areas can help to produce consistently high results and commitment.

## AN INDIVIDUAL'S GOALS

It is common for a sales manager to talk about 'the sales team'. It is the performance of the team that will determine your success; the team, of course, is a group of people with individual sales targets. Achieving and exceeding targets should create a positive feeling in each sales person. But you will also have to consider the different ambitions, desires and goals he/she wants to fulfill at work. These personal goals create expectations and if they are met, that person is more likely to perform well and remain enthusiastic about their role. A sales person's expectations should match those of your department and those of the company.

### Individual and company goals

There are two aspects to a sales person's development in a company:

- The achievement of sales targets (a financial goal).
- Personal fulfillment (a subjective set of goals).

Setting up personal development plans can be a positive motivational factor. It is important to encourage sales people to reveal their personal goals to you. These can then be monitored and acted upon alongside the company sales target. A sales manager can take an objective look at the company, team and individual goals by listing them and noting any marked differences.

Individual and company goals:

- Company goals:
  - To increase profit by 3% next year
  - To increase revenue by 9%
  - To bring at least two new products into the market
  - To reduce the time taken for new products to be built and to then get to market

- To prepare all company personnel for ten year business plan changes

- Sales manager's goals:
  - To gain at least 10% of new accounts
  - To ensure that all the sales team achieve 100% of their target
  - To help at least two team members win a large new account
  - To be the top sales team in the India
  - To spend more time with each individual account manager
- Examples of individual goals:
  - To meet 150% of annual company target
  - To develop bottom ten least profitable accounts
  - To be more thorough with internal company paperwork
  - To prepare for possible major account sales role
  - To spend more time preparing a sales call

You can then ensure that a sales person's goals match those of the company. Everyone in a sales team needs to be fully aware of the company's objectives and sales targets to enable you to:

- Build a team strategy that takes these into account
- Manage and monitor company, team and individuals' goals.

In order to maintain someone's level of motivation and enthusiasm you should ensure that they feel a goal is achievable. Also, every person's goals will differ in some way even if their overall sales objectives are the same. By making an effort to understand your sales people, achieving the targets and managing them becomes easier. You should treat your sales team as a group of individuals with different needs and different goals. This will help you understand their personal motivation. It will also:

- Help you become a better team leader
- Improve the quality of your communication
- Increase the team's confidence
- Encourage their desire to perform to the best of their ability.

In order to have a better understanding of what 'drives' sales people, we need to look at the theory of motivation.

## MOTIVATION THEORY AND PRACTICE

Motivation is a process that starts with a physiological or psychological need that activates a behavior or a drive that is aimed at a goal. Every employee is expected to show increased and qualitative productivity by the manager. To achieve this behavior of the employee is very important. The behavior of the employees is influenced by the environment in which they find themselves. Finally, an employee's behavior will be a function of that employee's innate drives or felt needs and the opportunities he or she has to satisfy those drives or needs in the workplace

**BEHAVIORS ON THE JOB DETERMINED BY:**

- NEEDS THE INDIVIDUAL BRINGS TO THE JOB
  UNIQUE TO EACH PERSON
- THE SITUATION "OUTSIDE THE PERSON"
- OPPORTUNITIES FOR SATISFYING NEEDS

If employees are never given opportunities to utilize all of their skills, then the employer may never have the benefit of their total performance. Work performance is also contingent upon employee abilities. If employees lack the learned skills or innate talents to do a particular job, then performance will be less than optimal. A third dimension of performance is motivation.

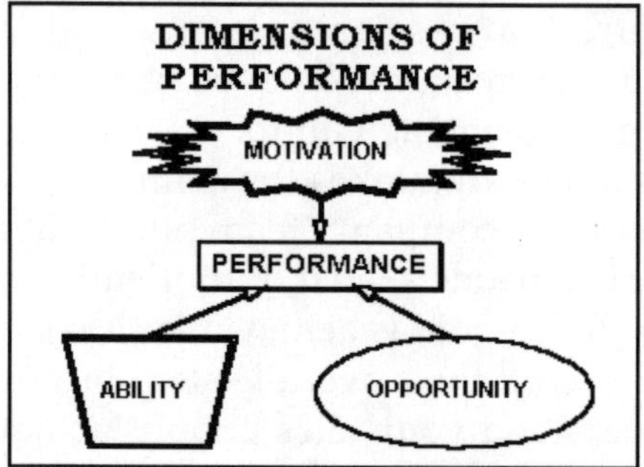


"Motivation is the act of stimulating someone or oneself to get desired course of action, to push right button to get desired reactions."

The following are the features of motivation:

- Motivation is an act of managers
- Motivation is a continuous process
- Motivation can be positive or negative
- Motivation is goal oriented
- Motivation is complex in nature
- Motivation is an art
- Motivation is system-oriented
- Motivation is different from job satisfaction

## MOTIVATIONAL FACTORS

There are several factors that motivate a person to work. The motivational factors can be broadly divided into two groups:

- MONETARY FACTORS:
  - Salaries or wages: Salaries or wages is one of the most important motivational factors. Reasonable salaries must be paid on time.

While fixing salaries the organization must consider such as :

(i) Cost of living

(ii) Company ability to pay

(iii) Capability of company to pay etc,

- Bonus: It refers to extra payment to employee over and above salary given as an incentive. The employees must be given adequate rate of bonus.
- Incentives: The organization may also provide additional incentives such as medical allowance, educational allowance, HRA, allowance, etc.
- Special individual incentives: The company may provide special individual incentives. Such incentives are to be given to deserving employees for giving valuable suggestions.

• NON MONETARY FACTORS :

- Status or job title: By providing a higher status or designations the employee must be motivated. Employees prefer and proud of higher designations.
- Appreciation and recognition: Employees must be appreciated for their services. The praise should not come from immediate superior but also from higher authorities.
- Delegation of authority: Delegation of authority motivates a subordinate to perform the tasks with dedication and commitment. When authority is delegated, the subordinate knows that his superior has placed faith and trust in him.
- Working conditions: Provision for better working conditions such as air-conditioned rooms, proper plant layout, proper sanitation, equipment, machines etc, motivates the employees.
- Job security: Guarantee of job security or lack of fear dismissal, etc can also be a good way to motivate the employees. Employees who are kept temporarily for a long time may be frustrated and may leave the organization.
- Job enrichment: Job enrichment involves more challenging tasks and responsibilities. For instance an executive who is involved in preparing and presenting reports of performance, may also asked to frame plans.
- Workers participation: Inviting the employee to be a member of quality circle, or a committee, or some other form of employee participation can also motivate the work-force.
- Cordial relations: Good and healthy relations must exist throughout the organization. This would definitely motivate the employees.
- Good superiors: Subordinates want their superiors to be intelligent, experienced, matured, and having a good

personality. In fact, the superior needs to have superior knowledge and skills than that of his subordinates. The very presence of superiors can motivate the subordinates.

- Other factors: There are several other factors of motivating the employees:
  (i) Providing training to the employees.
  (ii) Proper job placements.
  (iii) Proper promotions and transfers.
  (iv) Proper performance feed back.
  (v) Proper welfare facilities.
  (vi) Flexible working hours.

**Need and importance of motivation**

Motivation offers several importances to he organization and to the employees:

- Higher efficiency
- Reduce absenteeism.
- Reduces employee turn over.
- Improves a corporate image.
- Good relations.
- Improved morale.
- Reduced wastages and breakages.
- Reduced accidents.
- Facilitates initiative and innovation.

**Money as a motivator**

It is normally believed that money acts as a motivator. In general the role of money as a motivator depends upon certain factors:

- Money fails to motivate people, when there is no direct relationship between reward and effort.
- Economic conditions of people influence the Importance of money. For poor person, the value of certain amount of money is quite high as compared to rich.
- Money is a significant motivator at lower level of employee's level however money may not be a significant factor for senior executives who have already fulfilled their lower level needs.
- Employees are concerned not only with the amount of money paid to them, but it should be fair and equitable as paid to that of other employees of same level or status.
- Social attitudes towards money and wealth also decide the motivation to earn more and more.

**Motivational Theories**

Maslow's-Hierarchy of Needs Theory: This theory was proposed by Abraham Maslow and is based on the assumption that people are motivated by a series of five universal needs. These needs are ranked, according to the order in which they influence human behavior, in hierarchical fashion

- Physiological needs are deemed to be the lowest- level needs. These needs include the needs such as food & water.
  - So long as physiological needs are unsatisfied, they exist as a driving or motivating force in a person's life. A hungry person has a felt need. This felt need sets up both psychological and physical tensions that manifest themselves in overt behaviors directed at reducing those tensions (getting something to eat). Once the hunger is sated, the tension is reduced, and the need for food ceases to motivate. At this point (assuming that other physiological requirements are also satisfied) the next higher order need becomes the motivating need.
- Thus, safety needs -- the needs for shelter and security -- become the motivators of human behavior.
  - Safety needs include a desire for security, stability, dependency, protection, freedom from fear and anxiety, and a need for structure, order, and law... In the workplace this needs translates into a need for at least a minimal degree of employment security; the knowledge that we cannot be fired on a whim and that appropriate levels of effort and productivity will ensure continued employment.
- Social needs include the need for belongingness and love.
  - Generally, as gregarious creatures, human have a need to belong. In the workplace, this need may be satisfied by an ability to interact with one's coworkers and perhaps to be able to work collaboratively with these colleagues.
- After social needs have been satisfied, ego and esteem needs become the motivating needs.

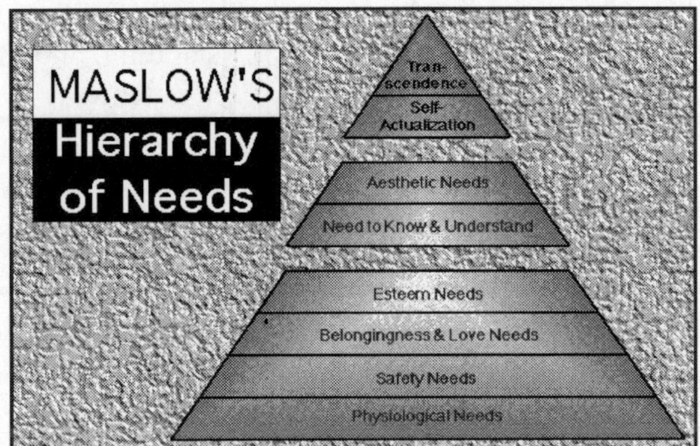


  - Esteem needs include the desire for self-respect, self-esteem, and the esteem of others. When focused externally, these needs also include the desire for reputation, prestige, status, fame, glory, dominance, recognition, attention, importance, and appreciation.

- The highest need in Maslow's hierarchy is that of self-actualization; the need for self-realization, continuous self-development, and the process of becoming all that a person is capable of becoming.

Aldermen's Hierarchy of Motivational Needs: Clayton Alerter reworked Maslow's Need Hierarchy to align it more closely with empirical research. Aldermen's theory is called the ERG theory -- Existence, Relatedness, and Growth.

- Existence refers to our concern with basic material existence requirements; what Maslow called physiological and safety needs.
- Relatedness refers to the desire we have for maintaining interpersonal relationships; similar to Maslow's social/love need, and the external component of his esteem need.
- Growth refers to an intrinsic desire for personal development; the intrinsic component of Maslow's esteem need, and self-actualization

**Alderfer's Hierarchy of Motivational Needs**

| Level of Need | Definition | Properties |
|---|---|---|
| Growth | Impel a person to make creative or productive effects on himself and his environment | Satisfied through using capabilities in engaging problems: creates a greater sense of wholeness and fullness as a human being |
| Relatedness | Involve relationships with significant others | Satisfied by mutually sharing thoughts and feelings: acceptance. confirmation. under-standing. and influence are elements |
| Existence | Includes all of the various forms of material and psychological desires | When divided among people one person's gain is another's loss if resources are limited |

Aldermen's ERG theory differs from Maslow's Need Hierarchy insofar as ERG theory demonstrates that more than one need may be operative at the same time. ERG theory does not assume a rigid hierarchy where a lower need must be substantially satisfied before one can move on. Alerter also deals with frustration-regression. That is, if a higher-order need is frustrated, an individual then seeks to increase the satisfaction of a lower-order need. According to Maslow an individual would stay at a certain need level until that need was satisfied. ERG theory counters by noting that when a higher-order need level is frustrated the individual's desire to increase a lower- level need takes place.

**A Reorganization of Maslow's and Alderfer's Hierarchies**

| Level | Introversion | Extroversion |
|---|---|---|
| Growth | Self-Actualization (development of competencies [knowledge, attitudes, and skills] and character) | Transcendence (assisting in the development of others' competencies and character: relationships to the unknown, unknowable) |
| Other (Relatedness) | Personal identification with group, significant others (Belongingness) | Value of person by group (Esteem) |
| Self (Existence) | Physiological, biological (including basic emotional needs) | Connectedness, security |

Inability to satisfy a need for social interaction, for instance, might increase the desire for more money or better working conditions. So frustration can lead to a regression to a lower need. In summary, ERG theory argues, like Maslow, that satisfied lower- order needs lead to the desire to satisfy higher-order needs; but multiple needs can be operating as motivators at the same time, and frustration in attempting to satisfy a higher- level need can result in regression to a lower- level need. Table. Alderfer's Hierarchy of Motivational Needs Level of Need Definition Properties Growth Impel a person to make creative or productive effects on himself and his environment Satisfied through using capabilities in engaging problems; creates a greater sense of wholeness and fullness as a human being Relatedness Involve relationships with significant others Satisfied by mutually sharing thoughts and feelings; acceptance, confirmation, under- standing, and influence are elements Existence Includes all of the various forms of material and psychological desires When divided among people one person's gain is another's loss if resources are limited

A Reorganization of Maslow's and Alderfer's Hierarchies Level Introversion Extroversion Growth Self-Actualization (development of competencies [knowledge, attitudes, and skills] and character) Transcendence (assisting in the development of others' competencies and character; relationships to the unknown, unknowable) Other (Relatedness) Personal identification with group, significant others (Belongingness) Value of person by group (Esteem) Self (Existence) Physiological, biological (including basic emotional needs) Connectedness, security

**Two-factor Theory**

Herzberg's Two Factor Theory, also known as the Motivation-Hygiene Theory, was derived from a study designed to test the concept that people have two sets of needs:

- Their needs as animals to avoid pain
- Their needs as humans to grow psychologically

Herzberg's study consisted of a series of interviews that sought to elicit responses to the questions:

- Recall a time when you felt exceptionally good about your job. Why did you feel that way about the job? Did this feeling affect your job performance in any way? Did this feeling have an impact on your personal relationships or your well- being?
- Recall a time on the job that resulted in negative feelings? Describe the sequence of events that resulted in these negative feelings.

***Research Resultlts***

It appeared from the research, that the things making people happy on the job and those making them unhappy had two separate themes.

**SATISFACTION (MOTIVATION)**

Five factors stood out as strong determiners of job satisfaction:

- Achievement
- Recognition
- Work itself
- Responsibility
- Advancement

The last three factors were found to be most important for bringing about lasting changes of attitude. It should be noted, that recognition refers to recognition for achievement as opposed to recognition in the human relations sense.

**DISSATISFACTION (HYGIENE)**

The determinants of job dissatisfaction were found to be:

- Company policy
- Administrative policies

- Supervision
- Salary
- Interpersonal relations
- Working conditions

From the results Herzberg concluded that the replies people gave when they felt good about their jobs were significantly different from the replies given when they felt bad. Certain characteristics tend to be consistently related to job satisfaction and others to job dissatisfaction. Intrinsic factors, such as work itself, responsibility and achievement seem to be related to job satisfaction. Respondents who felt good about their work tended to attribute these factors to themselves. On the other dissatisfied respondents tended to cite extrinsic factors such as supervision, pay, and company policies and working condition. Herzberg proposed that his findings indicated the existence of a dual continuum: the opposite of "satisfaction" is "No satisfaction" and the opposite of "Dissatisfaction" is "No Dissatisfaction. According to Herzberg, the factors leading to Job satisfaction are separate and distinct form those that lead to job dissatisfaction. Therefore, managers who seek to eliminate factors that can create job dissatisfaction may bring about peace but not necessarily motivation. They will be placating their workforce rather than motivating them.

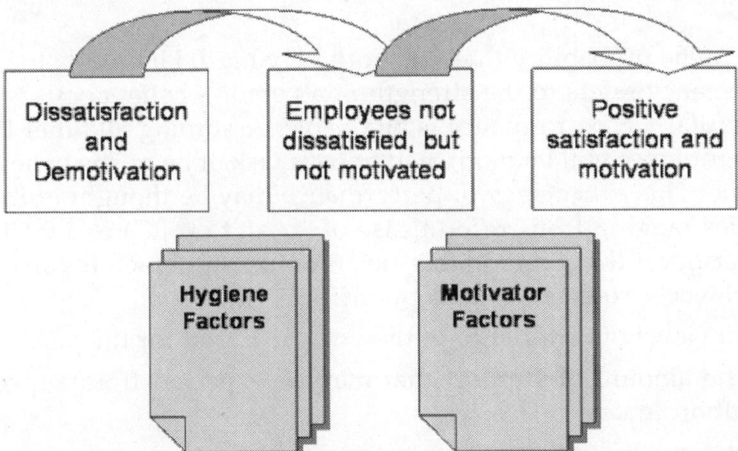


As a result, conditions surrounding the job such as quality of supervision, pay, company policies, physical working conditions relations with others and job security were characterized by Herzberg as hygiene factors, when they're adequate, people will not be dissatisfied; neither will they be satisfied. If we want to motivate people on their jobs, Herzberg suggested emphasizing factors associated with the work itself or to outcomes directly derived form it, such as promotional opportunities, opportunities for personal growth, recognition, responsibility and achievement. These are the characteristics that people find intrinsically rewarding.

**Expectancy Theory**

In recent years, probably the most popular motivational theory has been the Expectancy Theory (also known as the Valence-Instrumentality-Expectancy Theory). Although there are a number of theories found with this general title, they all have their roots in Victor Vroom's 1964 work on motivation.

***Alternatives and Choices***

Vroom's theory assumes that behavior results from conscious choices among alternatives whose purpose it is to maximize pleasure and minimize pain. The key elements to this theory are referred to as:

- Expectancy (E),
- Instrumentality (I), and
- Valence (V).

Critical to the understanding of the theory is the understanding that each of these factors represents a belief. Vroom's theory suggests that the individual will consider the outcomes associated with various levels of performance (from an entire spectrum of performance possibilities), and elect to pursue the level that generates the greatest reward for him or her.

*Expectancy*

"What's the probability that, if I work very hard, I'll be able to do a good job?" Expectancy refers to the strength of a person's belief about whether or not a particular job performance is attainable. Assuming all other things are equal, an employee will be motivated to try a task, if he or she believes that it can be done. This expectancy of performance may be thought of in terms of probabilities ranging from zero (a case of "I can't do it!") to 1.0 ("I have no doubt whatsoever that I can do this job!") A number of factors can contribute to an employee's expectancy perceptions:

- The level of confidence in the skills required for the task
- The amount of support that may be expected from superiors and subordinates
- The quality of the materials and equipment
- The availability of pertinent information

Previous success at the task has also been shown to strengthen expectancy beliefs.

*Instrumentality*

"What's the probability that, if I do a good job, that there will be some kind of outcome in it for me?"

If an employee believes that a high level of performance will be instrumental for the acquisition of outcomes which may be gratifying, then the employee will place a high value on performing well. Vroom defines Instrumentality as a probability belief linking one outcome (a high level of performance, for example) to another outcome (a reward). Instrumentality may range from a probability of 1.0 (meaning that the attainment of the second outcome -- the reward -- is certain if the first outcome -- excellent job performance -- is attained) through zero (meaning there is no likely relationship between the first outcome and the second). An example of zero instrumentality would be exam grades that were distributed randomly (as opposed to be awarded on the basis of excellent exam performance). Commission pay schemes are designed to make employees perceive that performance is positively instrumental for the acquisition of money. For management to ensure high levels of performance, it must tie desired outcomes (positive valence) to high performance, and ensure that the connection is communicated to employees. The VIE theory holds that people have preferences among various outcomes. These preferences tend to reflect a person's underlying need state.

*Valence*

The term Valence refers to the emotional orientations people hold with respect to outcomes (rewards). An outcome is positively valeted if an employee would prefer having it to not having it. An outcome that the employee would rather avoid (fatigue, stress, noise, layoffs) is negatively valeted. Outcomes towards which the employee appears indifferent are said to have zero valence. Valences refer to the level of satisfaction people expect to get from the outcome (as opposed to the actual satisfaction they get once they have attained the reward). Vroom suggests that an employee's beliefs about Expectancy, Instrumentality, and Valence interact psychologically to create a motivational force such that the employee acts in ways that bring pleasure and avoid pain. People elect to pursue levels of job performance that they believe will maximize their overall best interests (their subjective expected utility). ` There will be no motivational forces acting on an employee if any of these three conditions hold:

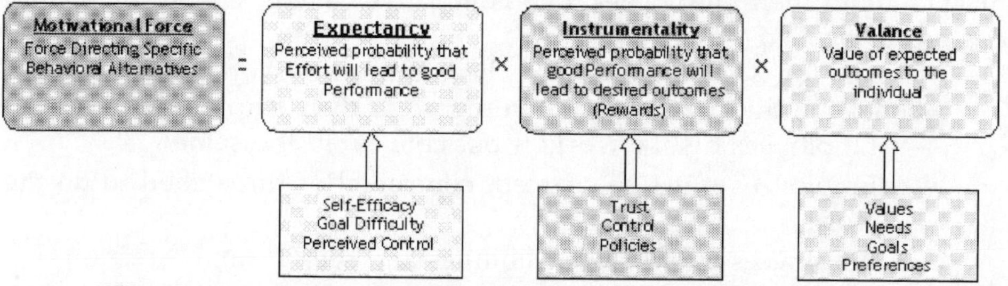


- The person does not believe that he/she can successfully perform the required task

- The person believes that successful task performance will not be associated with positively valet outcomes
- The person believes that outcomes associated with successful task completion will be negatively valet (have no value for that person)

**McClelland's Theory of Needs**

According to David McClelland, regardless of culture or gender, people are driven by three motives:

- Achievement,
- Affiliation, and
- Influence.

Since McClelland's first experiments, over 1,000 studies relevant to achievement motivation have been conducted. These studies strongly support the theory.

- *Achievement:* The need for achievement is characterized by the wish to take responsibility for finding solutions to problems, master complex tasks, set goals, and get feedback on level of success.
- Affiliation: The need for affiliation is characterized by a desire to belong, an enjoyment of teamwork, a concern about interpersonal relationships, and a need to reduce uncertainty.
- *Power:*The need for power is characterized by a drive to control and influence others, a need to win arguments, a need to persuade and prevail

According to McClelland, the presence of these motives or drives in an individual indicates a predisposition to behave in certain ways. Therefore, from a manager's perspective, recognizing which need is dominant in any particular individual affects the way in which that person can be motivated. Summary: People with achievement motives are motivated by standards of excellence, delineated roles and responsibilities and concrete, timely feedback. Those with affiliation motives are motivated when they can accomplish things with people they know and trust. And the power motive is activated when people are allowed to have an impact, impress those in power, or beat competitors.

**Theory of "X" and Theory of "Y"**

Douglas McGregor observed two diametrically opposing view points of managers about their employees, one is negative called "Theory of X" and one is positive called "Theory of Y"

- Theory of X: Following are the assumptions of managers who believe in the "Theory of X" in regard to their employees.
  - Employees dislike work; if possible avoid the same
  - Employees must be coerced, controlled or threatened to do the work
  - Employees avoid responsibilities and seek formal direction
  - Most employees consider security of job, most important of all other factors in the job and have very little ambition

- Theory of Y: Following are the assumptions of managers who believe in the "Theory of Y" in regard to their employees.
  - Employees love work as play or rest
  - Employees are self directed and self controlled and committed to the organizational objectives
  - Employees accept and seek responsibilities
  - Innovative spirit is not confined to managers alone, some employees also possess it.

Theory of X assumes Maslow's lower level needs dominate in employees. Whereas Theory of Y, assumes Maslow's higher level needs dominate in employees.

**Goal Setting Theory**

Edwin Locke proposed that setting specific goals will improve motivation. Salient features of this theory are the following:

- Specific goal fixes the needs of resources and efforts
- It increases performance
- Difficult goals result higher performance than easy job
- Better feedback of results leads to better to better performance than lack of feed back.
- Participation of employees in goal has mixed result
- Participation of setting goal, however, increases acceptance of goal and involvements.
- Goal setting theory has identified two factors which influences the performance. These are given below;
  - Goal commitment
  - Self efficiency
- Goal commitment: Goal setting theory presupposes that the individual is committed to the goal. This commitment depends on the following:
  - Goals are made public
  - Individual has an internal locus of control
  - Goals are self-set
- Self –Efficiency: Self Efficiency is the belief or self confidence, that he/she is capable of performing task. Persons with high self-efficiency put up extra-efforts when they face challenges. In the case of low self-efficiency level they will lessen or even abandon when meeting challenges.

**Reinforcement Theory**

This theory focuses its attention as to what controls behaviour. In contrast to goal setting theory, which is cognitive approach focus attention on what initiates behaviour? Behaviour, as per cognitive approach is initiated by internal events. Reinforcement theory argues that behaviour is reinforced and controlled by external events. The classical conditioning proposed by Pavlov which we have already studied in our earlier lessons explains this in a better way.

### Equity theory

This theory of motivation centers around the principle of balance or equity. According to this theory level of motivation in an individual is related to his or her perception of equity and farness practiced by management. Greater the fairness perceived higher the motivation and vice versa. In this assessment of fairness, employee makes comparison of input in the job (in terms of contribution) with that of outcome (in terms of compensation) and compares the same with that of another colleague of equivalent cadre.

## INFLUENCING BEHAVIOUR AND ATTITUDES

In chapter six we stated that understanding your sales people's attitude is a key element in influencing their response to different people. While you can make conscious efforts to match behavioural styles with others, the tone of your communication will affect how successful this is. In this section we will look at how we can influence other people's behaviour through the tone of our communication. People notice what attitude we have through the patterns of communication we adopt. All communication generates thoughts and feelings in others. In this section we will look at two ways of encouraging the responses we desire. These are:

- Questioning our own understanding about people at work.
- Understanding the different patterns of communication we can adopt and the effect they have.

### Understanding your sales team

We have mentioned the importance of understanding your sales people. In order to do this effectively you might want to look at a number of areas where they need to show improvement. These might include:

- Willingness to take responsibility
- Showing initiative
- Being committed
- Having a positive attitude
- Being 'solution' based in their approach
- Being customer focused
- Getting on well with colleagues.

A sales manager will need to be realistic about someone's true attitude and level of motivation. To do this you might want to look at your own beliefs and behaviour towards the team. This can affect the way they respond. For example:

- Have positive expectations of people
- Try to be consistent
- Ensure that your intentions are properly understood
- Remain flexible/adaptable.

Monitoring your own behaviour can also help you understand why you react the way you do to certain situations. This will help you manage them better in the future.

**Communication patterns**

Your level of motivation will be affected by your attitude. Your attitude is a reflection of what you are thinking and feeling at any given moment. What you are focused on and how you feel, will produce a pattern of communication. This, in turn, will influence how you say something. Your attitude and tone of communication can be a strong motivational factor in someone deciding whether to listen to what you say. By taking the time to consider:

- What a person will think
- How they might feel (in response to your communication)
- What you say and how it is interpreted by someone.

You will:

- Think more carefully about what you say
- Improve your chances of being properly understood.

You can do this by understanding the five common patterns that people adopt when communicating:

- Pattern 1: Being spontaneous, imaginative and lighthearted.
- Pattern 2: Showing concern and understanding.
- Pattern 3: Being rational, logical and calm. Inquiring about/seeking information.
- Pattern 4: Being resistant, calculating, or tactical.
- Pattern 5: Using forceful opinions and judgements.

All of these patterns have their place in communicating with people. While we can be flexible in the patterns we adopt, we will often use one of these patterns more than another. This can tend to be a 'learned' pattern of communication that is more impulsive than controlled. This will depend on the type of person we are and the situation we face. The challenge is to be able to assess a situation and adopt an appropriate pattern. This can be applied to the sales people you manage. You can monitor which pattern they use when communicating with people (externally) and colleagues (internally).You can then work on two fronts:

- Remain flexible so that you can find appropriate responses to situations and alter a pattern that is not working.
- Coach your sales people to raise their awareness of the patterns they adopt in selling situations.

You can then use different patterns to communicate with and influence people in different ways.

**Flexible communication**

Different levels of motivation determine which of these patterns we adopt in our communication. This will be different for each individual. It will also depend on the situation. As a manager of sales people, you should consider your preferred patterns and consider the effect of your communication on others. Your ability to be flexible in your patterns will determine the impact you have on others and how they respond to you. A common example of different patterns we adopt can be seen, for example, when a manager approaches a sales person regarding a poor monthly performance:

- Sales manager's communication: The sales manager points out the poor results and states that the sales person must address the situation– now!
- Sales person's response: The sales person becomes defensive, referring to lack of support and shows little sign of responding positively to this approach.

The sales person's 'resistant' response (pattern 4) indicates they do not value or appreciate this communication. The sales manager now has a choice – to stay in pattern 5 or to alter his/her approach to another pattern. Examples of other patterns the manager might now adopt are given below:

- Pattern 1: The manager refers to the results in an amusing and friendly manner. The sales person is reminded of their excellent recent results, which may have led them to become over confident this month.
- Pattern 2: The manager refers to current results in a concerned manner. The sales person is encouraged to discuss any problems.
- Pattern 3: The manager refers to the result in a matter-of-fact tone and asks for the sales person's view and explanation of the current situation. Further questions are asked to determine whether the sales person is taking the necessary steps to reverse the position.
- Pattern 4: The manager points out that inconsistency will not earn the sales person a high sales ranking and that their rivals in the team will lead by year-end.

Your goal is not necessarily to match someone else's pattern, but rather to select an appropriate pattern in response. The diagram opposite develops the above example. The sales manager has communicated forcefully and receives a resistant response. The manager now decides to take a more flexible line, selecting pattern 2.The sales person responds in pattern 3, allowing a more rational discussion to take place.

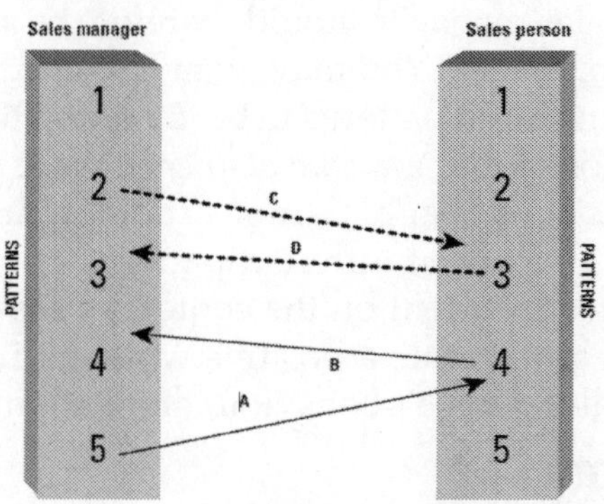


*Figure 18: Sales patterns*

Your communication to someone (in one pattern) will lead to a reaction in one of the five same patterns. No pattern or approach is necessarily wrong. How appropriate your communication is, will depend on:

- The circumstances
- The response you get.

Pattern 3 represents a rational approach to communication. Therefore, we can use it to be more objective about our delivery of the other patterns. You cannot guarantee the outcome of any communication with someone; however your effectiveness will rely on:

- Focusing on the outcome you want
- Recognizing when you receive a poor reaction (a sign that you may need to change your current communication pattern or challenge someone else's).

When we communicate, our body language, tone of voice and words combine to represent our current pattern. How we use these three elements, will influence the patterns and responses we receive from others. Remember, each pattern can be spoken and received in a positive or negative way. This applies to:

- The content
- The delivery.

The way we communicate will be dependent upon a number of factors:

- The context/urgency of the situation
- Our mood (attitude) and that of the person/people we are talking to
- The subject being discussed
- A person's desired outcome
- The relationship of the people involved.

When you are considering your own pattern of communication with people, consider what outcome you desire. This can provoke choices in our communication we may not have considered. (A lighthearted remark can make someone feel more relaxed in one context and receive a very negative reaction in another.) A sales manager should therefore be aware of the different types of people he/she manages. You may want to consider what you believe their individual communication patterns to be. By doing this you will improve your own communication skills. You can also encourage your sales people to do the same. Our beliefs about people's motivation can influence the way we behave with them. We also adopt different patterns of communication with different people. This is dependent on the context of the situation. A flexible approach to this will help to create a positive work environment. It will also help us to understand sales people's behaviour and current level of motivation.

## MOTIVATION AND REWARD

Motivation is a behavior that you can influence but not create. Even highly motivated individuals can get frustrated, discouraged, or tired on a project. Team members need to know they are valued, their efforts are noticed, and their good work is appreciated. Remember that each employee is different and motivated or rewarded by different things. The key is to be timely, creative, and authentic and that the motivation or reward matches the interests and goals of the employee, whenever possible.

### Creating Productive Work Environments

Today's workforce wants more than money – the traditional currency. Workers are looking for a "new currency" that can be found in the 5 Rest: Responsibility, Relationships, Respect, Recognition, Rewards. Managers have many options for implementing the 5 Rest in the workplace, and using them for planning, managing and evaluating performance.

#### *Responsibility*

Typical job descriptions look like extensive to-do lists ending with a catchall phrase such as "...other duties as assigned." The underlying message can be seen as "Do whatever I tell you." Today's workforce is much more interested in flexibility to add value in creating desired outcomes. Employees want to feel that what they do is important. What can managers do? Make sure jobs are properly profiled for employees and describe outcomes that are relevant to the unit's work. Eliminate tasks and activities that are unessential to your primary mission and talk to employees regularly about ways to increase alignment between what they do and where the unit is headed.

#### *Relationships*

Motivation is an inside job – something in each individual that is unleashed under the right circumstances. Effective managers can create these circumstances by building relationships and creating supportive environments. Coaching, teaching, supporting and guiding all are strategies for producing the right outcomes. Above all, managers need to be authentic, honest and ethical. Building trust is essential to helping employees are motivated to take risks and perform to their highest levels.

***Respect***

In a respectful environment, employees are valued and respected for the intellectual capital they contribute. Performance management and review systems are aimed at building confidence and competence. Feelings, ideas and actions are valued and attended to. As a supervisor, you may be part of a larger organization that has its "major league" rules, but how you manage your team is largely up to you. After all, you are the coach. Your expectations will shape the environment. Build on the concept of teamwork – respecting differences, solving problems collaboratively, and supporting one another. Avoid negative energy, such as gossiping or harassing. If the larger environment isn't supportive, engage employees in developing operating principles or defining a vision that expresses how everyone will work with one another, how customers are to be served, and how communications are to flow.

***Recognition***

For many employees, recognition is not so much about getting credit as it is about being appreciated. Focus on creating intrinsic rewards (genuine opportunities to contribute, become more knowledgeable and develop professionally) in addition to extrinsic rewards (prizes, incentive contest). Special assignments can be an effective form of recognition, but it can't just be more work. Offer more challenging work or work that utilizes the employee's strengths. It's essential to make sure the assignment is something the employee welcomes. If employees feel taken advantage of, special assignments will generate resentment and frustration rather than positive motivation.

***Rewards***

To provide optimum return on investment, rewards must be an integral part of an overall recognition and reward strategy linking business goals and objectives with the other 4 Rest. Effective rewards need to be linked to the individual's goals and preferences. "One size fits all" doesn't work for rewards.

**20 Ways to Motivate Employees**

- Use appropriate methods of reinforcement.
- Eliminate unnecessary threats and punishments.
- Adequately recognize accomplishments.
- Allow employees both flexibility and choice.

- Increase employee responsibility through delegation.
- Institute a program of goal setting.
- Clarify your expectations making sure that employees understand them.
- Design tasks and environments to be consistent with employee needs.
- Individualize your supervision.
- Provide immediate and relevant feedback that will help improve employee performance.
- Show that you have confidence in your employees.
- Show interest in each individual under your supervision.
- Allow individuals to participate in making decisions that affect them.
- Establish a climate of trust and open communication.
- Minimize the use of formal regulations and rules.
- Listen to and deal effectively with employee complaints.
- Point out improvements in performance, no matter how small.
- Criticize behavior, not people.
- Encourage employees to engage in novel and challenging activities.
- A certain level of stress is basic to motivation, so don't eliminate it completely.

**Core Elements of Employee Motivation**

The following questions "measure the core elements needed to attract, focus, and keep the most talented employees".

- Do I know what is expected of me at work?
- Do I have the materials and equipment I need to do my work right?
- At work, do I have the opportunity to do what I do best every day?
- In the last seven days, have I received recognition or praise for good work?
- Does my supervisor, or someone at work, seem to care about me as a person?
- Is there someone at work who encourages my development?
- At work, do my opinions seem to count?
- Does the mission/purpose of my company make me feel like my work is important?
- Are my co-workers committed to doing quality work?
- Do I have a best friend at work?
- In the last six months, have I talked with someone about my progress?
- At work, have I had opportunities to learn and grow?

**Rewarding Employees**

Rewarding your employees doesn't have to be costly. There are many things that supervisors can do to let staff members know that their efforts are noticed and their good work is appreciated. The key is to be timely, creative, and authentic. Remember that each employee is different. Match the reward to the interests and goals of the employee whenever possible. Make sure you know your employees well enough to be sure the reward will be appreciated. Here are some low cost suggestions:

- Take time to personally thank employees for doing a good job. Do it regularly, specifically and sincerely.
- Vary your approach when thanking employees. Some efforts merit formal letters of recognition with a copy to the employee's file. For others, a timely and specific e-mail message can be effective. A few sincere words of thanks delivered in person are almost always appreciated.
- Low-key recognition activities can be very effective. Take a few minutes during a staff meeting to recognize a successful project and present the participants with an appropriate token such as a certificate, a "congratulations" cake, or their favorite candy bar. Or bring in ice cream treats for everyone at the end of a particularly stressful week.
- When someone has been successful, offer them a chance to teach others what they did. This will allow the unit to learn from the successful experience, and will acknowledge the person's unique contribution to the work.
- Keep a supply of treats to be delivered with a short note. For example, a roll of Lifesavers saying "You were a lifesaver today" or a can of Orange Crush soda with a note saying "Thanks for helping out in the crush."
- Create a traveling trophy to be passed among team members whenever someone successfully completes a difficult task.

**Financial reward**

A sales person needs to be highly motivated to achieve a company's sales targets. The prospect of exceeding their target should make them feel very positive. However, this will depend on whether they believe they are receiving adequate reward for their effort and that their targets are clearly achievable. The S.M.A.R.T. acronym below provides a sales manager with a method of setting targets in a manner which will raise each person's commitment. Are they:

- S = Specific: Targets need to be clearly defined and easy to understand.

- M = Measurable: A formula for commission and bonuses needs to be easily measured. Individual results should be available to create a competitive element within the sales team.
- A = Agreed: Agreement should be reached with sales people on their individual target. This will help each person 'accept ownership' of the sales target.
- R = Realistic: Targets, commission and bonus levels should be achievable and realistic. The reward given is then a strong motivational factor for correct focus and effort.
- T = Timed: Create specific time periods for targets to be met. These should be communicated and adhered to.

**Incentives**

Incentives are an excellent way to focus a sales person's effort. They should be seen as an additional alternative to a sales person's financial remuneration. They are not a substitute for a good commission/ bonus structure. They are a means of creating a specific focus on products and services to increase sales revenue. The time period can extend from short monthly activity periods to an annual one. The type of incentive will depend on the investment you/the company decides to make. It will also depend on:

- The extra revenue you anticipate (during the campaign)
- The reasons for the incentive
- The amount you have budgeted for
- The product/service you are promoting
- The amount of time you want sales people to focus on it.

Incentives are a good way to focus attention providing they are fair, monitored correctly and achieve the result that was intended.

**Non-monetary rewards**

Most sales people are driven by opportunities to maximize their income. But they also respond positively to other forms of recognition. This can come in many forms:

- Acknowledgement from you and your senior management
- Special award ceremonies during conferences
- Using particular titles or accolades (such as 'winners' and 'trophies').

Other alternatives are to give different titles to those with particular sales responsibilities. You can also do this with people who have:

- Achieved a high level of results
- Consistently exceeded their level of performance
- The potential to become future sales managers.

A sales person's behaviour will often become more positive and focused when they are given a role with more responsibility. People respond well when they feel appreciated and when they see a way of developing themselves. In one organization, the desire to move from 'inside sales' (internal telephone support) to 'outside sales' (face to face selling) provides a steady stream of potential candidates. A sales manager can maintain a high level of motivation in the sales and support team by being aware of these factors and monitoring people's level of desire.

**Education, training and personal development**

The provision of training courses reflects the value you place on your team or an individual. Good training should be seen as an investment not a cost. By investing in your people and providing opportunities for their development you are demonstrating their value to your company. To achieve this you will need to determine what their specific needs are. You will also need to identify what relevant programmers are available. By taking the time to do this, you can increase the level of motivation in your sales people. Not only will you improve their skills but you will give someone more chance of improving the quality of their work. A manager can also select different educational opportunities that will help team members have a better understanding of their role. This will also contribute to a good team atmosphere. Many people learn more about the importance of trust and co-operation from an 'outward bound' exercise than they might do in the 'classroom'. Regular team meetings and 'corporate entertainment' days can help team members 'bond' with each other. It can also boost each sales person's morale. Time invested in preparing different methods of reward can produce high motivation and greater commitment from your sales team. Consider combining financial and other types of reward. In this way you will be maintaining focus on the sales target while meeting a person's personal goals and development needs.

## CONCLUSION

In this chapter we have looked at 'Motivating the team'. This included:

- An individual's goals
- Motivation theory and practice
- Influencing behaviour and attitudes
- Motivation and reward.

A sales manager's goal is to create an environment in which people motivate themselves. This will depend on the way you communicate with the sales team and whether your sales people are satisfied with their job role. Sales people need to feel that they are understood and appreciated. This forms the basis of them maintaining a high level of motivation.

# PROFESSIONAL COMMUNICATION AND TEAM COLLABORATION

## BACKGROUND

In today's health care system, delivery processes involve numerous interfaces and patient handoffs among multiple health care practitioners with varying levels of educational and occupational training. During the course of a 4-day hospital stay, a patient may interact with 50 different employees, including physicians, nurses, technicians, and others. Effective clinical practice thus involves many instances where critical information must be accurately communicated. Team collaboration is essential. When health care professionals are not communicating effectively, patient safety is at risk for several reasons: lack of critical information, misinterpretation of information, unclear orders over the telephone, and overlooked changes in status. Lack of communication creates situations where medical errors can occur. These errors have the potential to cause severe injury or unexpected patient death. Medical errors, especially those caused by a failure to communicate, are a pervasive problem in today's health care organizations. According to the Joint Commission, if medical errors appeared on the National Center for Health Statistic's list of the top 10 causes of death in the United States, they would rank number 5—ahead of accidents, diabetes, and Alzheimer's disease, as well as AIDS, breast cancer, and gunshot wounds.

The 1999 Institute of Medicine report, To Err Is Human: Building a Safer Health System, revealed that between 44,000 and 98,000 people die every year in U.S. hospitals because of medical errors. Even more disturbing, communication failures are the leading root cause of the sentinel events reported to the Joint Commission from 1995 to 2004. More specifically, the Joint Commission cites communication failures as the leading root cause for medication errors, delays in treatment, and wrong-site surgeries, as well as the second most frequently cited root cause for operative and postoperative events and fatal falls. Traditional medical education emphasizes the importance of error-free practice, utilizing intense peer pressure to achieve perfection during both diagnosis and treatment. Errors are therefore perceived normatively as an expression of failure. This atmosphere creates an environment that precludes the fair, open discussion of mistakes required if organizational learning is to take place. In the early 1990s, Donald Berwick wrote about patients needing an open communication system instead of experiencing adverse events stemming from communication failures. More than a decade later, this concept still has profound implications on our method of health care delivery. As such, this chapter will review the literature on the important role of communication and team collaboration in helping to reduce medical errors and increase patient safety.

## RESEARCH EVIDENCE

### What Are Communication and Team Collaboration

Webster's Dictionary defines communication as "the imparting or interchange of thoughts, opinions, or information by speech, writing, or signs." It is important to consider that communication is not just verbal in form. One study states that 93 percent of communication is more affected by body language, attitude, and tone, leaving only 7 percent of the meaning and intent based on the actual words said. Whereas the spoken words contain the crucial content, their meaning can be influenced by the style of delivery, which includes the way speakers stand, speak, and look at a person. However, critical information is often transmitted via handwritten notes, e-mails, or text messages, which can lead to serious consequences if there is miscommunication.

Collaboration in health care is defined as health care professionals assuming complementary roles and cooperatively working together, sharing responsibility for problem-solving and making decisions to formulate and carry out plans for patient care. Collaboration between physicians, nurses, and other health care professionals increases team members' awareness of each others' type of knowledge and skills, leading to continued improvement in decisionmaking. Effective teams are characterized by trust, respect, and collaboration. Deming is one of the greatest proponents of teamwork. Teamwork, he believes, is endemic to a system in which all employees are working for the good of a goal, who have a common aim, and who work together to achieve that aim.When considering a teamwork model in health care, an interdisciplinary approach should be applied. Unlike a multidisciplinary approach, in which each team member is responsible only for the activities related to his or her own discipline and formulates separate goals for the patient, an interdisciplinary approach coalesces a joint effort on behalf of the patient with a common goal from all disciplines involved in the care plan.

The pooling of specialized services leads to integrated interventions. The plan of care takes into account the multiple assessments and treatment regimens, and it packages these services to create an individualized care program that best addresses the needs of the patient. The patient finds that communication is easier with the cohesive team, rather than with numerous professionals who do not know what others are doing to mange the patient. It is important to point out that fostering a team collaboration environment may have hurdles to overcome: additional time; perceived loss of autonomy; lack of confidence or trust in decisions of others; clashing perceptions; territorialism; and lack of awareness of one provider of the education, knowledge, and skills held by colleagues from other disciplines and professions. However, most of these hurdles can be overcome with an open attitude and feelings of mutual respect and trust. A study determined that improved teamwork and communication are described by health care workers as among the most important factors in improving clinical effectiveness and job satisfaction.

Components of Successful Teamwork:

- Open communication
- Nonpunitive environment

- Clear direction
- Clear and known roles and tasks for team members
- Respectful atmosphere
- Shared responsibility for team success
- Appropriate balance of member participation for the task at hand
- Acknowledgment and processing of conflict
- Clear specifications regarding authority and accountability
- Clear and known decisionmaking procedures
- Regular and routine communication and information sharing
- Enabling environment, including access to needed resources
- Mechanism to evaluate outcomes and adjust accordingly

Extensive review of the literature shows that communication, collaboration, and teamwork do not always occur in clinical settings. For example, a study by Sutcliff, Lewton, and Rosenthal reveals that social, relational, and organizational structures contribute to communication failures that have been implicated as a large contributor to adverse clinical events and outcomes. Another study shows that the priorities of patient care differed between members of the health care team, and that verbal communication between team members was inconsistent. Other evidence shows that more than one-fifth of patients hospitalized in the United States reported hospital system problems, including staff providing conflicting information and staff not knowing which physician is in charge of their care. Over the past several years, we have been conducting original research on the impact of physician and nurse disruptive behaviors and its effect on staff relationships, staff satisfaction and turnover, and patient outcomes of care, including adverse events, medical errors, compromises in patient safety, poor quality care, and links to preventable patient mortality. Many of these unwanted effects can be traced back to poor communication and collaboration, and ineffective teamwork. Unfortunately, many health care workers are used to poor communication and teamwork, as a result of a culture of low expectations that has developed in many health care settings. This culture, in which health care workers have come to expect faulty and incomplete exchange of information, leads to errors because even conscientious professionals tend to ignore potential red flags and clinical discrepancies. They view these warning signals as indicators of routine repetitions of poor communication rather than unusual, worrisome indicators. Although poor communication can lead to tragic consequences, a review of the literature also shows that effective communication can lead to the following positive outcomes: improved information flow, more effective interventions, improved safety, enhanced employee morale, increased patient and family satisfaction, and decreased lengths of stay. Fuss and colleagues and Gittell and others show that implementing systems to facilitate team communication can substantially improve quality.

Effective communication among staff encourages effective teamwork and promotes continuity and clarity within the patient care team. At its best, good communication encourages collaboration, fosters teamwork, and helps prevent errors.

## BARRIERS TO EFFECTIVE COMMUNICATION

Health professionals tend to work autonomously, even though they may speak of being part of a team. Efforts to improve health care safety and quality are often jeopardized by the communication and collaboration barriers that exist between clinical staff. Although every organization is unique, the barriers to effective communication that organizations face have some common themes.

Common Barriers to Interprofessional Communication and Collaboration:

- Personal values and expectations
- Personality differences
- Hierarchy
- Disruptive behavior
- Culture and ethnicity
- Generational differences
- Gender
- Historical interprofessional and intraprofessional rivalries
- Differences in language and jargon
- Differences in schedules and professional routines
- Varying levels of preparation, qualifications, and status
- Differences in requirements, regulations, and norms of professional education
- Fears of diluted professional identity
- Differences in accountability, payment, and rewards
- Concerns regarding clinical responsibility
- Complexity of care
- Emphasis on rapid decisionmaking

However, most often the barriers manifest between nurses and physicians. Even though doctors and nurses interact numerous times a day, they often have different perceptions of their roles and responsibilities as to patient needs, and thus different goals for patient care. One barrier compounding this issue is that because the United States is one of the most ethnically and culturally diverse countries in the world, many clinicians come from a variety of cultural backgrounds. In all interactions, cultural differences can exacerbate communication problems. For example, in some cultures, individuals refrain from being assertive or challenging opinions openly. As a result, it is very difficult for nurses from such cultures to speak up if they see something wrong. In cultures such as these, nurses may communicate their concern in very indirect ways. Culture barriers can also hinder nonverbal communication. For example, some cultures ascribe specific meaning to eye contact, certain facial expressions, touch, tone of voice, and nods of the head.

Issues around gender differences in communication styles, values, and expectations are common in all workplace situations. In the health care industry, where most physicians are male and most nurses are female, communication problems are further accentuated by gender differences. A review of the organizational communication literature shows that a common barrier to effective communication and collaboration is hierarchies. Sutcliff and colleagues' research concurs that communication failures in the medical setting arise from vertical hierarchical differences, concerns with upward influence, role conflict, and ambiguity and struggles with interpersonal power and conflict. Communication is likely to be distorted or withheld in situations where there are hierarchical differences between two communicators, particularly when one person is concerned about appearing incompetent, does not want to offend the other, or perceives that the other is not open to communication.

In health care environments characterized by a hierarchical culture, physicians are at the top of that hierarchy. Consequently, they may feel that the environment is collaborative and that communication is open while nurses and other direct care staff perceive communication problems. Hierarchy differences can come into play and diminish the collaborative interactions necessary to ensure that the proper treatments are delivered appropriately. When hierarchy differences exist, people on the lower end of the hierarchy tend to be uncomfortable speaking up about problems or concerns. Intimidating behavior by individuals at the top of a hierarchy can hinder communication and give the impression that the individual is unapproachable. Staff who witness poor performance in their peers may be hesitant to speak up because of fear of retaliation or the impression that speaking up will not do any good. Relationships between the individuals providing patient care can have a powerful influence on how and even if important information is communicated. Research has shown that delays in patient care and recurring problems from unresolved disputes are often the by-product of physician-nurse disagreement.

Our research has identified a common trend in which nurses are either reluctant or refuse to call physicians, even in the face of a deteriorating status in patient care. Reasons for this include intimidation, fear of getting into a confrontational or antagonistic discussion, lack of confidentiality, fear of retaliation, and the fact that nothing ever seems to change. Many of these issues have to deal more with personality and communication style. The major concern about disruptive behaviors is how frequently they occur and the potential negative impact they can have on patient care. Our research has shown that 17 percent of respondents to our survey research in 2004-2006 knew of a specific adverse event that occurred as a result of disruptive behavior. A quote from one of the respondents illustrates this point: "Poor communication post-op because of disruptive reputation of physician resulted in delayed treatment, aspiration, and eventual demise." Leaders in both medicine and nursing have issued ongoing initiatives for the development of a cooperative rather than a competitive agenda to benefit patient care. A powerful incentive for greater teamwork among professionals is created by directing attention to the areas where changes are likely to result in measurable improvements for the patients they serve together, rather than concentrating on what, on the surface, seem to be irreconcilable professional differences. The fact that most health professionals have at least one characteristic in common, a personal desire to learn, and that they have at least one shared value, to meet the needs of their patients or clients, is a good place to start.

## PRACTICE IMPLICATIONS

### Known Benefits of Communication and Team Collaboration

A large body of literature shows that because of the complexity of medical care, coupled with the inherent limitations of human performance, it is critically important that clinicians have standardized communication tools and create an environment in which individuals can speak up and express concerns. This literature concurs that when a team needs to communicate complex information in a short period of time, it is helpful to use structured communication techniques to ensure accuracy. Structured communication techniques can serve the same purpose that clinical practice guidelines do in assisting practitioners to make decisions and take action. Research from aviation and wilderness firefighting is useful in health care because they all involve settings where there is a huge variability in circumstances, the need to adapt processes quickly, a quickly changing knowledge base, and highly trained professionals who must use expert judgment in dynamic settings. Research shows that in these disciplines, the adoption of standardized tools and behaviors is a very effective strategy in enhancing teamwork and reducing risks.

#### *Crew Resource Management*

Experts in aviation have developed safety training focused on effective team management, known as Crew Resource Management. Improvements in the safety record of commercial aviation may be due, in part, to this training. Realizing that 70 percent of commercial flight accidents stemmed from communication failures among crew members, CRM sought to standardize communication and teamwork. The concept originated in 1979, in response to a NASA workshop that examined the role that human error plays in air crashes. CRM emphasizes the role of human factors in high-stress, high-risk environments. John K. Lauber, a psychologist member of the National

Transportation Safety Board, deemed CRM as "using all available sources—information, equipment, and people—to achieve safe and efficient flight operations." CRM encompasses team training as well as simulation, interactive group debriefings, and measurement and improvement of aircrew performance. This represents a major change in training, which had previously dealt with only the technical aspects of flying. It considers human performance limiters and the nature of human error, and it defines behaviors that are countermeasures to error, such as leadership, briefings, monitoring and cross-checking, decisionmaking, and review and modification of plans. From a practical standpoint, CRM programs typically include educating crews about the limitations of human performance. Trainees develop an understanding of cognitive errors and how stressors contribute to the occurrence of errors. Operational concepts stressed include inquiry, seeking relevant operational information, advocacy, communicating proposed actions, conflict resolution, and decisionmaking. CRM is now required for flight crews worldwide.

The development and implementation of CRM in aviation over the last 25 years offers valuable lessons for medical care. Sexton and colleagues compared flight crews with operating room personnel on several measures, including attitudes toward teamwork. This landmark study included more than 30,000 cockpit crew members and 1,033 operating room personnel. Questionnaires were sent to crew members of major airlines around the world. The operating room participants were mailed an analogous questionnaire, administered over a period of 3 years at 12 teaching and nonteaching hospitals in the United States, Italy, Germany, Switzerland, and Israel.

The Sexton study and other analyses suggest that safety-related behaviors that have been applied and studied extensively in the aviation industry may also be relevant in health care. Study results show successful CRM applications in several dynamic decisionmaking health care environments: the operating room, labor and delivery, and the emergency room. As with aviation, the medical application of CRM has required tailoring of training approaches to mirror the areas in which human factors contribute to mishaps. In anesthesiology, 65–70 percent of safety problems have been attributed at least in part to human error. In response, several anesthesiologists from the Veterans Affairs Palo Alto Health Care System and Stanford University developed Anesthesia Crisis Resource Management, modeled on CRM. Kaiser Permanente, a nonprofit American health care system providing care for 8.3 million patients, has also adopted CRM with successful results. In response to the occurrence of a sentinel event—a medical error with serious consequences—Eglin U.S. Air Force Regional Hospital developed and implemented a patient safety program called Medical Team Management that was modeled on the aviation industry's CRM program and focused on communication, teamwork, and reporting to determine the impact of a patient safety program on patterns of medical error reporting. This study was a retrospective review of 1,102 incident reports filed at Eglin USAF Regional Hospital in Florida between 1997 and 2001. Collected data from the comparison periods were statistically analyzed using the chi-square test. This study indicates that, since the implementation of MTM, there has been a statistically significant increase in the number of reports filed at Eglin USAF Regional Hospital and a decline in the severity of incidents. These findings suggest that since the implementation of MTM, there have been changes in the patterns of error reporting, and with training, staff are able to prevent more serious incidents.

Application of a CRM Model to Medicine:

- Design of systems to absorb errors through redundancy, standardization, and checklists
- Movement from placing blame to designing safe processes and procedures, i.e., applying a systems approach
- Assurance of full immunity while implementing a nonpunitive approach
- Debriefing of all events, including near misses, that have learning potential. Focus on the severity of the potential risk rather than on the severity of the event's final outcome is more conducive to establishing effective prevention programs.
- Institutionalization of a permanent program for risk identification, analysis, and dissemination of the lessons learned throughout the professional community

## *SBAR*

Doctors and nurses often have different communication styles in part due to training. Nurses are taught to be more descriptive of clinical situations, whereas physicians learn to be very concise. Standardized communication tools are very effective in bridging this difference in communication styles.

Michael Leonard, physician coordinator of clinical informatics at Kaiser Permanente, along with colleagues, developed a technique called SBAR. This technique has been implemented widely at health systems such as Kaiser Permanente. Many other hospitals have embraced the SBAR communication tool or a similar tool created by the Studer Group. For example, the Queen's Medical Center in Honolulu has incorporated the SBAR tool as a key component of its patient safety program. The SBAR technique provides a framework for communication between members of the health care team about a patient's condition. SBAR is an easy-to-remember tool used to create mechanisms useful for framing any conversation, especially critical ones, requiring a clinician's immediate attention and action. It allows for an easy and focused way to set expectations between members of the team for what will be communicated and how, which is essential for information transfer and cohesive teamwork. Not only is there familiarity in how people communicate, but the SBAR structure helps develop desired critical-thinking skills. The person initiating the communication knows that before they pick up the telephone, they need to provide an assessment of the problem and what they think an appropriate solution is. Their conclusion may not ultimately be the answer, but there is clearly value in defining the situation.

Studer Group Communication Guidelines for Nurses

- Have I seen and assessed this patient myself before I call?
  - Are there standing orders?
  - Do I have at hand
    - (i) The chart?
    - (ii) List of current meds, IV fluids, and labs?
    - (iii) Most recent vital signs?
    - (iv) If reporting lab work, date and time this test was done and results of previous tests for comparisons?
    - (v) Code status?
  - Have I read the most recent MD progress notes and notes from the nurse who worked the shift ahead of me?
  - Have I discussed this call with my charge nurse?
  - When ready to call, Remember to identify self, unit, patient, room number.
    - (i) Know the admitting diagnosis and date of admission.
    - (ii) Briefly state the problem, what it is, when it happened or started, and how severe it is.
  - What do I expect to happen as a result of this call?
  - Document whom you spoke to, time of call, and summary of conversation.
  - Engage and treat physician with respect.

SBAR:

- SBAR – a technique for communicating critical information that requires immediate attention and action concerning a patient's condition
- Situation – What is going on with the patient? "I am calling about Mrs. Joseph in room 251. Chief complaint is shortness of breath of new onset."
- Background – What is the clinical background or context? "Patient is a 62-year-old female post-op day one from abdominal surgery. No prior history of cardiac or lung disease."
- Assessment – What do I think the problem is? "Breath sounds are decreased on the right side with acknowledgment of pain. Would like to rule out pneumothorax."

- Recommendation – What would I do to correct it? "I feel strongly the patient should be assessed now. Are you available to come in?"

STICC is another type of structured briefing protocol used by the U.S. Forest Service to give direction to firefighters. The following five steps are involved:

- Situation: Here's what I think we face.
- Task: Here's what I think we should do.
- Intent: Here's why
- Concern: Here's what we should keep our eye on.
- Calibrate: Talk to me. Tell me if you don't understand, can't do it, or see something I do not.

## ESTABLISHING CULTURE TO SUPPORT COMMUNICATION AND TEAM COLLABORATION

The literature reviewed shows that effective teams are characterized by common purpose and intent, trust, respect, and collaboration. Team members value familiarity over formality and watch out for each other to make sure mistakes are not made. Health care teams that do not trust, respect, and collaborate with one another are more likely to make a mistake that could negatively impact the safety of patients.

One of the first crucial steps is organizational commitment and willingness to address the situation. Commitment needs to come from the top down and bottom up, making a statement about the way the organization does business. The rallying point should be around behavioral standards and their relationship to patient safety. It's ironic that ever since the publication of the original IOM report, To Err Is Human, organizations have spent the bulk of their time and efforts in improving patient systems rather than addressing the human factor issues highlighted in the original report. Several recent reports have suggested that while we have made progress in the patient safety movement, we have a long way to go in meeting the IOM recommendations. Addressing defects in communication that affect collaboration, information exchange, appreciation of roles and responsibilities, and direct accountability for patient care are key components of any patient safety program. Clinical and administrative leaders must set the tone by establishing and adhering to behavioral standards that support agreed-upon code of conduct practices backed by a nonpunitive culture and zero-tolerance policy.

The next step in the process is recognition and self-awareness. Organizations must be able to assess the prevalence, context, and impact of behaviors to identify potential opportunities for improvement. Doing an internal assessment will help pinpoint the seriousness of the situation and provide clues to areas that need to be addressed. Assessment information can be gained from formal methods such as incident reports, survey tools, focus groups, department meetings, task forces or committees, direct observation, suggestion boxes, and hot lines. Informal methods such as casual meetings and gossip can also provide valuable surface information and should be evaluated more deeply as to the source, relevance, and significance of the events to determine next steps. In many organizations there are still remnants of reluctance to address the issue head on for fear of antagonizing a prominent surgeon or staff member. With growing concerns about workforce shortages, staff satisfaction and retention, hospital reputation, liability and patient safety, and the need for compliance to the latest Joint Commission proposed standards addressing disruptive behaviors, organizations can no longer afford to take a passive approach to the situation.

Creating opportunities for different groups to just get together is a highly effective strategy for enhancing collaboration and communication. These group interactions can be either formal or informal. Encouraging open dialogue, collaborative rounds, implementing preop and postop team briefings, and creating interdisciplinary committees or task forces that discuss problem areas frequently provides an upfront solution that reduces the likelihood of disruptive events. When a disruptive event does occur, some organizations have implemented a time-out, code white, or red light policy that addresses the issue in real time to prevent any further serious consequences. Developing and implementing a standard set of behavior policies and procedures is vital. These policies need to be consistent and universally applied. There should not be a separate policy for any one particular discipline or service. For the medical staff, the policies should become part of the medical staff bylaws with signed agreements to abide by these policies at the time of appointment and recredentialing. Included in the policies should be a standardized protocol outlining expected standards and the process for addressing disruptive behavior issues, recommendations, followup plans, and actions to be taken in the face of individual resistance or refusal to comply. Prior to implementation, make sure all employees are familiar with the existence, purpose, and intent of the policies and procedures.

For the process to unfold, the organization needs to encourage its employees to report disruptive behaviors. The organization needs to address issues related to confidentiality, fear of retaliation, and the common feelings that there is a double standard and that nothing ever gets done. Reporting mechanisms should be made easy and must be supported by the presence of a nonpunitive environment. The ideal vehicle for reporting is to address the situation in real time, but concerns about position, appropriateness, receptiveness, fear, hostility, and retaliation are significant impediments. Appropriate vehicles for reporting may include reporting of the incident to a superior, filing an incident report, using a complaint or suggestion box, or reporting directly to a task force or interdisciplinary committee with assigned responsibilities for addressing these issues. Besides maintaining confidentiality and reducing risks of retaliation, one of the most crucial aspects of the reporting system is to give recognition and assurance that the complaints will be addressed and actions will be taken. Responses should be timely, appropriate, consistent, and provide necessary feedback and followup.

Taking action though appropriate intervention strategies is next. On one level, generic educational programs can do a lot to spread the message and teach basic skills necessary to promote effective communication. Appropriate topics should include sessions on team dynamics, communication skills, phone etiquette, assertiveness training, diversity training, conflict management, stress management, and any other courses necessary to foster more effective team functioning and communication flow. Courses should be offered to all staff and employees at the organization: physicians, physicians in training, nurses, nursing students, and all other staff who have patient contact or play a role in the delivery of patient care. For individuals who have consistently exhibited disruptive behavior, education may need to be supported by more focused sessions and specific counseling. Another important strategy is to promote and assure competency training at all levels of the health care team. This is a key factor affecting trust and respect, which have such a strong influence on team collaboration.

Focused team training programs have been of particular value. One of the newer approaches to improving team collaboration and patient safety is through the principles learned from the aviation industry. Fostering an environment of trust and respect, accountability, situational awareness, open communication, assertiveness, shared decisionmaking, feedback, and education, interdisciplinary CRM training has brought significant improvements to communication flow in the perioperative setting. Having a clinical champion or early adopter who actively promotes the importance of appropriate behavior, communication, and team collaboration can be an extremely valuable asset. Champions can come from the executive ranks or through the voluntary interest and enthusiasm of other staff members. Co-champions may be even more effective. Some organizations have reported that having a nurse and physician go through a joint training program will help foster mutual cooperation and collaboration between the different disciplines. Followup and feedback bring closure to the process. It is important to let people know that their input is welcomed, followup actions will be taken, and appropriate feedback will be provided.

## RESEARCH IMPLICATIONS

The existing literature adequately outlines structured communication techniques that will help minimize medical errors. However, more research is needed on how to effectively deal with miscommunication and barriers to communication in real-time crisis situations. Also, the existing literature lacks concrete research confirming a cause-and-effect relationship between human factors and clinical outcomes of care.

## CONCLUSIONS

Effective clinical practice must not focus only on technological system issues, but also on the human factor. As shown in this chapter, good communication encourages collaboration and helps prevent errors. It is important for health care organizations to assess possible setups for poor communication and be diligent about offering programs and outlets to help foster team collaboration. By addressing this issue, health care organizations have an opportunity to greatly enhance their clinical outcomes.

# 8

# Learning as a Tool of Performance

## LEARNING PROCESS

To learn is to acquire knowledge or skill. Learning also may involve a change in attitude or behavior. Children learn to identify objects at an early age; teenagers may learn to improve study habits; and adults can learn to solve complex problems. Pilots and aviation maintenance technicians need to acquire the higher levels of knowledge and skill, including the ability to exercise judgment and solve problems. The challenge for the aviation instructor is to understand how people learn, and more importantly, to be able to apply that knowledge to the learning environment. This handbook is designed as a basic guide to educational psychology. This chapter addresses that branch of psychology directly concerned with how people learn.

## LEARNING THEORY

Learning theory may be described as a body of principles advocated by psychologists and educators to explain how people acquire skills, knowledge, and attitudes. Various branches of learning theory are used in formal training programs to improve and accelerate the learning process. Key concepts such as desired learning outcomes, objectives of the training, and depth of training also apply. When properly integrated, learning principles, derived from theories, can be useful to aviation instructors and developers of instructional programs for both pilots and maintenance technicians. Over the years, many theories have attempted to explain how people learn. Even though psychologists and educators are not in complete agreement, most do agree that learning may be explained by a combination of two basic approaches: behaviorism and the cognitive theories.

### Behaviorism

Behaviorists believe that animals, including humans, learn in about the same way. Behaviorism stresses the importance of having a particular form of behavior reinforced by someone, other than the student, to shape or control what is learned. In aviation training, the instructor provides the reinforcement. Frequent, positive reinforcement and rewards accelerate learning. This theory provides the instructor with ways to manipulate students with stimuli, induce the desired behavior or response, and reinforce the behavior with appropriate rewards. In general, the behaviorist theory emphasizes positive reinforcement rather than no reinforcement or punishment. Other features of behaviorism are considerably more complex than this simple explanation. Instructors who need more details should refer to psychology texts for a better understanding of behaviorism. As an instructor, it is important to keep in mind that behaviorism is still widely used today, because controlling learning experiences helps direct students toward specific learning outcomes.

**Cognative Theory**

Much of the recent psychological thinking and experimentation in education includes some facets of the cognitive theory. This is true in basic as well as more advanced training programs. Unlike behaviorism, the cognitive theory focuses on what is going on inside the student's mind. Learning is not just a change in behavior; it is a change in the way a student thinks, understands, or feels. There are several branches of cognitive theory. Two of the major theories may broadly be classified as the information processing model and the social interaction model. The first says that the student's brain has internal structures which select and process incoming material, store and retrieve it, use it to produce behavior, and receive and process feedback on the results. This involves a number of cognitive processes, including executive functions of recognizing expectancies, planning and monitoring performance, encoding and chunking information, and producing internal and external responses.

The social interaction theories gained prominence in the 1980s. They stress that learning and subsequent changes in behavior take place as a result of interaction between the student and the environment. Behavior is modeled either by people or symbolically. Cultural influences, peer pressure, group dynamics, and film and television are some of the significant factors. Thus, the social environment to which the student is exposed demonstrates or models behaviors, and the student cognitively processes the observed behaviors and consequences. The cognitive processes include attention, retention, motor responses, and motivation. Techniques for learning include direct modeling and verbal instruction. Behavior, personal factors, and environmental events all work together to produce learning.

Both models of the cognitive theory have common principles. For example, they both acknowledge the importance of reinforcing behavior and measuring changes. Positive reinforcement is important, particularly with cognitive concepts such as knowledge and understanding. The need to evaluate and measure behavior remains because it is the only way to get a clue about what the student understands. Evaluation is often limited to the kinds of knowledge or behavior that can be measured by a paper-and-pencil exam or a performance test. Although psychologists agree that there often are errors in evaluation, some means of measuring student knowledge, performance, and behavior is necessary.

**Combined Approach**

Both the behavioristic and the cognitive approaches are useful learning theories. A reasonable way to plan, manage, and conduct aviation training is to include the best features of each major theory. This provides a way to measure behavioral outcomes and promote cognitive learning. The combined approach is not simple, but neither is learning.

## DEFINITION OF LEARNING

The ability to learn is one of the most outstanding human characteristics. Learning occurs continuously throughout a person's lifetime. To define learning, it is necessary to analyze what happens to the individual. For example, an individual's way of perceiving, thinking, feeling, and doing may change as a result of a learning experience. Thus, learning can be defined as a change in behavior as a result of experience. This can be physical and overt, or it may involve complex intellectual or attitudinal changes which affect behavior in more subtle ways. In spite of numerous theories and contrasting views, psychologists generally agree on many common characteristics of learning.

## CHARACTERISTICS OF LEARNING

Aviation instructors need a good understanding of the general characteristics of learning in order to apply them in a learning situation. If learning is a change in behavior as a result of experience, then instruction must include a careful and systematic creation of those experiences that promote learning.

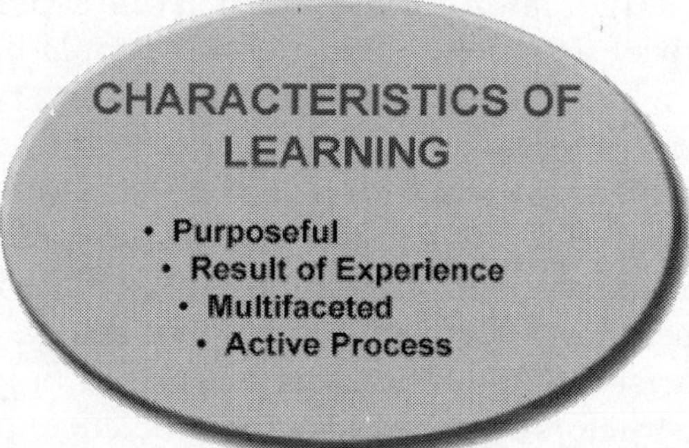


**Fig.** Effective Learning shares several common characteristics.

This process can be quite complex because, among other things, an individual's background strongly influences the way that person learns. To be effective, the learning situation also should be purposeful, based on experience, multifaceted, and involve an active process.

## LEARNING IS PURPOSEFUL

Each student sees a learning situation from a different viewpoint. Each student is a unique individual whose past experiences affect readiness to learn and understanding of the requirements involved. For example, an instructor may give two aviation maintenance students the assignment of learning certain inspection procedures. One student may learn quickly and be able to competently present the assigned material. The combination of an aviation background and future goals may enable that student to realize the need and value of learning the procedures. A second student's goal may only be to comply with the instructor's assignment, and may result in only minimum preparation. The responses differ because each student ads in accordance with what he or she sees in the situation.

Most people have fairly definate ideas about what they want to do and achieve. Their goals sometimes are short term, involving a matter of days or weeks. On the other hand, their goals may be carefully planned for a career or a lifetime. Each student has specific intentions and goals. Some may be shared by other students. Students learn from any activity that tends to further their goals. Their individual needs and attitudes may determine what they learn as much as what the instruc- tor is trying to get them to learn. In the process of learning, the student's goals are of paramount significance. To be effective, aviation instructors need to find ways to relate new learning to the student's goals.

## LEARNING IS A RESULT OF EXPERIENCE

Since learning is an individual process, the instructor cannot do it for the student. The student can learn only from personal experiences; therefore, learning and knowledge cannot exist apart from a person. A person's knowledge is a result of experience, and no two people have had identical experiences. Even when observing the same event, two people react differently; they learn different things from it, according to the manner in which the situation affects their individual needs. Previous experience conditions a person to respond to some things and to ignore others.

All learning is by experience, but learning takes place in different forms and in varying degrees of richness and depth. For instance, some experiences involve the whole person while others may be based only on hearing and memory. Aviation instructors are faced with the problem of providing learning experiences that are meaningful, varied, and appropriate. As an example, students can learn to say a list of words through repeated drill, or they can learn to recite certain principles of flight by rote. However, they can make them meaningful only if they understand them well enough to apply them correctly to real situations. If an experience challenges the students, requires involvement with feelings, thoughts, memory of past experiences, and physical activity, it is more effective than a learning experience in which all the students have to do is commit something to memory.

It seems clear enough that the learning of a physical skill requires actual experience in performing that skill. Student pilots learn to fly aircraft only if their experiences include flying them; student aviation maintenance technicians learn to overhaul powerplants only by actually performing that task. Mental habits are also learned through practice. If students are to use sound judgment and develop decision-making skills, they need learning experiences that involve knowledge of general principles and require the use of judgment in salving realistic problems.

## LEARNING IS MULTIFACETED

If instructors see their objective as being only to train their students' memory and muscles, they are underestimating the potential of the teaching situation. Students may learn much more than expected if they fully exercise their minds and feelings. The fact that these items were not included in the instructor's plan does not prevent them from influencing the learning situation.

Psychologists sometimes classify learning by types, such as verbal, conceptual, perceptual, motor, problem solving, and emotional. Other classifications refer to intellectual skills, cognitive strategies, and attitudinal changes, along with descriptive terms like surface or deep learning. However useful these divisions may be, they are somewhat artificial. For example, a class learning to apply the scientific method of problem solving may learn the method by trying to solve real problems. But in doing so, the class also engages in verbal learning and sensory perception at the same time. Each student approaches the task with preconceived ideas and feelings, and for many students, these ideas change as a result of experience. Therefore, the learning process may include verbal elements, conceptual elements, perceptual elements, emotional elements, and problem solving elements all taking place at once. This aspect of learning will become more evident later in this handbook when lesson planning is discussed.

Learning is multifaceted in still another way. While learning the subject at hand, students may be learning other things as well. They may be developing attitudes about aviation-good or bad-depending on what they experience. Under a skillful instructor, they may learn self-reliance. The list is seemingly endless. This type of learning is sometimes referred to as incidental, but it may have a great impact on the total development of the student.

## LEARNING IS AN ACTIVE PROCESS

Students do not soak up knowledge like a sponge absorbs water. The instructor cannot assume that students remember something just because they were in the classroom, shop, or airplane when the instructor presented the material. Neither can the instructor assume that the students can apply what they know because they can quote the correct answer verbatim. For students to learn, they need to react and respond, perhaps outwardly, perhaps only inwardly, emotionally, or intellectually. But if learning is a process of changing behavior, clearly that process must be an active one.

## LEARNING STYLES

Although characteristics of learning and learning styles are related, there are distinctions between the two. Learning style is a concept that can play an important role in improving instruction and student success. It is concerned with student preferences and orientation at several levels. For example, a student's information processing technique, personality, social interaction tendencies and the instructional methods used are all significant factors which apply to how individual students learn. In addition, today's culturally diverse society, including international students, must be considered.

The key point is that all students are different, and training programs should be sensitive to the differences. Some students are fast learners and others have difficulties; and, as already mentioned, motivation, experience, and previous training affect learning style. Any number of adjectives may be used to describe learning styles. Some common examples include:

- Right/left brain
- Holistic/serialist
- Dependent/independent
- Reflective/impulsive

Theories abound concerning right- or left-brain dominance. In general, those with right-brain dominance are characterized as being spatially oriented, creative, intuitive, and emotional. Those with left-brain dominance are more verbal, analytical, and objective. However, the separate hemispheres of the brain do not function independently. For example, the right hemisphere may recognize a face, while the left associates a name to go with the face. The term dominance is probably misleading when applied to brain hemispheres; specialization would be a more appropriate word.

Learning style differences certainly depend on how students process information. Some rely heavily on visual references while others depend more on auditory presentations. For example, visual students learn readily through reading and graphic displays, and auditory students have more success if they hear the subject matter described. Another difference is that some learn more easily when an idea is presented in a mathematical equation, while others may prefer a verbal explanation of the same idea. In addition, where hands-on activities are involved, students also learn by feel. This is sometimes called kinesthetic learning.

Information processing theories contain several other useful classifications. As an example, in the holistic/serialist theory, the holist strategy is a top-down concept where students have a big picture, global perspective. These students seek overall comprehension, especially through the use of analogies. In contrast, the serialist student focuses more narrowly and needs well-defined, sequential steps where the overall picture is developed slowly, thoroughly, and logically. This is a bottom-up strategy. Two additional information processing classifications describe deep-elaborative and the shallow-reiterative learners. Testing practices which demand comprehension, rather than a regurgitation of facts, obviously encourage students to adopt a deep-elaborative learning style. Detailed information on testing procedures, as well as curriculum design and instructor techniques, is included later in this handbook.

As indicated, personality also affects how students learn. Dependent students require a lot of guidance, direction, and external stimulation. These students tend to focus on the instructor. The more independent students require only a minimum amount of guidance and external stimulation. They are not overly concerned with how the lesson is presented. Students with a reflective-type personality may be described as tentative. They tend to be uncertain in problem-solving exercises. The opposite applies to impulsive students. Typically, they dive right in with enthusiasm and are prone to make quick, and sometimes faulty, decisions. The social interaction concept contains further classifications of student learning styles. Like most of the other information on learning styles, these classifications are derived from research on tendencies of undergraduate students.

Some generalizations about these classifications indicate that compliant students are typically task oriented, and anxious-dependent students usually score lower than others on standardized tests. Discouraged students often have depressed feelings about the future, and independent students tend to be older, intelligent, secure, and comfortable with the academic environment. Attention seekers have a strong social orientation and are frequently involved in joking, showing off, and bragging. In contrast, silent students usually are characterized by helplessness, vulnerability, and other disconcerting behaviorisms.

Other studies identify more categories that are easily recognized. Among these are collaborative, sharing students who enjoy working with others, and competitive students who are grade conscious and feel they must do better than their peers. Participant students normally have a desire to learn and enjoy attending class, and avoidant students do not take part in class activities and have little interest in learning. The existing learning environment also influences learning style. In real life, most students find it necessary to adapt to a traditional style learning environment provided by a school, university, or other educational/training establishment. Thus, the student's learning style may or may not be compatible. Instructors who can recognize student learning style differences and associated problems will be much more effective than those who do not understand this concept. Also, these instructors will be prepared to develop appropriate lesson plans and provide guidance, counseling, or other advisory services, as required.

## PRINCIPLES OF LEARNING

Over the years, educational psychologists have identitied several principles which seem generally applicable to the learning process. They provide additional insight into what makes people learn most effectively.

### READINESS

Individuals learn best when they are ready to learn, and they do not learn well if they see no reason for learning. Getting students ready to learn is usually the instructor's responsibility. If students have a strong purpose, a clear objective, and a definite reason for learning something, they make more progress than if they lack motivation. Readiness implies a degree of single-mindedness and eagerness. When students are ready to learn, they meet the instructor at least halfway, and this simplifies the instructor's job. Under certain circumstances, the instructor can do little, if anything, to inspire in students a readiness to learn. If outside responsibilities, interests, or worries weigh too heavily on their minds, if their schedules are overcrowded, or if their personal problems seem insoluble, students may have little interest in learning.

### EXERCISE

The principle of exercise states that those things most often repeated are best remembered. It is the basis of drill and practice. The human memory is fallible. The mind can rarely retain, evaluate, and apply new concepts or practices after a single exposure. Students do not learn to weld during one shop period or to perform crosswise landings during one instructional flight. They learn by applying what they have been told and shown. Every time practice occurs, learning continues. The instructor must provide opportunities for students to practice and, at the same time, make sure that this process is directed toward a goal.

### EFFECT

The principle of effect is based on the emotional reaction of the student. It states that learning is strengthened when accompanied by a pleasant or satisfying feeling, and that learning is weakened when associated with an unpleasant feeling. Experiences that produce feelings of defeat, frustration, anger, confusion, or futility are unpleasant for the student. If, for example, an instructor attempts to teach landings during the first flight, the student is likely to feel inferior and be frustrated. Instructors should be cautious. Impressing students with the difficulty of an aircraft maintenance problem, flight maneuver or flight crew duty can make the teaching task difficult. Usually it is better to tell students that a problem or maneuver, although difficult, is within their capability to understand or perform. Whatever the learning situation, it should contain elements that affect the students positively and give them a feeling of satisfaction.

**PRIMACY**

Primacy, the state of being first, often creates a strong, almost unshakable, impression. For the instructor, this means that what is taught must be right the first time. For the student, it means that learning must be right. Unteaching is more difficult than teaching. If, for example, a maintenance student learns a faulty riveting technique, the instructor will have a difficult task correcting bad habits and reteaching correct ones. Every student should be started right. The first experience should be positive, functional, and lay the foundation for all that is to follow.

**INTENSITY**

A vivid, dramatic, or exciting learning experience teaches more than a routine or boring experience. A student is likely to gain greater understanding of slow flight and stalls by performing them rather than merely reading about them. The principle of intensity implies that a student will learn more from the real thing than from a substitute. In contrast to flight instruction and shop instruction, the classroom imposes limitations on the amount of realism that can be brought into teaching. The aviation instructor should use imagination in approaching reality as closely as possible. Today, classroom instruction can benefit from a wide variety of instructional aids to improve realism, motivate learning, and challenge students. Chapter 7, Instructional Aids and Training Technologies, explores the wide range of teaching tools available for classroom use.

**RECENCY**

The principle of recency states that things most recently learned are best remembered. Conversely, the further a student is removed time-wise from a new fact or understanding, the more difficult it is to remember. It is easy, for example, for a student to recall a torque value used a few minutes earlier, but it is usually impossible to remember an unfamiliar one used a week earlier. Instructors recognize the principle of recency when they carefully plan a summary for a ground school lesson, a shop period, or a postflight critique. The instructor repeats, restates, or reemphasizes important points at the end of a lesson to help the student remember them. The principle of recency often determines the sequence of lectures within a course of instruction.

## HOW PEOPLE LEARN

Initially, all learning comes from perceptions which are directed to the brain by one or more of the five senses: sight, hearing, touch, smell, and taste. Psychologists have also found that learning occurs most rapidly when information is received through more than one sense.

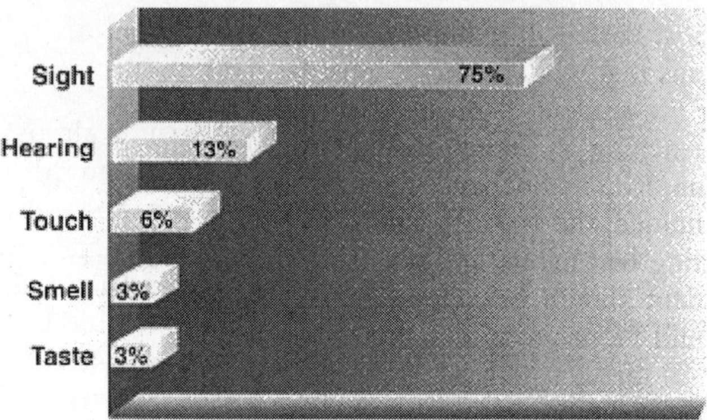


**Fig.** Most learning occurs through sights, but the combination of sight and hearing accounts for about 88 per cent of all perceptions.

## PERCEPTIONS

Perceiving involves more than the reception of stimuli from the five senses. Perceptions result when a person gives meaning to sensations. People base their actions on the way they believe things to be. The experienced aviation maintenance technician, for example, perceives an engine malfunction quite differently than does an inexperienced student. Real meaning comes only from within a person, even though the perceptions which evoke these meanings result from external stimuli. The meanings which are derived from perceptions are influenced not only by the individual's experience, but also by many other factors. Knowledge of the factors which affect the perceptual process is very important to the aviation instructor because perceptions are the basis of all learning.

## FACTORS WHICH AFFECT PERCEPTION

There are several factors that affect an individual's ability to perceive. Some are internal to each person and some are external.

- Physical organism
- Basic need
- Goals and values
- Self-concept

- Time and opportunity
- Element of threat

**Physical Organism**

The physical organism provides individuals with the perceptual apparatus for sensing the world around them. Pilots, for example, must be able to see, hear, feel, and respond adequately while they are in the air. A person whose perceptual apparatus distorts reality is denied the right to fly at the time of the first medical examination.

**Basic Need**

A person's basic need is to maintain and enhance the organized self. The self is a person's past, present, and future combined; it is both physical and psychological. A person's most fundamental, pressing need is to preserve and perpetuate the self. All perceptions are affected by this need. Just as the food one eats and the air one breathes become part of the physical self, so do the sights one sees and the sounds one hears become part of the psychological self. Psychologically, we are what we perceive. A person has physical barriers which keep out those things that would be damaging to the physical being, such as blinking at an arc weld or flinching from a hot iron. Likewise, a person has perceptual barriers that block those sights, sounds, and feelings which pose a psychological threat. Helping people learn requires finding ways to aid them in developing better perceptions in spite of their defense mechanisms. Since a person's basic need is to maintain and enhance the self, the instructor must recognize that anything that is asked of the student which may be interpreted by the student as imperiling the self will be resisted or denied. To teach effectively, it is necessary to work with this life force.

**Goals and Values**

Perceptions depend on one's goals and values. Every experience and sensation which is funneled into one's central nervous system is colored by the individual's own beliefs and value structures. Spectators at a ball game may see an infraction or foul differently depending on which team they support. The precise kinds of commitments and philosophical outlooks which the student holds are important for the instructor to know, since this knowledge will assist in predicting how the student will interpret experiences and instructions. Goals are also a product of one's value structure. Those things which are more highly valued and cherished are pursued; those which are accorded less value and importance are not sought after.

**Self-Concept**

Self-concept is a powerful determinant in learning. A student's self-image, described in such terms as confident and insecure, has a great influence on the total perceptual process. If a student's experiences tend to support a favorable self-image, the student tends to remain receptive to subsequent experiences. If a student has negative experiences which tend to contradict self-concept, there is a tendency to reject additional training. A negative self-concept inhibits the perceptual processes by introducing psychological barriers which tend to keep the student from perceiving. They may also inhibit the ability to properly implement that which is perceived. That is, self-concept affects the ability to actually perform or do things unfavorable. Students who view themselves positively, on the other hand, are less defensive and more receptive to new experiences, instructions, and demonstrations.

**Time and Opportunity**

It takes time and opportunity to perceive. Learning some things depends on other perceptions which have preceded these learnings, and on the availability of time to sense and relate these new things to the earlier perceptions. Thus, sequence and time are necessary. A student could probably stall an airplane on the first attempt, regardless of previous experience. Stalls cannot really be learned, however, unless some experience in normal flight has been acquired. Even with such experience, time and practice are needed to relate the new sensations and experiences associated with stalls in order to develop a perception of the stall. In general, lengthening an experience and increasing its frequency are the most obvious ways to speed up learning, although this is not always effective. Many factors, in addition to the length and frequency of training periods, affect the rate of learning. The effectiveness of the use of a properly planned training syllabus is proportional to the consideration it gives to the time and opportunity factor in perception.

**Element of Threat**

The element of threat does not promote effective learning. In fact, fear adversely affects perception by narrowing the perceptual field. Confronted with threat, students tend to limit their attention to the threatening object or condition. The field of vision is reduced, for example, when an individual is frightened and all the perceptual faculties are focused on the thing that has generated fear. Flight instruction provides many clear examples of this. During the initial practice of steep turns, a student pilot may focus attention on the altimeter and completely disregard outside visual references. Anything an instructor does that is interpreted as threatening makes the student less able to accept the experience the instructor is trying to provide. It adversely affects all the student's physical, emotional, and mental faculties. Learning is a psychological process, not necessarily a logical one. Trying to frighten a student through threats of unsatisfactory reports or reprisals may seem logical, but is not effective psychologically. The effective instructor can organize teaching to fit the psychological needs of the student. If a situation seems overwhelming, the student feels unable to handle all of the factors involved, and a threat exists. So long as the student feels capable of coping with a situation, each new experience is viewed as a challenge. A good instructor realizes that behavior is directly influenced by the way a student perceives, and perception is affected by all of these factors. Therefore, it is important for the instructor to facilitate the learning process by avoiding any actions which may inhibit or prevent the attainment of teaching goals. Teaching is consistently effective only when those factors which influence perceptions are recognized and taken into account.

## INSIGHT

Insight involves the grouping of perceptions into meaningful wholes. Creating insight is one of the instructor's major responsibilities. To ensure that this does occur, it is essential to keep each student constantly receptive to new experiences and to help the student realize the way each piece relates to all other pieces of the total pattern of the task to be learned. As an example, during straight-and-level flight in an airplane with a fixed-pitch propeller, the RPM will increase when the throttle is opened and decrease when it is closed. On the other hand, RPM changes can also result from changes in airplane pitch attitude without changes in power setting. Obviously, engine speed, power setting, airspeed, and airplane attitude are all related. True learning requires an understanding of how each of these factors may affect all of the others and, at the same time, knowledge of how a change in any one of them may affect all of the others.

This mental relating and grouping of associated perceptions is called insight. Insight will almost always occur eventually, whether or not instruction is provided. For this reason, it is possible for a person to become an electrician by trial and error, just as one may become a lawyer by reading law. Instruction, however, speeds this learning process by teaching the relationship of perceptions as they occur, thus promoting the development of the student's insight. As perceptions increase in number and are assembled by the student into larger blocks of learning, they develop insight. As a result, learning becomes more meaningful and more permanent. Forgetting is less of a problem when there are more anchor points for tying insights together. It is a major responsibility of the instructor to organize demonstrations and explanations, and to direct practice, so that the student has better opportunities to understand the interrelationship of the many kinds of experiences that have been perceived. Pointing out the relationships as they occur, providing a secure and nonthreatening environment in which to learn, and helping the student acquire and maintain a favorable self-concept are key steps in fostering the development of insight.

## MOTIVATION

Motivation is probably the dominant force which governs the student's progress and ability to learn. Motivation may be negative or positive, tangible or intangible, subtle and difficult to identify, or it may be obvious. Negative motivation may engender fear, and be perceived by the student as a threat. While negative motivation may be useful in certain situations, characteristically it is not as effective in promoting efficient learning as positive motivation.

Positive motivation is provided by the promise or achievement of rewards. These rewards may be personal or social; they may involve financial gain, satisfaction of the self-concept, or public recognition. Motivation which can be used to advantage by the instructor includes the desire for personal gain, the desire for personal comfort or security, the desire for group approval, and the achievement of a favorable self-image. The desire for personal gain, either the acquisition of possessions or status, is a basic motivational factor for all human endeavor. An individual may be motivated to dig a ditch or to design a supersonic airplane solely by the desire for financial gain. Students are like typical employees in wanting a tangible return for their efforts. For motivation to be effective, students must believe that their efforts will be suitably rewarded. These rewards must be constantly apparent to the student during instruction, whether they are to be financial, self-esteem, or public recognition.

Lessons often have objectives which are not obvious at first. Although these lessons will pay dividends during later instruction, the student may not appreciate this fact. It is important for the instructor to make the student aware of those applications which are not immediately apparent. Likewise, the devotion of too much time and effort to drill and practice on operations which do not directly contribute to competent performance should be avoided. The desire for personal comfort and security is a form of motivation which instructors often forget. All students want secure, pleasant conditions and a safe environment. If they recognize that what they are learning may promote these objectives, their attention is easier to attract and hold. Insecure and unpleasant training situations inhibit learning. Everyone wants to avoid pain and injury. Students normally are eager to learn operations or procedures which help prevent injury or loss of life. This is especially true when the student knows that the ability to make timely decisions, or to act correctly in an emergency, is based on sound principles.

The attractive features of the activity to be learned also can be a strong motivational factor. Students are anxious to learn skills which may be used to their advantage. If they understand that each task will be useful in preparing for future activities, they will be more willing to pursue it. Another strong motivating force is group approval. Every person wants the approval of peers and superiors. Interest can be stimulated and maintained by building on this natural desire. Most students enjoy the feeling of belonging to a group and are interested in accomplishment which will give them prestige among their fellow students.

Every person seeks to establish a favorable self-image. In certain instances, this self-image may be submerged in feelings of insecurity or despondency. Fortunately, most people engaged in a task believe that success is possible under the right combination of circumstances and good fortune. This belief can be a powerful motivating force for students. An instructor can effectively foster this motivation by the introduction of perceptions which are solidly based on previously learned factual information that is easily recognized by the student. Each additional block of learning should help formulate insight which contributes to the ultimate training goals. This promotes student confidence in the overall training program and, at the same time, helps the student develop a favorable self-image. As this confirmation progresses and confidence increases, advances will be more rapid and motivation will be strengthened.

Positive motivation is essential to true learning. Negative motivation in the form of reproofs or threats should be avoided with all but the most overconfident and impulsive students. Slumps in learning are often due to declining motivation. Motivation does not remain at a uniformly high level. It may be affected by outside influences, such as physical or mental disturbances or inadequate instruction. The instructor should strive to maintain motivation at the highest possible level. In addition, the instructor should be alert to detect and counter any lapses in motivation.

## LEVELS OF LEARNING

Levels of learning may be classified in any number of ways. Four basic levels have traditionally been included in aviation instructor training. The lowest level is the ability to repeat something which one has been taught, without understanding or being able to apply what has been learned. This is referred to as rote learning. Progressively higher levels of learning are understanding what has been taught, achieving the skill for application of what has been learned, and correlation of what has been learned with other things previously learned or subsequently encountered. For example, a flight instructor may explain to a beginning student the procedure for entering a level, left turn. The procedure may include several steps such as:

- Visually clear the area,
- Add a slight amount of power to maintain airspeed,
- Apply aileron control pressure to the left,
- Add sufficient rudder pressure in the direction of the turn to avoid slipping and skidding, and
- Increase back pressure to maintain altitude.

A student who can verbally repeat this instruction has learned the procedure by rote. This will not be very useful to the student if there is never an opportunity to make a turn in flight, or if the student has no knowledge of the function of airplane controls. With proper instruction on the effect and use of the flight controls, and experience in controlling the airplane during straight-and-level flight, the student can consolidate these old and new perceptions into an insight on how to make a turn. At this point, the student has developed an understanding of the procedure for turning the airplane in flight. This understanding is basic to effective learning, but may not necessarily enable the student to make a correct turn on the first attempt.

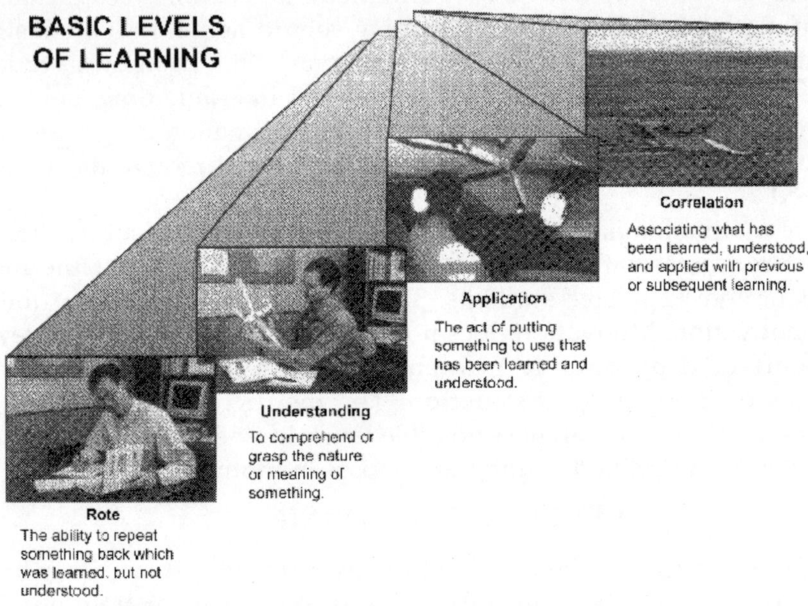


**Fig.** Learning is progressive and occurs at several basic levels

When the student understands the procedure for entering a turn, has had turns demonstrated, and has practiced turn entries until consistency has been achieved, the student has developed the skill to apply what has been learned. This is a major level of learning, and one at which the instructor is too often willing to stop. Discontinuing instruction on turn entries at this point and directing subsequent instruction exclusively to other elements of piloting performance is characteristic of piecemeal instruction, which is usually inefficient. It violates the building block concept of instruction by failing to apply what has been learned to future learning tasks. The building block concept will be covered later in more detail. The correlation level of learning, which should be the objective of aviation instruction, is that level at which the student becomes able to associate an element which has been learned with other segments or blocks of learning. The other segments may be items or skills previously learned, or new learning tasks to be undertaken in the future. The student who has achieved this level of learning in turn entries, for example, has developed the ability to correlate the elements of turn entries with the performance of chandelier and lazy eights.

## DOMAINS OF LEARNING

Besides the four basic levels of learning, educational psychologists have developed several additional levels. These classifications consider what is to be learned. Is it knowledge only, a change in attitude, a physical skill, or a combination of knowledge and skill? One of the more useful categorizations of learning objectives includes three domains:

- Cognitive domain (knowledge),
- Affective domain (attitudes, beliefs, and values), and
- Psychomotor domain (physical skills).
- Each of the domains has a hierarchy of educational objectives.

The listing of the hierarchy of objectives is often called a taxonomy. A taxonomy of educational objectives is a systematic classification scheme for sorting learning outcomes into the three broad categories and ranking the desired outcomes in a developmental hierarchy from least complex to most complex.

## COGNATIVE DOMAIN

### Cognative Domain

The cognitive domain, described by Dr. Benjamin Bloom, is one of the best known educational domains.

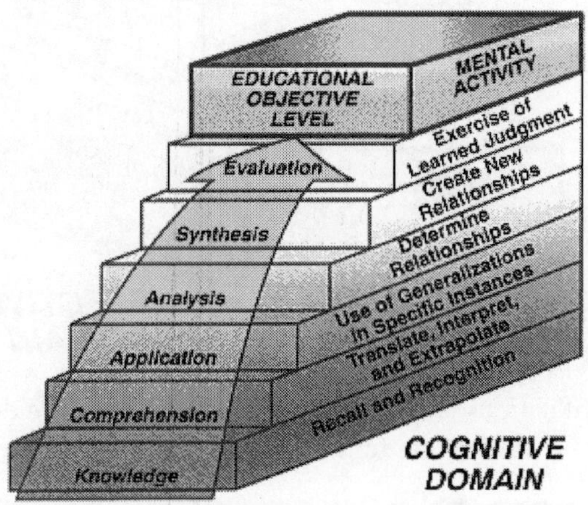


**Fig.** Dr. Bloom's hierarchical taxonomy for the cognitive domain (knowledge) includes six education objective levels.

It contains additional levels of knowledge and understanding and is commonly referred to as Bloom's taxonomy of educational objectives. In aviation, educational objectives in the cognitive domain refer to knowledge which might be gained as the result of attending a ground school, reading about aircraft systems, listening to a preflight briefing, reviewing meteorological reports, or taking part in computer-based training. The highest educational objective level in this domain may also be illustrated by learning to correctly evaluate a flight maneuver, repair an airplane engine, or review a training syllabus for depth and completeness of training.

## AFFECTIVE DOMAIN

The affective domain may be the least understood, and in many ways, the most important of the learning domains. A similar system for specifying attitudinal objectives has been developed by D.R. Krathwohl. Like the Bloom taxonomy, Krathwohl's hierarchy attempts to arrange these objectives in an order of difficulty. Since the affective domain is concerned with a student's attitudes, personal beliefs, and values, measuring educational objectives in this domain is not easy. For example, how is a positive attitude toward safety evaluated? Observable safety-related behavior indicates a positive attitude, but this is not like a simple pass/fail test that can be used to evaluate cognitive educational objective levels. Although a number of techniques are available for evaluation of achievement in the affective domain, most rely on indirect inferences.

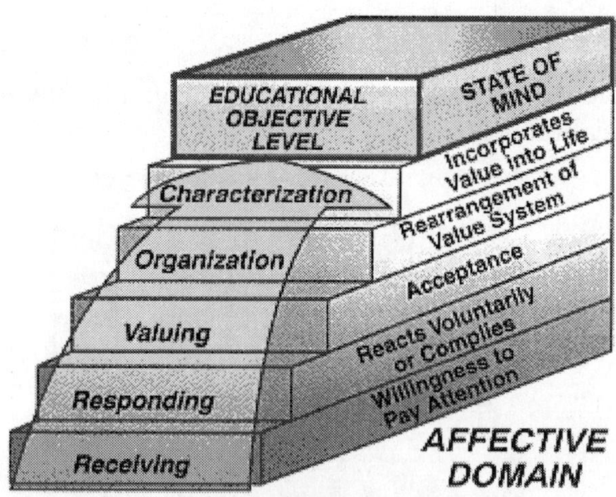


**Fig.** D.R. Krathwohl's hierarchical taxonomy for the affective domain (altitudes, beliefs, and values) contains five education objective levels.

## PSYCHOMOTOR DOMAIN

here are several taxonomies which deal with the psychomotor domain but none are as popularly recognized as the Bloom and Krathwohl taxonomies.

However, the taxonomy developed by E.J. Simpson also is generally acceptable. Psychomotor or physical skills always have been important in aviation. Typical activities involving these skills include learning to fly a precision instrument approach procedure, programming a GPS receiver, or using sophisticated maintenance equipment. As physical tasks and equipment become more complex, the requirement for integration of cognitive and physical skills increases.

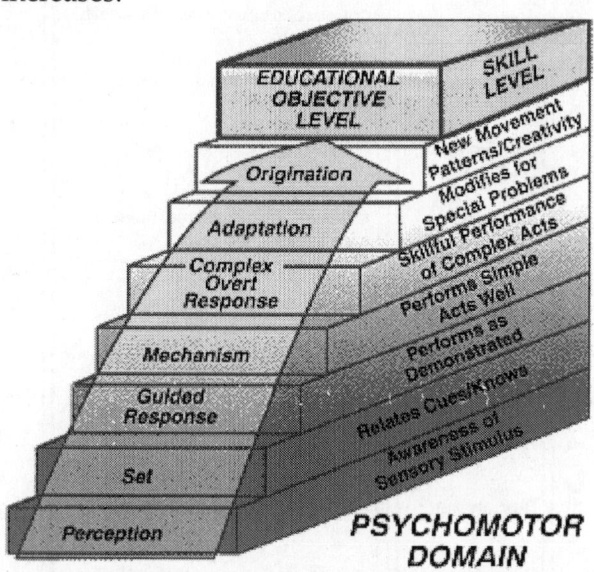


**Fig.** E.J. Simpson's hierarchical taxonomy for the psychomotor domain (physical skills) consists of seven educational objective levels.

## PRACTICAL APPLICATION OF LEARNING OBJECTIVES

The additional levels of learning definitely apply to aviation flight and maintenance training. A comparatively high level of knowledge and skill is required. The student also needs to have a well-developed, positive attitude. Thus, all three domains of learning, cognitive, affective, and psychomotor, are pertinent. These additional levels of learning are the basis of the knowledge, attitude, and skill learning objectives commonly used in advanced qualification programs for airline training. They also can be tied to the practical test standards to show the level of knowledge or skill required for a particular task. A list of action verbs for the three domains shows appropriate behavioral objectives at each level. Instructors who are familiar with curricula development will recognize that the action verbs are examples of performance-based objectives. Expanded coverage of the concept of performance-based objectives is included in Chapter 4 of this handbook.

| | OBJECTIVE LEVEL | ACTION VERBS FOR EACH LEVEL |
|---|---|---|
| COGNITIVE DOMAIN | Evaluation | assess, evaluate, interpret, judge, rate, score, or write |
| | Synthesis | compile, compose, design, reconstruct, or formulate |
| | Analysis | compare, discriminate, distinguish, or separate |
| | Application | compute, demonstrate, employ, operate, or solve |
| | Comprehension | convert, explain, locate, report, restate, or select |
| | Knowledge | describe, identify, name, point to, recognize, or recall |
| AFFECTIVE DOMAIN | Characterization | assess, delegate, practice, influence, revise, and maintain |
| | Organization | accept responsibility, adhere, defend, and formulate |
| | Valuing | appreciate, follow, join, justify, show concern, or share |
| | Responding | conform, greet, help, perform, recite, or write |
| | Receiving | ask, choose, give, locate, select, rely, or use |
| PSYCHOMOTOR DOMAIN | Origination | combine, compose, construct, design, or originate |
| | Adaptation | adapt, alter, change, rearrange, reorganize, or revise |
| | Complex Overt Response | same as below except more highly coordinated |
| | Mechanism | same as below except with greater proficiency |
| | Guided Response | assemble, build, calibrate, fix, grind, or mend |
| | Set | begin, move, react, respond, start, or select |
| | Perception | choose, detect, identify, isolate, or compare |

**Fig.** A listing such as the one shown here is useful for development of almost any training program

## LEARNING PHYSICAL SKILLS

Even though the process of learning is profound, the main objective or purpose of most instruction typically is teaching a concept, a generalization, an attitude, or a skill. The process of learning a psychomotor or physical skill is much the same, in many ways, as cognitive learning. To provide a real illustration of physical skill learning, try the following exercise: On a separate sheet of paper, write the word "learning" 15 times with your left hand or with your right hand, if you are left handed. Try to improve the speed and quality of your writing as you go along.

### PHYSICAL SKILLS INVOLVE MORE THAN MUSCLES

The above exercise contains a practical example of the multifaceted character of learning. It should be obvious that, while a muscular sequence was being learned, other things were happening as well. The perception changed as the sequence became easier. Concepts of how to perform the skill were developed and attitudes were changed.

### DESIRE TO LEARN

Thinking back over their past experiences in learning to perform certain skills, students might be surprised at how much more readily they learned those skills that appealed to their own needs. Shorter initial learning time and more rapid progress in improving the skill normally occurred. Conversely, where the desire to learn or improve was missing, little progress was made. A person may read dozens of books a year, but the reading rate will not increase unless there is a deliberate intent to increase it. In the preceding learning exercise, it is unlikely that any improvement occurred unless there was a clear intention to improve. To improve, one must not only recognize mistakes, but also make an effort to correct them. The person who lacks the desire to improve is not likely to make the effort and consequently will continue to practice errors. The skillful instructor relates the lesson objective to the student's intentions and needs and, in so doing, builds on the student's natural enthusiasm.

### PATTERNS TO FOLLOW

Logically, the point has been emphasized that the best way to prepare the student to perform a task is to provide a clear, step-by-step example. Having a model to follow permits students to get a clear picture of each step in the sequence so they understand what is required and how to do it. In flight or maintenance training, the instructor provides the demonstration, emphasizing the steps and techniques. During classroom instruction, an outside expert may be used, either in person or in a video presentation. In any case, students need to have a clear impression of what they are to do.

## PERFORM THE SKILL

After experiencing writing a word with the wrong hand, consider how difficult it would be to tell someone else how to do it. Even demonstrating how to do it would not result in that person learning the skill. Obviously, practice is necessary. The student needs coordination between muscles and visual and tactile senses. Learning to perform various aircraft maintenance skills or flight maneuvers requires this sort of practice. There is another benefit of practice. As the student gains proficiency in a skill, verbal instructions mean more. Whereas a long, detailed explanation is confusing before the student begins performing, specific comments are more meaningful and useful after the skill has been partially mastered.

## KNOWLEDGE OF RESULTS

In learning some simple skills, students can discover their own errors quite easily. In other cases, such as learning complex aircraft maintenance skills, flight maneuvers, or flight crew duties, mistakes are not always apparent. A student may know that something is wrong, but not know how to correct it. In any case, the instructor provides a helpful and often critical function in making certain that the students are aware of their progress. It is perhaps as important for students to know when they are right as when they are wrong. They should be told as soon after the performance as possible, and should not be allowed to practice mistakes. It is more difficult to unlearn a mistake, and then learn it correctly, than to learn correctly in the first place. One way to make students aware of their progress is to repeat a demonstration or example and to show them the standards their performance must ultimately meet.

## PROGRESS FOLLOWS A PATTERN

The experience of learning to write a word with the wrong hand probably confirmed what has been consistently demonstrated in laboratory experiments on skill learning. The first trials are slow, and coordination is lacking. Mistakes are frequent, but each trial provides clues for improvement in subsequent trials. The student modifies different aspects of the skill such as how to hold the pencil, or how to execute finger and hand movement. Graphs of the progress of skill learning, such as the one shown below, usually follow the same pattern. There is rapid improvement in the early stages, then the curve levels off and may stay level for a significant period of time. Further improvement may seem unlikely. This is a typical learning plateau.

A learning plateau may signify any number of conditions. For example, the student may have reached capability limits, may be consolidating levels of skill, interest may have waned, or the student may need a more efficient method for increasing progress. Keep in mind that the apparent lack of increasing proficiency does not necessarily mean that learning has ceased. The point is that, in learning motor skills, a leveling off process, or a plateau, is normal and should be expected after an initial period of rapid improvement. The instructor should prepare the student for this situation to avert discouragement. If the student is aware of this learning plateau, frustration may be minimized.

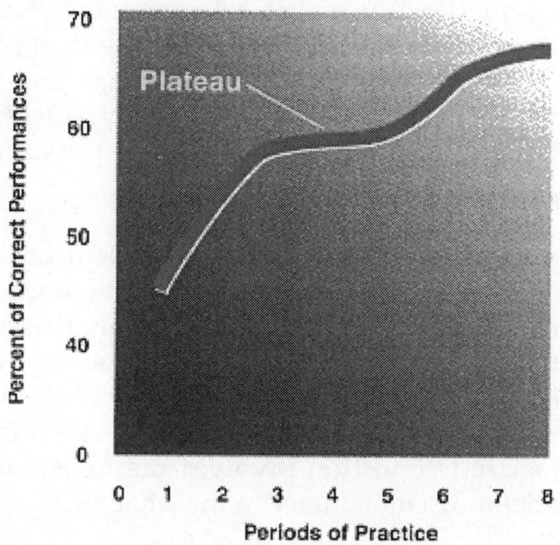


**Fig.** Students will more than likely experience a learning plateau at some point in their training.

## DURATION AND ORGANIZATION OF A LESSON

In planning for student performance, a primary consideration is the length of time devoted to practice. A beginning student reaches a point where additional practice is not only unproductive, but may even be harmful. When this point is reached, errors increase, and motivation declines. As a student gains experience, longer periods of practice are profitable.

Another consideration is the problem of whether to divide the practice period. Perhaps even the related instruction should be broken down into segments, or it may be advantageous to plan one continuous, integrated sequence. The answer depends on the nature of the skill. Some skills are composed of closely related steps, each dependent on the preceding one. Learning to pack a parachute is a good example. Other skills are composed of related subgroups of skills. Learning to overhaul an aircraft engine is a good example.

## EVALUATION VS CRITIQUE

If an instructor were to evaluate the fifteenth writing of the word "learning," only limited help could be given toward further improvement. The instructor could judge whether the written word was legible and evaluate it against some criterion or standard, or perhaps even assign it a grade of some sort. None of these actions would be particularly useful to the beginning student. However, the student could profit by having someone watch the performance and critique constructively to help eliminate errors.

In the initial stages, practical suggestions are more valuable to the student than a grade. Early evaluation is usually teacher oriented. It provides a check on teaching effectiveness, can be used to predict eventual student learning proficiency, and can help the teacher locate special problem areas. The observations on which the evaluations are based also can identify the student's strengths and weaknesses, a prerequisite for making constructive criticism.

### APPLICATION OF SKILL

The final and critical question is, Can the student use what has been learned? It is not uncommon to find that students devote weeks and months in school learning new abilities, and then fail to apply these abilities on the job. To solve this problem, two conditions must be present. First, the student must learn the skill so well that it becomes easy, even habitual; and second, the student must recognize the types of situations where it is appropriate to use the skill. This second condition involves the question of transfer of learning, which is briefly discussed later in this chapter.

## MEMORY

Memory is an integral part of the learning process. Although there are several theories on how the memory works, a widely accepted view is the multi-stage concept which states that memory includes three parts: sensory, working or short-term, and long-term systems. The total system operates somewhat like an advanced computer that accepts input from an external source, contains a processing apparatus, a storage capability, and an output function.

### SENSORY REGISTER

The sensory register receives input from the environment and quickly processes it according to the individual's preconceived concept of what is important. However, other factors can influence the reception of information by the sensory system. For example, if the input is dramatic and impacts more than one of the five senses, that information is more likely to make an impression. The sensory register processes inputs or stimuli from the environment within seconds, discards what is considered extraneous, and processes what is determined by the individual to be relevant. This is a selective process where the sensory register is set to recognize certain stimuli and immediately transmit them to the working memory for action. The process is called preceding. An example is sensory preceding to recognize a fire alarm.

No matter what is happening at the time, when the sensory register detects a fire alarm, the working memory is immediatly made aware of the alarm and preset responses begin to take place.

## WORKING OR SHORT-TERM MEMORY

Within seconds the relevant information is passed to the working or short-term memory where it may temporarily remain or rapidly fade, depending on the individual's priorities. Several common steps help retention in the short-term memory. These include rehearsal or repetition of the information and sorting or categorization into systematic chunks. The sorting process is usually called coding or chunking. A key limitation of the working memory is that it takes 5-10 seconds to properly code information. If the coding process is interrupted, that information is lost after about 20 seconds.

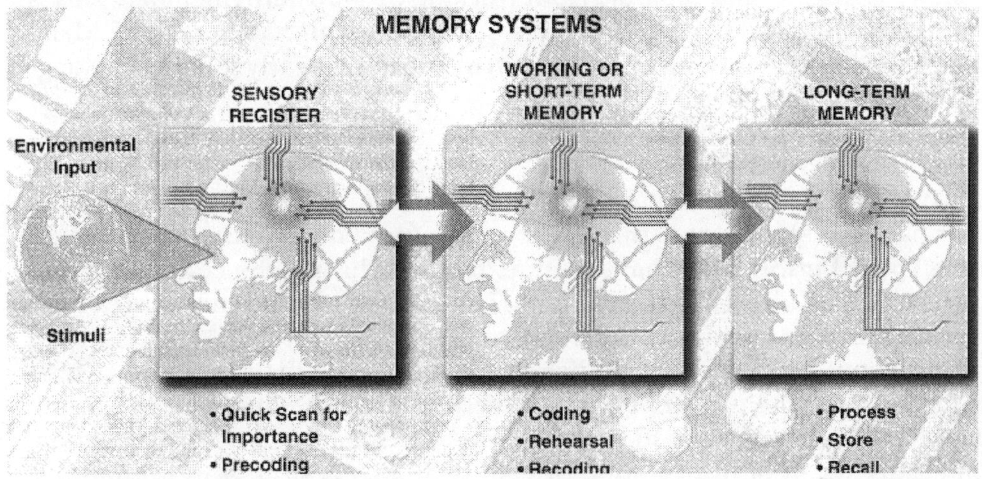


**Fig.** Information processing within the sensory register, working or short-term memory, and long-term memory includes complex coding, sorting, storing, and recall functions.

The working or short-term memory is not only time limited, it also has limited capacity, usually about seven bits or chunks of information. A seven-digit telephone number is an example. As indicated, the time limitation may be overcome by rehearsal. This means learning the information by a rote memorization process. Of course, rote memorization is subject to imperfections in both the duration of recall and in its accuracy. The coding process is more useful in a learning situation. In addition, the coding process may involve recoding to adjust the information to individual experiences. This is when actual learning begins to take place. Therefore, recoding may be described as a process of relating incoming information to concepts or knowledge already in memory.

Methods of coding vary with subject matter, but typically they include some type of association. Use of rhymes or mnemonics is common. An example of a useful mnemonic is the memory aid for one of the magnetic compass errors. The letters "ANDS" indicate:

- Accelerate
- North
- Decelerate
- South

Variations of the coding process are practically endless. They may consist of the use of acronyms, the chronology of events, images, semantics, or an individually developed structure based on past experiences. Developing a logical strategy for coding information is a significant step in the learning process. In this brief discussion of memory, it may appear that sensory memory is distinct and separate from working or short-term memory. This is not the case. In fact, all of the memory systems are intimately related. Many of the functions of working or short-term memory are nearly identical to long-term memory functions.

## LONG-TERM MEMORY

What then is distinctive about the long-term memory? This is where information is stored for future use. For the stored information to be useful, some special effort must have been expended during the coding process in working or short-term memory. The coding should have provided meaning and connections between old and new information. If initial coding is not properly accomplished, recall will be distorted and it may be impossible. The more effective the coding process, the easier the recall. However, it should be noted that the long-term memory is a reconstruction, not a pure recall of information or events. It also is subject to limitations, such as time, biases, and, in many cases, personal inaccuracies. This is why two people who view the same event will often have totally different recollections.

Memory also applies to psychomotor skills. For example, with practice, a tennis player may be able to serve a tennis ball at a high rate of speed and with accuracy. This may be accomplished with very little thought. For a pilot, the ability to instinctively perform certain maneuvers or other tasks which require manual dexterity and precision provides obvious benefits. For example, it allows the pilot more time to concentrate on other essential duties such as navigation, communications with air traffic control facilities, and visual scanning for other aircraft. As implied, one of the major responsibilities of the instructor is to help students use their memories effectively. Strategies designed to aid students in retention and recall of information from the long-term memory are included later in this chapter. At the same time, an associated phenomenon, forgetting, cannot be ignored.

## THEORIES OF FORGETTING

A consideration of why people forget may point the way to help them remember. Several theories account for forgetting, including disuse, interference, and repression.

### Disuse

The theory of disuse suggests that a person forgets those things which are not used. The high school or college graduate is saddened by the lack of factual data retained several years after graduation. Since the things which are remembered are those used on the job, a person concludes that forgetting is the result of disuse. But the explanation is not quite so simple. Experimental studies show, for example, that a hypnotized person can describe specific details of an event which normally is beyond recall. Apparently the memory is there, locked in the recesses of the mind. The difficulty is summoning it up to consciousness.

### Interference

The basis of the interference theory is that people forget something because a certain experience has overshadowed it, or that the learning of similar things has intervened. This theory might explain how the range of experiences after graduation from school causes a person to forget or to lose knowledge. In other words, new events displace many things that had been learned. From experiments, at least two conclusions about interference may be drawn. First, similar material seems to interfere with memory more than dissimilar material; and second, material not well learned suffers most from interference.

### Repression

Freudian psychology advances the view that some forgetting is repression due to the submersion of ideas into the subconscious mind. Material that is unpleasant or produces anxiety may be treated this way by the individual, but not intentionally. It is subconscious and protective. The repression theory does not appear to account for much forgetfulness of the kind discussed in this chapter, but it does tend to explain some cases.

## RETENTION OF LEARNING

Each of the theories implies that when a person forgets something, it is not actually lost. Rather, it is simply unavailable for recall. The instructor's problem is how to make certain that the student's learning is readily available for recall. The following suggestions can help. Teach thoroughly and with meaning. Material thoroughly learned is highly resistant to forgetting. This is suggested by experimental studies and it also was pointed out in the sections on skill learning. Meaningful learning builds patterns of relationship in the student's consciousness. In contrast, rote learning is superficial and is not easily retained. Meaningful learning goes deep because it involves principles and concepts anchored in the student's own experiences. The following discussion emphasizes five principles which are generally accepted as having a direct application to remembering.

**Praise Stimulates Learning**

Responses which give a pleasurable return tend to be repeated. Absence of praise or recognition tends to discourage, and any form of negativism in the acceptance of a response tends to make its recall less likely.

**Recall is Promoted by Association**

As discussed earlier, each bit of information or action which is associated with something to be learned tends to facilitate its later recall by the student. Unique or disassociated facts tend to be forgotten unless they are of special interest or application.

**Favorable Attitudes Aid Retention**

People learn and remember only what they wish to know. Without motivation there is little chance for recall. The most effective motivation is based on positive or rewarding objectives.

**Learning with All our Senses is most Effective**

Although we generally receive what we learn through the eyes and ears, other senses also contribute to most perceptions. When several senses respond together, a fuller understanding and greater chance of recall is achieved.

**Meaningful Repetition Aids Recall**

Each repetition gives the student an opportunity to gain a clearer and more accurate perception of the subject to be learned, but mere repetition does not guarantee retention. Practice provides an opportunity for learning, but does not cause it. Further, some research indicates that three or four repetitions provide the maximum effect, after which the rate of learning and probability of retention fall off rapidly.

Along with these five principles, there is a considerable amount of additional literature on retention of learning during a typical academic lesson. After the first 10-15 minutes, the rate of retention drops significantly until about the last 5-10 minutes when students wake up again. Students passively listening to a lecture have roughly a five percent retention rate over a 24-hour period, but students actively engaged in the learning process have a much higher retention. This clearly reiterates the point that active learning is superior to just listening.

## TRANSFER OF LEARNING

During a learning experience, the student may be aided by things learned previously. On the other hand, it is sometimes apparent that previous learning interferes with the current learning task. Consider the learning of two skills. If the learning of skill A helps to learn skill B, positive transfer occurs. If learning skill A hinders the learning of skill B, negative transfer occurs. For example, the practice of slow flight helps the student learn short-field landings. However, practice in making a landing approach in an airplane may hinder learning to make an approach in a helicopter. It should be noted that the learning of skill B may affect the retention or proficiency of skill A, either positively or negatively. While these processes may help substantiate the interference theory of forgetting, they are still concerned with the transfer of learning. It seems clear that some degree of transfer is involved in all learning. This is true because, except for certain inherent responses, all new learning is based upon previously learned Experience. People interpret new things in terms of what they already know. Many aspects of teaching profit by this type of transfer. It may explain why students of apparently equal ability have differing success in certain areas. Negative transfer may hinder the learning of some; positive transfer may help others. This points to a need to know a student's past experience and what has already been learned. In lesson and syllabus development, instructtors should plan for transfer by organizing course materials and individual lesson materials in a meaningful sequence. Each phase should help the student learn what is to follow.

The cause of transfer and exactly how it occurs is difficult to determine, but no one disputes the fact that transfer does occur. The significance of this ability for the instructor is that the students can be helped to achieve it. The following suggestions are representative of what educational psychologists believe should be done. Plan for transfer as a primary objective. As in all areas of teaching, the chance for success is increased if the teacher deliberately plans to achieve it. Make certain that the students understand that what is learned can be applied to other situations. Prepare them to seek other applications.

Maintain high-order learning standards. Overlearning may even be appropriate. The more thoroughly the students understand the material, the more likely they are to see its relationship to new situations. Avoid unnecessary rote learning, since it does not foster transfer. Provide meaningful learning experiences that build students' confidence in their ability to transfer learning. This suggests activities that challenge them to exercise their imagination and ingenuity in applying their knowledge and skills. Use instructional material that helps form valid concepts and generalizations. Use materials that make relationships clear.

## HABIT FORMATION

The formation of correct habit patterns from the beginning of any learning process is essential to further learning and for correct performance after the completion of training. Remember, primacy is one of the fundamental principles of learning. Therefore, it is the instructor's responsibility to insist on correct techniques and procedures from the outset of training to provide proper habit patterns. It is much easier to foster proper habits from the beginning of training than to correct faulty ones later. Due to the high level of knowledge and skill required in aviation for both pilots and maintenance technicians, training traditionally has followed a building block concept. This means new learning and habit patterns are based on a solid foundation of experience and/or old learning. Everything from intricate cognitive processes to simple motor skills depends on what the student already knows and how that knowledge can be applied in the present. As knowledge and skill increase, there is an expanding base upon which to build for the future.

# BEHAVIOR MANAGEMENT

Behavior management is similar to behavior modification. It is a less intensive version of behavior therapy. In behavior modification the focus is on changing behavior, while in behavior management the focus is on maintaining order. Behavior management skills are of particular importance to teachers in the educational system. Behavior management include all of the actions and conscious inactions to enhance the probability people, individually and in groups, choose behaviors which are personally fulfilling, productive, and socially acceptable.

There is a great deal of research related to "behavior change" and "behavior management". B.F. Skinner and Carl Rogers have given two distinctly different approaches for addressing behavior. Skinner's approach says that any one can manipulate behavior by first identifying what the individual finds rewarding. Once the rewards of an individual are known, then those rewards can be selected that the manager is willing to give in exchange for good behavior. Skinner calls this "Positive Reinforcement Psychology". Rogers proposes that in order to effectively address behavior problems, individual must be persuaded to want to behave appropriately. This is done by teaching the individual the difference between right and wrong including why he or she should do what is right. Rogers believes that the individual must have an internal awareness of right and wrong.

## USES OF BEHAVIOR MANAGEMENT

Many of the principles and techniques used are the same as behavior modification yet delivered in a less intensively and consistent fashion. Usually, behavior management is applied at the group level by a classroom teacher as a form of behavioral engineering to produce high rates of student work completion and minimize classroom disruption. In addition, greater focus has been placed on building self control. Brophy writes:

- "Contemporary behavior modification approaches involve students more actively in planning and shaping their own behavior through participation in the negotiation of contracts with their teachers and through exposure to training designed to help them to monitor and evaluate their behavior more actively, to learn techniques of self-control and problem solving, and to set goals and reinforce themselves for meeting these goals."

In general behavior management strategies have been very effective in reducing classroom disruption. In addition, recent efforts have focused on incorporating principles of functional assessment into the process.

While such programs can come from a variety of behavioral change theories, the most common practices rely on the use of applied behavior analysis principles such as positive reinforcement and mild punishments. Behavioral practices such as differential reinforcement are commonly used. Sometimes, these are delivered in a token economy or a level system. In general the reward component is considered effective. For example, Cotton reviewed 37 studies on tokens, praise and other reward systems and found them to be highly effective in managing student classroom behavior. The most comprehensive review of token procedures to match to children's level of behavioral severity was Walker's text "The acting out child."

## BUILDING PROSOCIAL BEHAVIOUR

Over the years, behavioral management principles such as reinforcement, modeling and even the use of punishment have been explored in the building of prosocial behavior. This area is sometimes referred to as "Behavioral Development" or Behavior analysis of child development. Midlarsky and colleagues used a combination of modeling and reinforcement to build altruistic behavior. Two studies exist in which modeling by itself did not increase prosocial behavior; however, modeling is much more effective than instruction giving. The role of rewards has been implicated in the building of self-control and empathy. Cooperation seems particularly susceptible to rewards. Sharing is another prosocial behavior influenced by reinforcement.

Reinforcement is particularly effective at least early in the learning series if context conditions are similar. Evidence exists to show some generalization. More controversial has been the role of punishment in forming prosocial behavior. One study found that donation rates of children could be increased by punishing episodes of failure to donate. The socialization process continues by peers with reinforcement and punishment playing major roles. Peers are more likely to punish cross-gender play and reinforce play specific to gender.

# LEARNING THEORIES AND ITS APPLICATION

## INTRODUCTION

Most people have been close to formal learning situations for a significant part of their lives. They are very curious to know about its dynamics and seek to clarify the following questions. To what extent can we attribute a person's behavior to learning? Will people learn things in spite of their environment? What is the difference between learning a behavior and acquiring it naturally? Can a skill be acquired or must an individual be born with such a talent as part their personality. These kinds of question demand that managers have a thorough understanding of what learning is and in what ways learning influences behavior.

## LEARNING PROCESS

Theories of Learning: Learning is part of every one's life. In our life, all complex behavior is learned. Learning is defined as any relatively permanent change in behavior that occurs as a result of experience. Whenever any change occurs learning is taken place in the individual. If an individual behaves, reacts, responds as a result of experience which is different from others, a person has encountered some new learning experience in his life. This definition consists of the following four key elements:

Change process: Learning involves some change in oneself in terms of observable actions explicitly shown to others or change in ones attitude or thought process occur with oneself implicitly. Change may be good or bad or positive or negative from an organization point of view. If a person is happened to experience some negative incidents, that person will hold prejudices or bias or to restrict their out put. On the contrary, if a person is encountering some good incident, that person is likely to hold positive attitude.

Permanent change: Due to whatever exposure a person encounters, the impact what it generates may be long lasting and permanent. Hence, the change must be of relatively permanent. If change occurs due to fatigue or alcohol consumption or temporary adaptation, it may be vanished once the goal is achieved. Setting behavioral actions: Explicit changes occurring in behavior is the main goal of learning process. A change in an individual's thought process or attitudes without any changes in any explicit behavior will not be considered as learning process. Need for meaningful experiences: Some form of experiences is necessary for learning. Experience may be acquired directly through observation or practice. If experience results in a relatively permanent change in behavior, one can confidently say that learning has taken place. Theories of Learning: There are three types of learning theories. These theories are classical conditioning, operant conditioning and social learning.

## CLASSICAL CONDITIONING THEORY

Russian physiologist Ivan Pavlov developed classical conditioning theory. When he was doing a research on the chemical properties of saliva of dog, he noticed accidentally that the dog started salivating the moment hearing the sound of a door of cupboard clinging. Based on his observation, he wanted to do some experiment whether the dog can be conditioned to respond to any neutral stimuli. He used a simple surgical procedure to operate the salivary glands of a dog to measure accurately the amount of saliva. Pavlov's Experiment: Pavlov conducted his experiment in three stages.

*Stage I:* When Pavlov presented the dog with a piece of meat, the dog exhibited a noticeable increase in salivation. The meat is unconditional stimulus and salivation is unconditional response.

*Stage II:* In this stage, the dog was not given a peace of meat but only exposed to a sound of ringing bell; the dog did not salivate to the mere sound of a ringing bell.

*Stage III:* Pavlov decided to link both the presentation of meat and the ringing of a bell one after the other with an interval of 5 minutes. After repeatedly hearing the bell before getting the meat, the dog began to salivate as soon the bell rang. There is an association or link between meat and ringing a bell. After repeating the association between meat and ringing a bell, the dog started salivating merely at the sound of the bell, even if no food was offered. The dog is now conditioned to respond to a sound of a bell and started salivating. This is called classical conditioning process.

Thus, classical condition is defined as the formation of S-R link or habit between a conditioned stimulus and a conditioned response through the repeated paring of conditioned stimulus with an unconditioned stimulus. In this experiment, the meat is unconditioned stimulus, and the expected response that is, salivating to the meat is called as unconditioned response. The sound of a bell is a neutral stimulus which does not have any property to elicit salivation, is called as conditioned stimulus. Although it was originally neutral, if the bell was paired with meat it acquired the same property as meat eliciting the salivation. The sound of a bell produced salivation when presented alone. This is called conditioned response, that is, now the dog is conditioned to respond to the sound of a bell. Learning conditioned response involves building up an association between a conditioned stimulus and unconditioned stimulus. When the stimuli, one is natural and the other one neutral are paired, the neutral one becomes a conditioned stimulus and hence takes on the properties of the unconditioned stimulus. Closely associated with classical conditioning as a vehicle for learning new behaviors are the phenomenon of extinction, spontaneous recovery, stimulus generalization and stimulus discrimination.

**Extinction**

Once a dog has learned to salivate to a bell, does this reflex continue to occur if the bell is sounded for many trails without the meat. Pavlov found that without meat, the bell elicits less and less salivation on each trail and eventually stopped salivating once for all. This phenomenon is called as extinction.

**Spontaneous Recovery**

But they also found that extinction does not return the animal fully to the unconditioned state. The mere passage of time following extinction can partially renew the conditioned reflex, a phenomenon is known as spontaneous recovery. And a single pairing of the conditioned stimulus with the unconditioned stimulus can renew the conditioned reflex, which can be abolished again only by another series of extinction trails. On the basis of such findings, Pavlov concluded that the conditioned reflex is not truly lost during the extinction, but is somehow inhibited, and that it can be disinhibited by such means as the passage of time or the recurrence of the unconditioned stimulus.

**Stimulus Generalization**

Learning research has demonstrated that individuals can respond to two separate stimuli in the same way on the basis of their similarities. Once the dog is conditioned to salivate to sound of a bell, the dog is also likely to respond to the sound of a buzzer sound which similar to the sound of a bell. In work life, for example, coffee taster must learn to respond appropriately to various flavor and aromas in deciding whether to accept or reject samples of coffee beans. Once they have learned what an ideal tastes and aroma should be, they must judge and compare samples to this standard. After conditioning, stimuli that resemble the conditioned stimulus will elicit the conditioned response even though they themselves are never paired with the unconditioned stimulus. This phenomenon is called generalization. The magnitude or likelihood of a response to the new stimulus is correlated with its degree of similarity to the original conditioned stimulus. Thus a dog conditioned to salivate to a 100-hertz tone also salivated to tones of other frequencies. But the farther the tone was in frequency from the original conditioned stimulus, the less the dog would salivate to it. For example, the acceptable or permissible level of standard is up to 4 degree variation, the taster will check to what extent the samples of coffee ordered is matching to this permissible within the 4 degree standard. On the basis of this similarity, the taster responds in a similar fashion to all samples and accepts those which are matching to that standard. If a person is learned to drive a car, and apply the same principles of driving to drive other mode of vehicles such as truck, van etc.

**Stimulus Discrimination**

Individuals can respond differently in the presence of two separate stimuli on the basis of differences in their characteristics. In the salivation experiment, the dog is conditioned to salivate to the sound of bell and not to the sound of any other sound. In due course of time, the dog is able to discriminate the sounds which are relatively different from the ideal bell sound. The dog, on the basis of stimulus dissimilarity, responds differently to the sounds of different tones by salivating only to the sound of a bell and not to any other mode of sound such as buzzer, metronome, musical note etc. The dog has shown stimulus discrimination. In another experiment, dog is conditioned to salivate to the sight of Black Square and not to any other colored square. After a series of trails in which presentation of gray square were never followed by food and the presentation of the Black Square were always followed by food, the dog stopped salivating to the gray square and continued to salivate to the black one.

The researchers continued this procedure with even-darker shades of gray, until the dog is conditioned to discriminate a Black Square from the gray shades. In traffic control, the drivers are learned to respond to different colors of signal and maintain the order in the traffic regulation. Stimulus generalization and discrimination are highly important as facilitator of learning through classical conditioning. Because of our ability to recognize similarities, individuals are able to transfer what we already know to new situations through the process of stimulus association and generalization. Classical conditioning is a major avenue of learning among individuals in work organizations. For example, trainer in organization take great care to make sure that conditions in the classroom or training facility are as similar as possible to actual work conditions in order to assure that what is learned can be transferred to the job.

**Application of Classical Conditioning Principles at Work**

Whenever President or Vice-President of Corporate Office visits factory site the employees in the shop floor will more attentive at work and look more prim, proper and active in their work life. It is quite natural that top management personnel visit evoking or eliciting a desired response- being prim and proper at work from the employees. The routine cleaning of windows or floor of the administrative office will be neutral stimulus never evoking any response from the employees. If the visit of the top management personnel is associated with such cleaning process, eventually the employees would turn on their best output and look prim and active the moment windows and floor are being cleaned up. The employees had learned to associate the cleaning of the windows with a visit from the head office. The cleaning process evoked attentive and active work behavior. Similarly,

Christmas Carols songs bring pleasant memories of childhood as these songs are being associated with the festive Christmas Spirit. Classical conditioning is passive. It is elicited in response to a specific, identifiable event.

## OPERANT CONDITIONING

Operant conditioned principle is proposed by B.F. Skinner, an American Psychologist. It is a type of conditioning in which desired voluntary behavior leads to a reward or prevent a punishment. Operant conditioning principle emphasizes strongly that the behavior of an individual is a function of its consequences. If the consequences are pleasant, the behavior associated with such consequences will be repeated again and again. If the consequences are unpleasant, the behavior will be in extinct. The rationale behind this theory is that people learn to behave in order to get something they want or to avoid something they don't want. Operant condition is learned process. The tendency to repeat such behaviouir is influenced by the reinforcement or lack of reinforcement brought about by the consequences of the behavior. The proper reinforcement strengthens a behavior and increases the likelihood that it will be repeated.

Skinner's Experiment: Skinner developed an apparatus to conduct a series of learning experiment using rats. He named that apparatus as Skinner's Box which has certain features such as a lever, bowl, light, water container etc. A highly deprived rat is placed in the box. Once a rat nudges or touches or hits the lever attached in the corner of the box, a piece of food pellet is dropped in the bowl. By trail and error, the rat learns that hitting the lever is followed by getting a food pellet in the bowl. Skinner coined the term operant response to any behavioral act such as pressing or hitting or nudging the lever that has some effect on the environment. Thus in a typical experiment with a skinner box, hitting or pressing the lever is an operant response, and the increased rate of lever hitting or pressing that occurs when the response is followed by a pellet of food exemplifies operant conditioning.

### Application of Operant Conditioning in Work Life

If a sales person who hits the assigned target of sales quota will be reinforced with a suitable attractive reward, the chances of hitting further sales target in future will be exemplified. Skinner argued that creating pleasant consequences to follow specific forms of behavior would increase the frequency of that behavior. People will most likely engage in desired behaviors if they are positively reinforced for doing so. Rewards are most effective if they immediately follow the desired response. In addition, behavior that is not rewarded is less likely to be repeated. A commissioned sales person wanting to earn a sizeable income finds that doing so is contingent on generating high sales in his territory.

## SOCIAL LEARNING THEORY

People learn through both observation and direct experience, which is called as sociallearning theory. Individual learn by observing what happens to other people and just by being told about something, as well as by direct experiences. By observing people around us, mostly from parents, teachers, peers, films and television performers, bosses, we learn new behavior pattern. Albert Bandura, who has most vigorously studied observational learning in humans, has emphasized that people observe others to learn not just specific motor skills but also more general modes or styles of behaving. Bandura demonstrated both of these functions of observational learning – acquiring specific actions and learning general styles of behavior – in experiments with children. Bandura proposed that people actively observe the behavior of other people to gain knowledge about the kinds of things that people do, and use that knowledge in situations where it is useful. Social learning theory gives much importance to perceptual process. People respond to how they perceive and defy consequences, not to the objective consequence themselves. The influence of models is key to the social learning process. The following four processes are vital to determine the influence that a model will have on an individual.

Attention Process: People learn from a model only when they recognize and pay attention to its critical features. People tend to be most influenced by models that are attractive, repeatedly available similar to us in our estimation. Retention Process: A model's influence will depend on how well the individual remembers the model's action after the model is no longer readily available. Motor Reproduction Process: After a person has seen a new behavior by observing the model, the watching must be converted to doing. This process then demonstrates that the individual can perform the modeled activities. Reinforcement Process: Individual will be motivated to exhibit they modeled behavior if positive incentives or rewards are provided. Behavior that is positively reinforced will be given more attention, learned better and performed more often.

## REINFORCEMENT THEORIES

Reinforcement theory is broadly based on learning theory and the works of B.F.Skinner. The foundation of this approach is on three fundamental factors. Firstly, it is believed that an individual is basically passive and merely mediates the relationship between the forces acting on him and their output. Secondly, reinforcement also rejects the explanation that behavior is based on an individual's needs, drives, or goals because they believe that such aspects are unobservable and hard to measure. The focus of attention is on behavior itself, which can be observed and measured. Finally, reinforcement theorists state that a relatively permanent change in behavior of an individual result from reinforced behavior or experience. By giving a proper reinforcement, the likely hood that desired behavior will be exhibited can be increased and the likelihood that the undesired behaviors will be exhibited can be reduced or both.

## TYPES OF REINFORCEMENT

In operant conditioning, the consequences of behavior are made to occur contingent on the individual's response or failure to respond. There are three basic components of operant conditioning: i) stimulus, ii) response or performance and iii) consequences or contingencies of reinforcement or rewards. The consequences or types of reinforcement determine the likelihood that a given behavior or response, will be performed in the future. Thus, to change the behavior of an individual, the consequences or reinforcement of the behavior must be changed. There are four types of reinforcement available to manage or modify an individual's behavior.

1. Positive Reinforcement
2. Punishment
3. Avoidance Learning
4. Extinction

### Positive Reinforcement

The application of this type of reinforcement to a given response or behavior increases the likelihood that the particular behavior by the individual will be repeated. For example, an engineer is given the task of designing a new piece of equipment. The engineer exerts a high level of effort and completes the project in time. The supervisor reviews the work and not only praises the engineer for his or her work, but recommends, for example, a pay increase for the excellent work. Negative reinforcement increases the frequency and strength of a desired behavior by making it contingent upon the avoidance of undesirable consequences for the employees. In order to avoid the heavy fine imposed for not wearing the helmet, the riders of two wheelers are likely to wear helmet continuously even though such an act is not so pleasant and voluntary. In order to avoid the firing of supervisor for late coming, the employee will ensure to report to office on time. Just to avoid the unpleasantness in the future, the person will try to exhibit the desired work behavior. Thus the negative reinforcement implies the mere anticipation of noxious stimuli from the environment by the employees will reinforce the desired behaviors.

### Punishment

The application of punishment is used to decrease the likelihood that the undesirable behavior or response by the individual will be repeated. Just as positive reinforcement strengthens a particular behavior, punishment weakens it. For example hourly workers in a plastics plant are given one hour for lunch. When a particular work continually takes an hour and thirty minutes for lunch, the supervisor will call the particular worker in his or her office and impose an half-a-day salary cut for their prolonged absent from work. The use of this punishment will hopefully change this worker's response back to acceptable behavior. The difference between punishment and negative reinforcement is that in the former case, noxious consequences is applied to decrease the frequency or strength of an undesired behavior, where as in the latter, a noxious consequences is withheld when a desired behavior is exhibited.

**Avoidance**

Just as with positive reinforcement, this type of reinforcement is a method used by managers to strengthen desired behavior. When a particular reinforcement can prevent the occurrence of an undesired stimulus, it is termed avoidance learning. As the same example cited above, in order to avoid reprimand and criticism, the worker makes a special effort to take only an hour for lunch. With the avoidance learning, the individual works hard to avoid the undesired consequences of the stimulus.

**Extinction**

Extinction is the withholding of positive reinforcement for a previously acceptable response. With continued non-reinforcement over time, the response or behavior will eventually disappear or be eliminated. Extinction involves three steps: i) identifying the behavior that needs to eliminated ii) identifying the reinforcers which encourage the behavior that is desired to be eliminated and iii) stopping the reinforcers. Behavior that is desired to be eliminated in an organizational setting, a company may offer their salespersons a bonus for every order from a new customer. This results in increased effort on the part of the salespersons to cultivate new sales outlets. After a period of time, the company evaluates this bonus system to be too costly to maintain, and there fore eliminates it. The sales force not seeing any further reward for extra effort in developing new sales, reduces their effort to normal levels. The company, by removing the reinforcement, caused an extinction of the behavior on the part of their sales persons. An undesirable behavior can thus be effectively extinguished by withholding the reinforcers.

## SHAPING BEHAVIOR

Shaping behavior is a process of changing an undesirable behavior to a desirable behavior by following a successive approximation of desirable targeted behavior with proper reinforcement. For example, the manager is interested to increase one of the customer service assistants' performances from 5 cases to 30 cases per day by properly following the reinforcement techniques. The managers can reinforce the new employee every time he makes incremental progress. For instance, the first time the customer service assistant process 10 cases, the manager can reward her through a word of praise with some cash incentive. When the customer service assistant started processing 15 cases, he would be reinforced further with double the incentive, and the reinforcement will continue every time a new target is achieved which is closer to the ultimate goal. The target set for attending 30 cases per day will be reached and the desired behavior will be shaped. If management rewarded the individual only when he or she showed desirable responses, there might be considerable improvement in their performance. The managers can shape behaviouir by systematically reinforcing each successive step that moves the individual closer to the desired response.

**Methods of Shaping Behavior**

There are four ways in which shaping of desirable behavior can be achieved: They are Positive Reinforcement, Negative reinforcement, punishment and extinction. The objective of each of the four reinforcement types is to modify an individual's behavior so that it will benefit the organization. Reinforcement will either increase the strength of desired behavior or decrease the strength of undesired behavior depending on the organization's needs and the individual's current behavior.

**Types of Reinforcement Methods**

| Types of Reinforcement | Stimulus | Response | Consequences or Reward |
|---|---|---|---|
| Positive Reinforcement: | High performance is rewarded in the organization | Individual performance at a high level (desired behavior) | Pay increase, recognition, praise |
| Punishment: | Only one hour is given for lunch each day | Individual continually takes more than one hour for lunch | Reprimand by Supervisor |
| Avoidance | Individuals who take more than one hour for lunch will be reprimanded by supervisor | Individuals take only one hour for lunch | No reprimand |
| Extinction | 1. Bonus given to sales person for each new customer order<br>2. Bonus removed for each new customer order | Sales person worked hard to get new orders<br>Sales persons exert only nominal effort to get new orders | Bonus<br>No bonus |

The impact of reinforcement on organizational behavior can be summarized as follows: Some type of reinforcement is necessary to reproduce a change in behavior. Some types or categories of rewards are more effective for use in organization than are others. The speed with which learning takes place and how lasting its effects will be determined by the timing of the reinforcement.

## SCHEDULES OF REINFORCEMENT

Reinforcement works effective when they follow some schedules or pattern. The two main types of reinforcement schedules are continuous or partial

### Continuous Reinforcement

This schedule reinforces the desired behavior each and every time it is demonstrated. Continuous reinforcement helps to direct behaviors toward desired goals quickly. However, it is more expensive to administer, especially if monetary rewards are used as reinforcement. Behaviors reinforced through a continuous reinforcement schedule are also likely to weaken very rapidly once the reinforcements are stopped.

### Intermittent or Partial Reinforcement

In this type of reinforcement not every instance of the desirable behavior is reinforced, but reinforcement is given often enough to make the behavior worth repeating. It is like a gambling house – poker machine in which people will continue to play even when they know the chances of winning is one in ten or hundred times. Intermittent reinforcement can be based on either a time frame or behavior response pattern. Intermittent schedules of reinforcement tend to be slow in establishing the desired behaviors. But once established, the behaviors also tend to be sustained after the reinforcements are stopped. There are four types of intermittent reinforcement schedule based on the intermittent intervals and intermittent behavioral responses.

#### *Fixed Internal Schedule*

Fixed interval schedule refers to the interval of time when behaviors will be rewarded. It could be hourly, weekly, daily, monthly and so on. For example, organizations reinforce desired behaviors in employees by paying their salaries on a monthly basis. Contractors pay daily wages to employees and other staff members by reinforcement their behaviors of doing a good day's work for a good day's pay. These are reinforcements based on a fixed interval schedule.

#### *Variable Interval Schedule*

A variable interval schedule rewards desired behaviors at random intervals of time. Instead of praising every day, a manager praises his employees occasionally, once in a ten days or fortnightly without a fixed time frame. An example of this schedule of reinforcement is a manager patting a good employee whenever he takes unscheduled visits to the shop floor. This kind of reinforcement is easy to administer and the desired behaviors are also sustained over time.

### *Fixed Ratio Schedule*

A fixed ratio schedule is followed when reinforcement are given every nth time a desired behavior occurs. An example of this will be suggestion scheme department giving a certificate of commendation" after every fifth suggestion accepted by the department from an employee.

### *Variable Ratio Schedule*

A variable ratio reinforcement schedule is followed when behaviors are rewarded randomly in terms of the number of times they occur. For example, some times employees are required to stay back at office to complete the required work. In such cases, a manager may reinforce an employee who is staying back to complete his job the first time the person stays late, and not reinforce the same behavior for the next four or five times, but reinforce it once again in the sixth time he stays back and again in fifteenth time he stays back and so on.

**Schedules of Reinforcement for Monetary Rewards:**

| Schedules of Reinforcement | Examples of Research |
|---|---|
| Fixed Interval | Weekly or monthly paycheck |
| Fixed Ratio | Piece-rate pay system based on number of units produced or sales commission |
| Variable Interval | Praise, recognition, or promotion awarded at variable time periods |
| Variable Ratio | Monitory bonuses for excellent performance awarded in small sums at various time periods. |

## BEHAVIOR MODIFICATION

An approach to motivation in organization that uses operant conditioning as its foundation is called behavior modification. The approach recommended by proponents of behavior modification is that of positive reinforcement. It is reported that positive reinforcers are more effective than negative reinforcers in achieving lasting changes in behavior. Behavior - modification programs in organizations generally follow at least five stages of development:

Stages I: Identifying Critical Behaviors: In this step, the managers has to identify the critical behaviors that make a significant impact on the employee's job performance. These are those 5 to 10 percent of behaviors that may account for up to 70 or 80 per cent of each employee's performance. This may be a difficult step for companies that use non-job related factors to measure performance.

Stage II: Developing a Baseline Data: This step requires the manager to develop some baseline performance data. This is obtained by determining the number of times the identified behavior is occurring under present condition. In this stage, specific goals for each employee are established. Lowering the absenteeism by 10 per cent is a typical example. Goals may concern such aspects as productivity improvement, decreased absenteeism and so on

Stage III: Identifying Behavioral Consequences: This step is to perform a functional analysis to identify the behavioral contingencies or consequences of performance. The employee keeps a record of his or her daily work. This acts ass a self-feedback mechanism

Stage IV: Developing and implementing an intervention strategy: The manager reviews the employee's performance record and then rewards the positive aspects of the performance, as determined by the goals set in Stage Two and recorded in Stage Three. Reinforcing with recognition, compliments or praise strengthens the desired behavior; withholding of such reinforcement should help make the employee aware of certain deficiencies in his or performance.

Stage V: Evaluating Performance Improvement: Finally, auditing of the effectiveness of this program is assessed

OB Modification has been used by a number of organizations to improve employee productivity and to reduce errors, absenteeism, tardiness and accident rates and to improve friendliness towards customers.

## IMPLICATIONS OF REINFORCEMENT THEORY

The reinforcement of the relationship between behavior and rewards is very important for maintaining motivated behavior on the part of the individual. Employees react positively when they perceive that rewards are contingent on good performance. When individuals are rewarded continually for their good performance, the employees tend to decrease their performance and motivation. The schedules of reinforcement are found to be very effective in sustaining motivated behavior and make them high productive in their work life. The implications of these results have direct application to the reward system used by organizations. It would be a good idea for manager to reinforce an employee on a continuous basis in the initial stages and after a while, the mangers must switch over to other types of schedules such as fixed interval or fixed ratio, and subsequently the implementation of variable schedules such as variable interval and variable ratio will be of much help to sustain the learned behavior firmly. For the manager, the most important factor in the application of operant conditioning is that employees should be rewarded contingent on their performance, not for the factors that are nonperformance based. Managers must learn how to design and implement effective reinforcement programs that will enable employees to be productive and satisfied with their work.

## CONTENT THEORIES OF MOTIVATION

### INTRODUCTION

Motivation is defined as individual's intention or willingness to put maximum effort in his/her work to reach organizational goals and enhance ones ability to satisfy some individual needs. The cyclic process of motivation starts from Unsatisfied needs??Tension??Drives??Search Behavior??Satisfied Need??to end with Reduced Tension. There are three major elements related to motivation: Effort, Goals and Needs.

#### Effort

It refers to an individual's intensity in reaching the stated goal. The intensity varies from individual to individual and also depends upon the extent to which individual assigns importance to various goals. If these efforts are channeled in proper direction consistent with organizational goals, the organization will maximize its profit and reach a state of excellence in their field.

#### Need

It refers to some internal state that makes certain outcomes appear attractive. It is also a state of deficiency and the organism tries to restore this deficiency to make it as equilibrium. An unsatisfied need creates tension that stimulates drives within an individual. These drives direct the individual in different directions or searching in different places to find a particular goal, If the goal is attained the organism will satisfy the need and reduce the tension.

#### Goals

Human behavior is always goal directed. Once the desired goal is satisfied, individuals will always restate the goals or look for other goals to get sastisfied. Goals will always be changing from one level to another. In order to motivate an individual, managers must ensure to set a goal in such a way which stimulates him or her to put more effort in their work. An effective way to set goals is to follow the SMART approach, which states that goals should meet five characteristics:

1. Specific
2. Measurable
3. Achievable

4. Relevant
5. Timely or Time Limited

If the chosen goal has these characteristics, the employee will have a highest level of motivation.

## CONTENT THEOREIS OF MOTIVATION

### Maslow's Hierarchy of Needs

Abraham Maslow formulated one of the most popular theories of human motivation.

Maslow's theory is based on the following propositions.

The needs are arranged in a hierarchy of importance, ranging from the lowest need to highest need level

All needs are never fully satisfied

Once a need is fairly well satisfied, it no longer motivates behavior

The needs are interdependent and overlapping

Maslow's theory of motivation explains five levels of needs.

#### *Physiological Needs*

The need for sunlight, sex, food, water and others, which are basic to human survival, are called physiological needs. At work level, this need can be met through by providing good working conditions, attractive wage or salary, subsidized housing, free catering etc.

#### *Safety Needs*

The safety needs include the need for freedom from threat caused by the environment, animals and people. It also includes the need for shelter, security and peace. At work level, this need can be met by providing private health insurance cover, attractive pension provisions, safe working conditions etc.

#### *Love and Belonging Needs*

These needs cover the need of relationships, affection, giving and receiving love and sense of belonging. The manager can provide the following facilities to take care of these needs: company sports and social clubs, office parties, barbeques, outings, permission for informal activities, and encouraging open communication

#### *Self Esteem Needs*

It is also known as ego needs, which fulfill the need for strength, achievement, recognition, appreciation, respect and prestige. The managers can provide regular positive feedback, prestigious job titles, photographs in company newsletter, promotions etc.

***Self-actualization Needs***

These are the need for full development of one's potential. Challenging job assignments, discretion over work activities, promotion opportunities and encouraging creativity can fulfill these needs. In terms of motivation, Maslow argued that each level in the hierarchy must be substantially satisfied before the next level is activated, and that once a need is fully satisfied, it may not motivate people. The next level in the hierarchy will be dominant only after the fulfillment satisfaction level. This theory has a lot of implication for managers. As a manager if you want to motivate an employee, first try to understand what level that person is on in the hierarchy and focus on satisfying those needs at or just above the level.

**Maslow's Need Hierarchy**

| General Factors | Need Level | Organizational Specific Factors |
|---|---|---|
| 1. Growth<br>2. Achievement<br>3. Advancement | Self-Actualization | 1. Challenging work<br>2. Creativity<br>3. Advancement in organization<br>4. Achievement in Work |
| 1. Recognition<br>2. Status<br>3. Self-esteem<br>4. Self-respect | Ego, Status and Esteem | 1. Job Title<br>2. Merit Pay Increase<br>3. Peer/Supervisory Recognition<br>4. Work Itself<br>5. Responsibility |
| 1. Companionship<br>2. Affection<br>3. Friendship | Social | 1. Quality of Supervision<br>2. Compatible Work Group<br>3. Professional Friendship |
| 1. Safety<br>2. Security<br>3. Competence<br>4. Stability | Safety and Security | 1 Safe Working Conditions<br>2. Fringe Benefits<br>3. General Salary Increases<br>4. Job Security |
| 1. Air<br>2. Food<br>3. Shelter<br>4. Sex | Physiological | 1. Heat and conditioning<br>2. Base Salary<br>3. Cafeteria<br>4. Working Conditions |

***Maslow's framework***

It is based on three fundamental assumptions

Individuals are goals oriented whose needs can influence their behavior. Only unsatisfied needs can influence behavior; satisfied needs do not act as motivator A person's needs are arranged in an order of importance, or hierarchy, from the basic the complex

The person advances to the next level of the hierarchy, or from basic to complex needs, only when the lower need is at least minimally satisfied. That is, the individual worker will first focus on satisfying a need for safe working conditions before motivated behavior is directed toward satisfying a need for achieving the successful accomplishment of a task.

Maslow classified these five needs into two broad categories as higher order needs and lower order needs. The basic needs such as physiological needs, safety needs and love and belonging needs were classified as lower order needs, where as self esteem, self actualization needs were described as higher order needs. The distinction between these two categories was made based on a single premise whether a person assigns much importance to the internal factors or the external factors. If a person gives much importance to the external factors such as salary, security, company policy, fringe benefits etc. the lower order needs are very dominant in him. On the other hand, if a person assigns challenging assignments, self-esteem, recognition, the higher order needs are very dominant in him. Employees, who are working in government organization likely to have fulfilled the basic needs, Maslow took a deprivation-gratification approach to need satisfaction.

That is, he contended that an unfulfilled or deprived need would activate a person to engage in behaviouir that would satisfy or gratify that need. Once one level of need is gratified, the next level of needs will emerge as the deprived needs seeking to be gratified. Maslow's need theory received wide recognition, particularly among practicing managers but it lacks empirical support substantially. Managers, who accepted Maslow's hierarchy attempted to change their organizations and management practices so that employees' needs could be satisfied. Maslow's theory is built on the framework that unsatisfied needs serve as factors arouse people to behavior. When a need has been minimally fulfilled, it then ceases to be a motivator of behavior. For example, as assembly line worker may have a desire or need to become a supervisor. Through training programs or part-time studies, this employee can be promoted to a supervisory role in the factory in due course of time. The need to become a supervisor no longer exists, and therefore, the behavior of the individual is altered to a new situating. An important point for managers to consider is that highly deficient needs, or needs that have gone unsatisfied for long period of time, serve to cause such behavioral responses as frustration, conflict and stress. Individual's reaction to frustration, conflict and stress differs from individual to individual depending upon environmental, organizational and personal factors. These reactions to need deficiency take the form of at least four different 'defensive behaviors'

Aggression: It is a physical or verbal defensive behavior that can be directed toward a person, object or the organizational. Physical aggression can take the form of such things as stealing or equipment sabotage. Verbal aggression can be the emotional outburst of an employee directed toward the supervisor concerning unsafe working conditions. Rationalization: It is defensive behavior that takes the form of such activities as placing the blame on other or having a "take ir or leave it" attitude. An employee may rationalize a small pay increase by attributing it to poor supervision or inadequate resources, when in fact it was the particular individual's unsatisfactory performance that caused the small pay increase.

Compensation: It concerns the behavior of a person going overboard in one area to make up for problems or need deficiency in another area. A person whose need for interaction with fellow employee's goes unsatisfied during normal working hours may compensate by being extremely active in company related social, recreational or civic activities. Regression: It is defense that significantly alters the individual's behavior. After being turned down for promotion to the position of a loan officer, the head cashier may change her behavior from being friendly and open to being tense, highly task oriented or temperamental. These defensive behaviors can result from the inability of an employee to satisfy a personally important need. These behaviors are realties in any organizational setting, and it's the responsibility of the manager to understand the cause, and if resources are available, provide a solution to correct defensive behavior.

### *Implications of Maslow's Hierarchy of Needs Theory*

This model helps the managers to understand and deal with issues of employee motivation at the workplace. This model can be applied to motivate people at all levels in the organization. Managers who understand the need patterns of their staff can help the employees to engage in the kinds of work activities and provide the types of work environment that will satisfy their needs at work. For instance, the employees love and belonging needs can be fully satisfied by organizing yearly dinner and dance program, office week end parties, creating recreation clubs or social clubs etc. Fortunately, the workplace has the potential to offer need gratification for several different types of needs, and mangers can motivate employees by giving appropriate organizational support which will gratify individual's needs. Thus, despite its drawbacks, Maslow's theory offers managers a good technique on understanding the motives or needs of individuals and how to motivate organizational members.

## Herzberg Two-Factor Theory of Motivation

Herzberg's two-factor theory of motivation suggests that there are two sets of factors which either led to job satisfaction or dissatisfaction. They are Motivating factors and Hygiene factors. Herzberg collected data from 200 accountants and engineers asking a simple question such as "Can you describe, in detail, when you feel exceptionally good about your job" Similarly, Can you describe, in detail, when you feel exceptionally bad about your job? Good feelings about the job were reflected in comments concerning the content and experiences of the job bad feelings about the job were associated with context factors, that is, those surrounding but not direct involving in the work itself. This study revealed two distinct types of motivational factors: satisfiers and dissatisfiers. Herzberg resulted in two specific conclusions:

1. There is a set of extrinsic job conditions that, when not present, result in dissatisfaction among employees. If these conditions are present, this does not necessarily motivate employees. These conditions are the dissatisfiers or hygiene factors because they are needed to maintain at least a level of no dissatisfaction. These factors are related to the context of the job and are called dissatisfiers. These include:
   - job security
   - salary
   - working condition
   - status
   - company policies
   - supervision
   - Interpersonal supervision
   - Fringe benefits
2. A set of intrinsic job conditions exist that help to build levels of motivation, which can result in good job performance. If these conditions are not present, they do not result in dissatisfaction. These set of aspects are related to the content of the job and are called satisfiers. These include:
   - Achievement
   - Recognition
   - Work itself
   - Responsibility
   - Advancement
   - Personal growth and development

### *Motivating Factors*

The presence of motivating factors always ensures job satisfaction and happiness among the employees. They are: achievement, recognition, responsibility, advancement, growth and the work itself. These motivating factors are relating to the work content factors.

### *Hygiene Factors*

The other set, which leads to dissatisfaction, is the hygiene factors such as salary, company policy, supervision, status, security and working conditions. These hygiene factors are relating to the work contextual factors.

Herzberg argued that improvement in the hygiene factors would only minimize dissatisfaction but not increase satisfaction and motivation.

### *Implications for Managers*

In order to motivate employees, the managers must ensure to provide the hygiene factors and then follow the motivating factors. Hertzberg's motivation-hygiene theory proposes that intrinsic factors are related to job satisfaction and motivation, whereas extrinsic factors are associated with job dissatisfaction. According to Herzberg, the factors that led to job satisfaction were separate and distinct from those that led to job dissatisfaction. Therefore, manages who sought to eliminate factors that created job dissatisfaction could bring about workplace harmony but not necessarily motivation. Because they do not motivate employees, the extrinsic factors that create job dissatisfaction were called hygiene factors. When these factors are adequate, people will not be dissatisfied; but at the same time they may not be fully satisfied. They will be in neutral state. If we want to motivate people on their jobs, it is suggested to give much importance on those job content factors such as opportunities for personal growth, recognition, responsibility, and achievement. These are the characteristics that people find intrinsically rewarding. Herzberg model sensitizes that merely treating the employees well through the good company policies is not sufficient to them motivated. Managers should utilize the skills, abilities, and talents of the people at work through effective job designing. In other words, the work given to employees should be challenging and exciting and offer them a sense of achievement, recognition, and growth. Unless these characteristics are present in the job, employees will not be motivated. In Herzberg's framework, these managerial reactions have focused primarily on the hygiene factors surrounding the job, which has resulted in bringing individual to the theoretical "zero point" of motivation. The two-factor theory would predict that improvements in motivation would only appear when managerial action focused not only the factors surrounding the job but on the inherent in most assembly line jobs and developing jobs that can provide increased levels of challenge and opportunities for a sense of achievement, advancement, growth and personal development.

## McGregor's Theory X and Theory Y

McGregor's theory is based on how a manager feels about human nature. In general, people tend to have either positive or negative assumptions about human nature. Based on these assumptions, McGregor proposed two sets of theories as Theory X (negative assumptions) and Theory Y (positive assumptions).

### *Theory X*

Theory X represents the traditional approach to managing and is characterized by the following basic assumption about human beings. The average human being has an inherent dislike of work and will avoid it if he can. Because of human characteristic of dislike of work, most people must be coerced, controlled, directed, and threatened with punishment to get them to put forth adequate effort towards the achievement of organizational objectives. The average human being prefers to be directed, wishes to avoid responsibility, has relatively little ambition, and wants security above all.

Once the team leaders tend to have the above-mentioned negative assumptions about their members, consequently, they will adopt the following strategies to influence them. Control measures or strict supervision are properly exercised to get results from them. Such control can be achieved by the appropriate use of rewards and punishment.

### *Implications of X Theory*

The implication for a manger working in an organization with these premises is that the group will be strictly controlled and supervised. Decisions will be made largely by the manager and communicated in writing or verbally in a formal situation. Members of the group will rarely be involved in determining their own tasks. Theory X usually operates in traditional, highly centralized organizations.

### *Theory Y*

Theory Y is more people oriented. It refers to Maslow's hierarchy of needs, particularly the higher-order needs and the motivation to fill these needs at work. It is based on the following assumptions. The following are some of the assumptions of Theory Y. The expenditure of physical and mental effort is as natural as play or rest. External control and threat of punishment are not the only means for bringing about effort toward organizational objectives. People will exercise self-direction and self-control in the services of objectives to which they are committed. Commitment to objectives is a function of rewards associated with their achievement. The average human beings learn, under proper condition, not only to accept but to seek responsibility. The capacity to exercise a relatively high degree of imagination, ingenuity, and creativity in the solution of organizational problems is widely, not narrowly, distributed in the population. Under the conditions of modern industrial life, the intellectual potentialities of the average human being are only partially utilized.

### *Implications of Y Theory*

Leaders operating under these assumptions will be more likely to consult the group, encourage members to contribute to decision making and work without strict supervision. Communication between the group and the leader will be two of the members of the group. The acceptance of the Theory Y approach, with its tenets of participation and concern for worker morale, encouraged managers to begin practicing such activities as i) delegating authority for many decision, ii) enlarging and enriching jobs of workers by making them less repetitive, iii) increasing the variety of activities and responsibilities and iv) improving the free flow of communication within the organization. The major criticisms are that too much emphasis was put on informal group process with knowledge of the complexities of group dynamics. Also the strategies evolved based on Theory Y may be successful in one organization and may not be successful in another.

**ERG Theory**

Alderfer proposed a modified version of Maslow's need hierarchy and labeled as ERG theory. Alderfer's ERG refers to three groups of core needs – Existence, Relatedness and Growth.

***Existence Needs***

These needs are all the various forms of physiological and material desires, such as hunger, thirst and shelter. In organizational settings, the need for pay, benefits, and physical working conditions are also included in this category. This category is comparable to Maslow's physiological and certain safety needs.

***Relatedness Needs***

These needs include all those that involve interpersonal relationships with others in the workplace. This types of need in individuals depends on the process of sharing and mutuality of feelings between others to attain satisfaction. This category is similar to Maslow's safety, social and certain ego-esteem needs.

***Growth Needs***

These needs involve a person's efforts toward creative or personal growth on the job. Satisfaction of growth needs results from an individual engaging in tasks that not only require the person's full use of his or her capabilities, but also may require the development of new capabilities. Maslow's self-actualization and certain of his egoesteem needs are comparable to those growth needs.

***ERG theory is based upon three major propositions***

The less each level of need has been satisfied, the more it will be desired. For example, the less existence needs have been satisfied on the job, the more they will be desired. The more lower level needs have been satisfied, the greater the desire for higher level needs. For example, the more existence needs have been satisfied for the individual worker, the greater the desire for relatedness needs. The less the higher level need have been satisfied, the more the lower level needs will be desired for example, the less growth needs have been satisfied, the more relatedness needs will be desired.

### *Difference between Alderfer's ERG and Maslow's Need Hierarchy*

ERG theory differs from Maslow's need hierarchy in two aspects:

Alderfer highlighted that once an individual's higher level need is not fully satisfied or encounters difficulty in fulfilling these needs resulting in frustrations and disappointment, the person will exhibit a strong desire to regress to a lower level needs where he/she finds more comfort and satisfaction. Alderfer further stated that an individual may have an intention to fulfill more than one need at the same time. In other words, individuals may be working towards fulfilling both their relatedness needs and growth needs or their existence and related needs simultaneously.

### *Implications of ERG Theory*

Alderfer has proposed two sets of views on individual's aspirations and fulfillment. One is satisfaction-progression and other frustration-regression. Satisfaction-progression is similar to Maslow's model in which once an individual's basic needs are satisfied, he/she will progress to the next level to satisfy the succeeding higher level to have them satisfied. Alderfer proposed yet another view of individual's aspirations and fulfillment. If people eventually become frustrated in trying to satisfy their needs at one level, their next lower level needs will re-emerge and they will regress to the lower level to satisfy more basic needs. This is called as frustration-regression. For manages, ERG theory provides a more workable approach to motivation in organization. Because of the frustration-regression approach component, it provides the manager with the opportunity of directing employee behavior in a constructive manner even though higher order needs are temporarily frustrated. In summary, ERG theory argues that satisfied lower-order needs lead to the desire to satisfy higher-order needs; but multiple needs can be operating as motivators at the same time and frustration in attempting to satisfy a higher-level need can result in regression to a lower-level need.

## McClelands THREE – NEEDS THEORY

McClelland proposed three types of needs common in work life. They are Need for Achievement, Need for Power and Need for Affiliation.

### *Need for Achievement*

This refers to the drive to excel, to achieve in relation to a set of standards and to strive to succeed. People with a high need for achievement are striving for personal achievement rather than for trappings and rewards of success. They have a desire to do something better or more efficiently than it has been done before. They prefer jobs that offer personal responsibility for finding solutions to problems, in which they can, received rapid and unambiguous feedback on their performance in order to tell whether they are improving or not and in which they can set moderately challenging goals. High achievers are not gamblers, they dislike succeeding by chance. They are motivated and prefer the challenge of working at a problems and accepting the personal responsibility for success or failure.

### *Implications for Need for Achievement Theory*

Too little challenge will bore them since there is no opportunity to satisfy their urge to achieve, and too much challenge would mean that the job is difficult and hence will induce the fear of failure in them. Since their need for achievement and accomplishment are high, high Need for Achievement individuals will not try to work on jobs that are so challenging that successful task accomplishment become doubtful. Also, high achievers avoid very easy or very difficult tasks instead they show willingness to take a moderate level of difficulty which will have much challenge in accomplishing them. They like to set goals that require stretching themselves a bit.

### *Need for Power*

This refers to the need to make others behave in a way that they would not have behaved otherwise. Individuals high in Need for Power enjoy being 'in-charge', strive for influence over others, and prefer to be in competitive and status oriented situations. McClelland distinguished two types of power – Personal Power and Institutional Power. Individuals high in personal power like to inspire subordinates and expect that latter to respect and obey them. Such behaviors gratify their own need for power in a personal sense. Managers, who are high in institutional power, tend to exert authority and influence so as to achieve the goals of the organization rather than to gain any personal ego satisfaction. McClelland describes the institutional power managers as "organizationminded" and getting things done in the interest of the organization. That is, the institutional power manager exercises power in the interests and welfare of the organization. Institutional power managers are said to be very effective since they are willing to somewhat sacrifice their own interests for the organization's overall wellbeing. McClelland feels that institutional or social power is good for the organization and personal power is detrimental to the overall interests of the organization.

### *Implications for Need for Power*

Persons with high need for power would naturally be turned on by holding positions of authority and influence in the organization. They like to take charge and be in control of situations. Placing such individuals in high level positions will help them to gratify their own needs as well as get many of the organization's policies and orders followed and carried out by employees.

***Need for Affiliation***

This refers to the desire for friendly and close interpersonal relationships. Individuals high in Need for Affiliation like to interact with colleagues in the organization. They have a strong desire for approval and reassurance from others and they are willing to conform to the norms of groups to which they belong. In effect, they have needs to develop affinity and warm relationships with people in the work system. They are usually gregarious by nature and like to work with others in a friendly atmosphere. Team work, co-operative efforts, and joint problem-solving sessions, and committee assignments are all suited for those high in Need for Affiliation.

***Implications for Need for Affiliation***

People high in need for affiliation are said to perform better in their jobs when they are given supportive feedback. Thus, friendly manages and supervisors can influence individuals high in Need for Affiliation and motivate them to work harder.

## PROCESS THEORIES OF MOTIVATION

The content theories of motivation provided managers with a better understanding of the particular work-related factors that arouse employees to motivate employees' behavior. However, these theories provide very little understanding of why people choose a particular behavioral pattern to accomplish work goals. The process theories will help understand the dynamics of cognitive aspects such as comparison, probability of maximizing benefits etc. Expectancy theory and equity theories are the two major theories that concern this approach to motivation in organization. Cognitive models of motivation are based on the notion that individual make conscious decision about their job behavior. Thus understanding the process by which individual make decision about how much effort they will put on the job will help manages to motivate people better.

### PROCESS THEORIES OF MOTIVATION

#### Equity Theory

Adams proposes equity theory of motivation based on the proposition that every one tend to compare the ratio of his/her input and out come with input-outcome ratio of other person. The comparison process is highly inevitable. The reference person or comparison person will always be in the same group, class, age, category etc. For example, a manager will always compare himself/herself with other fellow manages. A worker will always compare with other worker in the same organization. In the comparison process, if a person feels that his ratio of input-outcome is more or less equal to that of his comparison person's ratio of input-outcome, a state of equity exists. Then he perceives the situation as just and fair. If a person perceives the ratio as unequal, he will experience inequity that will lead to tension and stress. Inequity exists under two conditions: 1. the person feels a negative inequity, when he has been rewarded less for his efforts than another and 2. The person experiences a positive inequity, when he finds himself rewarded more than another for a similar degree of effort. Both kinds' of inequities produce cognitive dissonance or internal tensions and propel people to action in order to reduce the dissonance.

***Selection of Reference Person or Comparison Person***

The selection of comparison person adds to the complexity of equity theory. Research studies reveal that the type of reference person chosen plays an important role in equity theory. There are four referent comparisons that an employee can use.

1. Self-inside: An employee's experiences in a different position inside his or her present organization.
2. Self-outside: An employee's experiences in a situation or position outside his or her present organization.
3. Other-inside: Another individual or group of individuals inside the employee's organization
4. Other-outside: Another individual or groups of individuals outside the employee's organization.

Employees might compare themselves with other friends, neighbors, co-workers, colleagues in other organizations. The type of reference person or comparison person an employee chooses will be influenced by the information the employee holds about referents, as well as by the attractiveness of the referent. There are many factors which moderate the selection of reference person such as age, sex, education, tenure, nature of job etc. The positive and negative inequities can be denoted as follows:

Positive Inequity

$$\frac{\text{Outcomes for Person}}{\text{Inputs of Person}} > \frac{\text{Outcomes for Other}}{\text{Inputs of Other}}$$

Negative Inequity

$$\frac{\text{Outcomes for Person}}{\text{Inputs of Person}} < \frac{\text{Outcomes for Other}}{\text{Inputs of Other}}$$

Based on equity theory, the employees who perceive inequity in the occupation may have many options to choose to restore balance

1. Changing their input by putting more effort in their job, updating skills, knowledge or talents etc.
2. Changing their outcomes by increasing their output such as

producing more volume of output, high quality of output, conserving more resources. Saving more time, minimizing downtime etc.

3. Distorting self perception by rationalizing certain things such as due to sickness the amount of effort put in is very low or acquisition of some degrees or certificates will make a person feel that I am working harder than anyone else.
4. Distorting perception of the reference person by assuming that the person has more contacts with influential superiors and gets more benefits.
5. Choosing a different referent person and seeking comfort with that person. For instance, if A used B as her comparison point till now, she might after feeling negative inequity, change her comparison point to C by persuading herself that B is now bound to enjoy special favors since she has married the boss's nephew.
6. Leaving the field once for all.

There are two types of justice emphasized in equity theory such as Distributive Justice and Procedural justice. Distributive Justice: It refers to the perceived fairness of the amount and allocation of rewards among individuals. Procedural Justice: It refers to the perceived fairness of the process used to determine the distribution of rewards. Research results indicate that distributive justice has a grater influence on employee satisfaction than procedural justice, while procedural justice tends to affect employees organizational commitment, trust in their boss and intention to quit.

### *Implications of Equity Theory*

Equity theory sensitizes managers to the fact that individuals often make equity comparisons and that sometimes the rewards given by managers may have consequences which might be reflected in subordinates' behaviors. This is especially true when visible rewards such as promotions, pay increases and bonuses are given to employees. Managers must anticipate when the employees experience inequities and try to adjust the behavior in such a way by communicating the performance appraisal process to their employees. The proper explanation of how the performance appraisal process is being carried out must be explained to all the employees. Further, the types of rewards dispensed and creating a well established system which takes care of the anomalies in the reward systems are essential in maintaining inequity in the organization. Felt inequities are common in all organizations and hence it is important for managers to manage equity dynamics intelligently and carefully. Managers should consider openly sharing information on how allocation decisions are made, following consistent and unbiased procedures and engaging in similar practices to increase the perception of procedural justice. By increasing the perception of procedural fairness, employees are likely to view their bosses and the organization as positive even if they have dissatisfied with pay, promotions and other outcomes. Equity theory proves at lease three guidelines for managers to consider:

- It emphasizes on equitable rewards for employees. When individuals believe that they are not being rewarded in an equitable fashion, certain morale and productivity problems may arise.
- The concerning equity or inequity is not made solely on a personal basis but involves comparison with other workers, both within and outside the organization. In other words, it is not only important how much an employee is being paid, but how much he or she is being paid compared to other employees who have the same or similar jobs.
- Individual reaction to inequity can include changes in inputs and changes in outcomes, with the level or direction depending on whether the inequity was perceived to be underpaying or overpaying.

**Vroom Expectancy Model**

Expectancy theory relates to choice behavior. The theory states that individuals will evaluate various strategies of behavior and then choose the particular strategy that they believe will lead to those work related rewards that they value. If the individual workers believe that working hard each day will lead to a pay increase, expectancy theory would predict that this will be the behavior he will choose. The main postulates of expectancy theory are centered on the belief systems of an individual. Expectancy theory argues that the strength of a tendency to act in a certain way depends on the strength of an expectation that the act will be followed by a given outcome and on the attractiveness of the that outcome to the individual. There are three key concepts in Expectancy theory.

***Expectancy I***

Effort?Performance Relationship: Expectancy is the perceived belief concerning the likelihood that a particular behavioral act will be followed by a particular outcome. The degree of belief can vary between 0 and 1. That is, the extent to which an individual's belief system links effort-performance relationship, that is, exerting a given amount of effort will lead to corresponding level of performance. For instance, a student has a strong belief that if he puts 10 hours of reading per day, the chances of getting distinction in his examination is very high and at the same time if he believes that just putting only 2 hours of reading per day, the chances of getting a pass mark is very remote. The main emphasis is the differential levels of efforts in work will lead to differential level of outcome. He might decide to put forth his best effort and perform an excellent job, or he might decide to put forth a moderate level of effort and do an acceptable job. If he pouts in moderate effort, the final performance may be either acceptable or less acceptable. Hence, for each of the effort – performance contingencies, the individual will attach some kind of probability which would range from 0 to 1. For example, the individual might attaché a probability of.7 that he would do an excellent job if he puts in superior efforts and a probability of.3 that it would end up to be only an acceptable job even when he puts in superiors performance.

***Expectancy II Performance àReward Relationship***

It refers to the relationship between first and second – level outcomes. According to Vroom, instrumentality can vary between +1.0 and -1.0. If the first-level outcome always leads to a pay increase, the instrumentality would be perceived as having a value of +1.0. If there is no perceived relationship between first and second-level outcome, then the instrumentality approaches zero. That is, the extent to which an individual's belief system links performance – reward relationship, that is, getting a desired level of performance will lead to the attainment of desired outcome. For instance, insurance agent beliefs strongly that getting policies worth of 10 crores will lead to getting a club membership and attractive cash incentive. The main emphasis is the differential level of performance in work will lead to differential level of reward outcome.

***Valence***

Attractiveness of rewards: The degree to which organizational rewards satisfy an individual's personal goals or needs and the attractiveness of those potential rewards for the individual. Expectancy theory helps to analyze the extent to which the belief system facilitates to maximize the amount of effort put in their work. For instance, if a person feels that his skill level is very deficient, no matter how hard he tries in his work, he is not likely to be a high performer. Similarly if a person believes if his boss is biased or partial, he expects to get a poor appraisal regardless of his level of effort. These examples suggest that one possible source of low employee motivation is the belief that no matter how hard he or she works, the likelihood of getting a good performance appraisal is very low. Similarly if a person feels that there is a weak relationship between performances – reward relationship in their job, the chances of getting outstanding performance will be poor. The reason is that organizations reward system is not solely based on the performance criteria but on the other non-performance factors. For example, when pay rise is given to employees based on factors such as seniority, being cooperative; employees are likely to see weak performance-reward relationship and feel demotivated. Since Vroom's initial model, expectancy theory has undergone at least four developments.

- The theory was extended by making the distinction between extrinsic outcomes and intrinsic outcomes. Extrinsic valence refers to outcomes that come to the individual from others because of his performance; intrinsic valences are associated with the job itself.
- A further distinction was made between two types of expectancies. Expectancy I is concerned with the perceived relationship between effort and performance. Expectancy II, similar to Vroom's concept of instrumentality is concerned with the relationship between first level outcomes and second-level outcomes or reward. These expectancies have come to be known as EI and EII
- It also concerns the broadening to the theory to include the possible effects of other work-related variable on the major variables of expectancy such as: a) the possible impact of personality variables in the formation of expectancy perceptions. B) the effect of past experiences on expectancy development and c) the inclusion of ability and role perception as possible moderating effects on the relationship between motivation and actual performance.
- The expectancy model is also extended to include the variables of workrelated satisfaction. Satisfaction is viewed as being a function of actual performance and the real rewards gained from that performance.

***Implications of Vroom Expectancy Model***

As mentioned above, if the employees feel that the rewards are not so attractive to fulfill his goals, he or she may not put much effort in his or her work. For example, the employee works hard in the hope of getting a promotion but gets a pay rise instead which he is not interested in will make him demotivated. Or the employee wants a more interesting and challenging job but receives only a few words of praise. It is desirable to assess what attracts employees in their work. But some managers incorrectly assume that all employees want the same thing, thus overlooking the motivational effects of differentiating rewards. In summary, the key to expectancy theory is the understanding of an individual's goals and the linkage between effort and performance, between performance and rewards and finally, between rewards and individual goal satisfaction.

**Porter and Lawler Model**

Porter and Lawler proposed a comprehensive model of motivation encompassing the moderating effects of abilities and traits and role perception and accelerating roles of perceived equitable rewards and perceived Effort-Reward probability. Porter and Lawler Model: The model highlights two important factors which facilitate or influence to put more effort in work. They are the valence and perceived EffortàReward probability

- *Valence:* The first factor concerns the extent to which the value of reward that is likely to be received from their job influences the amount of effort. For instance, if a person is showing more interest towards the reward or expected outcome, the chances of putting more effort in his or her work will be very high. If the expected reward is not attractive enough, he will lower his effort.
- *Perceived EffortàReward probability:* The second factor states the influence of perceived effortà.reward probability. If a person feels that the probability of getting reward is very high for given level of effort, he will more likely to put high level of effort in his work.

There are other two significant factors which facilitate to maximize the amount of performance.

- Abilities and Traits: If an individual has requisite abilities, skills and traits to perform the assigned job, he will produce more results than others who do not have such skills to such type of tasks. Traits include endurance, perseverance and goal-directedness which are relevant for doing any tasks. These abilities and traits will moderate the effort?performance relationships.
- Role Perception: If an individual has very clear role perception, that is, very clear job descriptions of what he is supposed to do in his tasks without any ambiguity or confusion, the person will deliver more output. The accuracy of role perception is another variable that moderate the effort?Performance relationship. That is, only those who perceived their role as it is defined by the organization will be able to perform when they put forth the required effort in their job.

Types of rewards: Performance will result in getting various rewards. This can be classified into intrinsic and extrinsic rewards. Intrinsic rewards are those which are derived within oneself by getting the feelings of job satisfaction, self-esteem, sense of competence and realizing ones own potentialities. Extrinsic rewards are those external rewards that are given by others in the work environment such as money, promotion, security, incentives etc. Both these types of rewards will result in satisfaction. Once again, the Reward??Satisfaction relationships is moderated by the perceived equitable rewards, that is, satisfaction will be experienced only when the person feels fairly and rewarded for his efforts.

### *Implications of Porter and Lawler Model*

Porter and Lawler's model is of great significance to managers since it sensitizes them to focus attention on the following to keep their employees motivated.

- Assigning right type of jobs to right types of person, ensuring perfect match between person and job.

- Providing a clear job descriptions and highlighting what a person is expected of in his work
- Assigning the proper performance levels such s quantity, waste control number of customer attended etc.
- Ensuring that the rewards given to their employees are very attractive to them.

If high levels of motivation are to be induced, managers should ensure that the employees perceive a direct link between performance and desired rewards. If significant changers in performance levels are desired, the rewards given must also be significant and valued enough by the employees to change their effort levels. The Porter and Lawler model is useful in understanding by the dynamic of motivation at the work place.

## GOAL SETTING AND JOB SATISFACTION

The basic framework of goal setting theory is that it deals with the relationship between conscious goals or intentions and task performance. A goal is defined as what the individual is consciously trying to do. The basic premise of the approach is that an individual's conscious goals or intentions influence his behavior. Specific, concrete or harder goals result in a higher level of individual performance than do easy goals. Goal setting involves four steps: i) It involves the establishment of target results and the clarification of potential rewards that are associated with goal accomplishment ii) goal setting aspects such as the degree of goal difficulty and goal challenges iii) goal-setting intension made by the individual involving the acceptance and commitment to the previously established goals iv) task performer's interest, personality characteristics..

### GOAL SETTING THEORY

Locke proposed that intentions to work towards a goal are major source of work motivation. The goals facilitate employees what needs to be done and how much effort will need to be put forth in their tasks. The evidence shows the work values and goals will determine strongly the performance of an individual. Actual work behavior then becomes a function of values and goals set by the individual. The manager can motivate employees between goals which jointly decided by both. The following are the four important requirements for setting the goal in such a way to elicit a desired performance. They are: goal specificity, goal difficulty, goal acceptance and feedback.

- Goal Specificity: Setting specific goals with clear expectations both in terms of quantitatively as well as qualitatively will reduce the ambiguity or confusion among the employees. Then the employee can put forth more effort and concentrate the achievement of a well-defined output. Research findings revealed that setting specific performance goals is a better motivator and achieves better results than asking employees to do their best in general.

- Goal Difficulty: If the goals are too easy to finish the required task, the employee will not be motivated enough and get bored in due course of time. Similarly if the goals are too difficult to complete, he will get high level of frustration and not able to complete the task in time. Hence, it is desirable to set the goal with moderate difficult level that will provide much challenge and motivate people to do work better than easy goals.
- Participation in Goal Setting Process: If the employees are allowed to participate in setting their work goals with clear directions, the likelihood getting full acceptance and participation in their task will be very high. Further, the goals must be so consonance with the employee's attitudes and values that is there must be a perfect harmonization of individual values system and nature of work. Once there is an acceptance and commitment to the goal, the employees will be motivated to put forth greater effort and perform well.
- Feedback on Goal Effort: Once the knowledge of the results of their work is known to the employees periodically, they will realize their shortcomings, errors, and adjust their work behavior accordingly to meet the required expected output. Feedback helps in as much as is it keeps the employee's goal directed behavior on target and stimulates the person to put in greater efforts.

**Self- Efficacy**

Self-efficacy refers to an individual's belief that he is capable of performing a task. If an individual's self-efficacy is very high, he will have more confidence in his ability to succeed in a task. So, in difficult situations, people with low selfefficacy are more likely to lessen their effort or given up altogether, while those with high self-efficacy will try harder to master the challenge. In addition, individual's high in self-efficacy seem to respond to negative feedback with increased effort and motivation, whereas those low in self-efficacy are likely to lessen their effort when given negative feedback. Research indicates that individual goals setting does not work equally well on all tasks. The results showed that goals seem to have a more substantial effect on performance when tasks are simple rather than complex, well learned rather than novel, and independent rather than interdependent goals.

**Implications of Goal Setting Theory**

The success of goal setting as a motivational technique is largely a function of designing the goals with all four characteristics. Goal setting is a powerful motivator and can be used even in service organizations where the output is not easily quantifiable. Goals can be set in such organizations in terms of servicing time, customer complaints, customer satisfaction levels, and other factors as would be appropriate to the managerial responsibilities at hand.

**Management by Objectives**

It is a program that encompasses specific goals set with cooperation of employees, for an explicit time period, with feedback on goal progress. MBO emphasizes setting goals participatively that are tangible, variable, measurable, realistic and timely. The main focus of MBO is converting overall organizational objectives into specific objectives for the organizational units and individual members. The objectives are flowing from top to bottom in the hierarchy as corporate goals, divisional goals, departmental goals and individual goals in the organization. Lower unit managers jointly participate in setting their own goals. MBO works from the bottom up as well as from the top down. The result is a hierarchy of objectives that links objectives at one level to those at the next level. Each individual employee will have some specific personal performance objectives. There are four common elements in the MBA program: They are: goals specificity, participative decision making, time frame and feedback process.

- Goal Specificity: Listing a set of goal statements of what employees are expected of in their work life. Instead of highlighting vague and general statements such as improve service or increase the quality, converting those into a specific and measurable statements such as 20 customers are attended with one hour, rejection rate or error rate in the quality must be less than 1 per 10000 pieces produced will help to achieve the goals.
- Participative Decision Making: The objectives of MBO program are set unilaterally by the top managers. The employees are invited to share their ideas and consulted periodically to list the desired objectives. MBO replaces imposed goals with participatively determined goals.
- Time Frame: Each objective must have a specific time period to accomplish with a strict deadline by stating the time and date. The time period can be one month, three months which facilitate to complete the tasks in time.
- Feedback on Performance. MBO system will facilitate to provide the knowledge of results to the concerned employees immediately by their supervisors whether it is positive or negative. In case the performance will be inferior or below the level of set objective, the same will be appraised to the employees immediately and corrective action will be taken accordingly. This can be supplemented by periodic managerial evaluations, when progress is reviewed.

### Comparison of Goal Setting and MBO

MBO directly advocates specific goals and feedback. MBO implies that goals must be perceived as feasible. Consistent with goal setting, MBO would be most effective when the goals are difficult enough to require the person to do some stretching. The only area of difference between MBO and goal setting is on the issue of participation. MBO advocates strongly the participation is part of the setting objectives, while goal setting theory states that supervisors can set and assign goals to subordinates frequently. As the participation is elicited form the employees periodically, employees can be induced to set even more difficult goals themselves.

### Failures of MBO

When MBO programmes do not work well, it is often due to one or more of the following reasons:

1. The managers unilaterally set the goals and expect the subordinates to accept them without reservation.
2. Adequate resources are not provided, lack of top management commitment
3. Feedback is not provided to the subordinates on how well or poorly the individual is making progress towards goals attainment
4. When the goals are met, the subordinates are not appropriately rewarded.

### Employee Recognition Programs

Even if the nature of work is repetitive and boring such as working as waiter in fast food restaurant, attending to customer complaints in departmental stores, the employees can be motivated further and retain them within their organization by giving proper recognition. The following are the ways to recognize the employees:

- Complementing regularly in front of the other employees
- Displaying 'Employees of the Month' in the notice board prominently
- Giving special attractive incentives – free lunch, travel, bonus etc
- Employees are referred as 'associates' as a mark of respect for their contribution
- Celebrating the positive aspects of each employees work once in a month
- Everyone wears same type of uniform

### Linking Recognition and Reinforcement

If the desired behavior is rewarded or recognized immediate quite often or periodically that behavior is likely to encourage its repetition. Recognition can take many forms:

- Sending a personal note congratulating an employee
- Sending e-mail note acknowledging commendable work.
- Recognize accomplishments openly.
- Celebrate team success
- Use of suggestion system

**Employee Involvement Program**

Employee Involvement: It is a participative process that uses the entire capacity of employees and is designed to encourage increased commitment to the organization's success. The key issues involved in the involvement process are as follows:

- Involving workers in those decision that affect them
- Increasing their autonomy and control over their work life
- Opportunity to interact with customers and get adequate feedback directly from them regarding their work
- Introducing a flat structure with flexible rules and regulations within the unit

The following are the various types of Employment Involvement Programs: Workers Participation in Management, Quality Circles, and Employee share ownership plans

**Workers Participation in Management**

It is a process in which workers share a significant degree of decision-making power with their immediate supervisors. It promotes high level of morale and productivity within the organization. More participation can be elicited from the employees by providing some facilities such as giving adequate time to participate, issues must be relevant to their interest, and employees must have the ability to participate and conducive work culture supporting employee involvement. Seeking participation is vital for the organization as the nature of job is very complex and the managers may not know everything their employees do.

As the employees know the operational difficulties and the ways to overcome, they can provide better decision than the managers. Further, the nature of tasks are interdependent requiring frequent consultation with concerned people in other departments, which demanding to form teams, committee and group meetings to resolve issues that affect them jointly. Participation also facilitates to enhance employees commitment to the collective decision. Finally, participation provides intrinsic rewards for employees and it can make their jobs more interesting and meaningful. Instituting suitable reward system, creating flexible organic organizational structure with more flexibility will help significantly enhance participative decision-making. However, research results showed that participation typically has only a modest influence on employee productivity, motivation and job satisfaction. The following are the types of workers representation:

- Representative Participation: It refers to workers participatio n i n organizational decision making through a small group of representative employees. The goal of representative participation is to redistribute power with in an organization, putting employees on a more equal footing with the interest of management and shareholders.
- Works Council: It refers to groups of nominated or elected employees who must be consulted when management makes decisions involving personnel.
- Board Representative: This is a form of representative participation. Here the employees sit on a company's board of directors and represent the interests of the firm's employees.

**Quality Circle**

It refers to a work group of employees who meet regularly to discuss their quality problems, investigate causes, recommend solutions and take corrective actions. The members meet regularly typically once a week, during office time within the company premises to discuss their quality problems, investigate causes of the problem, recommend solutions and take corrective actions. The QC members take over the responsibility for solving quality problems and they generate and evaluate their own feedback. In general, management typically retains control over the final decision regarding implementation of recommended solutions. QC concept includes teaching participating employees group communication skills, various quality strategies, and measurement and problem analysis. The formation of QC is more likely to positively affect productivity. The failure of many QC to measurable benefits has also led to abandoning of QC system. There are two possible disappointment results. i) lack of time to get full involvement among employees ii) lack of planning and top-management commitment often contributed to quality circle failures. Employee share ownership plans: It refers to company-established benefit plans in which employee acquire shares as part of their benefits.

**JOB SATISFACTION**

It is defined as an individual's general attitude towards his or job. If an individual holds a positive attitude and livingness towards various elements of job, he is likely to have more job satisfaction. It involves interaction with fellow employees and bosses, following organizational rules, and policies, working conditions, job itself, recognition from superiors etc.

**Factors that lead to Job Satisfaction**

The following important factors such as conducive work environment such as mentally challenging work, equitable rewards, supportive working conditions, supportive colleagues, the personality-job fit etc. will enhance the level of job satisfaction.

- Mentally Challenging Jobs: Employees tend to prefer jobs that give them opportunities to use their skills and abilities and offer a variety of tasks, freedom on how well they are doing. Jobs that have too little challenge create bordom. Most employees will experience more pleasure and satisfaction if they have moderate level of challenge in their work.
- Equitable rewards: When pay is seen as fair and based on job demands, individual skill level and the prevailing market pay standards, job satisfaction is likely to result. Promotion provides opportunities for personal growth, more responsibilities and increased social status. Employees who perceive that promotion decisions are made in a fair and just manner are likely to experience satisfaction from their jobs.
- Supportive Working Conditions: Comfortable working conditions such as temperature, light and other environmental factors facilitate to enhance satisfaction level of the employees. Most employees prefer working relatively close to home, in clean and relatively modern facilities and with adequate, safe and well-maintained tools and equipment.
- Supportive Fellow Employees: Employees satisfaction is increased when the immediate supervisor understands and friendly, offers praise for good performance, listens to the employee's opinions and shows a personal interest in them.
- Personality-job fit: High agreement between an employee's personality and occupation results in more satisfaction. People with personality types congruent with their chosen vocations find that have the right talents and abilities to meet the demands of their jobs. Such people are more likely to be successful at those jobs.

***Effect job satisfaction on employee performance***

- Satisfaction and Productivity: The general notion is that a happy employee is a productive employee. The relationship between productivity and satisfaction is very high when the employee behavior is not constrained or controlled by the outside factors.
- Satisfaction and Absenteeism: Research results reported that the employees with high satisfaction scores had much higher attendance than those with lower satisfaction levels.
- Satisfaction and Turnover: Satisfaction is also negatively related to turnover. People with low level of job satisfaction are likely to leave the organization.

# 9

# Control Management

## MANAGEMENT SYSTEM: AN INTRODUCTION

### AN OVERVIEW

Management is an action procedure composed of some vital functions, for getting the objective of any enterprise accomplished through the efforts of its personnel. Wherever and whenever objectives are to be achieved through organized and co-operative endeavour, management becomes essential for directing and unifying the group efforts towards a general purpose. As human aims and beliefs are mostly realized through the establishment of diverse associations in our civilization, management is universally needed for operating all such organisation. Management, viewed as a functional concept, is of equal necessity to the educational religious, charitable, and other non-business organizations as it is required for business Organizations. Furthermore, the greatest and the mainly comprehensive of our social organizations, viz., the Government of all kinds require management as others require, perhaps more than all other social organizations. That the Government without requires a management procedure has been applied pointed out in the statement: A Government without good management is a home built on sand. Put in short, management is an essential accompaniment of all social organizations, and it is to be establish everywhere as a separate, separate and control action.

The nature and significance of the action do not change even if it is described management in some social in situations and management in others. Management is the only activating unit of any enterprise for getting things done through it personnel. The job of management is to give dynamic leadership that combines the productive but passive possessions into a fruitful organization. Not only does it adapt itself to existing opportunities, restrictions and pressures, but it exercises a positive power as well as to create the future events favorable for the enterprise. With a view to getting the expected results and seeing that things happen as they should, management has to become a creator of the economy rather then its creature. Management forges ahead through innovations in operating situation and the adoption of distant-sighted scheduling. It visualizes the future, initiates changes, and achieves the purpose of any enterprise under highly dynamic circumstances. As an action procedure, management plans the future course of action, organizes people and their work, directs the operation and controls the performance, and therefore ensures the accomplishment of enterprise objectives. Adaptations and innovations permeate through each of these phases of the management procedure. Management acts as a creative and invigorating force in the organization. It makes result that is better than the sum total of efforts put in through the group. Management adds real plus value to the operation of any enterprise through enlisting as small extra value out of each person.

It gives new ideas, imaginations and visions to the group working integrate its efforts in such a manner as to explanation for better results. It ensures a smooth flow of work in the organization through focusing on strong points, neutralizing weak link, overcoming difficulties, and establishing team spirit. Management strives to secure the maximum result through the use of minimum possessions. Management is old as culture and it has been of some concern to organized civilization thought civilized history. Several examples exist today to remind us the result of the organized behaviors of the past. Though, the principles of such organized behaviors are either not accessible or not applicable in present day social structure. In information, no organized effort towards developing management principles was accepted on before the present century and mainly of the earlier contributions towards raising the efficiency of organized clusters were scattered. Another important point in the context of the development of thought is that the contributions have been made through practicing managers as well as academicians. Therefore the total contribution is the result of practical experience as well as the organized researches. If we examine several thought from era point of view, the role of organized researches successively augment in the development of management principles. For the sake of analysis, the management thoughts have been classified as:

- Systems approach.
- Human dealings approach, and
- Classical Approach

This classification is based on the grouping of several thoughts which have parallel in the approach of how managers get the things done.

## SYSTEM APPROACH OF MANAGEMENT

The systems approach, also labeled as contemporary theory of management, is a relatively new approach though neither the conditions management and organisation nor the system is a new concept. In excess of the past tow decades or so the systems approach has appeared as vigorous and lively. Now, we are bombarded with reference to system in several walks of life. Everything is a system and the system thinking is the through work. We have entered an era that forces man to discover more accurate answers to questions involving the 'wholeness' of an operation.

This age of synthesis forces management to think out in new and dissimilar ways- as suggested through the systems approach. In this view the whole is not merely a combination of the system but separate from it s parts. Before analyzing how an organisation functions as a system, it is imperative to examine the concept, and working of the system. A system is defined as the assemblage of things linked or interdependent, so as to form an intricate unity; a whole composed of parts in orderly arrangement just as to some scheme or plan. This has been defined as 'an organized' or intricate whole; an assemblage or combination of things or parts forming an intricate unitary whole. Several authors on systems approach have attempted to develop a generalized theory which can be applied to any system-physical, biological, or social. They have termed is as Common Systems Theory (GST). The theory is concerned with developing a systematic, theoretical framework for describing the empirical world. Buckley describes its role as such, 'A which functions as a whole through virtue of the inter-dependence of its parts described a system and the method which aims at discovering how this is brought in relation to the in widest diversity of systems has been described Common Systems Theory. Common Systems Theory seeks to classify systems through the way their components are organized and to derive the laws, or typical patterns of behaviour, for the dissimilar classes of systems singled but through the taxonomy.

The first vital level in system management is the determination of organisation system. Since organisation is a deliberate and purposive creation, the vital objectives of the organisation should be determined before its creation. Determination of objectives is significant because every effort is directed towards realization of these objectives. In the second level, each unit of the organisation is arranged in some combination to give desired results. Systems design gives the overall framework for implementing systems concepts. It comprises strategic and comprehensive scheduling for the whole organizational system, as well as the development of operation and facilitating sun-system. The third level-operation and control-refers to conversion of inputs into outputs. Inputs may be in the form of information, materials, and power. The inputs are allocated to plan, though it is possible to eliminate parts of the scheduling required throughout operations through designing system with predetermined input allocation structuring the system to operate in a specified fashion and with more predictable results. Operation of the system requires some sort of control, that is, a mechanism for output or related features, comparing his measurement with the average, and activating the element to adjust inputs to correct the deficiency. This is necessary to uphold the equilibrium of the system close to the ideal point. The fourth level pertains to review and evaluation, that is, to ascertain how well the system has performed. This is dissimilar from the control in the sense that control refers to operating efficiency, while the concept of review and evaluation is more comprehensive, and always relates the functioning of the system to its objectives. The review and evaluation happen at periodic intervals throughout the life cycle of a system and lead to design changes in the present system or recommendations for changes which may be operated in future systems

**Human Relation Approach of Management**

The classical approach which focused attention on the mechanical physiological variables of organizational functioning was tested on the field to augment the efficiency of organisations. Surprisingly, positive characteristics of these variables could not evoke positive response in work behaviour, and researchers tried to investigate the reasons for human behaviour at the work. They exposed that the real cause of human behaviour was something more than physiological variables. Such findings generated a new phenomenon in relation to the human behaviour and focused attention of the human beings in the organisations. As such, this new approach his been described 'human approach of management'. Even in the writings of classical approach, notably, Taylor, Fayol, Henry Gantt, Follet, Urwick, and others, the human unit in the organisation was recognized, but they emphasized it very small. The human dealings approach was born out of a reaction to classical approach and throughout the last four decades, a lot of literature on human dealings had been urbanized. The essence of the human dealings contributions is contained in two points;

- Organizational situation should be viewed in social conditions as well as in economic and technological conditions,
- The social procedure of group behaviour can be understood in conditions of clinical method analogous to the doctor's diagnosis of the human organism.

In the middle of human dealings approach, there are several contributions and several more researches are being accepted on. These contain contributions form well-known 'Hawthorne Experiments', several sociologists-Bakke, Selznic, Homans, dubin, and Dalton; several psychologists-McGregor, Likert, Argyris, March and Simon, Leavitt, Blake, Sayles, Brown, etc. There will be relatively lengthy discussion of the results and implications of the Hawthorne studies because of their historical importance to the behavioral approach to the analysis of management troubles. In information, for the first time, a rigorous and systematic analysis of human factor in organisations was made in the form of Hawthorne experiments.

## CONTRIBUTION OF HENRY FAYOL OF CLASSICAL APPROACH

Perhaps, the real father of contemporary management theory is Henry Fayol. He was a French mining engineer, who after obtaining engineering degree joined a French coal firm as technician in 1880. Fayol observed the organizational functioning from manager's point of view.

He establishes that all behaviors of the organisation could be divided into six clusters:

- Technological (relating to manufacture)
- Commercial (buying, selling, and swap)
- Financial (search of capital and its optimum use)
- Accounting (including statistics)
- Managerial (scheduling, organisation, command, co-ordination, and control).

He points out that these behaviors exist in every organisation. He further observes that first five behaviors. Fayol has divided his approach of learning management in three parts:

- Managerial qualities and training.
- Common principles of management,
- Units of management.

Management in all business and human organization action is the performance of getting people jointly to accomplish desired goals and objectives. Management comprises scheduling, organizing, staffing, leading or directing, and controlling an organization (a group of one or more people or entities) or effort for the purpose of accomplishing a goal. Resourcing encompasses the deployment and manipulation of human possessions, financial possessions, technological possessions, and natural possessions. Because organisations can be viewed as systems, management can also be defined as human action, including design, to facilitate the manufacture of useful outcomes from a system. This view opens the opportunity to 'manage' oneself, a pre-requisite to attempting to manage others. Management can also refer to the person or people who perform the act(s) of management. The verb manage comes from the Italian maneggiare (to handle — especially apparatus), which in turn derives from the Latin manus. The French word mesnagement influenced the development in meaning of the English word management in the 17th and 18th centuries. Some definitions of management are:

- Organisation and coordination of the behaviors of an enterprise in accordance with sure policies and in attainment of clearly defined objectives. Management is often incorporated as a factor of manufacture beside with machines, materials, and money. The management guru Peter Drucker, the vital task of a management is twofold: marketing and innovation.
- Directors and managers who have the power and responsibility to create decisions to manage an enterprise. As a discipline,

> management comprises the interlocking functions of formulating corporate policy and organizing, scheduling, controlling, and directing the firm's possessions to achieve the policy's objectives. The size of management can range from one person in a little firm to hundreds or thousands of managers in multinational companies. In big firms the board of directors formulates the policy which is implemented through the chief executive officer.

Mary Parker Follett, who wrote on the topic in the early twentieth century, defined management as "the art of getting things done through people"? She also described management as philosophy. One can also think of management functionally, as the action of measuring a quantity on a regular foundation and of adjusting some initial plan; or as the actions taken to reach one's planned goal. This applies even in situations where scheduling does not take lay. From this perspective, Frenchman Henri Fayol considers management to consist of seven functions:

- Scheduling
- Organizing
- Leading
- Coordinating
- Controlling
- Staffing
- Motivating

Some people, though, discover this definition, while useful, distant too narrow. The phrase "management is what managers do" occurs widely, suggesting the difficulty of defining management, the shifting nature of definitions, and the connection of managerial practices with the subsistence of a managerial cadre or class. One habit of thought regards management as equivalent to "business management" and therefore excludes management in spaces outside commerce, as for instance in charities and in the public sector. More realistically, though, every organization necessity manages its work, people, procedures, technology, etc. in order to maximize its effectiveness. Nonetheless, several people refer to university departments which teach management as "business schools." English speakers may also use the condition "management" or "the management" as a communal word describing the managers of an organization, for instance of a corporation. Historically this use of the condition was often contrasted with the condition "Labor" referring to those being supervised. In for-profit work, management has as its primary function the satisfaction of a range of stakeholders. This typically involves creation a profit, creating valued products at a reasonable cost (for customers), and providing rewarding employment opportunities (for employees).

In nonprofit management, add the importance of keeping the faith of donors. In mainly models of management/governance, shareholders vote for the board of directors, and the board then hires senior management. Some organizations have experimented with other methods (such as employee-voting models) of selecting or reviewing managers; but this occurs only very rarely. In the public sector of countries constituted as representative democracies, voters elect politicians to public office. Such politicians hire several managers and officers, and in some countries like the United States political appointees lose their jobs on the election of a new president/governor/ mayor. Difficulties arise in tracing the history of management. Some see it (through definition) as a late contemporary (in the sense of late modernity) conceptualization. On those conditions it cannot have a pre-contemporary history, only harbingers (such as stewards).

Others, though, detect management-like-thought back to Sumerian traders and to the builders of the pyramids of ancient Egypt. Slave-owners through the centuries faced the troubles of exploiting/motivating a dependent but sometimes unenthusiastic or recalcitrant workforce, but several pre-industrial enterprises, given their little level, did not feel compelled to face the issues of management systematically. Given the level of mainly commercial operations and the lack of mechanized record-keeping and recording before the industrial revolution, it made sense for mainly owners of enterprises in those times to carry out management functions through and for themselves. But with rising size and complexity of organizations, the split flanked by owners (individuals, industrial dynasties, or clusters of shareholders) and day-to-day managers (self-governing specialists in scheduling and control) slowly became more general. While management has been present for millennia, many writers have created a background of works that assisted in contemporary management theories.

**Sun Tzu's The Art of War**

Written through Chinese common Sun Tzu in the 6th century BC, The Art of War is a military strategy book that, for managerial purposes, recommends being aware of and acting on strengths and weaknesses of both a manager's organization and a foe's.

**Niccolò Machiavelli's The Prince**

Believing that people were motivated through self-interest, Niccolò Machiavelli wrote The Prince in 1513 as advice for the leadership of Florence, Italy. Machiavelli recommended that leaders use fear—but not hatred—to uphold control.

**Adam Smith's The Wealth of Nations**

Written in 1776 through Adam Smith, a Scottish moral philosopher, The Wealth of Nations aims for efficient organization of work through Specialization of labor. Smith described how changes in procedures could boost productivity in the manufacture of pins. While individuals could produce 200 pins per day, Smith analyzed the steps involved in manufacture and, with 10 specialists, enabled manufacture of 48,000 pins per day.

## 19TH CENTURY

Classical economists such as Adam Smith (1723 - 1790) and John Stuart Mill (1806 - 1873) provided a theoretical background to resource-allocation, manufacture, and pricing issues. In relation to the similar time, innovators like Eli Whitney (1765 - 1825), James Watt (1736 - 1819), and Matthew Boulton (1728 - 1809) urbanized units of technological manufacture such as standardization, excellence-control procedures, cost-accounting, interchangeability of parts, and work-scheduling. Several of these characteristics of management lived in the pre-1861 slave-based sector of the US economy. That environment saw 4 million people, as the modern usages had it, "supervised" in profitable quasi-mass manufacture. Through the late 19th century, marginal economists Alfred Marshall (1842 - 1924), Léon Walras (1834 - 1910), and others introduced a new layer of complexity to the theoretical underpinnings of management. Joseph Wharton offered the first tertiary-stage course in management in 1881.

## 20TH CENTURY

Through in relation to the 1900 one discovers managers trying to lay their theories on what they regarded as a thoroughly scientific foundation. Examples contain Henry R. Towne's Science of management in the 1890s, Frederick Winslow Taylor's The Principles of Scientific Management, Frank and Lillian Gilbreth's Applied motion revise, and Henry L. Gantt's charts (1910s). In 1912 Yoichi Ueno introduced Taylorism to Japan and became first management consultant of the "Japanese-management approach". His son Ichiro Ueno pioneered Japanese excellence assurance. The first comprehensive theories of management appeared approximately 1920. The Harvard Business School invented the Master of Business Management degree (MBA) in 1921. People like Henri Fayol (1841 - 1925) and Alexander Church described the several branches of management and their inter-relationships. In the early 20th century, people like Ordway Tead (1891 - 1973), Walter Scott and J. Mooney applied the principles of psychology to management, while other writers, such as Elton Mayo (1880 - 1949), Mary Parker Follett (1868 - 1933), Chester Barnard (1886 - 1961), Max Weber (1864 - 1920), Rensis Likert (1903 - 1981), and Chris Argyris (1923 - ) approached the phenomenon of management from a sociological perspective. Peter Drucker (1909 – 2005) wrote one of the earliest books on applied management: Concept of the Corporation (published in 1946).

It resulted from Alfred Sloan (chairman of Common Motors until 1956) commissioning a revise of the organisation. Drucker went on to write 39 books, several in the similar vein. H. Dodge, Ronald Fisher (1890 - 1962), and Thornton C. Fry introduced statistical techniques into management-studies. In the 1940s, Patrick Blackett combined these statistical theories with microeconomic theory and gave birth to the science of operations research. Operations research, sometimes recognized as "management science" (but separate from Taylor's scientific management), attempts to take a scientific approach to solving management troubles, particularly in the regions of logistics and operations. Some of the more recent growths contain the Theory of Constraints, management through objectives, reengineering, Six Sigma and several information-technology-driven theories such as agile software development, as well as group management theories such as Cog's Ladder. As the common recognition of managers as a class solidified throughout the 20th century and gave perceived practitioners of the art/science of management a sure amount of prestige, so the way opened for popularized systems of management ideas to peddle their wares. In this context several management fads may have had more to do with pop psychology than with scientific theories of management. Towards the end of the 20th century, business management came to consist of six separate branches, namely:

- Human resource management
- Operations management or manufacture management
- Strategic management
- Marketing management
- Financial management
- Information technology management responsible for management information systems

## 21ST CENTURY

In the 21st century observers discover it increasingly hard to subdivide management into functional categories in this way. More and more procedures simultaneously involve many categories. Instead, one tends to think in conditions of the several procedures, tasks, and objects subject to management. Branches of management theory also exist relating to nonprofits and to government: such as public management, public management, and educational management. Further, management programs related to civil-civilization organizations have also spawned programs in nonprofit management and social entrepreneurship. Note that several of the assumptions made through management have approach under attack from business ethics viewpoints, critical management studies, and anti-corporate activism. As one consequence, workplace democracy has become both more general, and more advocated, in some spaces distributing all management functions in the middle of the workers, each of whom takes on a portion of the work. Though, these models predate any current political issue, and may happen more naturally than does a command hierarchy. All management to some degree embraces democratic principles in that in the extensive condition workers necessity provide majority support to management; otherwise they leave to discover other work, or go on strike. Despite the move toward workplace democracy, command-and-control organization structures remain commonplace and the de facto organization structure. Indeed, the entrenched nature of command-and-control can be seen in the way that recent layoffs have been mannered with management ranks affected distant less than employees at the lower stages of organizations. In some cases, management has even rewarded itself with bonuses when lower stage employees have been laid off.

## MANAGEMENT TOPICS

### Vital Functions of Management

Management operates through several functions, often classified as scheduling, organizing, leading/directing, and controlling/monitoring.

- Scheduling: Deciding what requires to happen in the future (today, after that week, after that month, after that year, in excess of the after that 5 years, etc.) and generating plans for action.
- Organizing: (Implementation) creation optimum use of the possessions required to enable the successful carrying out of plans.
- Staffing: Job analyzing, recruitment, and hiring individuals for appropriate jobs.
- Leading/directing: Determining what requires to be done in a situation and getting people to do it.
- Controlling/Monitoring: Controlling/Monitoring checking progress against plans, which may require modification based on feedback.

These functions are closely interlinked and interwoven in character. These functions are the identifying marks through which a manger can be differentiated form a non-manager.

Of the four functions, though, the upper or top executives are mostly preoccupied with the first two functions-scheduling and organization, while the lower-ranking executives are mainly busy with direction and mainly busy with direction and control. But the thinking functions of scheduling and organisation cannot be separated in to water-tight compartments from the doing functions of direction and control. Irrespective of their stages and spheres of action, executives are required to perform all the four functions in varying degrees.

- Scheduling: Is the rational and orderly thinking in relation to the ways and means for the realization of sure goals. It involves thought and decision pertaining to a future course of action. It anticipates and precedes action rather than creation a reflective thinking abuts the past events. Absence of scheduling before doing implies rashness, imprudence, or shortsightedness in the performance of work. Before undertaking any work, is to be done, and who is to do the work. In considering these points, managers have to clarify objectives or goals and to evolve policies and procedures for guiding those who do the work; they have to chart the proposed rows of action with proper time schedules for the execution of work. For providing a factual foundation for future action, managers have to map out a programmed indicating the best course of action to be followed, fixing the targets and standards of work performance there in, and evolving the strategies and remedies for possible hindrances to the smooth flow of work. In other words, programmes give a complete road map for the guidance of managers to get things done through operators. In a sense, scheduling and decisions creation are synonymous. Like decision creation, scheduling is made for providing guide to action in problem regions. There is much general ground flanked by the steps scheduling and of decision creation -diagnosis of the problem, development of alternative, evaluation of alternative and selection of the best course of action. The decision stage of scheduling is so significant that several writers have treated scheduling as a synonym of decision creation.

- Organization: Gives the mechanism or tools for purposive, integrated, and co-operative action through two or more persons with a view to implementing any plan. With a few persons, organization calls for the allocation of tasks to individuals and requires the efforts of several people, many departments approach into subsistence under the charge of dissimilar managers who are tied jointly neatly through power relationships for integrated action. That is, organization involves the division and subdivision of behaviors, into departments, parts and jobs as well as the integration of behaviors and positions into a coordinated whole. The division of behaviors entails three thing, viz., determination of Total behaviors, grouping of such behaviors and assignment of jobs to both managers and operators. The integration of behaviors is effected through positions which are bound jointly in a constant pattern through the fabric of inter-relationships in the middle of enterprise functions, jobs, and personnel. Delegation of power is the cement that holds the positions jointly as one entity. The concept of organization has a number of implications.
- First, it has two characteristics: Technological or mechanistic aspect pertaining to behaviors and social or humanistic aspect pertaining to people. For the personal contentment and social satisfaction of people, organization calls for the matching of jobs with individuals and vice-versa. Secondly, as a mechanism for action, organization

is required to be changed when either the volume and nature of action or the personnel change. Although some amount of reorganization takes lay with every personnel change, upper-stage personnel change is more important in effect. Thirdly, delegation of power takes lay not only flanked by management members, but it extends to operators as well. In addition to managerial jobs, the operating jobs are also put to the similar procedure of delegation.

- Direction: Is mainly a function of human dealings and motivation. This function is, of course, denoted variously through dissimilar writers, such as command, leadership, motivation, execution or actuating. The organizational mechanism is to be energized, activated, or put into action for carrying out the management plan. This is what is actually done through directing function to set the organization in motion. But human beings are not inanimate cogs in a machine; they have emotions, aspirations, sentiments, capability to participate or to withhold such participation. Like a machine, they could not be ordered to do a predetermined work. With the purpose of inducing the members of the organization to put forth their best endeavour, managers direct the employees through the medium of leadership, guidance, supervision, communication, and counseling. Direction involves personal and social-group relationships. The working conditions are inspired and motivated to do the work willingly and whole-heartedly because of providing desirable job satisfaction and wanted team spirit.
- Control: Ensures qualitative and quantitative performance of work in the organization for completing plans and achieving objectives. Under the control function, measuring standards or yardsticks are recognized and communicated to managers so that they can regulate employee performance and can work through self-control. Moreover, control brings to light any management lapses that hinder satisfactory work progress, and therefore it gives the managers with an opportunity to take remedial action before it is too late. The control function furnishes new data and facts that enable the managers to verify the accuracy of their decisions with regard to scheduling, organizing, and directing functions. Controlling as a procedure involves measurement, evaluation, and correction of performance in the light of standards recognized through scheduling. That scheduling and controlling are inter-dependent can be explained form the nature of either function. Likewise, plans are not capable of self-achieving without the exercise of controlling function. In the past, control was work-focused rather than work-focused,

Regions and categories and implementations of management:

- Accounting management
- Agile management
- Applied Engineering (field)
- Association management
- Capability Management
- Change management
- Disagreement management
- Commercial operations management
- Communication management
- Constraint management
- Cost management
- Crisis management
- Critical management studies
- Customer connection management
- Decision creation styles
- Design management
- Disaster management
- Distributed management
- Earned value management
- Educational management
- Engineering Management
- Environmental management
- Facility management
- Financial management
- Forecasting
- Human possessions management
- Hospital management
- Hospitality management
- Hotel management
- Information technology management
- Innovation management
- Interim management
- Inventory management
- Knowledge management
- Land management
- Leadership
- Logistics management
- Lifecycle management
- Marine fuel management
- Marketing management
- Materials management
- Office management

- Operations management
- Organization development
- Perception management
- Practice management
- Program management
- Project management
- Procedure management
- Performance management
- Product management
- Public management
- Public management
- Excellence management
- Records management
- Connection management
- Resource management
- Restaurant management
- Risk management
- Rural management
- Skills management
- Social entrepreneurship
- Spend management
- Strategic management
- Stress management
- Supply chain management
- Systems management
- Talent management
- Time management
- Technology Management

## STRATEGIES AND MANAGEMENT CONTROL

### CONCEPT OF STRATEGY

The top management of an organization is concerned with the selection of a course of action from in the middle of dissimilar alternatives to meet the organizational objectives. The procedure through which objectives are formulated and achieved is recognized as strategic management and strategy acts as the means to achieve the objective. Strategy is the grand design or an overall 'plan' which an organization chooses in order to move or react towards the set of objectives through by its possessions. Strategies mainly often devote a common programme of action and an implied deployed of emphasis and possessions to attain comprehensive objectives. An organization is measured efficient and operationally effective if it is characterized through coordination flanked by objectives and strategies. There has to be integration of the parts into a complete structure. Strategy helps the organization to meet its uncertain situations with due diligence. Without a strategy, the organization is like a ship without a rudder. It is like a tramp, which has no scrupulous destination to go to. Without an appropriate strategy effectively implemented, the future is always dark and hence, more are the chances of business failure.

**Meaning of Strategy**

The word 'strategy' has entered in the field of management from the military services where it refers to apply the forces against an enemy to win a war. Originally, the word strategy ha s been derived from Greek, 'strategos' which means generalship. The word as used for the first time in approximately 400 BC. The word strategy means the art of the common to fight in war. The dictionary meaning of strategy is "the art of so moving or disposing the instrument of warfare as to impose upon enemy, the lay time and circumstances for fighting through one self" In management, the concept of strategy is taken in broader conditions. Just as to Glueck, "Strategy is the unified, comprehensive, and integrated plan that relates the strategic advantage of the firm to the challenges of the environment and is intended to ensure that vital objectives of the enterprise are achieved through proper implementation procedure"

This definition of strategy lays stress on the following:

- Unified comprehensive and integrated plan
- Strategic advantage related to challenges of environment
- Proper implementation ensuring attainment of vital objectives

Another definition of strategy is which also relates strategy to its environment. "Strategy is organization's pattern of response to its environment in excess of an era of time to achieve its goals and mission". This definition lays stress on the following:

- It is organization's pattern of response to its environment
- The objective is to achieve its goals and missions

Though, several experts do not agree in relation to the precise scope of strategy. Lack of consensus has lead to two broad categories of definitions: strategy as action inclusive of objective setting and strategy as action exclusive of objective setting.

**Strategy as Action, Inclusive of Objective Setting**

In 1960's, Chandler made an effort to describe strategy as "the determination of vital extensive condition goals and objective of an enterprise and the adoption of the courses of action and the allocation of possessions necessary for carrying out these goals"

This definition gives for three kinds of actions involved in strategy:

- Determination of extensive condition goals and objectives
- Adoption of courses of action
- Allocation of possessions

**Strategy as Action Exclusive of Objective Setting**

This is another view in which strategy has been defined. It states that strategy is a way in which the firm, reacting to its environment, deploys its principal possessions and marshalls its efforts in pursuit of its purpose. Michael Porter has defined strategy as "Creation of a unique and valued location involving a dissimilar set of behaviors. The company that is strategically positioned performs dissimilar behaviors from rivals or performs alike behaviors in dissimilar ways". The people who consider this version of the definition call strategy a unified, comprehensive, and integrated plan relating to the strategic advantages of the firm to the challenges of the environment After considering both the views, strategy can basically be put as management's plan for achieving its objectives. It basically comprises determination and evaluation of alternative paths to an already recognized mission or objective and eventually, choice of best alternative to be adopted

**Nature of Strategy**

We can understand the nature of strategy. A few characteristics concerning nature of strategy are as follows:

- Strategy is a major course of action through which an organization relates itself to its environment particularly the external factors to facilitate all actions involved in meeting the objectives of the organization
- Strategy is the blend of internal and external factors. To meet the opportunities and threats provided through the external factors, internal factors are matched with them
- Strategy is the combination of actions aimed to meet a scrupulous condition, to solve sure troubles or to achieve a desirable end. The actions are dissimilar for dissimilar situations
- Due to its dependence on environmental variables, strategy may involve a contradictory action. An organization may take contradictory actions either simultaneously or with a gap of time. For instance, a firm is occupied in closing down of some of its business and at the similar time expanding some
- Strategy is future oriented. Strategic actions are required for new situations which have not arisen before in the past
- Strategy requires some systems and norms for its efficient adoption in any organization
- Strategy gives overall framework for guiding enterprise thinking and action

The purpose of strategy is to determine and communicate a picture of enterprise through a system of major objectives and policies. Strategy is concerned with a unified direction and efficient allocation of an organization's possessions. A well made strategy guides managerial action and thought. It gives an integrated approach for the organization and aids in meeting the challenges posed through environment

**Essence of Strategy**

Strategy, just as to a survey mannered in 1974, comprises the determination and evaluation of alternative paths to an already recognized mission or objective and eventually, choice of the alternative to be adopted. Strategy is characterized through four significant characteristics:

- Extensive condition objectives
- Competitive Advantage
- Vector
- Synergy

## STRATEGIES AND CORE COMPETENCIES

The Core Competence of the Corporation, C.K. Prahalad and Gary Hamel coined the condition core competencies, or the communal learning and coordination skills behind the firm's product rows. They made the case that core competencies are the source of competitive advantage and enable the firm to introduce an array of new products and services. Just as to Prahalad and Hamel, core competencies lead to the development of core products. Core products are not directly sold to end users; rather, they are used to build a superior number of end-user products.

Diagram Core Competencies to End Products

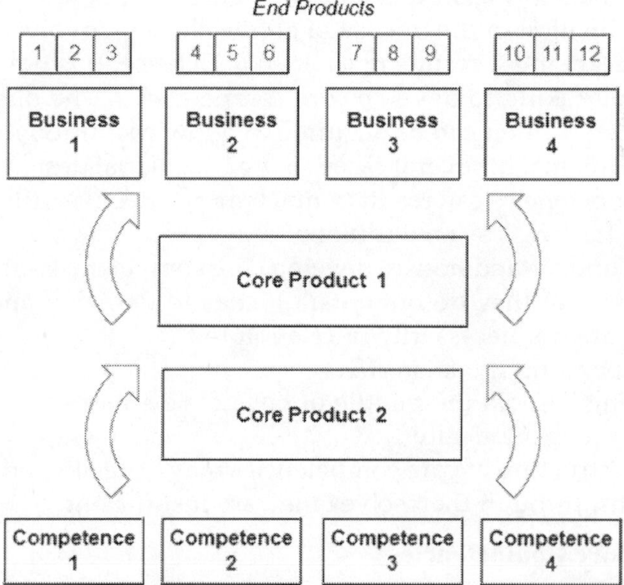


For instance, motors are a core product that can be used in wide array of end products. The business elements of the corporation each tap into the relatively few core products to develop a superior number of end user products based on the core product technology. This flow from core competencies to end products is shown in the following diagram :

The intersection of market opportunities with core competencies shapes the foundation for launching new businesses. Through combining a set of core competencies in dissimilar ways and matching them to market opportunities, a corporation can launch a vast array of businesses. Without core competencies, a big corporation is presently a collection of discrete businesses. Core competencies serve as the glue that bonds the business elements jointly into a coherent portfolio.

**Developing Core Competencies**

Just as to Prahalad and Hamel, core competencies arise from the integration of multiple technologies and the coordination of diverse manufacture skills. Some examples contain Philip's expertise in optical media and Sony's skill to miniaturize electronics. There are three tests useful for identifying a core competence. A core competence should:

- Give access to a wide diversity of markets, and
- Contribute significantly to the end-product benefits, and
- Be hard for competitors to imitate.

Core competencies tend to be rooted in the skill to integrate and coordinate several clusters in the organization. While a company may be able to hire a team of brilliant scientists in a scrupulous technology, in doing so it does not automatically gain a core competence in that technology. It is the effective coordination in the middle of all the clusters involved in bringing a product to market those results in a core competence. It is not necessarily an expensive undertaking to develop core competencies. The missing pieces of a core competency often can be acquired at a low cost through alliances and licensing agreements. In several cases an organizational design that facilitates sharing of competencies can result in much more effective utilization of those competencies for small or no additional cost.

To better understand how to develop core competencies, it is worthwhile to understand what they do not entail. Just as to Prahalad and Hamel, core competencies are not necessarily in relation to the:

- Outspending rivals on R&D
- Sharing costs in the middle of business elements
- Integrating vertically

While the structure of core competencies may be facilitated through some of these actions, through themselves they are insufficient.

**The Loss of Core Competencies**

Cost-cutting moves sometimes destroy the skill to build core competencies. For instance, decentralization creates it harder to build core competencies because autonomous clusters rely on outsourcing of critical tasks, and this outsourcing prevents the firm from developing core competencies in those tasks since it no longer consolidates the know-how that is spread throughout the company. Failure to recognize core competencies may lead to decisions that result in their loss. For instance, in the 1970's several U.S. manufacturers divested themselves of their television manufacturing businesses, reasoning that the industry was mature and that high excellence, low cost models were accessible from Distant East manufacturers. In the procedure, they lost their core competence in video, and this loss resulted in a handicap in the newer digital television industry. Likewise, Motorola divested itself of its semiconductor DRAM business at 256Kb stage, and then was unable to enter the 1Mb market on its own. Through recognizing its core competencies and understanding the time required building them or regaining them, a company can create better divestment decisions.

**Core Products**

Core competencies manifest themselves in core products that serve as a link flanked by the competencies and end products. Core products enable value creation in the end products. Examples of firms and some of their core products contain:

- 3M - substrates, coatings, and adhesives
- Black & Decker - little electric motors
- Canon - laser printer subsystems
- Matsushita - VCR subsystems, compressors
- NEC - semiconductors
- Honda - gasoline powered engines

The core products are used to launch a diversity of end products. For instance, Honda uses its engines in automobiles, motorcycles, lawn mowers, and portable generators. Because firms may sell their core products to other firms that use them as the foundation for end user products, traditional events of brand market share are insufficient for evaluating the success of core competencies. Prahalad and Hamel suggest that core product share is the appropriate metric. While a company may have a low brand share, it may have high core product share and it is this share that is significant from a core competency standpoint. Once a firm has successful core products, it can expand the number of uses in order to gain a cost advantage via economies of level and economies of scope.

**Implications for Corporate Management**

Prahalad and Hamel suggest that a corporation should be organized into a portfolio of core competencies rather than a portfolio of self-governing business elements. Business element managers tend to focus on getting immediate end-products to market rapidly and usually do not feel responsible for developing company-wide core competencies. Consequently, without the incentive and direction from corporate management to do otherwise, strategic business elements are inclined to under invest in the structure of core competencies. If a business element does manage to develop its own core competencies in excess of time, due to its autonomy it may not share them with other business elements. As a solution to this problem, Prahalad and Hamel suggest that corporate managers should have the skill to allocate not only cash but also core competencies in the middle of business elements. Business elements that lose key employees for the sake of a corporate core competency should be recognized for their contribution.

## CORPORATE STAGE STRATEGY

Corporate stage strategy covers the strategic scope of the organization as a whole. For mainly organizations the corporate strategic plan is the only strategic plan required. Often strategy at the corporate stage is basically referred to as corporate strategy, or in unified companies the corporate business strategy. The procedure that produces it is described corporate strategic scheduling, or sometimes basically corporate scheduling. In a few situations though, it may be justified to speak of corporate stage strategy to distinguish it from other types of scheduling.

### Strategy Stages

In the first case the organisation may be multidivisional in nature to the extent that in principle or even in law, separate parts of the enterprise could operate as viable entities in their own right. These 'group structures' may undertake strategic scheduling as group exercise where under the corporate stage strategy, each separate subsidiary or division has its own strategic scheduling procedure and strategic plan. In these cases though, one of the mainly important inputs to each divisions' strategic scheduling is the output of the corporate strategic scheduling. These outputs from corporate stage strategy; usually in the form of performance targets for the divisions cannot be ignored through the subsidiary element. The corporate business strategy may also set down a little number of other factors that the divisions, or strategic business elements as they may sometimes be described. These might contain guidance on market definition, including geographic scope. For instance the subsidiaries of a multinational bank may be defined through the country they operate in. In this case the corporate business strategy would set profit targets for each country bank.

The corporate strategy would yield to the country banks as to the strategies they pursue in generating these profits. The country stage banks would have their own business element stage strategies. In the second case corporate stage strategy is used to distinguish it from the several other plans and scheduling procedures that get the condition 'strategic' in their names.

The word strategy has acquired a type of aura that appears to create several people want to use it, regardless of how actually strategic the matter at hand is in relation to the overall performance of an organisation. So we can end up with strategic plans for every stage, part and functional procedure in the organization. Strategic scheduling is a systematic, formally documented procedure for deciding the handful of key decisions that an organisation, viewed as a corporate whole, necessity get right in order to thrive in excess of the after that few years. Though, because of this wide spread usage in a diversity of contexts we also use the account 'corporate stage strategy' or 'corporate strategy', and refer sometimes to 'corporate strategic scheduling' to create it clear we are not talking in relation to the all these other partial or 'non corporate' shapes. Because the successful implementation of corporate stage strategy relies on cooperation and alignment crossways the organization as a whole, it is useful to distinguish the several stages of strategy.

**Decisions in Corporate Stage Strategy**

Keep in mind that at the beginning we said that corporate-stage strategies address the whole strategic scope of the enterprise. This is the "big picture" view of the organization and may contain deciding in which product or service markets to compete and the geographic boundaries of the organizations' operations. For multi-divisional organizations or enterprises, how capital, staffing, and other possessions are allocated is usually recognized at the corporate stage. Additionally, because market definition is usually the domain of corporate-stage strategy, the responsibility for diversification, or the addition of new products or services to the existing offerings, also mostly comes within the responsibility of corporate-stage strategy. Also, whether to compete head on with other companies or to selectively set up cooperative partnering arrangements, or 'strategic alliances' is a decision for corporate-stage strategy, while requiring ongoing input from business element or divisional stage managers.

**Corporate Stage Strategic Questions**

So crucial questions addressed through corporate-stage strategy, in the middle of other possibilities may contain:

- What should be the scope of operations; i.e.; what businesses should the firm be in? And where should it be in business?
- How should the organization allocate its possessions its several existing rows of business or business elements?
- What stage of diversity should exist in the business as it moves into the future? Are there other behaviors the enterprise should be in or are there current behaviors that should be targeted for stopped or sold off to others?
- What should be the nature of this diversity or how diversified should the organization be? Should it diversify in alike product or

service markets, or into totally dissimilar regions; becoming a more conglomerate entity.

- How should the firm be organized? What will be the boundaries of the enterprise? How will these boundaries impact relationships in the middle of parts of the business, with suppliers, customers and other interest clusters? How will the organizational functions such as product development, manufacture, sharing finance, marketing, sales customer service, etc. fit jointly? Are the responsibilities for each business element clearly recognized and is accountability recognized? Which will be accepted out in-home, and which will be contracted out?
- Should the firm enter into cooperative, mutually-beneficial relationships or alliances with others? If so, on what foundation? If not, what impact might this have on future organizational performance?

As these questions illustrate, corporate strategies address the extensive-condition direction for the organization as a whole. Corporate strategies deal with plans for the whole organization and change as the capabilities of the organization develop and as the environment of the organization changes. Top management has primary decision creation responsibility in developing corporate strategies and these managers are directly responsible to providers of capital to the organization, whether shareholders, donors, members, and so on depending on the kind of organization. The role of the governing board of is to ensure that top managers actually act to address these owner or primary beneficiary interests.

**Business-Stage Strategies**

Business-stage strategies are alike to corporate-strategies in that they focus on overall performance. As separate from corporate-stage strategy, though, they focus on presently one instead of a range of businesses. The corporate stage strategy of a multi division operation is like a strategy for managing an investment portfolio. Business elements are usually individual enterprise-like entities oriented toward a scrupulous industry, product or service kind, and or market. Business-stage strategies are therefore primarily concerned with:

- Managing element behaviors so they conform to organizational corporate stage strategies, sometimes including cooperation with other business elements to achieve 'strategic synergy'.
- Developing distinctive capabilities, possessions and competitive advantage in each element.
- Identifying product or service-market opportunities and developing strategies for succeeding in each.
- Monitoring the business industry environment so that strategies conform to requires of the markets at the current level of development.

In a single-product company, corporate-stage and business-stage strategies are the similar. Business-stage strategies seem at the business element strengths, weaknesses, opportunities and threats; much like corporate-stage strategies, except for the emphasis in business-stage strategies is on the specific product or service, not on the corporate stage investment portfolio. Business-stage strategies therefore contribute to corporate-stage strategies. Corporate-stage strategies effort to deliver benefits to the primary beneficiaries, such as raising the wealth of shareholders through profitability of the overall corporate portfolio, and business-stage strategies are concerned wit:

- Matching their operations with the overall objectives of corporate-stage strategy while simultaneously
- Navigating the environment in which they are active in such a way that they are in the middle of the better performers in their industry.

**Functional-Stage Strategies**

Functional-stage strategies are concerned with managing the functional regions of the organization, such as product or service development and design, marketing and sales, finance, human possessions, manufacture, research and development, etc., so that each function upholds contributes to individual business element strategies and the overall corporate-stage strategy. Functional strategies are primarily concerned with:

- Efficiently deploying specialists within the functional region.
- Integrating behaviors within the functional region
- Creation sure that functional strategies link effectively and efficiently with business strategies and the overall corporate-stage strategy.

## BUSINESS ELEMENT STRATEGIES

In an effort to create the traditional business model less bureaucratic and more flexible, some organizations have begun implementing business element strategy. Instead of forcing a new department into the average chain of command, companies form differently sized autonomous business elements that statement directly to top management. Now the role of the corporation is to manage its business elements and coordinate their efforts into the overall corporate strategy.

**Elements**

A business element is a part or department of a business that runs as an autonomous entity. Their profits are usually treated separately than those of the business as a whole. "All SBUs (little business elements) are a single business (or collection of businesses), have their own competitors and a manager accountable for operations, and can be independently planned for," reports Reference for Business.

**Objectives**

Each business element necessity meets five criteria. First, their mission and focus necessity be dissimilar from all other organization SBUs. Second, they should have an easily and clearly defined group of competitors. Third, its scheduling and development should be accepted out quite independently of any other business unity. Finally, each SBU necessity has a separate manager with decision-creation power who is fully responsible for the operation.

**Approach**

While there is no generic approach that works best all the time, once you determine an approach that works, it's best to stick with it. A collaborative approach builds business elements through relying on employee input combined with corporate strategy. A corporate led approach relies on the executives to plan the element and the goals focus on growth, profit and market share. Thirdly, the business element may form its own strategic plan that is approved, edited or disapproved through corporate management.

**Analysis**

Business element strategy relies on answering two questions: what are an element's strengths and what is the best way to improve performance. This analysis allows you to set up "the SBU's mission, setting objectives, and determining strategy to use to meet these objectives," reports MAB Paradigms Consulting Firm. SBUs require constant analysis through reports and financial projections to determine if they remain productive or if their strategy necessitates alteration to better improve performance.

## DESIGNING MANAGEMENT CONTROL SYSTEM

The three purposes of this level are to give a review of empirical, contingency-based research as it has urbanized since the early 1980s, to critically evaluate this work, and consider a diversity of theoretical foundations that may assist in developing future research. The review is based, in the main, on research employing survey-based methods that has been published in a broad selection of accounting and management journals. The review is selective and illustrative of issues pertinent to the development of a contingency-based framework for the design of MCS, and does not effort a comprehensive coverage of relevant research The chapter is structured as follows. The after that part introduces the region of contingency-based MCS research and gives an overview of findings in excess of the past 20 years. The following nine parts review articles in conditions of their contribution to understanding topics measured within contingency-based research. These are: the meaning of MCS, outcomes of MCS, and the contextual variables of external environment, technology (traditional and modern), organizational structure, size, strategy and national civilization. Each part comprises two parts: first, findings from the extant literature are presented and a series of propositions summarizing these findings are offered; and second, critical issues concerning each variable are examined with a view to identifying regions that give challenges for improvement and opportunities for future research. Following these parts, issues concerning theory development are examined. Finally, the potential role of a diversity of theories in progressing understanding of contingency-based research in MCS is measured.

## AN ORGANIZATIONAL FRAMEWORK FOR CONTINGENCY BASED MCS RESEARCH

The identification of contextual variables potentially implicated in the design of effective MCS can be traced to the original structural contingency frameworks urbanized within organizational theory. Theorists such as Burns and Stalker, Perrow, Thompson, Lawrence and Lorsch, and Galbraith focused on the impact of environment and technology on organizational structure. Early accounting researchers drew on this work to investigate the importance of environment, technology, structure and size to the design of MCS. Reviews mannered 20 years ago through Waterhouse and Tiessen and Otley were able to structure their commentaries through categorizing the early research into these key variables. In considering MCS research since 1980, it is apparent that these key variables have been confirmed as descriptors of fundamental, generic units of context. Several recent studies, incorporated in this review, focus on modern characteristics of the environment, technologies and structural arrangements.

They draw on the original organizational theorists to develop arguments that help explain how the effectiveness of MCS depends on the nature of modern settings. Also, recent research has measured the relevance of additional contextual variables to the design of MCS. Perhaps the mainly significant new stream of literature has been that related to the role of strategy. This has been assimilated within the traditional organizational model in ways that suggest significant links flanked by strategy, the environment, technology, organizational structure and MCS. The importance of technology to MCS design has been enriched through research drawing on the manufacturing literature, and the work of economists such as Milgrom and Roberts. Issues concerning the role of MCS within advanced manufacturing settings such as Total Excellence Management, Presently-in-Time and Flexible Manufacturing have been explored. Researchers have gained new insights into the role of MCS within new structural arrangements, such as teams, through drawing on the human resource management literature which investigates the dynamics of teams including issues concerning performance evaluation. National civilization has been recognized as a unit of context following the development of multi-national operations in several organizations. In reviewing the past 20 years of contingency based research it is significant to consider the extent to which progress has been made in developing an empirical body of literature relating MCS to units of context. The conventional, functionalist contingency-based approach to research assumes that MCS are adopted to assist managers achieve some desired organizational outcomes or organizational goals.

The appropriate design(s) of MCS will be influenced through the context within which they operate. The following nine parts consider: the meaning of MCS, the outcomes of MCS and the key contextual variables as they have evolved, historically, in the literature. First, the connection flanked by MCS and the external environment is measured. This is followed through technology (both traditional and modern), structure and size. After that, strategy is examined. Finally, the role of national civilization in MCS design is reviewed. On the foundation of the empirical findings, propositions are offered which relate contextual variables to the MCS. Assessing these propositions requires considering shortcomings in contingency-based research, identifying the extent to which progress has been made in addressing these issues and noting opportunities for improvements and future directions.

## THE MEANING OF MCS

The conditions management accounting (MA), management accounting systems (MAS), management control systems (MCS), and organizational controls (OC)are sometimes used interchangeably. MA refers to a collection of practices such as budgeting or product costing, while MAS refers to the systematic use of MA to achieve some goal. MCS is a broader condition that encompasses MAS and also comprises other controls such as personal or clan controls. OC is sometimes used to refer to controls built into behaviors and procedures such as statistical excellence control, presently-in-time management. The condition MCS is used, in the main, throughout this chapter. The definition of MCS has evolved in excess of the years from one focusing on the provision of more formal, financially quantifiable information to assist managerial decision creation to one that embraces a much broader scope of information.

This comprises external information related to markets, customers, competitors, non-financial information related to manufacture procedures, predictive information and a broad array of decision support mechanisms, and informal personal and social controls. Conventionally, MCS are perceived as passive apparatus providing information to assist managers. Though, approaches following a sociological orientation see MCS as more active, furnishing individuals with power to achieve their own ends. Contingency-based research follows the more conventional view that perceives MCS as a passive tool intended to assist manager's decision creation. Contingency-based research has focused on a diversity of characteristics of MCS. These contain dimensions of budgeting such as participation, importance of meeting budgets, formality of communications and systems sophistication, links to reward systems, budget slack, post completion audits and variance analysis. Examples of modern innovations in MCS contain ABC/ ABM, non-financial performance events and economic value analysis. Researchers are likely investigating progress concerning balanced scorecards and target costing. At a more common stage, studies have measured sophistication of controls, reliance on accounting performance events, dimensions of information such as scope, timeliness and aggregations, sophisticated capital budgeting, cost consciousness, competitor focused accounting, strategic interactive controls and diagnostic controls, information which is related to issues concerning customers, product design, time, cost, possessions and profitability which is distinguished on stage of detail, updating frequency and interactive use with operational personnel.

**Critical Evaluation**

Overall, assessing findings from contingency based research involves judging how the results accumulate to give generalizable findings concerning MCS. As is general in several social sciences, MCS researchers are faced with decisions on whether to build on an existing region of revise, such as the role of formal budgets, or identify emerging characteristics of MCS, such as balanced scorecards or target costing, and investigate the settings within which they may be mainly beneficial. Within the body of literature reviewed in this paper there is a mixture of studies focused on single themes, and studies exploring unconnected units of MCS and context. Both kinds of studies are required. Learning the role of novel MCS practices within modern settings is necessary to ensure that MCS research is relevant. Given that several dimensions of MCS and their contexts change, novel studies will always be required to address emerging issues. There is a pressing require for studies into situations in which modern MCS may be best suited. Research is presently starting to be published identifying contingencies nearby the design and implementation of ABC/ABM.

Though, there is very small published contingency work on balanced scorecards, target costing, life cycle costing, the broad array of non-financial performance indictors including those related to assessing human resource management initiatives. Examples of the latter contain measurement to guide and evaluate the learning capabilities of the organization, events such as team maturity indexes and organizational climate surveys that effort to assess the effectiveness of administrative innovations. Recent growths in global operations, strategic risk management (including real options), corporate social reporting (including triple bottom row), economic value analysis, 360 degree performance evaluation, knowledge-based organizations, forensic accounting, intellectual capital, competitor accounting and value chain are only presently beginning to be understood through researchers. There is a require for more research into service and not-for-profit organizations as these entities become increasingly significant within mainly economies Notwithstanding the importance of learning controls that are relevant to modern settings, it is significant to develop knowledge in ways that ensure coherence in the revise of units of MAS and contextual variables, and in the findings of these studies. Such confidence can be derived from replication studies which enhance the validity and reliability of findings and thereby give a strong base to move forward through way of model development.

Commentators have been critical that in mainly regions of MCS research, studies have not urbanized enough 'critical mass' to confirm findings. The way in which studies evolved within the region of RAPM helps illustrate many difficulties in isolating the meaning and measurement of MCS variables. First, the precise meaning of the concept of RAPM has been confused through lack of definition of what is accounting and non-accounting and what is reliance. Given the ambiguity with the concept, it is not surprising that researchers sought to gain clarification through modifying their studies as understanding of RAPM and its measurement urbanized. Such refining of concepts and measurement is general in other social sciences, such as psychology. It is unfortunate that it is not part of the MCS research custom to spend more time on developing robust events of the units of MCS, particularly when there is ambiguity in the meaning of constructs. For instance, it is not clear how balanced scorecards should be measured.

It appears likely that the content and implementation of balanced scorecards vary widely flanked by organizations. It would appear useful to develop a valid measure of balanced scorecards that could then be used through researchers to explore its context. While such a valid measure would enhance consistency flanked by studies, a difficulty exists in the dynamic nature of MCS practices. MCS that are valid today may lose validity as they evolve through time. Certainly, because of advances in information technology (IT)software, some kinds of balanced scorecards being employed today are more comprehensive and strategic in nature than those being used 5 years ago. Likewise, the concept of RAPM and how it relates to broader controls has changed since the early work in the 1970 and 1980s. Without accommodating changes in modern control systems, concepts and events of MCS are unlikely to address pertinent, modern issues. A research climate that encouraged the development of valid concepts and events of MCS would have to recognize require for modification to incorporate the development of MCS. Participative budgeting has also been studied widely. Unlike RAPM, participation in budgets has approximately universally been conceptualized and measured following Milani.

In some studies, additional events are employed to give some validation of the primary measure. Other studies of budget related behaviour have drawn on attitudes and satisfaction with budgets, as urbanized through Swieringa and Moncur. There have been a considerable number of studies that have confirmed the measurement of the generic MCS features of broad scope, timeliness, aggregation, and integration. These studies have employed concepts and events urbanized through Chenhall and Morris, sometimes with minor adjustments to suit the scrupulous setting, and appear to be robust crossways a diversity of settings. Though, there has been small replication or coherence in measurement development in studies examining MCS practices of modern interest such as static flexible budgets, non-financial performance events, action-based accounting, competitor focused accounting, and product development information. Likewise, while studies have explored significant regions of MCS such as social controls, personnel control, sophisticated integrative mechanisms, administrative controls, interpersonal controls, sophisticated controls, there has been very small replication. A further criticism related to the nature of accounting controls within contingency-based research is that these form only part of broader control systems. Contingency-based research has focused on specific units of accounting controls, generic information dimensions of MCS, with a limited number of studies examining broader units of control, such as clan and informal controls, or integrative mechanisms. A difficulty in learning specific units of MCS in separation from other organizational controls is the potential for serious model under specification.

Therefore, if specific accounting controls are systematically connected with other organizational controls, studies that exclude or do not control for these units within the research method may statement spurious findings. For instance, a revise focused only on formal budget systems may argue that they are unsuitable in uncertain operating circumstances as they contain partial information and lack flexibility. Though, proof may indicate that successful organizations rely extensively on formal budgets. This unexpected finding occurs as a consequence of limiting the revise to budgets without considering broader control and information networks. It may be that successful organizations operating in uncertain circumstances have formal budgets but they are systematically combined with open and flexible informal communications flanked by managers. The formal budgets are useful in assisting scheduling and curbing excessive innovation, while the informal communications give broader information in flexible ways. Simons showed that formal budgets can give interactive controls in uncertain circumstances whereby the budgets generate intelligence data to build internal pressure to break out of narrow search routines and encourage the emergence of new strategic initiatives. Chapman also argues that in uncertain circumstances effective organizations can employ formal accounting but they should take lay within a situation that involves intense verbal communication flanked by organizational clusters. A way of addressing these concerns is to identify a diversity of control taxonomies and consider how they relate to several characteristics of MCS. One such taxonomy involves classifying controls as ranging from mechanistic to organic.

Mechanistic controls rely on formal rules, standardized operating procedures and routines. Organic systems are more flexible, responsive, involve fewer rules and standardized procedures and tend to be richer in data. These taxonomies are useful for addressing concerns of how MCS relate to broader control systems and can guide research into how scrupulous characteristics of MCS are constant with the control 'civilization' of organizations. Finally, it should be noted that there is a distinction flanked by the adoption of MCS and the implementation of the systems. Much can be learned in relation to the success or otherwise of MCS through examining how the control civilization, organic or mechanistic, powers the procedures of implementation. This becomes particularly significant when learning the adoption of innovative MCS such as action-based accounting and balanced scorecards which are closely connected to the organization's control civilization and the extent of change in MCS, in common. It appears clear that broader issues of control are likely to have implications for research into understanding MCS design.

There have been advances in excess of the past 20 years in demonstrating the importance of considering management accounting practices as characteristics of MCS. Understanding how specific characteristics of management accounting relate to broader control concepts assists in researching the complementary or substitution effects of non-accounting controls. A significant part of the research agenda is to understand how combinations of controls can be combined, to suit the scrupulous circumstances of the organization. In learning broad controls, it is necessary to be aware of the boundaries that some organizations and accountants lay approximately MAS and MCS. Without such awareness, there can be confusion as to what formal accounting control is, what structural control is, and what are personnel and informal controls.

## OUTCOMES OF MCS

Outcomes may be separated into issues related to the use or usefulness of the MCS, behavioral and organizational outcomes. There is an implied connection flanked by these outcomes. If the MCS are establish to be useful then they are likely to be used and give satisfaction to individuals, who then presumably can approach their tasks with enhanced information. As a consequence, these individuals take improved decisions and better achieve organizational goals. Clearly, there are broad leaps in logic from useful MCS, to improved job satisfaction and enhanced organizational performance. Moreover, there is no compelling proof to suggest that such links exist. Even within contingency-based research, the link flanked by enhanced organizational performance and usefulness of some aspect of MCS may well depend on the appropriateness of the useful MCS to the context of the organization.

Thoughts of interest to designers and researchers of MCS have been the extent to which the systems give information, the degree of use, the usefulness of the information or the beneficial nature of the MCS; the importance in creation operational decisions; importance to product development, whether they are helpful to the organization, and satisfaction with the systems. Behavioral outcomes such as job satisfaction have been significant in human resource management. The provision of a work laid environment to enhance employee welfare or job satisfaction is seen through some as a worthwhile goal in its own right. Moreover, other things equal, it may be presumed that individuals who are satisfied with their jobs will identify with organizational goals and work more effectively. Interestingly, there have not been several MCS studies that have examined the effects of MCS on job satisfaction. A diversity of studies have examined the effect of MCS on job related tension or stress. Unlike job satisfaction, stress appears to be more closely related to the nature of the MCS and is implicated in associations with performance. Organizational outcomes in contingency-based research have been dominated through self assessment procedures where individuals give an indication of their performance, or their organizational element, crossways a range of potentially significant managerial procedures or goals of the organization.

The issue of the validity of self-assessment is often raised as a concern. Proof suggests that a subordinate's self-assessment correlates with objective assessments and with a superior's subjective assessment. Notwithstanding this proof, it is always reassuring when a superior's performance rating of the respondent is incorporated in the revise. Curiously, there has been small work relating MCS change to share prices. Larcker establish that firms adopting incentive performance plans experienced an augment in capital investment and a positive security market reaction on disclosure of the plan to the market. Gordon and Smith accounted that returns to investors were higher for firms employing post completion reviews when matched with asymmetric information, capital intensity, capital expenditure and insider ownership. Smith recognized that positive returns were associated with post completion reviews in abandonment decisions.

Though, Gordon and Silvester establish no important association flanked by the installation of ABC and important stock market reaction. This poses the question as to whether improved understanding would follow from learning these associations within a diversity of organizational contexts. These studies do not employ contingency-based approaches as they explore only the main effects flanked by share price movement and the adoption of units of MCS. Progress in this region may be limited due to the difficulties in extracting the effects of adopting dissimilar MCS on share prices from other events that may be associated with share price movements. With the numerous possible events effecting share prices, control troubles can become acute. Also, data collection is complicated through require to collect data on the adoption and implementation of MCS through survey methods and to then match these with share price changes. Also, perhaps the lack of research in the region says something in relation to the dissimilar kinds of training flanked by researchers in finance and management accounting.

**Critical Evaluation**

Contingency-based studies have examined MCS as both dependent and self-governing variables. To look at fit flanked by MCS and context, some commentators have claimed that the outcome variables should be some dimension of desired organizational or managerial performance. Good fit means enhanced performance, while poor fit implies diminished performance. While the ultimate goal of MCS research is to give findings that assist managers achieve their goals or those of their organization, MCS research has sustained to contain dimensions of MCS, their use and usefulness, as the outcome variable. Also, it is noteworthy that performance has been incorporated as a self-governing variable explaining some features of MCS. While not explicit in mainly studies with MCS as the outcome variable, it is implied that associations flanked by context and MCS reflect equilibrium circumstances, or indicate optimal solutions because of survival of the fittest circumstances. If equilibrium is assumed, then learning performance is inappropriate as every firm has optimal performance given its situation. Researchers learning MCS as the outcome variables, also, note that this approach is justified through assuming that rational managers are unlikely to adopt or use MCS that do not assist in enhancing performance.

Alternatively, some argue that links flanked by MCS, context and performance can be tenuous as they involve several factors concerning the excellence of managing the manufacture procedures. In common, if disequilibrium circumstances are assumed, then it may be useful for contingency based studies to first set up adoption and use of MCS, then to look at how they are used to enhance decision excellence and finally investigate links with organizational performance. Care is required when interpreting studies that have outcome variables related to the features of MCS, such as 'use' and 'usefulness' of the systems. Individuals may be forced to use MCS systems, such as budgets or DCF analysis in decision creation, even though they discover them of small use. A scrupulous MCS may be perceived as not useful, rate low in satisfaction or benefits but organizational performance may be high due to the supply of required information from other sources, either formal or informal. These issues can be resolved through careful attention to the research question. It is quite legitimate to revise the adoption of systems and their use. Though, it may not be appropriate to claim that these outcomes are of value in improving organization performance.

Likewise, the extent to which MCS are perceived as useful may not imply improved organizational performance.

If learning one aspect of the MCS in separation from other sources of information, researchers should ensure that the studied attribute is the sole source of the information being studied. If an aspect of the MCS is being measured within situations that contain broader information and controls, the potential power of these other controls should be incorporated or controlled within the research design. In summary, despite the critique that contingency- based studies should contain organizational performance as the dependent variable, studies still follow approaches with MCS as the dependent variable. Care in theory construction is required in following either approach. Studies can give significant insights into the extent of adoption, use and usefulness of MCS, though, it should not be assumed that the models necessarily lead to enhanced organizational performance. Likewise, if performance is the dependent variable then compelling theory is required to illustrate how the combination of MCS and context enable managers to take more effective decisions that enhance organizational performance. Given the assumption that research should identify organizational performance as the criterion variable, a critical issue is what constitutes organizational performance? Distinguishing official and operative goals would appear an essential aspect of MCS research that comprises consideration of goals, mainly as it flags that the issue of organizational goals is distant from unproblematic. Investigating these goals requires a dynamic approach that examines the goal formulation procedure.

There are many issues that become significant. First, goal formulation or change often involves the power of new powerful players, either within or outside the organization, who can dramatically change official goals. MCS can act either as a tool to effect such changes or hinder their acceptance within the organization. For instance, a new Chief Executive Officer may stipulate that improved shareholder value is a priority. Consequently, performance measurement based on Economic Value Analysis may be introduced in an effort to align the actions of all employees with the single objective of improving economic value. Second, changes in the regions of organizational effectiveness can redirect goals to those regions of effectiveness. The unplanned detection of a new technology that potentially increases throughput can result in the adoption of 'timely' delivery as a goal of the organization. Third, it is apparent that the measurement of goals can have explicit effects on goal formulation, both planned and unintended. Goals may be selected or evolve as they can be measured readily through the MCS. A preoccupation with formal, 'hard' events may direct attention to those events at the expense of the subtleties of the situation.

For instance, measuring characteristics of customer or employee satisfaction, the organizational civilization or intellectual capital often require more subjective assessments of progress and, as such, may receive less attention than behaviors subjected to hard events such as manufacture rejects or throughput. Fourth, in addition to influencing kinds of goals, MCS may affect goal attainment through establishing standards or benchmarks for performance. Goals that are too hard may cause frustration and withdrawal, while standards that are too easy may not give enough challenge. Standards that are achievable but with enough stretch to give a challenge are often recommended as ideal. Though, in today's environment of intense competition and global operations, necessities for substantial continuous improvement may mean that hard standards based on continuous improvements are required to survive. Performance events can readily set up targets that require continuous improvement. Fifth, recently several organizations have recognized require to satisfy multiple and potentially competing goals. Mission statements identify the necessities to draw and uphold shareholders, employees, and customers and to do so in ways that are socially acceptable. Accountants have responded through refining triple bottom row reporting, environmental accounting, social corporate reporting and corporate sustainability. Sixth, aligning operative goals with official goals is a significant aspect of strategic management.

This is the essence of performance hierarchies and balanced scorecards that effort to capture the interactive effects of official goals associated with the interests of shareholders, customers, the internal procedures and the potential for the organization to sustain itself through learning and innovation. Of course, connections flanked by official and operative goals can be quite dissimilar in same organizations. Achieving shareholder welfare might require organizations to follow dissimilar operative goals concerning decisions on excellence, cost, delivery and the like. Linkages flanked by MCS and organizational goals are quite explicit, as a primary function of MCS is to measure progress towards achieving desired organization ends. It is a useful exercise when evaluating features of MCS used for reporting on goals to judge the extent to which they accommodate the following: consider multiple stakeholders; measure efficiency, effectiveness and equity; capture financial and non-financial outcomes; give vertical links flanked by strategy and operations and horizontal links crossways the value chain; give information on how the organization relates to its external environment and its skill to adapt. Presumably, balanced scorecards or performance hierarchies give a methodology to tackle several of these issues. The complexities of achieving these expectations may help to explain why several firm that effort to adopt balanced scorecards have difficulty in implementing them.

## CONTEXTUAL VARIABLES AND MCS

Before examining the contextual variables, a distinction is noted flanked by generic and specific definitions. When considering environment, specific definitions refer to scrupulous attributes such as intense price competition from existing or potential competitors, or the likelihood of a change in the availability of materials. Generic definitions effort to capture the effects of specific attributes in a more generalized way. Generic definitions enable designers and researchers of MCS to talk about the power of contextual variables without having to identify the scrupulous details of individual organizations. Constructing taxonomies of context and theories relating these to the use of MCS and organizational outcomes becomes more tractable. Clearly, to create prescriptive recommendations to a scrupulous organization it is necessary that the specific attributes of the environment be recognized. Moving flanked by the generic and specific should not be problematic providing the generic definitions are robust. Chapman gives a discussion of the deal-offs flanked by simplicity, accuracy and generalizability in variable definition.

**The External Environment**

The external environment is a powerful contextual variable that is at the base of contingency- based research. Perhaps the mainly widely researched aspect of the environment is uncertainty. Early contingency research in organization design focused on the effects of uncertainty on organizational structure. Examples contain Burns and Stalker, Galbraith, Lawrence and Lorsch and Perrow . It is significant to distinguish uncertainty from risk. Risk is concerned with situations in which probabilities can be attached to scrupulous events occurring, whereas uncertainty defines situations in which probabilities cannot be attached and even the units of the environment may not be predictable. The importance of uncertainty as a fundamental variable in MCS contingency-based research has been stressed recently through Chapman and Hartmann.

Both reinterpret characteristics of MCS research through examining the impact of environmental uncertainty. Uncertainty and risk do not give a comprehensive account of the environment. Khandwalla gives a useful taxonomy of environmental variables. These contain turbulence (risky, unpredictable, fluctuating, ambiguous), hostility (stressful, dominating, restrictive), diversity (diversity in products, inputs, customers), complexity (rapidly developing technologies). Other units of the environment that may generate pressure or give opportunities contain complexity and dynamism, controllable and uncontrollable, ambiguity or equivocality. Findings: external environment and MCS In accounting, uncertainty has been related to the usefulness of broad scope information and timely information; performance evaluation characterized through a more subjective evaluation approach; less reliance on incentive- based pay, non-accounting approach of performance evaluation rather than either a budget constrained or profit oriented approach and participative budgeting. Functional region, particularly research and development combined with budgetary participation was shown to enhance performance.

Some proof suggests combinations of traditional budgetary controls and more interpersonal and flexible controls in circumstances of environmental uncertainty. Ezzamel accounted that high environmental uncertainty was associated with an emphasis on budgets for evaluation and required explanation of variances but also high participation and interpersonal interactions flanked by superiors and subordinates. Merchant establish that environmental uncertainty was connected to pressure to meet financial targets but there was some flexibility through way of higher manipulation of information. In a revise of four cases, Chapman proposed that accounting has a scheduling role to play in circumstances of uncertainty but there necessity be substantial interactions flanked by accountants and other managers to cope with changing circumstances as they unfold in unpredictable ways. Environmental hostility has been associated with a strong emphasis on meeting budgets. Hostility from intense competition has been related to a reliance on formal control and sophisticated accounting, manufacture and statistical control. Though, sure specific units of competitive location, such as strength of market location and levels in product life cycles were not associated with the importance of budgets or participation. Also, environmental complexity, self-governing of function, was associated with a reduced emphasis on budgets. From these illustrations it can be seen that a constant steam of research in excess of the past 20 years has confirmed that uncertainty has been associated with a require for more open, externally focused, non-financial styles of MCS. Though, hostile and turbulent circumstances appear, in the main, to be best served through a reliance on formal controls and an emphasis on budgets. The question may be posed, what is the appropriate MCS for organizations operating in circumstances of uncertainty, turbulence and hostility? The organizational design literature proposes that organizations facing extreme pressure will initially tighten control as such pressure is likely to threaten short-term survival and then adopt more organic controls. Small is recognized in relation to the appropriate design of MCS to assist in managing intricate and competing forces from the external environment. It would be useful to look at how modern, interactive information systems can give a blend of tight controls with the opportunity to source more open, informal and subjective information. Certainly there is proof that effective organizations combine tight controls with more open, informal and flexible information and communication systems.

The following propositions summarize the research findings relating MCS to the external environment. Propositions concerning the external environment and MCS:

- The more uncertain the external environment the more open and externally focused the MCS.

- The more hostile and turbulent the external environment the greater the reliance on formal controls and an emphasis on traditional budgets.
- Where MCS focused on tight financial controls are used in uncertain external environments they will be used jointly with an emphasis on flexible, interpersonal interactions.

**Critical Evaluation**

The distinction flanked by dimensions within the external environment, such as uncertainty, hostility and complexity is significant to MCS design. More mechanistic, formal MCS tend to give partial information in uncertain circumstances and require rapid reformulation to cope with the unfolding unpredictability. Clear specification of the environmental dimensions of interest is required, as dissimilar theories are required to consider the effects of dissimilar dimensions. There are rich research opportunities to investigate appropriate MCS design for settings that are uncertain and also hostile and intricate. Interpreting studies that have examined the power of the external environment is complicated through the use of dissimilar events of the similar environmental construct. For instance, Gordon and Narayanan's revise of the association flanked by perceived environmental uncertainty and more broadly scoped MCS used a measure of uncertainty that captured the intensity of competition, the dynamic and unpredictable nature of the external environment, and units of change.

In learning the similar kind of MCS variables, Chenhall and Morris used a measure of uncertainty which measured lack of information on environmental factors, inability to assign probabilities on how the environment will affect success or failure, and not knowing the outcome of decisions on how the organization would lose if the decision was incorrect. The measure used through Gordon and Narayanan is more specifically focused on the external situation than Chenhall and Morris which has a composite of external components and implications for internal decisions. Even within the Gordon and Narayanan measure units of unpredictability are combined with difficulty. Tymond, Stout, and Shaw give a comprehensive review of MCS research investigating the role of environmental uncertainty providing recommendations that the events should involve top managers' perceptions of the external environment. The application of a single valid and reliable measure of environmental uncertainty would assist in comparing the results of studies examining uncertainty and help build a coherent body of knowledge on the effects of this variable of MCS design. The environment will continue to be a central unit of context in contingency-based research. The specific attributes of the environment are changing and should be incorporated in future studies. The external environment that mainly organizations face comprises increased social pressure on issues such as environmental ecology and the economic and social well being of employees and civilization. The implications for management and MCS of global competition and operations are increasingly significant. As organizations become involved in networks involving other entities such as joint ventures and supplier and customer alliances, the boundaries flanked by what is internal and external become blurred and consequently the role of MCS will likely change. Additionally, the way in which the environment exerts pressure should be explored. Granlund and Lukka note that pressure may approach from economic causes, coercion from organizations, normative pressure derived from appropriate social conduct, and the tendency to mimic apparently successful practices.

**Generic Concepts of Technology**

Technology has several meanings in organization behavior. At a common stage, technology refers to how the organization's work procedures operate (the way tasks change inputs into outputs)and comprises hardware (such as machines and apparatus), materials, people, software and knowledge. Three generic kinds of technology of importance to MCS design maybe recognized from the organizational literature: complexity, task uncertainty and interdependence. By these notions of technology, many key attributes that may power MCS design can be derived. First, organizations producing highly dedicated, non-average, differentiated products are likely to employ intricate element/batch technologies.

These will tend to involve procedures that have low analyzability of procedures and several exceptions. Also, managers are likely to have imperfect knowledge of procedures and low skill to measure outputs. A require for flexible responses to specific customers increases interdependencies crossways the value chain involving reciprocal interactions with customers, suppliers and functional elements such as marketing, manufacture, purchasing and research and development. It might be expected that these kinds of technologies would require controls to encourage flexible responses, high stages of open communication within the work force and systems to manage the interdependencies. Traditional, mechanistic MCS based on financial controls would not appear to suit these circumstances. Second, organizations that produce average, undifferentiated products employing capital rigorous, automated procedures are likely to employ mass manufacture and procedure technologies. These will involve highly analyzable procedures and few exceptions. Knowledge of procedures and events of output will be more readily accessible. Interdependencies are moderate being sequential. This technology requires standardized, administrative controls such as traditional, formal financial MCS.

A variant of this technology is where there are non-average products but the procedures are well understood. Interdependencies with customers are likely to be reciprocal. This technology is typical of an organization producing customized products but employing reasonably automated procedures. Controls are required that are flexible and that are constant with managing interdependencies. A reliance on traditional administrative controls, including financial MCS, is unlikely to give required flexibility and more open, informal controls will be more appropriate to manage interdependencies. At the similar time traditional, formal controls may assist in controlling procedures that are well understood.

**Findings: Standardized-Automated Procedures and MCS**

Technologies characterized through more standardized and automated procedures are served through more traditional formal MCS with highly dev eloped procedure controls; high (low) budget use and high (low) budgetary controls. High budgetary slack gives a buffer against low predictability within the procedures and is establish less in more predictable, automated procedures with high workflow integration. Alternatively, slack will be positively related to less automated, less predictable job/batch kind technologies.

**Task Uncertainty and MCS**

Technologies with high (low)task analyzability are related to a high (low)reliance on average operating procedures, programs and plans; tasks high in difficulty and variability are associated with a low reliance on accounting performance events; knowledge of task transformations is associated with behavior control; technologies with few exceptions that are high (low)in analyzability are associated with accounting (personnel)control s. Mia and Chenhall demonstrated that marketing departments faced more task uncertainty than manufacture departments and consequently used broad scope information to enhance performance. Brownell and Dunk showed that there was a fit flanked by circumstances of low task difficulty, participative budgeting and a high budget emphasis; while high task difficulty suited participation with or without a strong budget emphasis. Lau et al provided alike results, although they establish that high participation and high task difficulty provided a fit irrespective of budget emphasis, while high participation and high budget emphasis enhanced performance in low task difficulty situations. Brownell and Merchant establish that higher (lower) standardization of products (high knowledge of input/output dealings) combined with flexible (static) budgets and low participation to enhance performance. Brownell and Merchant's findings that low task uncertainty combined with more flexible budgets is somewhat inconsistent with other findings linking high task uncertainty with more informal, open MCS.

**Interdependence and MCS**

Low stages of interdependence have been connected to budgets, operating procedures and statistical reports; with statistical reports used for scheduling and informal coordination used in highly interdependent situations. In low interdependent public sector organizations there was an emphasis on budget analysis and managers' power on budgets but infrequent interactions with superiors and small required explanation from budgets. In more intricate situations there was less emphasis on budgets and more frequent interaction flanked by subordinates and superiors. High (low)inter dependence was establish to be associated with broad (narrow) scope MCS that focuses on appropriate aggregations and integrative information.

Strategies of customization were associated with high stages of interdependence with the latter correlating with the importance for operational decisions of the information features of integration, aggregation and timeliness. Propositions concerning generic concepts of technology and MCS:

- The more technologies are characterized through standardized and automated procedures the more formal the controls including a reliance on procedure control, and traditional budgets with less budgetary slack.
- The more technologies are characterized through high stages of task uncertainty the more informal the controls including: less reliance on average operating procedures, programmes and plans, accounting performance events, behaviour controls; higher participation in budgeting; more personal controls, clan controls, and usefulness of broad scope MCS.
- The more technologies are characterized through high stages of interdependence the more informal the controls including: fewer statistical operating procedures; more statistical scheduling reports and informal coordination; less emphasis on budgets and more frequent interactions flanked by subordinates and superiors; greater usefulness of aggregated and integrated MCS.

**Modern Technologies**

In excess of the past 20 years MCS research has urbanized to consider the role of advanced technologies such as Presently in Time (JIT), Total Excellence Management (TQM)and Flexible Manufacturing (FM)as dimensions of context. To set up the importance of these units of technology, accounting researchers have dawn on theories from manufacturing urbanized through theorists such Hayes et al., Skinner and from economics such as notions of complementarities as modeled through Milgrom and Roberts. Young and Selto give a review of new manufacturing practices and some implications for performance events and incentive schemes, arguing require considering technology changes within their organizational context. Notwithstanding the importance of manufacturing theories, understanding the appropriate fit flanked by MCS and advanced technologies is assisted through reflecting on the vital, generic notions of technology addressed above.

Kalagnanam and Lindsay argue that JIT is best suited to open, informal, organic shapes of controls.

They claim that organic systems can best manage the secure linkages or coupling within JIT that can cause variability (task uncertainty due to several exceptions) between units of manufacture procedures (interdependence). Organic systems are also required to manage require for flexible responses to customers, which involves coordinating reciprocal interdependencies crossways the value chain. Finally, JIT implies continuous improvement that is best served through commitment to change from the shop floor which is encouraged through organic systems. Alike arguments may be made for implementing innovative MCS in TQM and FM situations. These technologies have high variability and low analyzability. The low analyzability derives from require to continually use potential complementarities flanked by the several units of TQM practices. Also, TQM and FM involve the effective management of interdependencies within manufacture procedures including relationships with customers, suppliers and other external parties. Controls are required to encourage managers and shop floor employees to focus on the critical units of variability within the TQM programmes and to give effective links crossways the value chain. This information is generated at both the procedure (cybernetic kind controls such as statistical procedure controls)and strategic stages (i.e. linking procedures to strategic outcomes). Continuous improvement requires access to knowledge on world's best practice and systems to encourage innovation. Appropriate control systems should be open and informal, contain broad scope information, benchmarking, and performance events that indicate links flanked by strategy and operations such as balanced scorecards and strategic integrative controls.

**Findings: Advanced Technologies and MCS**

Ittner and Larcker demonst rated that product focused TQM was connected to timely problem solving information and flexible revisions to reward systems. They establish for advanced (holistic) TQM, external benchmarking and the integration of excellence and strategic information is significant. Ittner and Larcker examined the association flanked by excellence programmes and a diversity of strategic controls related to implementation, internal and external monitoring. Links flanked by excellence and strategic controls were established, with differences flanked by countries. Also, example-wide performance effects were restricted to controls concerning manager's participation in approving excellence programmes and team formulation, with other associations contingent on industry effects. Sim and Killough establish that customer and excellence performance was higher in TQM and JIT situations where there was customer and excellence related performance goals and incentives compared to where fixed pay was used. Ittner, Larcker, Nagar, and Rajan reported that performance gains from supplier partnership practices were associated with extensive use of non-price selection criteria, frequent meetings and interactions with suppliers and supplier certification.

These controls were not effective for arms length supplier dealings. Kalagnanam and Lindsay establish that organic MCS were associated with effective JIT systems. Some studies have examined the role of non-financial performance events in advanced technologies. Banker et al. establish that JIT, excellence and teamwork were associated with the provision of non-financial, excellence and productivity events to shop floor employees. There is some proof suggesting that relying on non-financial events to evaluate managers in TQM situations gives interactive strategic control. Mia establishes that the provision of broadly based MCS enhanced organizational performance in JIT settings. The broad MCS incorporated performance targets related to non-financial manufacturing indicators, actual performance on those targets, organizational financial indicators and industry and organizational trends on overall performance. Customer focused manufacturing, jointly with advanced manufacturing technology (AMT), have been associated with non-financial events. It is noteworthy that there is ambiguity in findings related to the extent to which associations flanked by usefulness of non-financial performance events and advanced technologies are related to enhanced performance. For instance, Chenhall establish positive performance effects flanked by combinations of non-financial events and TQM, while Perera et al. did not. One explanation for these differing findings is in the use of the performance events. Chenhall related the events to reward and compensation systems, whereas Perera et al. did not create this linkage. Perhaps the extent to which non-financial events are used to evaluate and reward managers may be significant in understanding links flanked by performance events, advanced technologies and performance.

This suggestion is constant with Sim and Killough's findings that incentive pay enhanced the positive effects of TQM and JIT on customer and excellence performance. Also, Larcker's market -based revise establish that the combination of incentive schemes and capital investment was associated with improved investor return. A recent revise, reporting a laboratory revise, demonstrated the importance of incentive schemes to enhance both absolute performance and rates of improvement through encouraging individuals to spend more time on tasks and to use and examine information. Foster and Horngren found that flexible manufacturing systems (FMS) were associated with performance events focused on time, excellence, operating efficiency and flexibility. There was also a change in the costing methods (allocations, treatment of costs as era and changes in the components of direct costs). Though, flexible manufacturing (FM)has been connected to a de-emphasis of efficiency-based events with control derived from integrative liaison devices. It is to be noted that there is a variation flanked by FMS which are technological systems such as computer assisted design and computer assisted manufacturing (CAD/CAM) and FM which is a generic notion of technology emphasizing a strategy of flexible response and customization. More research is needed to explore whether both focused formal controls at the operational stage and more intricate integrative devices can coexist to assist control within TQM and FM situations. Also, links flanked by dissimilar kinds of controls for operational, managerial and strategic decisions should be explored. For instance, Chenhall and Langfield-Smith (1998b)link performance with combinations of several traditional and modern controls with a range of strategies and manufacturing practices. Propositions concerning advanced technologies and MCS:

- TQM is associated with broadly based MCS including timely, flexible, externally focused information; secure interactions flanked by advanced technologies and strategy; and non-financial performance measurement.
- The extent to which combinations of advanced technologies and non-financial performance events are associated with enhanced performance depends on the degree to which the events are used as part of reward and compensation schemes.
- The advanced technologies of JIT and FMS are associated with broadly based MCS such as informal controls and greater use of non-financial performance events.
- FM is associated with the use of informal, integrative mechanisms.
- Supplier partnership practices are associated with non-financial events, informal meetings and interactions crossways the value chain.

**Critical Evaluation**

The three generic concepts of technology that have been used in MCS research (complexity, task uncertainty and interdependence)a re separate constructs but there are some general themes concerning uncertainty. It appears likely that conversion of inputs into outputs within less intricate, mass manufacture technologies is more programmable and predictable than in job or batch styled technologies servicing customized products. High stages of predictability are associated with the throughput of procedure technologies but not for the management of breakdowns and other exceptions. The construct of task uncertainty concerns lack of information and is a combination of variability or lack of knowledge in relation to the alternatives and uncertainty in relation to the how to examine the variations, or measure outputs, that happen throughout the conversion of materials into output. A higher stage of interdependence, where the work of one sub-element is complicated through having to rely on another, raises the possibility of more uncertainty derived from lack of control in excess of the supplying sub-element. The importance of uncertainty as an aspect of both environment and technology has lead to some ambiguity flanked by environmental and technological uncertainty in MCS research. For instance, Hirst argued that accounting performance events would be inappropriate in circumstances of environmental uncertainty but measured uncertainty with a composite measure comprising both units of task and environmental uncertainty arguing that the concepts are measuring the similar thing. Ross theorizes effects flanked by task uncertainty and performance events but uses events of environmental uncertainty. Clarification of links flanked by environmental and technological uncertainty is required to isolate potentially dissimilar effects of these variables on MCS design. For instance, external uncertainty implies a lack of information which creates it hard to plan kinds of products and services, stages of output and make contingency plans. Also, it creates evaluation hard as demand may change in ways beyond the control of managers.

This suggests that more flexible, interactive MCS are required to encourage learning and version and evaluate managers on the foundation of more subjective events or against adjustable criteria dependent on changing circumstances. The uncertainty associated with technology is, in part, derived from the environment with the technology being responsive to the uncertainty associated with markets and product necessities. Therefore, technology may respond to environmental uncertainty through becoming more flexible or through employing JIT techniques. The appropriate MCS design is likely to be more flexible and organic. Though, uncertainty, also, is caused directly within the technological procedures, independently from environmental circumstances. This may be derived from a search for improvements in product design and cost efficiencies and is likely to augment concern with managing uncertainty and complexity associated with the manufacture procedures.

These circumstances may prompt the adoption of scheduling and evaluation systems such as action- based accounting, non-financial manufacturing performance events and supplier networks. Despite the links flanked by environmental and task uncertainty, where possible researchers should draw on work that has tried to resolve issues related to the validity and reliability of events concerning these contextual variables. An instance of this is Brownell and Dunk who sought to reconcile findings related to the role of task uncertainty in the revise of budgetary related behaviours. Studies through Brownell and Hirst and Hirst used a measure of task uncertainty that aggregated the separate dimensions of task difficulty (analyzability)and variability (number of exceptions). Brownell and Dunk argued that such a composite measure is inappropriate as it mixes up the potential effects of difficulty and analyzability. They establish that task difficulty and not task variability moderated the effects of budget behaviours on performance. The region of modern manufacturing practices, such as JIT, TQM, FM and AMT, has provided several opportunities for contingency-based research. Ideas from economics concerning complementarities are likely to prove useful in modeling the way multiple characteristics of manufacturing can be combined optimally. Developing an understanding of best manufacturing practices and the way in which manufacturing aligns with or gives the impetus for strategy would appear to be a necessary step in ensuring that MCS design maintains relevance to the technological core of organizations. Closer cooperation flanked by MCS researchers and manufacturing technology experts and industrial engineers would be fruitful.

The importance of advances in IT cannot be underestimated. The adoption of interactive IT systems, such as SAP R/3, often triggers the adoption of scrupulous performance and costing systems. As the average life span of products decrease, consideration of the life cycle of products has become a concern in manufacturing. Short product life cycles lay demands for new product initiatives and alter cost structures. Also, decreasing life cycles augment operating risk and require increased capital investment. Understanding how MCS innovations, such as target costing, can assist management within these settings will likely become increasingly significant. There has been small work that has investigated how MCS are best suited to dissimilar levels in the growth of firms. Significant topics are the role of more formal systems at the levels of new firm formation, early growth, maturity and decline.

Questions arise concerning the necessities of MCS at these dissimilar levels, particularly the extent to which MCS can assist in the transition from early growth to more mature levels. Moores and Yuen provide an examination of issues concerning dissimilar characteristics of MCS that are significant for dissimilar levels of the growth cycle of firms. Finally, it is noteworthy, that mainly contingency based MCS research has involved big, manufacturing organizations. There have been some studies in the hospital and hospitality sectors but, on the whole, there has been small research investigating the service and government sectors. Some examples contain studies within government agencies, hospitals, research and development and marketing departments. The growth in importance of service industries such as hospitality and tourism, and the introduction of managerial approaches to public sector management give several opportunities for future research.

**Organizational Structure**

Organizational structure is in relation to the formal specification of dissimilar roles for organizational members, or tasks for clusters, to ensure that the behaviors of the organization are accepted out. Structural arrangements power the efficiency of work, the motivation of individuals, information flows and control systems and can help form the future of the organization. There have been several definitions of organizational structure.

A significant distinction is the variation flanked by the outcomes of structure and the structural mechanisms. Lawrence and Lorsch refer to structure, generically, as the way in which the organization is differentiated and integrated. Differentiation is concerned with the extent to which sub-element manager's act as quasi entrepreneurs, while integration is defined as the extent to which the subunits act in ways that are constant with organizational goals. The mechanisms to achieve differentiation involve decentralizing power, while integration involves rules, operating procedures, committees and the like. Pugh, Hickson, and Turner and Pugh, Hickson, Hinings, & Turner empirically recognized examples of structural mechanisms that have been used commonly in contingency-based research, including centralization, standardization, formalization and configuration.

Burns and Stalker discus s structure, generically, in conditions of mechanistic and organic approaches. The means to achieve these shapes of structure involve mechanisms such as rules, procedures and openness of communications and decision procedures. Perrow identified structure in conditions of bureaucratic and non-bureaucratic approaches. Designers of MCS have been concerned with formulating MCS to be constant with the intent of organizational structure. Consequently, it is useful to consider the extent to which MCS are mechanistic or organic, or to which they differentiate or integrate. The choice of structure in organizational contingency research has focused on the appropriate structure to fit the stages of uncertainty in the environment, strategy and the organization's technology. Usually, it is whispered that more organic structures are suited to uncertain environments. Though, it should be noted that Lawrence and Lorsch recognized require for higher stages of differentiation to cope with diverse and uncertain environments and that this causes potential integration troubles which require sophisticated liaison mechanisms (integrative personnel, meetings), rather than rules and procedures.

This kind of response is something of a hybrid flanked by mechanistic (for differentiation)and organic kinds of structure (for integration)to manage uncertainty. A big body of literature suggests that strategies characterized through diversification require differentiated, divisional structures. Also, it may be argued that once scrupulous structures are in lay then decisions will be influenced through the opportunities afforded managers from power granted to them and, perhaps, the political interests of those individuals. Therefore, strategy might follow structure. Often the structural arrangements have significant implications for information flows that may form or bias the future directions of the organization. In the prior part extensive links flanked by technology and kinds of controls were drawn. It is, also, noteworthy that early studies of organizational design recognized significant links flanked by technology and structure. Particularly, early research establishes that changing to more efficient technologies did not necessarily lead to enhanced effectiveness accepted. Implementing the technically efficient technologies required reformulating roles and structures with dynamic negative effects on the way individuals related to the new technologies, and consequently, deterioration in performance. It was apparent that socio-technological approaches were required to ensure improved organizational performance. These early observations are significant to several recent structural innovations such as work-based team that effort to harness growths in technology with the efficient blending of appropriate skills and the motivating force of teamwork. When evaluating contingency relationships flanked by MCS and structure, units of environment, technology and strategy are likely to be implicated in the relationships and, as such, much can be gained through considering them at the similar time.

## Findings: Organizational Structure and MCS

Big firms with sophisticated technologies that are decentralized have been associated with a strong emphasis on formal MCS; and big, diverse, decentralized firms used more administrative controls. Decentralized organizations were recognized as perceiving aggregated and integrated information as useful. Managerial performance was associated with the interaction flanked by decentralization and each of the features of broad scope, integrated, aggregated and timely information received/obtained from MCS. There is some proof linking MAS to functional differentiation. Functional differentiation (more responsibility in excess of regions of manufacturing)was connected to formality of budgetary procedures. Hayes establishes that the importance of evaluating factors related to internal operations, external circumstances and interdependencies depended on the functional nature of departments.

In manufacture departments, overall effectiveness was associated with factors related to the performance of internal factors. For marketing, performance of factors related to the external operating circumstances and interdependencies were mainly significant. Functional differentiation has been connected to environmental uncertainty to demonstrate how research and development elements, compared to marketing, are better suited to participative budgeting. Mia and Chenhall establish that marketing, compared to manufacture, involves higher task uncertainty that explained why marketing managers used broad scope information more effectively than those in manufacture. Concerning scrupulous functional decisions, Foster and Gupta recognized that improvements in MCS would be valued for pricing decisions, customer mix, sales force/promotions and product mix. Costing information was perceived as useful for decisions concerning products and customers. There was a variation flanked by potential and actual use of MCS in the region of marketing. Budgetary participation has been studied extensively and associated with a wide diversity of contextual units. Structural contingencies connected to effective participative budgeting have incorporated functional differentiation, specifically research and development compared to marketing; leadership approach employing high compared to low budget emphasis; a consideration rather than initiating approach of leadership; as well as the findings related to decentralization. As noted, the theories used to look at functional differentiation relied on links to external environmental uncertainty, rather than structure, per se.

The ways in which MCS combine with units of organizational structure to give differentiation and integration within modern organizational structures give several opportunities for worthwhile research. Particularly, there are few studies that have measured the fit flanked by organic structures and MCS. Organizational theory would suggest require for flexible, open information systems rather than tight budgetary systems. Gordon and Narayanan establish that organic structures were best served through broad scope and future oriented information. Some researchers have established that more organic, behaviorally oriented implementation is required to ensure the success of action-based accounting. Gosselin establish that action-based costing is adopted and implemented in organizations with more mechanistic structures. Particularly, mechanistic structures (vertical differentiation or bureaucratic decision procedures)facilitate adoption of activity based costing (an administrative innovation)and centralization and formalization were associated with implementing action-based costing. Organic structures were more suited to action analysis and action-cost analysis (technological innovation).

Presumably, organizations proceeding from action analysis to action-based costing would require units of organic and mechanistic structures to carry them through the levels of action analysis to action-based costing. A significant unit of modern structures is teams. As yet there are few studies that have measured the role of MCS within team based structures. Young and Selto predicted that teamwork and problem solving abilities of shop floor employees would be associated with high performance related to JIT outcomes. Their revise in a single organization did not reveal these associations due, in part, to an inability of workers to address procedure troubles and poor implementation of JIT-compatible management controls. Scott and Tiessen statement that team based structures were associated with high task complexity and that team performance was associated with use of comprehensive performance events (financial and non-financial), formulated participatively and used for compensation. In an experimental revise, Drake, Haka, and Ravenscroft establish that in team structures the interaction flanked by ABC and rewards based on group incentives was associated with cooperative innovations, lower costs and higher profits. Propositions concerning organizational structure and MCS:

- Big organizations with sophisticated technologies and high diversity that have more decentralized structures are associated with more formal, traditional MCS (e.g. budgets, formal communications).
- Research and development departments compared to marketing departments, which face higher stages of task uncertainty, are associated with participative budgeting; and marketing compared to manufacture departments, which face higher stages of external environmental uncertainty, are associated with more open, informal MCS.
- The structural features of functional differentiation based on research and development compared to marketing, leadership approach characterized through a consideration compared to initiating approach, and higher stages of decentralization are associated with participative budgeting.
- Decentralization is associated with the MCS features of aggregation and integration.
- Team based structures are associated with participation and comprehensive performance events used for compensation.
- Organic organizational structures are associated with perceptions that future orientated MCS are more useful, and with the effective implementation of action analysis and action-cost analysis.

**Critical Evaluation**

Structural mechanisms have been conceived of as involving differentiation and integration. Concerning differentiation, conventional thinking in management accounting proposes that decentralization should be combined with profit center responsibility accounting systems. To achieve integration easy mechanisms, such as operating procedures and formal budgets, have been recommended. It is of interest to observe the extent to which these recommendations appear somewhat inconsistent with the suggestions of Lawrence and Lorsch that highly differentiated organizations should employ intricate liaison mechanisms to achieve integration. Closer inspection of empirical findings suggests that comprehensive and formal mechanistic controls might be only one aspect of coordinative efforts in differentiated organizations. Khandwalla establish that big decentralized companies employed sophisticated controls but also utilized high stages of participation and human dealings approaches to coordinate behaviors. Certainly, participation in budgeting has been connected to decentralized organizations. Merchant establish participation was one aspect of administrative controls. Gul, Tsui, Fong, and Kwok establish an association flanked by decentralization and participative budgeting. How the participation of individuals in formal budgets might link to more organic shapes of control is a motivating region for further research. The role of budgets within organizations that have urbanized structures based on delayering, developing teams and empowering employees should be investigated. Galbraith allude s to the require to focus on the procedure of decision creation and disagreement resolution in situations in which there is ambiguity and disagreement flanked by the several structural elements and roles within organizations.. Care should be employed in selecting measurement instruments related to structure. Structure has been measured in conditions of decentralization of power, structuring of behaviors, interdependence and organic-mechanistic orientations. Events of decentralization, structuring of behaviors and interdependence have relied, in the main, on those urbanized through the Aston school.

The organic-mechanistic nature of structure has been derived from Khandwalla. The Aston events have been subjected to considerable scrutiny and empirical testing for validity and reliability in the organizational literature. The use of more novel events, such as those related to team-based structures, will require consideration of work that has urbanized these events. As with other units of context, in modern settings, structure remnants a significant factor in understanding MCS design. Several argue that adjustments to structure are required to ensure employee commitment to organizational goals related to continuous improvement. Structural innovations, such as delayering, flat structures, networking, procedure orientations and team-based work clusters concern the removal of barriers flanked by organizational behaviors. Such seamless organizational structures appear to be inconsistent with traditional profit centers and responsibility accounting, yet several organizations uphold these hierarchical structures. Empowerment and teamwork have replaced participation as the appropriate concept for understanding the efforts of several organizations to gain employee involvement. Issues of coordination, performance evaluation and reward systems in team-based organizations are significant research regions. Much can be learned from linking MCS research agendas with work of human resource management researchers.

**Size**

Growth in size has enabled firms to improve efficiency, providing opportunities for specialization and the division of labour. Big organizations tend to have more power in controlling their operating environment, and when employing large-scale mass manufacture techniques have reduced task uncertainty. Though, as an organization becomes superior the require for managers to handle greater quantities of information increases to a point where they have to institute controls such as rules, documentation, specialization of roles and functions, extended hierarchies and greater decentralization down hierarchical structures. Modern big organizations often develop secure associations with suppliers and customers, which blur the boundaries flanked by organizations, thereby rising further the size of the entity. Size has also provided organizations with the possessions to expand into global operations, sometimes through way of mergers, takeovers, licensing or other collaborative arrangements. These growths make additional administrative concerns due to increased stages of complexity within the manufacture procedures and with managing interdependencies with global partners.

***Findings: Size and MCS***

Few MCS studies have explicitly measured size as a contextual variable. In the main, studies have examined relatively big organizations, usually justifying this as it is big firms that tend to adopt the kind of practices incorporated within more formal MCS. Studies that have examined size have measured its effects jointly with other units of context such as technology, product diversity and have examined an array of controls. Khandwalla (1972, 1977)establish that big firms were more diversified in product rows, employed mass manufacture techniques, were more divisionalized and made greater use of sophisticated controls and environmental information gathering such as forecasting and market research. The papers through Bruns and Waterhouse and Merchant, discussed earlier in conditions of organizational structure, give proof related to size.

Bruns and Waterhouse identified two shapes of control associated with size: administrative with big firms and personal with little firms. Administrative control comprised more sophisticated technologies, formalized operating procedures, high stages of specialists and work related rules. Managers perceived that employees had high stages of control and had high stages of participation in setting standards and spent more time in budgeting. They perceived budgets as limiting innovation and flexibility in structuring organizations. Interpersonal control involved centralized decision creation, individuals saw themselves as having more interaction on budget related matters, not having their methods of reaching budgets accepted and being required to explain budget variances. Individuals were satisfied with their superior–subordinate relationships. Merchant's revise also measured size as an aspect of a multiple variable approach. Big, diverse firms were more decentralized, used sophisticated budgets in a participative way and employed more formal communications. Propositions concerning size and MCS

- Big organizations are associated with more diversified operations, formalization of procedures and specialization of functions.
- Big organizations are associated with more divisionalized organizational structures.
- Big size is associated with an emphasis on and participation in budgets and sophisticated controls.

**Critical Evaluation**

Mainly contingency-based MCS research has studied superior organizations but has not measured size difference within superior entities. This is unfortunate as there is proof from early organizational contingency studies that the connection flanked by size and administrative arrangements such as specialization, formalization and the vertical span increases with size but at a declining rate. Therefore, while it is reasonable to assume that big firms employ formal MCS, it is possible that dissimilar kinds of controls will be appropriate within these big firms, depending on size. The role of MCS in smaller or medium sized entities has not received small attention in the contingency- based MCS literature, nor has the role of MCS in firms that change size due to rapid internal growth, take-in excess of or merger been explored. It appears likely that the role of formal and interpersonal controls would differ depending on size and rate of change in size. Several opportunities for MCS, contingency-based research are likely to be establishing in the region of little and medium sized business. An impact of technological change and structural reform has been to reduce the number of employees, both shop-floor employees and the number of middle stage managers. In as much as the number of employees is associated with coordination and control issues, reduced size, due to the substitution of capital for labour, will have implications for MCS.

For instance, the combination of procedure controls to monitor machines and informal controls for evaluating people will likely become more significant where there are fewer employees operating and managing capital rigorous technologies. Concerning measurement, there are many ways of estimating size including profits, sales volume, assets, share valuation and employees. The use of financial events can create comparisons flanked by organizations hard as dissimilar accounting treatments can be establish flanked by firms. Mainly contingency-based MCS studies have defined and measured size as the number of employees. Numbers of employees has been establishing to correlate with net assets. It is possible that the precise measure of size could be significant depending on the unit of context and dimensions of MCS being studied. If the theory is considering the effectiveness of budgets to coordinate individuals behaviors then employees is appropriate. If, though, the revise is examining the effects of environment on the effectiveness of customer focused accounting then sales and assets might be more appropriate as these events capture market power that can lead to barriers to entry or industry concentration. Khandwalla argues that forecast sales are the best indicator or how size may relate to scheduling, budgeting and structural modification.

**Strategy**

Strategy is somewhat dissimilar from other contingency variables. In a sense it is not a unit of context, rather it is the means whereby managers can power the nature of the external environment, the technologies of the organization, the structural arrangements and the control civilization and the MCS. The role of strategy is significant as it addresses the criticism that contingency based research assumes that an organization's MCS is determined through context and that managers are captured through their operating situation. Recently, MCS research has recognized that managers have 'strategic choice' whereby they can location their organizations in scrupulous environments.

Therefore, if the current product range is too uncertain, reformulating product strategy into a market that is more predictable may remove the pressure from the environment. It may, also, limit potential opportunities and so require the organization to look at its attitudes to the tradeoff flanked by potential returns and acceptable risk and uncertainty. Notwithstanding the strategic direction selected through the organization, contingency- based research predicts that sure kinds of MCS will be more suited to scrupulous strategies. The powerful power of strategy is evidenced through the popular use of conditions such as strategies of TQM, the strategic imperative of an empowered workforce and strategic management accounting. Langfield-Smith gives a summary of research into MCS and strategy. Much generic taxonomy has been urbanized including entrepreneurial-conservative; prospecters-analysers-defenders; build-hold-harvest; and product differentiation- cost leadership.

Proof from the strategy-organizational design research suggests that strategies characterized through a conservative orientation, defenders, harvest and cost leadership are best served through centralized control systems, dedicated and formalized work, easy co-ordination mechanisms and attention directing to problem regions. Strategies characterized through an entrepreneurial orientation, prospectors, build and product differentiation are connected to lack of standardized procedures, decentralized and results oriented evaluation, flexible structures and procedures, intricate co-ordination of overlapping project teams, and attention directing to curb excess innovation. Simons argues that four dimensions of MCS link to strategy: belief systems to communicate and reinforce vital values and missions, boundary systems to set up limits and rules to be respected, diagnostic controls to monitor outcomes and correct deviations, and interactive controls to enable top managers to personally involve themselves with subordinates and operations with a view to forcing dialogue and learning.

### *Findings: Strategy and MCS*

From MCS research, proof suggests links flanked by strategy and cost control and to formality of performance evaluation. The studies are focused on strategy at the strategic business element stage, rather than corporate or functional stages. Mainly of the studies explore the association flanked by

MCS and strategic typologies. Conservatives, defenders and cost leadership strategies discover cost control and specific operating goals and budgets more appropriate than entrepreneurs, prospectors and product differentiation strategies. Simons establish that entities with small sense of urgency in relation to the creating a vision, did not employ interactive controls. These generalizations are fairly simplistic. Merchant establish no association flanked by dissimilar growth strategies and pressure to meet financial targets. Simons demonstrated that tight controls were apparent in more entrepreneurial strategies, perhaps to balance excessive innovation and to help learning in uncertain environments.

Chenhall and Morris found that tight control was appropriate for conservative strategies; though, tight control was also establish in entrepreneurial situations but, importantly, operating jointly with organic decision styles and communications. Again, the apparent paradox can be explained through require for organic systems to encourage innovation and tight control to curb excessive innovation. Concerning performance measurement, build compared to harvest strategies, which involve low specialization and difficulty in measuring outcomes, suit more subjective and extensive-condition controls e.g. Product differentiation was associated with a low emphasis on meeting budgets, and when combined with high service sharing was associated with a reliance on more subjective behavioral control. A revise through Abernethy and Brownell establish that hospitals undergoing strategic change (a more prospector kind of strategy) used budgets interactively, focusing on dialogue, communication and learning (more organic styles of control). Van der Stede showed that product differentiation strategies were associated with less rigid budgetary control, which in turn, was associated with increased budgetary slack, although there were no direct effects flanked by strategy and slack. Proof on the usefulness of more broad scope scheduling information for prospector companies and for those following build compared to harvest strategies was establish through Guilding. In this revise, the scope of the information related to competitor-focused accounting which incorporated competitor cost assessment, competitive location monitoring, competitor appraisal based on published financial statements, strategic costing and strategic pricing. Bouwens and Abernethy found that the stage of importance to operational decision creation of more integrated, aggregated and timely information was correlated with customization strategies. While associations with broad scope information were not establish, the revise focused on importance for 'operational' decisions, which presumably excluded decisions concerning markets and customer necessities which are more likely to involve broad scope information. Propositions concerning strategy and MCS:

- Strategies characterized through conservatism, defender orientations and cost leadership are more associated with formal, traditional

MCS focused on cost control, specific operating goals and budgets and rigid budget controls, than entrepreneurial, build and product differentiation strategies.

- Concerning product differentiation, competitor focused strategies are associated with broad scope MCS for scheduling purposes, and customization strategies are associated with aggregated, integrated and timely MCS for operational decisions.
- Entrepreneurial strategies with both formal, traditional MCS and organic decision creation and communications.
- Strategies characterized through defender and harvest orientations and following cost leadership are associated with formal performance measurement systems including objective budget performance targets, compared to more prospector strategies which require informal, open MCS characterized through more subjective extensive condition controls and interactive use of budgets focused on informal communications.

**Critical Evaluation**

Ideally, the role of strategy is dynamic involving managers in continually assessing the way combinations of environmental circumstances, technologies and structures enhance performance. MCS has the potential to aid managers in this procedure through assisting them in formulating strategy related to markets and products, required technologies and appropriate structures. MCS can then be implicated in the implementation and monitoring of strategies, providing feedback for learning and information to be used interactively to formulate strategy. Few studies in MCS have investigated these issues, rather mainly have been restricted to identifying MCS that are appropriate for dissimilar strategic archetypes. While there are some general units in these dissimilar strategic archetypes, there are important differences, consequently care is needed in developing theory that is specific to the archetypes employed in the revise. For instance, Fisher and Govindarajan develop theory to look at strategy and alternative controls based on the dissimilar requires derived from combinations of strategic mission, by concepts of build, hold and harvest, and competitive strategy, by product differentiation and low cost taxonomies. The extent to which these archetypes, which were urbanized in the 1970s and 1980s, uphold their relevance to modern settings is questionable. Strategies are being complicated through require for mainly organizations to be both low cost producers and to give customers with high excellence, timely and reliable delivery. More meaningful associations flanked by strategy, environment and internal operations may become apparent if specific units of strategic priorities are investigated. Relevant research is accessible based on modern strategic priorities and has been applied in management accounting research. The role of MCS in organizations involved in strategic change is a significant topic.

Some insights can be gained through examining movement crossways dimensions of archetypes, such as a change from harvest to prospector orientations, Though, greater understanding of how MCS is implicated in strategic change is possible through considering theories that relate to differences flanked by incremental, synthetic and discontinuous change, the role of strategic intent and strategic possessions, the variation flanked by planned and emerging strategies, styles of management that encourage change, the impediments to change of any formal resource allocation procedure, and the way MCS can be used to manage both evolutionary and revolutionary change. There have been concerns with the measurement of strategy. Events used to revise strategy have been criticized as mixing up units of the environment with organizational attributes (therefore studies of strategy and environment would be invalid). Events tend not to relate to competitors which create comparisons crossways industry clusters problematic. Managers have difficulty relating to descriptions used to capture generic typologies such as build, harvest and prospect. Strategy research should consider work that has attempted to validate strategy events such as Dess and Davis, Kotha et al., Miller and Friesen, Miller and Roth and Shortell and Zajac.

**Civilization**

The connection flanked by the design of MCS and national civilization symbolizes an extension of contingency-based research from its organizational foundations into more sociological concerns. The vital proposition is that dissimilar countries possess scrupulous cultural features. This predisposes individuals from within these cultures to respond in distinctive ways to MCS. Civilization has becomes significant in the design of MCS, in excess of the past 20 years, as several companies have urbanized multi-national operations. These companies face the issue of whether to transfer their domestic MCS overseas, or redesign their systems to fit the cultural features of the offshore entities. Compared to studies of other contextual variables, research into civilization has been limited and is somewhat exploratory. There is a plethora of meanings of civilization.

Though, Kaplan claims there is consensus in the middle of anthropologists that civilization is composed of patterned and interrelated traditions, which are transmitted in excess of time and legroom through non-biological mechanisms based on man's uniquely urbanized linguistic and non-linguistic symbolizing capabilities. Civilization can be described through inherent traits such as knowledge, belief, art, morals, law, custom, and other capabilities and habits acquired through man as a member of civilization. Though, often civilization is conceptualized as a set of features in accessible to suit the methodological and scientific requires of the research society. The mainly widely used features were urbanized through Hofstede who described the cultural values as power aloofness (acceptance of unequal sharing of power), individualism vs. collectivism (placing self-interest ahead of the group), uncertainty avoidance (preference to avoid uncertainty and rely on rules and structures), masculinity vs. femininity (attainment, assertiveness and material success vs. modesty and preference for excellence of life)an d, subsequently, confucian dynamism. Virtually all MCS contingency-based studies have used these values to revise the power of civilization.

### *Findings: Civilization and MCS*

Contingency-based research in MCS has examined associations flanked by cultural dimensions and units of structure such as standardization, decentralization, and control system features such as formality on controls, reliance of accounting performance events and budgetary participation. Overall, the research has provided mixed results as to whether civilization does have effects crossways characteristics of MCS. There are few regions where consensus can be drawn. This is because studies have examined dissimilar combinations of cultural dimensions and have measured characteristics of MCS in dissimilar ways. As a consequence there is small overlap flanked by studies to enable themes to be drawn or comparisons made and generalizations urbanized. The following are examples of studies that have examined accounting controls. Harrison demonstrated that differences flanked by Singapore and Australian managers did not moderate the connection flanked by budget emphasis in evaluation and either job related tension or job satisfaction.

Though, the connection flanked by reliance on accounting performance events and low job related tension and high job satisfaction was stronger for Singapore managers, the explanation being that these managers had low individualism and high power aloofness compared to Australian managers. O'Conner argued that the low power aloofness establish in western parent companies would control in excess of high power aloofness establish in their local Singapore subsidiaries, thereby enhancing the effectiveness of the parent MCS. By these arguments he establishes that the connection flanked by role ambiguity and superior/subordinate relationships (perceptions of competence and trustworthiness) and both participation in budgeting and in performance evaluation was stronger in foreign subsidiaries than local Singapore entities. Merchant, Chow, and Wu studied Taiwanese and US firms and establish that civilization was not significant in explaining use or effectiveness of the degree of subjectivity in profit center manager's performance evaluation. Only use of extensive-condition incentives was more significant in Taiwanese firms. Many studies have measured broader characteristics of MCS with less equivocal results. Snodgrass and Grant establish that Japanese, compared to US, companies experience less explicit controls and more implicit controls in monitoring, evaluation and rewarding. Ueno and Wu also establish differences flanked by Japanese and US managers on MCS features. They theoretically connected individualism with US managers and establish, empirically, that they used more formal communications, built slack, used controllability in budgeting and extensive-condition horizons for performance evaluation. Uncertainty avoidance was connected to Japanese firms to explain a preference for broad time horizons and structured budgetary procedures. These associations were not supported empirically leading to the conclusion that individualism is the dominant predictor of MCS. Vance, McClaine, Boje and Level studied formality of controls, team development, appraisal systems, intrinsic/extrinsic rewards and frequency of feedback in Indonesian, Malaysian, Thai and US firms. Important differences were establish flanked by US and Asian firms but also flanked by the dissimilar Asian firms. This revise is distinctive as it used both Hofstede's dimensions plus other concepts of civilization drawn from anthropology. Finally, studies by experimental methods have failed to support expected effects and have revealed ambiguous findings. Given the exploratory nature of research examining civilization and the lack of consensus on findings, only a common proposition relating civilization to MCS is presented. Proposition concerning civilization and MCS:

- National civilization is associated with the design of MCS.

### *Critical Evaluation*

The dominant notion of civilization employed in MCS-civilization research has been the Hofestede values. Though, many criticisms can be made as to how this approach to defining and measuring civilization has been employed. First, it assumes that the dissimilar values have the similar intensity within a civilization. If this is not the case, then some value may be more dominant than others and have a prominent effect. Second, some studies do not consider all of Hofstede's values. It is possible that omitted values may have effects that are relevant to the revise. Third, mainly studies assume that countries differ on values and proceed to test for differences flanked by countries without directly assessing cultural values. It is, so, significant to check that the assumed values of a country are still apparent in modern studies. Fourth, while Hofstede's values give a convenient tool for research, it does symbolize a restricted view of civilization. Its exclusive use has prohibited development of understanding how behaviour is influenced through the fundamental traits that power how individuals think, feel and respond. More subtle notions of civilization involving myths and ritual, language and narrative are not measured. It appears likely that theories and methods drawn from anthropology and sociology are more suited to understanding how these subtle factors combine to power how individuals respond to MCS. While national civilization has been studied extensively, it appears likely that other variables such as markets and technologies may interact with cultures in systematic ways to affect MCS design. For instance, the adoption of sure kinds of advanced technologies appears to work mainly effectively if attributes of collectivism are apparent. This combination of technology and civilization may suggest that sure kinds of performance events, suited to the technology but constant with collectivism, would be more appropriate. One variable that offers promise in the revise of civilization is organizational civilization. It is possible that a strong organizational civilization may control national civilization in the work situation. Small work has been completed in the region of organizational civilization and MCS design. As with national civilization, the meaning of organizational civilization and its revise are well served through the application of the research paradigms and methods from sociology and anthropology.

### Continuing Relevance of Traditional Units of Context

Insights into the present-day context of MCS can be gained through reflecting on the issues drawn from traditional contingency-based work. The environment will become more uncertain, hostile and intricate as a result of modern pressures. There will be requiring for organizations to develop increased environmental responsibility. Technologies will be established to have varying degrees of complexity, uncertainty and interdependencies that promote control issues. Structures will be employed that assist in developing more organic ways to communicate, but also give enhanced differentiation to motivate and location individuals secure to the business operations. Additionally, structures will be sought that empower individuals, with the purpose of providing a healthy and fulfilling work environment while better equipping the organization to achieve best practices. The challenges to coordination derived from size will increasingly become significant as organizations enlarge due to developing secure relationships with suppliers and customers and engaging in global operations through direct expansion, acquisition and merger. Notions of strategy are likely to be redefined and it will be necessary for MCS researchers to stay abreast of strategy commentators who reflect on the relevance of concepts urbanized through earlier writers. Civilization will augment in relevance as firms continue to develop multi-national operations and will likely best be researched through conceiving civilization in richer conditions than the value systems of Hofestede.

## ISSUES RELATED TO THEORY DEVELOPMENT

There are several shapes of theoretical fit that have been used to classify contingency-based research in MCS: selection, interaction and systems. Selection studies look at the way contextual factors are related to characteristics of MCS with no effort to assess whether this association is connected to performance. Interaction approaches contain studies that look at how organizational context moderates the connection flanked by MCS and organizational performance. Systems models consider the way in which multiple characteristics of controls systems and dimensions of context combine in a diversity of ways to enhance performance. Luft and Shields give a refinement to classify and talk about theories employed in contingency-based MCS research. This involves considering the structural dealings flanked by variables, the nature of the causality flanked by the variables and the stages of analysis.

**Structural Relationships Flanked by Variables**

There are many shapes of structural relationships. Linear additive models look at the association of several units of MCS with outcomes or of context with MCS. These theories give separate arguments for variable acting in separation with no attention to the explicit connection flanked by the explanatory variables. The inclusion of variables is justified as they assist in improving the prediction of the outcome criteria. The dominant form of analysis has been easy correlations or linear regression. Interaction models are used where the nature or strength of a connection flanked by MCS and an outcome criterion will depend on the power of scrupulous characteristics of context. Interaction variable models have been the dominant shapes in contingency- based research. For linear interaction models, moderated regression analysis or analysis of variance is appropriate. Hartmann and Moers give an extensive review of the shortcomings of interaction or moderated regression models as applied to budgetary research in excess of the past 20 years. Intervening models involve the specification of causal paths flanked by MCS, context and outcomes.

Studies may identify the antecedents to MCS, or they may demonstrate how the connection flanked by MCS and outcomes are explained through intervening variables. It is often significant to decompose the association flanked by MCS and outcomes into indirect effects operating through the intervening variable and direct effect which captures all remaining effects influencing the association flanked by MCS and outcomes. Initially, studies examining intervening models used a combination of linear regression and easy correlations to identify paths flanked by variables and then used these paths to decompose correlations of interest into direct and indirect effects. More recently, powerful structural equation models, such as EQS, LISTREL, AMOS and PLS, have been employed which enable latent variables to be constructed from multi-thing questionnaires and to identify, simultaneously, statistical significance with multiple dependent variables. It is possible to combine moderating variables within an intervening model through examining the extent to which a variable moderates the effects on one or more of the paths.

Given the recent criticism directed towards moderating variable models there is a danger that researchers will attempt and force arguments in relation to the interaction effects into intervening variable models. A fourth form of modeling involves systems approaches which also describe fit but do so through testing multiple fits simultaneously, involving a wider diversity of dimensions of context and MCS. Difference in performance stems from variations in overall systemic fit, with multiple, equally effective alternatives being possible. Techniques to test systems models contain the use of Euclidean aloofness and cluster analysis. These approaches are less rigorous than regression and require several decisions in conditions of the kind of analysis, and given the complexity of the relationships flanked by variables, interpretation and theory structure can be hard. They do, though, give a way of addressing the criticism that contingency-based research gives only a partial understanding of MCS and its context. For exploratory research, Ittner and Larcker note the potential of recursive partitioning to split samples into a sequence of sub-clusters thereby generating a treelike structure that describes a nesting of self-governing variables. It is noteworthy that to gain acceptable statistical power in more intricate models big example sizes are required. Therefore, the relatively little samples in some contingency-based studies limits the statistical power of the results. Moreover, it is unusual for contingency-based studies to statement statistical power.

**Causality**

Concerning causality, contingency-based MCS research has, in the main, been survey based and this tends to limit the scope of the studies to consider situations involving unidirectional relationships (MCS determines outcomes)or bi-directional relationships (MCS determines outcomes which then determines MCS).Mainly of the MCS research implicitly assumes unidirectional relationships. If the relationships are bi-directional, then it is possible that they are simultaneously determined on behalf of a situation in equilibrium, or they are related cyclically where MCS determines outcomes, then outcomes determine MCS, followed through MCS effecting outcomes and so on. Given the subsistence of cyclical relationships, the predictions from contingency-based theory may differ depending on which level of the cycle is being proposed. Moreover, given that mainly contingency- based research has used cross-sectional survey methods, the results are relevant to only one level of the cycle.

**Stages of Analysis**

The issue of stages of analysis is significant to theory construction within contingency-based research. Care is required in maintaining consistency flanked by the theory, the element or stage of analysis and the source of measurement. Consider examining the usefulness of budgets to evaluate sub-element performance. Budget usefulness is measured to depend on environmental uncertainty and managers' experience with budgets. The usefulness of budgets may be measured as a sub-element variable and the appropriate concept of environment is one that applies to the scrupulous subunits, such as uncertainty with sub-element products or suppliers. The assumption is that all managers within the sub-element will be expected to respond in the similar way to the environmental uncertainty. Any differences at the individual stage that may potentially affect budget usefulness are noise. Though, if individuals within the sub-element are expected to respond differently because of dissimilar experience with budgets the issue arises of what is the appropriate stage of analysis?

The usefulness of budgets and environmental uncertainty are sub-element variables and experience with budgets is individual stage. If an individual stage is adopted then the usefulness of budgets at the sub-element stage and the environmental uncertainty facing the subunit are inappropriate as the uncertainty is assumed to be the similar for all individuals within the subunit. If the theory comprises both sub-element and individual stages, then the sub-element stage of analysis can be preserved through splitting the existing sub-elements into new sub-elements based on dissimilar degrees of the individual stage variable. For instance, new sub-elements would be created which capture the four combinations of high/low uncertainty and high/ low experience with budgeting. More usually, the appropriate model for this is an interaction model.

# Index